INVENTING A DISCIPLINE

Richard E. Young

Inventing a Discipline

Rhetoric Scholarship in
Honor of Richard E. Young

Edited by

MAUREEN DALY GOGGIN
Arizona State University

National Council of Teachers of English
1111 W. Kenyon Road, Urbana, Illinois 61801-1096

Staff Editor: Bonny Graham
Interior Design: Jenny Jensen Greenleaf
Cover Design: Evelyn C. Shapiro
Cover Photograph: Copyright 1999 Karen DeWig

NCTE Stock Number: 23759-3050

It is the policy of NCTE in its journals and other publications to provide a forum for the open discussion of ideas concerning the content and the teach-ing of English and the language arts. Publicity accorded to any particular point of view does not imply endorsement by the Executive Committee, the Board of Directors, or the membership at large, except in announcements of policy, where such endorsement is clearly specified.

Every effort has been made to provide current URLs and e-mail addresses, but because of the rapidly changing nature of the Web, some sites and ad-dresses may no longer be accessible.

Library of Congress Cataloging-in-Publication Data

Inventing a descipline: rhetoric scholarship in honor of Richard E. Young/ edited by Maureen Daly Goggin.
    p. cm.
Includes bibliographical references and index.
ISBN 0-8141-2375-9 (pbk.)
    1. Rhetoric. I. Goggin, Maureen Daly. II. Young, Richard E. (Richard Emerson), 1932–

PN175.I58 2000
808—dc21

00-020225

CONTENTS

Contents

FOREWORD

RICHARD LEO ENOS

Holder of the Lillian Radford Chair of Rhetoric and Composition
Texas Christian University

M ost of us look forward to receiving our academic journals in the mail, but the November 1983 issue of *College English* turned out to be more gratifying than anyone at Carnegie Mellon University could ever have hoped for—including Richard E. Young. In that issue, Carnegie Mellon was recognized as having one of the premier rhetoric programs in the country. At the time, the rhetoric program was only in its fourth year, if you count one year of planning (1979) and three years in operation. I still recall how modest Richard was when he mentioned this achievement to me in his office. As the director of graduate studies, however, I saw this validation in anything but casual terms. While my expectations had been high, I was in a state of euphoria that our program was being recognized at such an early stage of its existence. Consequently, I only remember the next two hours as a blur. I photocopied the essay, highlighted the important parts regarding Carnegie Mellon, and personally hand-carried the results over to the administrative assistant of our university president, Richard M. Cyert. Not long after I had walked back across campus and returned to my office, my telephone rang. President Cyert was requesting that I give him an unhighlighted copy of *College English* so that he could distribute the essay to the trustees of the university! Of course, those who know Richard Young know that his contributions were well underway before he left the University of Michigan to found the rhetoric program at Carnegie Mellon, and that his contributions would continue long after that moment in November of 1983. Yet, as Richard Young's colleague and friend during both our Michigan and Carnegie

Mellon days, I would say that if I had to select one moment when all of Richard Young's hard work, genius, and diligence were first realized, it would be that morning in Pittsburgh, Pennsylvania.

Despite his modesty, it is nonetheless evident to me that Richard Young's vision was no less ambitious than to change the landscape of the field of English studies. Young's effort was not merely to "reclaim" rhetoric for English but to reconceptualize what rhetoric is and, in doing so, change forever our idea of what English is, does, and offers. As editor Maureen Daly Goggin points out, Young's contributions, broadly cast, fall into two major groups: the study of writing and the teaching of writing. That is, Young sought to improve the discipline by studying writing seriously and to implement that knowledge by refining heuristic procedures that qualitatively enhance the teaching of writing. These two groups provide the basis for the three major rubrics of this volume. The first, Field: Reflections on the Past, Present, and Future of the Discipline, offers four essays that take up issues of disciplinarity. The second, Wave: Temporal and Spatial Explorations of Rhetorical Theory and Practice, offers an extensive collection of essays that reconceptualize rhetoric. This rubric certainly reflects Young's own scholarly profile, for much of the inspiration for his own research draws on sources ranging from literature, linguistics, history, and psychology. Finally, Particle: Pedagogical Applications of Rhetoric reflects Young's interest in research applications, useful not only in the English classroom but in classrooms across the university. Central to that reform, particularly in the latter years of his career, was the teaching of writing across the curriculum (WAC). In this respect, and reflected in the essays that constitute these three rubrics, Young sought to change the field by changing the idea of the university itself; seeing WAC as a site for study is yet another manifestation of Young's efforts to implement the study of rhetoric into the teaching of writing. The impact of WAC is macroscopic, for it transforms the entire university into a research-based classroom.

As is evident by the contributions that make up this collection, the benefits Richard Young brought about for the universities in which he taught, as well as for the field of rhetoric and composition, are only just beginning to be realized. In one respect, these benefits have already been thoroughly explored by one of his most distinguished students and a contributor to this volume, Janice Lauer, in the *Encyclopedia of Rhetoric and Composition* (775–76). Lauer's account of Richard E. Young's ideas and work describes clearly the qualities that make this volume such an appropriate tribute. As a scholar, Young worked with Alton Becker and Kenneth Pike to pioneer a line of research in rhetoric and composition that would emerge as a paradigm for our field. Their text, *Rhetoric: Discovery and Change*, has become one of the cornerstones of research-based instruction that has revolutionized the field of composition. The organizing rubrics for this volume—field, wave, and particle—echo the heuristics of their tagmemic rhetoric.

As stellar as his scholarly accomplishments are, many argue that it is Richard Young's successful development of the doctoral program in rhetoric at Carnegie Mellon that ranks among his greatest contributions to our field. Young was also influential in making the improvement of the teaching of writing a major commitment of the National Endowment for the Humanities (NEH). For several years, Young coordinated NEH seminars, adjudicated the merits of NEH proposals, and advised NEH on the direction of writing research in the humanities. Out of his NEH seminars have emerged some of the most influential leaders of rhetoric and composition. In this collection, in fact, readers will be able to see for themselves just how acutely aware the authors are of their NEH experiences with Richard Young. One of Young's former NEH students, the late James A. Berlin, spoke of his former mentor's pedagogical contributions in his 1996 NCTE book, *Rhetorics, Poetics, and Cultures: Refiguring College English Studies*. Here also, in the area of application, we see the authors of this collection building on the research inspired by Young in ways that improve the teaching of writing and the integration of writing within the curricula of colleges across the country.

Finally, with Richard Young's direction and influence, rhetoric and composition once again has come to be seen as a serious enterprise within English studies. Young's educational contributions in graduate education have made a major and enduring impact on the field. Students who have earned doctorates in rhetoric in Young's programs at Michigan and Carnegie Mellon have gone on to establish and contribute to rhetoric and composition programs throughout the country. The measure of Young's success can be easily ascertained by the contributions of students and faculty. His most pervasive impact, however, may have been the indirect influence of his educational reforms on writing instruction. Young directed that research and teaching be both scholarly and serviceable; students learned not only through the richness of historical studies and the close analysis of empirical research but also through applying such knowledge to the teaching of writing.

According to an old saying, "There is no significant change without resistance." Perhaps that morning in November of 1983 is so clearly fixed in my mind because I appreciate the affirmation that was due Richard Young and those scholars of his generation who had worked so hard to bring about changes not only in the teaching and research of rhetoric but in the very mentality of English studies. Rhetoric and composition has now returned as a full, contributing partner to the field of English. Those of us who have been associated with Richard Young for decades realize the numerous personal sacrifices he has made to secure the achievements outlined here. It would indeed be difficult to imagine what rhetoric and composition would be like without his substantial contributions. We are all in his debt, and there is no better rhetorical moment to acknowledge this contribution than a *Festschrift* which, appropriately, celebrates his contributions through writing.

ACKNOWLEDGMENTS

As those who have edited collections know, this kind of valuable but difficult work depends on the efforts of lots of people. I owe a debt of gratitude to many. First and foremost, I want to thank Richard Young, my mentor and the inspiration for this project; his influence is woven everywhere throughout this collection. I am also most grateful to Richard Enos, who not only generously agreed to write the foreword but who also was a constant source of inspiration and support throughout this project. The twenty-two contributors to this volume also deserve acknowledgment for their patience with and dedication to this collection. I want to thank Michael Greer, former senior editor at NCTE, for his unwavering support, guidance, and help throughout the greater part of this project. Zarina Hock, current senior editor, deserves recognition for her significant efforts in seeing the project through to the end. I also want to thank the anonymous reviewers and members of NCTE's Editorial Board for their insights and suggestions. I am also grateful to NCTE staff editor Bonny Graham, under whose keen eye and sensitive reading this volume benefited. Also deserving mention are Beth Pearce, Steve Beatty, and Susan Miller Heck, who provided invaluable help in locating research materials and in conducting important administrative tasks so necessary to bringing a collection to fruition. Finally, Peter Goggin deserves special recognition for his never-ending intellectual and emotional support.

PERMISSIONS

Photo Credit: Department of English, Carnegie Mellon University, Pittsburgh, PA.

Page 215 (Chapter 10): Veronica Murayama, "Schizophrenia: What It Looks Like, How It Feels." Copyright ©1997 by Bedford/St. Martin's Press, Inc. From *St. Martin's Guide to Writing* 5E by Axelrod/Cooper. Reprinted with permission of Bedford/St. Martin's Press, Inc.

Page 228 (Chapter 10): Reprinted with permission from "Linking Mind and Brain in the Study of Mental Illnesses: A Project for a Scientific Psychopathology" by Nancy C. Andreasen, *Science* 275 (14 Mar. 1997): 1586–93. Copyright 1997 American Association for the Advancement of Science.

Pages 376 and 378 (Chapter 16): Figures 16.1 and 16.2 reprinted from *Computers and Composition* 12, Mike Palmquist et al., "Enhancing the Audience for Writing Across the Curriculum: Housing WAC in a Network-Supported Writing Center," pp. 335–53, Copyright 1995, with permission from Elsevier Science.

Pages 389–391 (Chapter 16): Netscape Communicator browser window© 1999 Netscape Communications Corporation. Used with permission.

Pages 411 and 415 (Chapter 17): The tables "Evaluation Design" and "Teacher Attitudes toward Planning Writing Assignments" by Jo-Ann Sipple were originally published in *Programs That Work: Models and Methods for Writing Across the Curriculum* edited by Toby Fulwiler and Art Young (Boynton/Cook, A subsidiary of Reed Elsevier Inc., Portsmouth, NH, 1990).

INTRODUCTION

A Genealogy on Genealogies

MAUREEN DALY GOGGIN
Arizona State University

*One of the most effective remedies to the divisiveness in
our profession over writing is what we know how to do
best. That is, we can investigate, seriously, as scholars,
the assumptions that underlie established practices and
habits about writing, and then allow what we learn to
guide the conduct of our professional lives.*

RICHARD E. YOUNG, "'Tracing Round the Frame':
Thinking about Writing in Departments of English"

*Inventing a Discipline: Rhetoric Scholarship in Honor of Rich-
ard E. Young* presents a collection of scholarly essays written
to pay tribute to Richard E. Young. Each contributor to this volume has heeded Young's call to "investigate, seriously, as scholars, the assumptions that underlie established practices and habits
about writing" ("'Tracing'" 164). The term *inventing* in the title
turns on multiple meanings. It invokes not only Young's important contributions to research, scholarship, and pedagogy on invention, and the rich body of scholarship sparked by his work,
but it also highlights his influence in the profession as a mentor
and colleague.

Richard E. Young deserves recognition for the many significant contributions he has made to the discipline of rhetoric and
composition. And as anyone well acquainted with Young would
certainly know, the best way to pay tribute to him is through a

collection of rigorous scholarly articles that explore vital questions concerning literate practices—that is, multiple, complex, interdependent reading and writing practices. This book, however, is not a *Festschrift* in the *traditional* sense of that term. Rather, in the spirit of Young's advocacy for careful and rigorous scholarship on significant problems, the essays in this book tackle, through a variety of perspectives and methods, complex questions concerning theories and pedagogies of literate practices.

A Brief Consideration of Richard Young's Contributions

As a scholar, teacher, and mentor, Young manifests the qualities of *vir bonus dicendi peritus*, the good man speaking well. As Scott Consigny observes, "the rhetor's task is not to answer questions and solve well-formulated problems, but rather to be able to *ask* good questions and to formulate or *discover* relevant problems in an indeterminate situation" (61). Throughout his career, Young has asked good questions that have helped to refocus attention on rhetorical invention as a dynamic process worthy of scholarly and pedagogical attention. This is the Young many know from his publications. But his influence and contributions extend far beyond the material that has appeared under his name in print. This volume may be understood as a partial genealogy of that influence.

In "Working on the Margin," Richard Young recalls some of the forces that motivated his scholarly and professional interest in rhetoric and specifically in rhetorical invention. Shortly after completing his Ph.D. in 1964 in Victorian literature at the University of Michigan, Young attended a seminar devoted to the study of rhetoric that was authorized in December of that year by the Conference on College Composition and Communication (CCCC) Executive Committee (Gorrell 138). A few years later, he became one of the founding members of the Rhetoric Society of America (RSA). (See Goggin, "Composing" 332 and "Rhetoric" on the origins of RSA and Young's contributions to the organization.) What is important is that Young turned his attention to rhetoric at a time when, in his words, "to work in the field of rhetoric was really to be on the margin" ("Working" 325). It was a time when those in rhetoric and composition were struggling to construct a disciplinary identity (Goggin, *Authoring*, "Composing" 329–34). As Young observes of his early work with Kenneth Pike and Alton Becker, "we saw ourselves as part of a widespread collaboration to create a new rhetoric and with that a new discipline that would take its place beside linguistics and literary studies" ("Working" 329). Indeed, Young's scholarship, professional interactions, and mentoring have contributed in a very literal sense to inventing the discipline of rhetoric and composition.

Karen Burke LeFevre notes that "invention in any field is a continuous process of problem-solving. . . . Inventors in any sphere are fortunate if they inherit good problems that serve as an impetus for invention" (90). Many in our field have been fortunate in inheriting good problems from Young (e.g., "Invention"; "Paradigms"; "Problems"; "Recent"; "'Tracing'"; and Young and Liu). His questions have sparked important scholarship such as LeFevre's *Invention as a Social Act*, in which she acknowledges that "Richard E. Young's exemplary work first drew me to the topic of rhetorical invention" (xiv). As a teacher and a mentor, Young has inspired other significant contributions, particularly through his National Endowment for the Humanities (NEH) seminars. For example, in *Rhetoric and Reality* James Berlin explicitly acknowledges his "year with Richard Young at Carnegie-Mellon University" for contributing to his monograph, and he acknowledges Young's influence less explicitly in *Writing Instruction in Nineteenth-Century American Colleges* when he thanks the NEH for "a fellowship in residence for college teachers in 1978–1979" (xi). Similarly, in their landmark essay "Audience Addressed/Audience Invoked," Lisa Ede and Andrea Lunsford trace the genesis of this work to the very same seminar when they write, "one of us became interested in the concept of audience during an NEH Seminar" (255). The "one of us" was Lisa Ede, who attended the 1978–79 seminar. Finally, Victor Vitanza, who attended the same year-long NEH seminar, explains the inception of the scholarly journal *Pre/Text* in this way: "We were all working with Richard Young, who in part created the conditions for the possibilities of *P/T*" (xvii). (These are only a handful of the many examples; for a study of Young's contributions to the field through his NEH seminars, see Almagno.)

The NEH seminars, and Richard Young's leadership in them, were crucial for helping to establish the nascent discipline of rhetoric and composition. They were offered at a time when only a few budding graduate programs were available in the field, thus providing an opportunity for many scholars, most of whom had been trained in literary studies, to retool themselves in rhetoric and composition. Perhaps less visible but no less important was Young's creation of the graduate program in rhetoric at Carnegie Mellon University, an accomplishment Richard Enos addresses more fully in his Foreword to this collection. Young designed the program to link the study of rhetoric with multiple disciplinary lenses from the sciences, social sciences, and humanities that encourage a variety of empirical, historical, hermeneutical, and theoretical approaches, and in so doing he anticipated the cross-disciplinary work and blurring of boundaries that is becoming increasingly common in academia today.

Crossing methodological boundaries is a hallmark of Young's own scholarship. His work has spanned multiple and diverse modes of inquiry, including, among others, theoretical (Young and Becker "Toward"), historical (Young and Goggin), and empirical (Palmquist and Young); he has also tackled multiple objects of study, including invention ("Paradigms," "Recent"), rhetorical theory and pedagogy (Young, Becker, and Pike), discourse (Young and Becker, "The Role"), writing across the curriculum ("Designing"), writing program administration ("Some Presuppositions"), and the profession of rhetoric and composition ("'Tracing,'" "Working").

In this multimodal work, one sees a dynamic paradigm for the discipline today, the roots of which Young helped to plant. Anne Ruggles Gere rightly characterizes the discipline of rhetoric and composition not as "a bounded territory, one that can be distinguished and set apart," but rather as "'a complex of forces,' . . . a kind of charged space in which multiple 'sites' of interaction appear" (4); Lynn Bloom defines it as a "multidisciplinary, eclectic, widely inclusive rather than exclusive" endeavor (274); and Janice Lauer has accurately described our field as a "dappled discipline" because researchers and scholars in rhetoric and composition explore complex questions and problems regarding literate practices through a variety of methodological and theoretical lenses ("Composition," "Rhetoric").

Young's scholarly work has both implicitly and explicitly advocated converging multiple perspectives to address these kinds of complex problems. For example, in his landmark article "Concepts of Art and the Teaching of Writing," Young traces two apparently incompatible concepts of art in rhetoric, what he terms *art as glamour* (or mystery) and *art as grammar* (or techne). Young concludes that given the durability of these two competing concepts of art, they may both be true on some level. He recommends the following:

> [We] [as scholars] can respond by considering the possibility that behind art as glamour and art as grammar there may be a more adequate conception of rhetorical art that does not lead us to affirm the importance of certain psychological powers at the cost of denying the importance of others. If we choose this last course of action, we might begin with a scholarly investigation of the role of heuristic procedures in the rhetorical process, since they call into play both our reason and our imagination. (202)

Young is not advocating a naive yoking of incompatible perspectives but rather a dynamic epistemology that recognizes the complexities of language, thought, action, context, and rhetorical practices. In this view is an argument for what Vitanza in this collection describes as a third term that disrupts the binary constructs of modernity.[1] It is a perspective that Young advocated as early as 1965, when with Alton Becker he wrote: "A tagmemic rhetoric stands somewhere between the rigorous theories of science and the almost purely intuitive theories of the humanities. We see no reason to reject the insights of either the former or the latter, believing that all new knowledge—like the process of writing itself—involves both intuitive analogy and formal precision" ("Toward" 468). Here rhetoric is understood as encompassing both *noesis* (knowledge making—science) and *poiesis* (creation—art) and therefore does not fit neatly into the modernist categories of arts and sciences that academia has used to define its endeavors. In this robust rhetoric, as in Young's whole oeuvre, lies the potential for conceiving of a discipline and pedagogy of rhetoric.

This collection not only acknowledges the powerful and influential contributions Richard Young has made, but it also responds to his invitation, offered with Becker and Pike, "to participate in the process of creating a rhetoric adequate to our times" (361). This book is not a final word—that would be antithetical to the principles of Young and the scholars writing here—but rather a generative tool, a heuristic, if you will, for future teachers and scholars who will take up the challenge of creating new rhetorics adequate to their times and places.

The Contributors and Their Contributions

Each of the contributors to this collection has heeded Young's call to engage in serious scholarly investigations of the "assumptions that underlie established practices and habits about writing" ("'Tracing'" 164). Further, as Young's own range of scholarship demonstrates, the contributors study a diverse array of disciplinary objects, situate their work in a wide matrix of theoretical perspectives, and engage in multiple modes of inquiry and multiple discourses. As such, they represent a microcosm of the discipline. This collection contains essays that are historical (Bazerman; Goggin and Beatty; Lauer; Paul and Blakeslee; Horner; Schnakenberg), philosophical and theoretical (Garver; Inkster; Vitanza; Watson), and empirical (Berkenkotter; Long; Greene and Nowacek; Palmquist; Sipple, Sipple, and Carson). The objects of study tackled also intersect with those to which Young has devoted his scholarly life: invention (Vitanza), rhetorical pedagogy (Petraglia; Berkenkotter; Greene and Nowacek; Palmquist; Schnakenberg; Sipple, Sipple and Carson), rhetorical theory (Inkster; Garver; Horner; Vitanza), discourse (Odell and McGrane), writing across the curriculum (Watson; Palmquist; Sipple, Sipple, and Carson; Greene and Nowacek), and the discipline and profession of rhetoric and composition (Bazerman; Goggin and Beatty; Lauer; Petraglia; Schnakenberg). These essays further support a tripartite epistemic view of rhetoric as concerned with *creating knowledge* (Bazerman; Lauer; Inkster;

Garver), *preserving knowledge* (Horner; Garver; Schnakenberg), and *using knowledge* (Long; Watson; Palmquist; Sipple, Sipple, and Carson). (See Goggin and Beatty in this volume for a fuller discussion of these three ideals in light of the field of rhetoric and composition.) This trinity echoes that offered in Young, Becker, and Pike's description of tagmemic rhetoric:

> Perhaps never before in our history has there been such a need for effective communication, but the old formulations of rhetoric seem inadequate to the times. We have sought to develop a rhetoric that implies we are all citizens of an extraordinarily diverse and disturbed world, that the "truths" we live by are tentative and subject to change; that we must be *discoverers of new truths* as well as *preservers and transmitters of the old*, and that *enlightened cooperation is the preeminent ethical goal of communication.* (emphasis added, 8–9)

Thus, although most of the contributors express their indebtedness to Young explicitly within their chapters, all express it implicitly.

That Young's influence pervades these chapters is not surprising. Virtually all of the contributors are linked in a common bond as former students of Young, having studied under him either at the University of Michigan (Lauer; Horner; Odell) or later at Carnegie Mellon University (Goggin; Petraglia; Blakeslee; Schnakenberg; Long; Greene; Palmquist; J. Sipple; Carson) as doctoral students, or as participants in his NEH seminars (Bazerman; Berkenkotter; Garver; Inkster; Vitanza; Watson). Spanning several generations of scholars now active in the discipline, the contributors offer a partial genealogy not only of Young's students and his influence but also of the field itself. Their chapters resonate with one another, sometimes in harmony and sometimes in discord. The resulting scholarly symphony is one which Young no doubt would applaud.

Together, the scholarly articles in this collection offer a window on the dynamic and richly diverse inquiries that constitute the profession today. In so doing, they capture the discipline of rhetoric and composition in the process of constructing itself. In other words, they demonstrate *rhetoric and composition in action.*

A Note on the Organization of Chapters

In deciding how to organize the chapters in this volume, I was guided by Young, Becker, and Pike's sixth and final maxim of tagmemic rhetoric: "*Linguistic choices are made in relation to a universe of discourse.* . . . [W]e must have either a conscious or a subconscious awareness of the particular universe of discourse that constrains our choices if we are to choose intelligently" (301).[2] The arrangement of the chapters has been very conscious. But I must quickly add that this organization, like any, is a convenient fiction. That is to say, one might choose to order these readings in many different ways. For example, I might have chosen a chronological scheme, dividing the sections into Our Past, Our Present, and Our Future. Or I might have divided the collection into sections that echo the kinds of issues Richard Young has dealt with in his scholarship: Problems, Invention, WAC.

The order resides not in the collection but in the lens I brought to bear on these essays. As Young, Becker, and Pike note, "units have contexts, variant forms, contrastive features, and parts. But units can not take different perspectives; only perceivers can do this" (122). The organizing principle I selected comes from yet another maxim of tagmemic rhetoric: "Maxim 4: *A unit of experience can be viewed as a particle, or as a wave, or as a field. That is, the writer can choose to view any element of his experience as if it were static, or as if it were dynamic, or as if it were a network of relationships or part of a larger network*" (122).

This maxim provides a powerfully robust framework for these essays. First, it is one of two that combine to create the powerful invention tool—the elegant nine-celled tagmemic heuristic. (The other is Maxim 3: "*A unit, at any level of focus, can be adequately understood only if three aspects of the unit are known: (1) its contrastive features, (2) its range of variation, and (3) its distribution in larger contexts*" [Young, Becker, and Pike 56].) Each cell in the heuristic can prompt multiple questions designed to help a writer view a problem from a variety of perspectives. In the universe of discourse inhabited by many of the potential readers of this book, this heuristic is well known. In fact, if one knows anything of Young, Becker, and Pike's rhetoric, one is likely to be familiar with the complex and powerful nine-celled heuristic of particle, wave, and field. It appears in various guises in numerous writing textbooks (e.g., Axelrod and Cooper, *The St. Martin's Guide to Writing* 439–40) and has been used by scholars such as Erika Lindemann in "Three Views of English 101" to organize disciplinary discussions. This scheme thus invokes one of Young's major contributions to our field, namely, the revival of invention, and it echoes the primary title of this collection, *Inventing a Discipline*. Second, as Young, Becker, and Pike point out, "note carefully that a unit is not either a particle *or* a wave *or* a field, but can be viewed as all three" (122). Since the three concepts are not meant to be thought of in isolation, this scheme calls attention to the echoing threads of arguments running through all the chapters—again, some in harmony and others in discord—and challenges readers to listen for these reverberations.

As the heading for the first part—Field: Reflections on the Past, Present, and Future of the Discipline—may suggest, the chapters in this section treat issues that concern rhetoric and composition as "a system itself, composed of interrelated subsystems" (Young, Becker, and Pike 123). Here contributors consider the history, present state, and potential future directions in research, scholarship, and pedagogies of our field (Bazerman; Goggin and Beatty; Lauer; Petraglia). The second section—Wave: Temporal and Spatial Explorations of Rhetorical Theory and Practice—contains theoretical, historical, and empirical investigations of particular kinds of rhetorical theories and practices. Some consider influences and potential influences of specific rhetorical theories (Inkster; Garver; Schnakenberg); others consider particular rhetorical practices, such as memory and delivery (Horner), invention (Vitanza), and visual and verbal rhetoric (Odell and McGrane); and still others consider the contexts of literate practices, such as scientific communities (Paul and Blakeslee; Berkenkotter). The final section—Particle: Pedagogical Applications of Rhetoric—clusters scholarly discussions of specific writing programs and pedagogical approaches. In other words, they "select from the dynamic whole [the profession] some part . . . and 'take a snapshot' of it" (Young, Becker, and Pike 123). These snapshots include a thoughtful analysis of a community literacy center and its implications for understanding the complexities of literate practices (Long); specific considerations of content and methodologies for teaching literate practices, considerations that hold important implications especially for writing-across-the-curriculum programs (Watson; Greene and Nowacek), and meaty discussions of the trials and tribulations of and lessons emerging from the development of two very different WAC programs (Palmquist; Sipple, Sipple, and Carson).

The chapters in these three sections offer multiple perspectives on and methodologies for the pressing issues surrounding the study and teaching of literate practices. In short, they offer a road map "to guide the conduct of our professional lives" (Young, "'Tracing'" 164).

Notes

1. Postmodernism has challenged strict binaries that insist on defining one thing as against and opposite another. (For a fuller discussion of this challenge, see Vitanza in this volume.) The biochemist Cyril Ponnamperuma, for example, argues:

> The division of matter into living and nonliving is perhaps an artificial one, convenient for distinguishing such extreme cases as a man and a stone but quite inappropriate when describing other cases such as a virus particle. Indeed, the crystallization of a virus by Wendell Stanley in the 1960s brought about the need for revising our definition of "life" and "living." Pirie has compared our use of the terms *living* and *nonliving* to the words *acid* and *base* as used in chemistry. While sodium hydroxide is distinctly alkaline [i.e., base] sulfuric acid is a powerful acid. But in between these two extremes is a whole variation in strength. The chemist has overcome the confusion arising from these rigid categories by inventing the nomenclature of "hydrogen ion concentration" (pH). In this way, all the observed phenomena can be described in terms of one quantity. We may have to invent a similar quantity to avoid any vagueness that might arise in applying the term "life" to borderline cases such as the virus. (qtd. in Stoff and Pellegrino 21)

A useful analogy can be drawn here between the complexities of trying to define matter and trying to delimit the enterprise of rhetoric and composition. Just as a new term had to be invented to describe the multiple properties of chemicals not captured by the dichotomy of acid and base, we probably need to invent new language that acknowledges that rhetoric and composition is both a science of art and an art of science.

2. Tagmemic rhetoric is comprised of six interrelated maxims. For a discussion of these maxims and of tagmemic rhetoric more generally, see Goggin's re-review essay of *Rhetoric: Discovery and Change*.

Works Cited

Almagno, Stephanie A. "An NEH Fellowship Examined: Social Networks and Composition History." Diss. U of Rhode Island, 1994.

Axelrod, Rise B., and Charles R. Cooper. *The St. Martin's Guide to Writing*. 5th ed. New York: St. Martin's, 1997.

Berlin, James A. *Rhetoric and Reality: Writing Instruction in American Colleges, 1900–1985*. Carbondale: Southern Illinois UP, 1987.

———. *Writing Instruction in Nineteenth-Century American Colleges*. Carbondale: Southern Illinois UP, 1984.

Bloom, Lynn Z. "Conclusion: Mapping Composition's New Geography." *Composition in the Twenty-First Century: Crisis and Change*. Ed. Lynn Z. Bloom, Donald A. Daiker, and Edward M. White. Carbondale: Southern Illinois UP, 1996. 273–80.

Consigny, Scott. "Rhetoric and Its Situations." Young and Liu 59–68.

Ede, Lisa, and Andrea Lunsford. "Audience Addressed/Audience Invoked: The Role of Audience in Composition Theory and Pedagogy." *The Writing Teacher's Sourcebook*. 3rd ed. Ed. Gary Tate, Edward P. J. Corbett, and Nancy Myers. New York: Oxford UP, 1994. 243–57.

Enos, Theresa, and Stuart C. Brown, eds. *Defining the New Rhetorics*. Newbury Park: Sage, 1993.

Gere, Anne Ruggles, ed. *Into the Field: Sites of Composition Studies*. New York: MLA, 1993.

Goggin, Maureen Daly. *Authoring a Discipline: Scholarly Journals and the Post–World War II Emergence of Rhetoric and Composition*. Mahwah, NJ: Erlbaum, 2000.

———. "Composing a Discipline: The Role of Scholarly Journals in the Disciplinary Emergence of Rhetoric and Composition since 1950." *Rhetoric Review* 15 (1997): 322–49.

———. *"Rhetoric: Discovery and Change"* by Richard E. Young, Alton L. Becker, and Kenneth L. Pike. *Rhetoric Review* 17 (1998): 188–94.

———. "Rhetoric Society of America." *Encyclopedia of Rhetoric and Composition: Communication from Ancient Times to the Information Age.* Ed. Theresa Enos. New York: Garland, 1996. 629.

Gorrell, Robert M. "Very Like a Whale—A Report on Rhetoric." *College Composition and Communication* 16 (1965): 138–43.

Lauer, Janice M. "Composition Studies: Dappled Discipline." *Rhetoric Review* 3 (1984): 20–29.

———. "Rhetoric and Composition Studies: A Multimodal Discipline." Enos and Brown 44–54.

LeFevre, Karen Burke. *Invention as a Social Act.* Carbondale: Southern Illinois UP, 1987.

Lindemann, Erika. "Three Views of English 101." *College English* 57 (1995): 287–302.

Palmquist, Michael, and Richard E. Young. "The Notion of Giftedness and Student Expectations about Writing." *Written Communication* 9 (1992): 137–68.

Stoff, Jesse A., and Charles R. Pellegrino. *Chronic Fatigue Syndrome: The Hidden Epidemic.* New York: Random, 1988.

Vitanza, Victor J. "A Retrospective and Two Prospectives." *Pre/Text: The First Decade.* Ed. Victor J. Vitanza. Pittsburgh: U of Pittsburgh P, 1993. xi–xxix.

Young, Richard E. "Concepts of Art and the Teaching of Writing." Young and Liu 193–202.

———. "Designing for Change in Writing Across the Curriculum Programs." *Balancing Acts: Essays on the Teaching of Writing in Honor of William F. Irmscher.* Ed. Chris Anderson et al. Carbondale: Southern Illinois UP, 1991.

———. "Invention: A Topographical Survey." *Teaching Composition: Twelve Bibliographical Essays.* Ed. Gary Tate. Fort Worth: Texas Christian UP, 1976. 1–43.

———. "Paradigms and Problems: Needed Research in Rhetorical Invention." *Research on Composing: Points of Departure.* Ed. Charles R. Cooper and Lee Odell. Urbana, IL: NCTE, 1978. 29–47.

————. "Problems and the Composing Process." *Visible Language* 14 (1980): 341–50.

————. "Recent Developments in Rhetorical Invention." *Teaching Composition: Twelve Bibliographical Essays.* Ed. Gary Tate. Fort Worth: Texas Christian UP, 1987. 1–38.

————. "Some Presuppositions in Decision-Making for Writing Programs." *An Oleo of Notions Concerning the Politics of Writing Instruction.* Ed. Robert D. Narveson. Lincoln: U of Nebraska–Lincoln, 1987. 44–63.

————. "'Tracing Round the Frame': Thinking about Writing in Departments of English." *Discourse Studies in Honor of James L. Kinneavy.* Ed. Rosalind J. Gabin. Potomac, MD: Scripta Humanistica, 1995. 149–67.

————. "Working on the Margin: Rhetorical Studies and the New Self-Consciousness." *Rhetoric Society Quarterly* 20 (1990): 325–32.

Young, Richard E., and Alton L. Becker. "The Role of Lexical and Grammatical Cues in Paragraph Recognition." *Studies in Language and Language Behavior* 11 (1966): 1–6.

————. "Toward a Modern Theory of Rhetoric: A Tagmemic Contribution." *Harvard Educational Review* 35 (1965): 450–68.

Young, Richard E., Alton L. Becker, and Kenneth L. Pike. *Rhetoric: Discovery and Change.* New York: Harcourt, 1970.

Young, Richard E., and Maureen Daly Goggin. "Some Issues in Dating the Birth of the New Rhetoric in Departments of English: A Contribution to a Developing Historiography." Enos and Brown 22–43.

Young, Richard E., and Yameng Liu, eds. *Landmark Essays on Rhetorical Invention in Writing.* New York: Hermagoras, 1995.

I

FIELD: REFLECTIONS ON THE PAST, PRESENT, AND FUTURE OF THE DISCIPLINE

To take a field perspective on a unit means to focus on the relationships (patterns, structures, organizational principles, networks, systems, functions) that order the parts of the unit and connect it to other units within a larger system.

YOUNG, BECKER, AND PIKE, *Rhetoric: Discovery and Change*

The essays in this section explore the discipline of rhetoric and composition within larger historical and systemic frameworks. Each looks, to one degree or another, to the past of the field to offer explanations for its present conditions and its relationship to other academic fields and to issue calls for much needed future research, theories, and pedagogies in rhetoric. To this extent, each essay in this section responds in its own way to the invitation Young, Becker, and Pike issued at the end of *Rhetoric: Discovery and Change* "to participate in the process of creating a rhetoric adequate to our times" (361). On the very last page of their book, Young, Becker, and Pike give the final sentence to John Dewey, who observed: "Not perfection as the final goal, but the ever enduring process of perfecting, maturing, refining, is the aim of living" (370). We might substitute the term "rhetoric" for "living" in Dewey's observation. As the essays in this section make clear, rhetoric as a system is contingent; that is to say, rhetoric systems, like rhetoric itself, are both responses to and shapers of the material conditions in which they operate.

Charles Bazerman traces the history of both rhetoric and literacy in search of a "new rhetoric for literacy needs." He outlines the tensions between rhetoric and literacy studies that he notes have been building for the past two centuries and argues for expanding the theoretical terrain of rhetoric and literacy to open a space for new research on and learning of complex, multiple literate practices—a space that will accommodate the complicated intersections among reading and writing practices as socially situated activities. As he notes, "It is a new world, and it needs a new rhetoric." For Bazerman,

> the way to move toward that rhetoric is through continued research into the forces actually at play in the many texts that circulate in the social spaces created by the print and electronic worlds, and into the ways individuals and their activities are influenced by their engagement with mediating texts. By watching what these texts do and what people do with them, without assuming that they are simply reproducing the activities of the agora, we can move toward a rhetoric that will illuminate the great diversity of our communicative world.

Maureen Daly Goggin and Steve Beatty are also concerned with creating a space for a new rhetoric that can accommodate theories, practices, and pedagogies of multiple literate practices. In tracing the history of writing instruction, they make a case for why the site of that new rhetoric may not be able to be constructed in writing programs as they are currently configured. Prompted by a question Young has posed, "[W]hy does our profession persist in relegating the study and teaching of writing to an inferior status despite what is by now more than a generation of serious theoretical, historical, and applied work in rhetorical studies in English Departments?" ("'Tracing'" 150), Goggin and Beatty explore why, despite a century of complaints and decades of dedicated efforts to unseat it, the compulsory first-year composition system established over a century ago remains impervious to any substantial change. They draw on the powerful economic theory of self-reinforcing mechanisms (a theory that accounts for why suboptimal systems often win out over more promising systems) to offer one explanation for the tenacity of this system and to speculate on ways to swerve from its groove.

Janice Lauer tackles the question "to what extent rhetorical scholarship in rhetoric and composition, speech communication, and classics coheres and interrelates or whether these fields study different problems, [or whether these] are motivated by distinct issues and are governed solely by their own guiding perspectives and interpretive practices." She demonstrates that although these fields have dealt with similar topics such as invention and the rhetorical situation, those in these fields have been "motivated for the most part by different issues and consequences." She shows that while rhetoric and composition scholars and teachers have drawn on the research from speech communication and classics, the reverse is not true, although there are signs of a growing intertextuality among the fields. She questions the unidirectionality of this pattern and ends with the provocative question, "If these disciplines take seriously the questions they pose about rhetorical theory, practice, and pedagogy, should they not welcome all cross-disciplinary research and scholarship that contributes to new understandings of these questions?"

Petraglia explores the question: What impact has the "rhetorical turn" in academia had? And what potential does it have for reforming how we teach complex literate practices? In the rhetorical turn, Petraglia argues, lies the potential for closing the gap between pedagogical practices and rhetorical theories—a gap Goggin and Beatty deal with in their chapter. He outlines the kinds of rhetoric questions being posed in a variety of fields, including, for instance, rhetoric and composition, speech communication, and rhetoric of inquiry. Such questions and the work spawned by them, Petraglia suggests, draw painful attention to the fact "that composition and public speaking classes are pale reflections of what we know about rhetoric and the demands for rhetorical training emanating from elsewhere in the academy as a result of the rhetorical turn." Petraglia's chapter resonates, as do the other chapters in this section, with Bazerman's call for a new rhetoric and prepares the way for the essays in the next section, which explore particular rhetorical theories, practices, and contexts.

Works Cited

Young, Richard E. "'Tracing Round the Frame': Thinking about Writing in Departments of English." *Discourse Studies in Honor of James L. Kinneavy.* Ed. Rosalind J. Gabin. Potomac, MD: Scripta Humanistica, 1995. 149–67.

Young, Richard E., Alton L. Becker, and Kenneth L. Pike. *Rhetoric: Discovery and Change.* New York: Harcourt, 1970.

CHAPTER ONE

A Rhetoric for Literate Society: The Tension between Expanding Practices and Restricted Theories

CHARLES BAZERMAN
University of California, Santa Barbara

Address an abiding social need.
RICHARD YOUNG

The day is short, the task is long.
SAYINGS OF THE FATHERS

During Richard Young's career, the teaching of writing has made enormous strides in knowledge and practice, in funding, and in institutional respect. Richard's vision, scholarship, and institutional leadership have been central to that story. Though the task is begun, however, it is hardly finished. We have only begun to sense how truly important writing and literacy are to the modern world and how partial and preliminary are our tools to speak to the need.

If those of us engaged in composition may have at first thought we just wanted to help some students articulate their thoughts and succeed in college, we soon were drawn into the ways our students participate in society and the ways literate practices hold

I would like to thank Carol Berkenkotter, Theresa Enos, Janice Lauer, Tom Miller, James Porter, Paul Prior, David Russell, Patricia Sullivan, and members of the rhetoric colloquia at Purdue University and the University of Arizona for their comments on earlier versions of this essay.

our world together. Writing practices, it now appears, are integral to the complex forms of social organization that maintain what prosperity, amity, and health we have on this crowded planet. This expanded challenge calls for new research and new theoretical perspectives that will help us navigate through the enlarged landscape we are beginning to notice. As we make good on the challenge, we increase our claim on the resources, authority, and professional respect that will allow us to do the job properly.

The Social Space of Literate Activity

Work on academic and professional writing[1] has sensitized us to the way writing is deeply embedded within intertextual networks (see Bakhtin; Selzer, "Intertextuality"; Bazerman, "Intertextual"). How we use our reading in our writing positions us in relation to previous texts, displaying the meaning and value we find in those texts, the relationships we see among them, and their role in the formation of the current moment. Every proposal for a new bridge rests on engineering textbooks, prior proposals, urban planning projections, internal corporate financial statements, contracts and materials catalogs, government policy and project documents, and many other sorts of files, reports, books, and correspondence—only a few of which may be explicitly referred to, but all of which make the proposal what it is.

Interactions mediated by literacy occur in no single physical space and time but in a space of mutual imaginings that we visit every time we pick up a document or begin to fill a blank page (as early as the fifteenth century, this virtual place was nominated the Republic of Letters [Eisenstein 137, n. 287]). Nonetheless, textually mediated relations draw sustenance and motive from our more immediate, embodied relations with the people and things that physically surround us (the problem of how to get us and our neighbors across a particular canyon every morning sets in motion the intertextually complex paperwork of trying to get a bridge built). In turn, the circulation of texts alters the course of immediate events by dint of the altered knowledge, skills, perceptions, affect, thoughts, and commitments brought about by our reading and writing. We return from our reading and writing altered in ways that change our local behavior—we build far different bridges than we did five thousand years ago. The technologies of literacy and print culture, evolving over the last fifty or so centuries (supplemented in the last two centuries by rapidly changing, but still letter-reliant, electronic communications technologies, beginning with the telegraph) have provided means for our local society to be pervaded by what sociologist Anthony Giddens has called time-space distanciation.

These specialized, highly elaborated forms of social participation abstracted from the immediate moment require literacy skills that extend beyond the text coding and decoding skills we associate with the lower grades of schooling, remediation, or adult literacy programs. In ever more challenging circumstances, people spend their whole careers developing specialized reading and writing skills—such as examining a legal brief for salient legal principles and relevant case details in relation to precedent and prior court rulings, or, on the basis of a few hours of information gathering and a few minutes of actual drafting, writing an engaging, reasonably accurate news story that conforms to current standards of the profession. Because such skills have been developed and passed on within their specialized fields of practice, however, they are often thought of as professional skills rather than literacy skills.

These specialized skills (e.g., reading and writing as judges do); the textual forms through which they are enacted (the opinion, the brief, the law review article); the social and cognitive means of text production (the appeals procedures that bring together documents for review and adjudication); the physical and economic means of text reproduction and distribution (the mixed government, private, and professional association systems of legal publication that distribute the judge's opinion to legal offices, courts, and law schools throughout the country); the social arrangements and roles developed in conjunction with the elaboration of texts (law clerks and law librarians; state bars and bar exams; law companies and legal clients; lawyer-client privilege and obligations of lawyers as officers of the court)—in short, the entire social, material, economic, symbolic apparatus of our multiformed textual culture, are historical inventions, becoming ever more pervasive and complex as the number of people, texts, and social organizations has increased.

We know, for example, some of the outlines of the development of the system of scientific publication, which perhaps has been studied more intensively than other literate systems because of recent interest in writing across the curriculum and the rhetoric of science (Bazerman and Russell; Harris). The scientific article was a latecomer—not even a possibility until the invention of the scientific journal in 1665 provided an occasion to develop particular text forms to circulate among specialized readers (Bazerman, *Shaping*; Atkinson). The kinds of arguments engaged in and the kinds of evidence, reasoning, and demonstrations brought to bear evolved over time, as did the social systems of referees and editors. Even the character and role of journal reader evolved over time as readers' interests, professional positions, critical criteria, and uses of the literature in daily practice changed. The social circulation and function of the journal also interacted with the changing character of the sponsoring societies and their relation to economic, political, and class systems within which they resided.

Around the nineteenth century, as literatures, investigative methods, and professionalization of authors and readers developed along with the critical challenge of the argument, articles began to approximate familiarly modern forms. Specialties and journals proliferated, each with its own special character and discursive challenge. Today there are many kinds of journals, articles, and forms of writing in physics, geology, ecology, psychology, anthropology, and every other of the specialized domains. Skilled producers of one kind of text in a specialty are not necessarily skilled producers of other kinds of text in that specialty, let alone in other specialties. The accomplished individual authors, editors, and publishers participate in an extensive system of book, journal, and other format production, circulation, and storage involving libraries, Internet, universities, societies, and for-profit publishers. These specialized forms of knowledge production then intersect with many other discursive systems—corporate and financial, governmental, defense, industrial, legal, psychological practice, education (see, for example, van Nostrand). Each of these systems has its own complex history of forms, institutions, and practices, and each has its own cadre of skilled and not-so-skilled practitioners.

Technology has an even more complex story interpenetrated with relations to other discursive systems, as I have learned in the course of examining the emergence of Edison's system of incandescent light and power. While science has tried to remove itself into specialized worlds of inquiry conducted by experts, technology is regularly in the business of gathering financial backers and clients, keeping stockholders and financial markets happy, gaining the cooperation of governments and publics, applying for and protecting patents and other legal statuses, positioning itself against the representations of competitors, drawing on increasingly sophisticated technical and scientific literatures, coordinating internal organizational work of development and production, managing public relations through the press, and positioning its products in the cultural market (Bazerman, *Languages*).

Though distanced and abstracted from the local moment, these textually mediated interactions are deeply embedded in our sociality. Many of the elaborate forms and systems of literate communication grew out of the transparently social forms of letter writing—emperors' correspondence with generals, governors, and emissaries formed the basis for bureaucratic forms of writing. Newspapers developed from letters of correspondence. Business memos, reports, orders, and sales documents in the eighteenth century were still all simply business correspondence (Yates). That is, large, distanced organizations grew from individual people sending messages at a distance to other individuals. Similarly, letter writing remains an important part of children's writing education because teachers need to find comprehensible human motives and situations beyond the logic of school performance to draw students into this curious practice of inscribing signs.

The historically evolved systems of literate activity create elaborate textual underpinnings to our daily lives and social relations, even when we are engaged in face-to-face events or experiences of the most material and physical kind. In the courtroom, oral arguments made before judges and juries rely on boxes of documents, are located within a system of laws and precedents, and produce a court record and a written opinion (Stratman). Similarly, doctors' interactions with patients and medical interventions are informed by medical school textbooks and the current clinical literature, to which practical experience (such as clinical outcomes of surgical procedures) must be reduced if that experience is to be of general use. Politicians' handshaking is embedded within the electoral system established by laws and within a system of politics fed by news and party documents. Our semiotic understanding and organization of events and social order, as produced within special domains of knowledge and practice and as stabilized in texts, pervade all aspects of our life.

The Consequences of Literacy Revisited

The consequences of literacy are manifold. In the seventies and eighties when scholars such as Goody, Havelock, Olson, and Ong started to outline a coherent set of interpersonal and intellectual changes that accompanied the introduction of literacy, they were caught up short by the argument that the consequences of literacy depended on how literacy practices were used within their contexts. This argument was made forcefully by Scribner and Cole through their observations of the varied consequences of the multiple literacies of the Vai in West Africa. Those individuals who used literacy in Western schools to work through puzzles in formal logic increased their abilities in formal logic; those who learned Arabic as part of Koranic scriptural practices increased their ability to repeat verbatim texts; and those who used the local rebus-like written language for letter writing were good at solving rebus puzzles. Literate Vai showed gains in cognitive skills corresponding only to the specific literacy practices they engaged in. Additionally, linguistic research pointed out that the spoken and the written language were connected by a continuity of forms and functions, so that the social and cognitive habits of oral and of literate people would not be distinguished across a sharp divide (Chafe; Tannen).

Yet, that the picture is more complex does not mean there is no picture. Rather, we need to look at the specific social practices and forms that have developed around literacy. This is a direction that anthropologist Jack Goody was heading in one of his last books on the subject: *The Logic of Writing and the Organization of Society*. While this text still assumes something of a unitary logic of writing, it nonetheless points toward a great variety of social consequences in different spheres, paying close attention to the historical and anthropological evidence from different societies. With respect to religions, Goody sees historical evidence that the concept of distinct religions that are similar and affiliated over substantial geographic regions, as opposed to varieties of local beliefs and practices, is tied to the emergence of scriptures that are central to religious practices—scriptures that can define a set of beliefs stably and recognizably over time and distances. Textually organized beliefs raise the possibility of universalism and the global applicability of beliefs. Literate priestly classes, having access to texts and control over doctrinal issues, may form bureaucracies of geographically dispersed belief practices and may aggregate the wealth and political power that often accompany geographic expansion. Further, attention to perceivable religious change (as opposed to the historical evolution of practice which remains unnoticed by practitioners) is a function of recorded beliefs and recorded history—increasing the saliency of doctrinal questions, differences among sects, decreed belief changes, changes of allegiance, and the like.

Government likewise faces new possibilities with the introduction of literacy. Goody notes such phenomena as the facilitation of emissaries and clerks over geographically dispersed areas, kept in communication by both written rule and correspondence. Literate government functionaries, engaged in taxation, census, and accounting, extend government control. Treaties can regularize relations with surrounding states. With centralization of power through literate communication, extended geographic areas may become reorganized into center/periphery relations, with the consequence that national ceremonies, rituals, and forms of loyalty come to supplement, if not replace, local loyalties. Goody provides similar accounts of legal and economic systems.

These literacy-facilitated institutional systems may develop in varying relationship with each other. Sometimes they may coincide, as when economic power is centralized in the state or church, or the church or the justice system becomes an organ of state policy. On the other hand, complex tensions may arise among the church, state, justice, and economic systems, each affording certain social protections and opportunities based on their separate principles and methods of bringing texts to bear on the local moment.

While Goody attends to only four of the major institutional systems of societies, we may consider similar developments in all aspects of affiliation and activity—for example, numismatic clubs rely on international newsletters, catalogs, reference works, and correspondence; sports leagues, even at the amateur level, have rules and rule-making bodies, league organization and bureaucracies, records and competitive rankings, publicity and news. Consider then the deeply literate practices of such institutions as hospitals and schools. Even the public sphere consists of complex networks of newspapers, magazines, press releases, political consultants, video news and commentary (which themselves are surrounded by paper, scripts, and bureaucracy), and other highly articulated systems which run on the written word. Even the supposed privacy of our bedrooms has been saturated by psychology, social science, and popular self-help publications, not to speak of the technology and economics of mattress making and the communications at a distance that have created the fashion market that influences the patterns on our bedsheets.

Literacy does not require or inexorably lead to any particular development, but it is a powerful tool available for organizing, extending, providing resources for, and transforming all of our social endeavors. Once transformed, these endeavors embed literate practices within their fundamental mechanisms of organization. These practices, as Scribner and Cole (drawing on Vygotsky) point out, are associated with specific forms of cognition. As people use the various tools of literacy, they learn to think with these tools: as discourse about law develops, we think more about the law, and to think, we use precisely those discursive terms of the law—so that if we want to discuss with our friend a court case in which we have been embroiled, we need to draw on the terms and events of the law to explain what is happening and why it is important that the opposing attorney filed a motion to dismiss before the depositions rather than after. If we want to escape the stabilized terms of the literate institution so as not to be constrained by the institution's own assumptions, we need to develop or draw on a critical vocabulary, most likely to be found in a critical literature, as in critical law studies. That is, even to inspect and query one literate system we may need the resources and strength of another.

Literate practices also embed specifics of the processes of text production, distribution, and use. By pursuing the situated practices within a discursive sphere, we can find new direction for writing process research, which lost some steam with the recognition that processes vary across individuals and circumstances. When viewed as embedded within specialized literacy systems, writing processes can be seen to be shaped and modeled in part by the institutional history and activity; further, atypical processes can inform us about the particularity of specific events and of each individual's form of participation (see Bazerman, *Shaping;* Blakeslee; Prior, *Writing/Disciplinarity;* Swales, *Other Floors*).

Directions for Research

The complex but sketchy picture that is emerging of how literacy works in structuring the modern way of life only points to the need for more research and theory to help fill out, extend, and clarify that picture. Goody points toward one direction for fundamental research into the history of specialized literacy practices and their consequences within the many different societies—starting from less elaborated social forms and observing how literacy enters into their expansion, transformation, and complex organization (see also Besnier). Such chronological investigation can help unpack the complex of current practices and systems. This kind of research complements rhetoric and composition's recent research into writing and literacy across the curriculum, in the disciplines, in the professions, and in the workplace. These inquiries start at the other end, with highly developed literate systems which the student or neophyte must learn in order to participate in. These participations may range from the most routine practices to core decision making or innovation that transforms the nature of the endeavor. The success of one's literacy socialization into specialized practices may be measured by how much access one has to the most central resources and mechanisms of communication, and how one makes use of that access.

In the historical middle, we have some allies in and resources from scholars engaged in the history of the book and print culture (building on the pioneering work of Eisenstein and of Chartier), as well as historians of specialized domains, such as the history of science and technology (for example, Dear) and the history of journalism and the news (for example, Schudson). Help also may be gained from a few scholars who have entered into parallel studies of other paper-and-ink symbolic practices, such as the history of numeracy (see Cohen; Porter) and the history of drawing as an everyday practice (Bermingham). The thriving profession of the history of literacy (see Kaestle), though it is not yet focused on the rise of literate systems of social organization nor on the advanced skills of specialized literacies, provides much data on the extent of literacy and the circulation of popular texts. We have allies also in current sociological, anthropological, and situated psychological studies of various forms of work and affiliation (see, for example, Engestrom and Middleton); the puzzles presented by the recent introduction of electronic media into a range of activities has brought particular attention to the embedding of symbolic activity within social arrangements.

Using these interdisciplinary resources to frame research projects can help us develop a truly fundamental understanding of the importance, mechanisms, and consequences of writing in society. Such a research program would broaden the basis of our discipline from its current marginal hold on students' writing as they make the transition from high school to the university (a hold which for many reasons we should not give up [Bazerman, "Response"]). First-year writing, or academic writing at all levels of undergraduate and graduate education, is the point at which students' personal literacy development meets the range of specialized literacy practices of contemporary professionalism. However, the tensions between individuals' actual writing skills and the professional demand for specialized writing skills are hard to understand and respond to without having in front of us the larger picture puzzle of literacy and society into which these moments, or pieces, of educational demand fit.

The Limited Domain of Classical Rhetoric

Rhetoric has historically developed as a reflective, practical, strategic art of language use. As such it provides a theoretical model and a theoretical starting point for considering how we can effectively operate in this emerging world of increasingly specialized literate interaction. To develop theoretical terms that are appropriate to literacy, we need to develop new rhetorical categories that extend beyond the limited vision of classical rhetoric, which was concerned with a small range of historically particular oral performances that were embedded in societies which differed substantially from ours. Not of least significance, in the ancient world the novel technology of literacy had not entered so deeply into the major institutions of social organization. In the last two millennia, there have been some attempts to address rhetorical challenges created by the growing pervasiveness of literate communication, but no truly coherent set of categories has yet emerged that is both literate and rhetorical.

Of all the spontaneous talk that people engage in every day with only limited forethought and reflection in response to immediately perceived circumstances, only a small and unusual subset gave rise to the intellectual apparatus of classical rhetoric and a class of professional rhetoricians who provided advice and instruction for successful speech. The special class of speech events that ancient Greeks and Romans worried enough about to support the formation of a rhetorical profession was high-stakes competitive debate presented to influence public evaluations or decisions. These triadic communications appealed to the third-party audience for preference over one's opponent or opponents.

If you were accused in public of appropriating your neighbor's land, or if you wanted your neighbors to take up arms against a neighboring state, or if you wanted to advance the leadership and trust of a political ally, you might spend some time reflecting on the nature of the situation, how you might best speak to that occasion, and how you might disarm your opponents' position. You might well ask for advice from the most skilled of speakers and review people's memories of the most effective such talks in the past. If you anticipated a public future for your citizen child, you might even want the child to be educated in the arts of public influence. Rhetoric, consequently, was designed to address oral, high-stakes public forums on forensic, deliberative, and epideictic matters.

Without the professional class and its social roles of advice giving and education, the literature on rhetorical theory would not have developed. Consider some contrasting cases. In the classical world, interpersonal conversation was not considered problematic enough or of sufficient stakes, so a reflective art on their conduct never developed; research and pedagogy on personal talk became a substantial industry only with the rise of modern clinical psychology, which gave us reasons to value the quality of communication with intimates. Similarly, in the classical world market negotiation and sales talk may have been learned in the family and in daily practice, but no highly reflective art developed at that time, no schools of marketing were formed, no advertising agencies provided lunch trade to the restaurants of Athens, and the language of commerce had no role in the formation of rhetoric. The reasons of power, class, and social motive that led to the selection of speech types that developed intellectual, social, and economic apparatuses for their refinement are interesting to consider, but here I need only point out the fact of selectivity.

In the classical world, although there was some teaching of writing (Murphy, *Short History*) and written texts did present principles of rhetoric, grammar, and logic, and while accounts and records were kept, laws were written, and legates and embassies were communicated with, no extensive system of reflection and strategy developed around writing, except as a form of scripting oratory, or around reading, except as a means of access to past oratorical performances, to be imitated and learned from (for example, Quintilian, bk. X). Literature, consisting mainly of scripted public performance of dramas and odes, drew the attention of the philosophers but primarily to evaluate the effect of communal performance on the emotional state and moral character of the citizen audience. The art of poetics was a spottier affair, the concern of the small subset of people engaged in creating the literature.

Following the lead of Quintilian, educators up through the nineteenth century continued to teach writing primarily as a means of scripting oratory. Accordingly, rhetorical teaching remained directed toward public performance concerned with high-stakes, highly visible issues of justice, deliberation, and communal formation. In the medieval period, a rhetoric was also articulated for preaching, another highly public, scripted, high-stakes performance concerned with instilling values and commitments and directing communal behavior.

Ars Dictaminis as a Literate Rhetoric

The narrowness of rhetorical focus prevailed despite the proliferation of forms of writing in increasingly elaborate social systems, as suggested earlier. Within separate faculties of law, medicine, philosophy, and the other arts, students practiced a variety of literacies but considered their practices to be law or medicine or philosophy rather than a form of language use. Few masters of specialized language thought about the communicative nature of their disciplines, and if they did provide support for neophyte writing, it tended to be through untheorized books of forms and models for imitation.

One of the more sophisticated attempts to develop a reflective art of a specialized literacy practice was the *ars dictaminis*.[2] This medieval art of letter writing, as exemplified in one of its most well-developed texts, the anonymous *Principles of Letter Writing*, pays particular attention to issues of class and role (foregrounded in the extensive treatment of the salutation), establishing cooperative relations through a secure bond of sentiment and obligation (considered in the section on "The Securing of Good Will"), establishing the situation (in the adaptation of the Ciceronian narration), and identifying a specific point of cooperation (in the new rhetorical section called "The Petition").[3] Seeking cooperative action in an essentially dyadic relationship, the letter aims to strengthen social bonds, which are attenuated by the distances of place, time, and acquaintanceship that writing mediates. Further, because the occasion of the request is not immediately in front of the correspondent's eyes, the letter must represent the situation so as to orient the reader toward the requested transaction. While the narration in a persuasive speech may cast a current and visible situation in a particular light, the narration in the letter must itself evoke the situation in the reader's imagination. With the situation evoked—and the reader appropriately respected according to hierarchy, with its obligations and loyalties, and with no opponent present or evoked—there is likely to be little need for persuasion; accordingly, the Ciceronian speech elements of division, proof, and refutation are not present in this form. Thus the art of letter writing begins to reframe the problems of strategic communication away from oral contest toward new social dynamics and difficulties of literate interaction, particularly as they take shape within a hierarchical society.

Audience attention, trust, and goodwill are particularly fragile in written communication. Readers face difficult work in imaginatively and favorably reconstructing the situation, activity, and author's presence from the texts they are reading; as a consequence, ruptures of misunderstanding, mistrust, or just indifference may rapidly lead to inattention, twisted meanings, lack of sympathy, or the framing of objections and accounts of the writer's shortcomings. A reader's alignment with the text is not easily regained once the bond between writer and reader is broken; furthermore, the writer has no way of monitoring the reader to sense a rupture and attempt a repair strategy. Speakers often regain wandering audiences, but writers rarely do. The *ars dictaminis* pays particular attention to the social, personal, and linguistic resources available to ensure such a rupture does not take place, and counsels risking the displeasure of the reader only when the writer's hierarchical authority is adequate to assure compliance and continuing obedience.

The Renaissance Pleasures of the Textualized Word

Although the *ars dictaminis* was a powerful force in the medieval world and eventually provided the foundations for later commercial and government correspondence, it did not have a long-term effect on the rhetorical traditions. Nor did the literate and graphic forms of Ramism influence rhetoric, despite Ramism's displacement of dialectic within philosophy and its offsprings of natural philosophy, social philosophy, political philosophy, and philosophy of the mind—each in turn developing into sciences with their own peculiar practices.

During the Renaissance, literate composition and the circulation of manuscripts and books may have fostered the concern for style, which extended far beyond the moderate classical concern for figures and tropes intended for oral delivery. Writing facilitates the polishing of individual phrases and sentences as well as the elaboration and amplification of thoughts by insertion, as Quintilian had already recognized. Copiousness and elegance are far more amusing and tempting when one is sitting alone in a study than when one is speaking on the forum steps to a fidgety audience. Style and copiousness also influenced face-to-face manners, but only in the court as an indication of refinement. As such it also was associated with the refined literary practices of the court, where it found perhaps its highest form in the poetry, prose, and verse drama of the period.

At that time, refinement of phrasing was not theorized as a literate practice but instead was seen simply as an extension of style in the scripted oral tradition (soon to extend in eighteenth-century oratory to scripted gesture mapped out in graphic form). In the latter part of the twentieth century, however, such verbal play was specifically associated with the pleasures of the text and the highly textualized imagination of deconstructionist literary criticism, which sees disrupted texts as formed from small stylistic gestures carried out separately from any social or referential contexts they may give the illusion of evoking (Barthes). In any event, the literate inclinations of stylistic rhetoric did not lead to an examination of the basic communicative conditions of textuality or of the social functions being carried out by literacy, except as a marker of the personal refinement and witty amusement of equally refined audiences. In this aspect, rhetoric became a marker of social distinction—a formulation that even its practitioners might have accepted.

New Literate Practices and Literature's Subsumption of Literate Rhetoric

At the same time that rhetoric was attending to courtly display—or rather at the same time that those interested in courtly display had appropriated the rhetorical tradition and the name of rhetoric—other forms of literate practice were developing outside the official purview of rhetoric and even overtly distinguishing themselves from the flowers of rhetoric. The systems of bureaucratic, commercial, and scientific literacy that were expanding rapidly during this period of colonial expansion engaged in stylistic eloquence only insofar as they addressed issues of class, court patronage, or policy. While, for example, the early members of the Royal Society did engage in elaborate praise and metaphoric argument, particularly in relation to patronage and policy issues, as well as in efforts to maintain social respect within a still largely gentlemanly endeavor (Shapin; Atkinson), other kinds of language use were being developed to carry out their new communal investigative labor, within which they saw the remnants of eloquence as a hindrance. Accompanying this overt hostility to what was then called rhetoric, these new practices were not theorized in rhetorical terms, nor did they influence the concepts that formed the rhetorical conceptual canon.

Only in the eighteenth century did print communication become a serious topic of rhetorical analysis. Here my story narrows to Great Britain and the United States, the two countries which most directly influenced the tradition of writing instruction in the United States. In Great Britain, outsiders such as the instructors at the dissenting academies, most notably Joseph Priestley, and the Scots rhetoricians, beginning with Edward Aytoun and John Stevenson and continuing with Adam Smith, Thomas Reid, George Campbell, and Hugh Blair, recognized the new print culture of newspapers, journals, pamphlets, and books as the locus of social power. They noted that accomplished writers—people such as Addison, Dryden, Johnson, Mandeville, Pope, and Swift—wielded much influence. The rhetorics of the late eighteenth century, written for aspiring Scots and dissenters, included criticism of contemporary literary models in order to identify the character of effective prose. Further, they began to note that plain style and plain speaking, avoiding extravagant art, were important in maintaining readers' faith. Priestley went so far as to recommend a halting style for speech, to demonstrate contemplativeness and sensibility, which were particularly prized by the literate and educated.

An audience, indeed that is wholly *illiterate* may have all their passions actuated by means of admiration, or astonishment, and mechanical communication but then there are few English audiences composed wholly of persons of so little reading and reflection as makes that practicable. And it is hardly possible that a person whose reading has lain among modern English books, or has conversed with persons of liberal education, should not have acquired more *delicacy of taste*, than to be taken with that gross and direct address of the passions, which Cicero adopted with applause. (emphasis in original, Priestley 114.)

Some of the same rhetoricians who were noting the social power of belles lettres also noted other influential written genres that did not rely on classical persuasion. Smith in his rhetoric discussed didactic writing, and in other publications he considered the psychological sources and consequences of the force of philosophic discourse (Bazerman, "Money Talks"). Similarly, Priestley contemplated the nature of historical and scientific writing, presenting proposals for the most effective means of participating in and organizing such discourses (Bazerman, "How Natural"). Even these rhetoricians who reached out to a range of higher-status forms of literacy, however, did not attend to the even then powerful languages of commerce, law, or government bureaucracy. The focus of their expanded rhetoric remained on issues of public persuasion in areas of fundamental values, belief, and policy associated with the leisured ruling class.

In a further break with prior rhetorics, these new print-oriented works abandoned previous assumptions about natural political order and human nature to begin with minimalist Lockean views of human experience and associations. These rhetorics reconceived how humans used symbols to make sense of their own experience, to mediate between each other, and to form social order.

Sympathy, sensibility, and access to the experiences of others became in this line of thinking important capacities for building human bonds. Belles lettres was seen as the key to successful public discourse, both for individual success in touching others for one's own ends and for communal cooperation rising above meanness of spirit, narrow self-interest, and the limits of individual experience. In this newly stabilized literary public realm, power and influence were associated with the new educated classes of sensibility and letters in a nineteenth-century Britain engaged in administering an empire. In nineteenth- and early twentieth-century United States, belles lettres (in alliance with the new research orientation of the university) held sway over secondary and university higher literacy practices, which were no longer called rhetoric. However, in the more protean U.S. society of the period, commercial, corporate, journalistic, technical, scientific, and professional forms of literacy (entirely outside more traditional liberal education) gathered increasing importance and sophistication. A good index of the increasingly complex terrain of literate practices is the variety of magazines and newspapers that flooded the U.S. market in the century following the Civil War.

During this time, however, formal rhetorical teaching in Britain had vanished, and in the United States it had gone into a decline, stabilized under the simplified psychological assumptions of faculty and modes (Mulderig) and a simplified model of expository transmission of knowledge (Connors), both taught only to those who were viewed as not yet having reached adequate competence to take part in the literary literacy of liberal education. The theory that accompanied these pedagogic practices was in a fundamental sense arhetorical, in that it aimed at the development of the individual writer's cognitive faculties rather than at the effective interaction with an audience. Improved communication and persuasion were assumed to come from the increased shared understanding and approbation of those whose faculties were similarly developed. People of reason and refinement would come to a common understanding through intelligent writing. Composition became a mental discipline rather than a strategic art.

Until the revival of composition, new elaborations of rhetorical theory in this century rose primarily out of literary concerns and bear the marks caused by addressing literary problems (as in the work of Burke, Booth, and, by after-the-fact appropriation, Bakhtin). The formation of speech departments preserved a rhetoric aimed at spoken performance, with strong continuing allegiance to classical models. Technical, business, organizational, and journalistic writing developed their own trainings within the professional schools and separate from English departments, composition, or rhetoric.

Composition's Rhetoric

In the United States in the post–World War II decades, the new field of composition, devoted to university writing, attempted to develop new rhetorics out of communication and linguistics, seeking new grounds for considering the form and interactions of writing.[4] After these impulses faltered, however, classical rhetoric, reimported from speech departments, became the only alternative to literary models for considering what one would want to write, to whom, for what purposes, and in what form. The investigation of writing processes and the psychology of writing did provide new energy, research, and theory for composition, but it has not provided much guidance as to what kinds of texts those processes might produce and what the consequences of those texts might be (see Russell, "Activity Theory and Process Approaches").

The issues of what one might write, for whom, for what purpose, and in what form have, however, been reengaged by writing across the curriculum, in the disciplines and professions, and in the workplace, which have opened up the perspective presented here. The descriptive work of located writing practices has opened up new questions calling for new theory to guide people reading and writing in these new domains. Genre theory (drawing on linguistics, sociology, anthropology, history, and rhetoric [see Bazerman, "Life"; Bhatia; Freedman and Medway]) and activity theory (with its roots in psychology [see Russell, "Activity Theory and Its Implications," "Rethinking Genre"]) have started to provide some shape to what we have found. Although orienting us to the social and personal dynamics of writing, however, these theories have not yet provided a comprehensive practical rhetoric to help guide people in their literate interactions.

Whether on the basis of these or other theories, a new rhetoric for literacy needs to be built hand in hand with our growing knowledge of how modern society has come to work through the written word. And that new rhetoric needs to be flexible enough to address the transformations of literacy in electronic media—where word, sound, visuals, and calculation are being integrated and moved rapidly and cheaply across great distances in environments structured by the technology. It is a new world, and it needs a new rhetoric. The way to move toward that rhetoric is through continued research into the forces actually at play in the many texts that circulate in the social spaces created by the print and electronic worlds, and into the ways individuals and their activities are influenced by their engagement with mediating texts. By watching what these texts do and what people do with them, without assuming that they are simply reproducing the activities of the agora, we can move toward a rhetoric that will illuminate the great diversity of our communicative world.

Notes

1. For overviews and collections, see Russell, "Writing and Genre"; Bazerman and Paradis; Freedman and Medway; Odell and Goswami; Spilka; Swales, *Genre*.

2. For overviews, see Murphy, *Rhetoric in the Middle Ages,* and Perelman.

3. For a translation of this text, see Murphy, *Three Medieval Rhetorical Arts.*

4. Young, Becker, and Pike's *Rhetoric: Discovery and Change* can be well understood as the culminating work of this period.

Works Cited

Atkinson, Dwight. *Scientific Discourse in Sociohistorical Context: The Philosophical Transactions of the Royal Society of London, 1675–1975.* Mahwah, NJ: Erlbaum, 1999.

Bakhtin, Mikhail. *The Dialogic Imagination: Four Essays.* Austin: U of Texas P, 1981.

Barthes, Roland. *The Pleasure of the Text.* New York: Hill, 1975.

Bazerman, Charles. "How Natural Philosophers Can Cooperate." *Textual Dynamics of the Professions: Historical and Contemporary Studies of Writing in Professional Communities*. Ed. Charles Bazerman and James Paradis. Madison: U of Wisconsin P, 1991. 13–44.

———. "Intertextual Self-Fashioning: Gould and Lewontin's Representations of the Literature." *Understanding Scientific Prose*. Ed. Jack Selzer. Madison: U of Wisconsin P, 1993. 20–41.

———. *The Languages of Edison's Light*. Cambridge: MIT P, 1999.

———. "The Life of Genre, the Life in the Classroom." *Genre and Writing: Issues, Arguments, Alternatives*. Ed. Wendy Bishop and Hans Ostrom. Portsmouth, NH: Boynton, 1997. 19–26.

———. "Money Talks: The Rhetorical Project of Adam Smith's Wealth of Nations." *Economics and Language*. Ed. Willie Henderson, Tony Dudley-Evans, and Roger Backhouse. New York: Routledge, 1993. 173–99.

———. "Response: Curricular Responsibilities and Professional Definition." *Reconceiving Writing, Rethinking Writing Instruction*. Ed. Joseph Petraglia. Mahwah, NJ: Erlbaum, 1995. 249–60.

———. *Shaping Written Knowledge: The Genre and Activity of the Experimental Article in Science*. Madison: U of Wisconsin P, 1988.

Bazerman, Charles, and James Paradis, eds. *Textual Dynamics of the Professions: Historical and Contemporary Studies of Writing in Professional Communities*. Madison: U of Wisconsin P, 1991.

Bazerman, Charles, and David R. Russell, eds. *Landmark Essays on Writing Across the Curriculum*. Davis, CA: Hermagoras P, 1994.

Bermingham, Ann. "'An Exquisite Practice': The Institution of Drawing as a Polite Art in Britain." *Towards a Modern Art World*. Ed. Brian Allen. New Haven: Yale UP, 1995. 47–66.

Besnier, Niko. *Literacy, Emotion, and Authority: Reading and Writing on a Polynesian Atoll*. Cambridge: Cambridge UP, 1995.

Bhatia, Vijay K. *Analyzing Genre: Language Use in Professional Settings*. Essex, Eng.: Longman, 1993.

Blakeslee, Ann M. "Activity, Context, Interaction, and Authority: Learning to Write Scientific Papers *In Situ*." *Journal of Business and Technical Communication* 11 (1997): 125–69.

Booth, Wayne C. *The Rhetoric of Fiction*. Chicago: U of Chicago P, 1961.

Burke, Kenneth. *A Rhetoric of Motives*. Berkeley: U of California P, 1969.

Chafe, Wallace. "Information Flow in Speaking and Writing." *The Linguistics of Literacy*. Ed. Pamela Downing, Susan D. Lima, and Michael Noonan. Amsterdam: Benjamins, 1992. 17–30.

Chartier, Roger. *The Cultural Uses of Print in Early Modern France*. Princeton: Princeton UP, 1987.

Cohen, Patricia Cline. *A Calculating People: The Spread of Numeracy in Early America*. Chicago: U of Chicago P, 1982.

Connors, Robert J. *Composition-Rhetoric: Backgrounds, Theory, and Pedagogy*. Pittsburgh: U of Pittsburgh P, 1997.

Dear, Peter, ed. *The Literary Structure of Scientific Argument: Historical Studies*. Philadelphia: U of Pennsylvania P, 1991.

Eisenstein, Elizabeth L. *The Printing Press as an Agent of Change: Communications and Cultural Transformations in Early Modern Europe*. Cambridge: Cambridge UP, 1979.

Engestrom, Yrjo, and David Middleton, eds. *Cognition and Communication at Work*. Cambridge: Cambridge UP, 1996.

Freedman, Aviva, and Peter Medway, eds. *Genre and the New Rhetoric*. London: Taylor, 1994.

Giddens, Anthony. *The Constitution of Society: Outline of the Theory of Structuration*. Berkeley: U of California P, 1984.

Goody, Jack. *The Logic of Writing and the Organization of Society*. Cambridge: Cambridge UP, 1986.

Harris, Randy, ed. *Landmark Essays on Rhetoric of Science: Case Studies*. Mahwah, NJ: Erlbaum, 1997.

Havelock, Eric A. *The Literate Revolution in Greece and Its Cultural Consequences*. Princeton: Princeton UP, 1982.

Kaestle, Carl F. *Literacy in the United States: Readers and Reading since 1880*. New Haven: Yale UP, 1991.

Mulderig, Gerald P. "Nineteenth Century Psychology and the Shaping of Alexander Bain's English Composition and Rhetoric." *The Rhe-*

torical Tradition and Modern Writing. Ed. James J. Murphy. New York: MLA, 1982. 95–104.

Murphy, James J. *Rhetoric in the Middle Ages: A History of Rhetorical Theory from Saint Augustine to the Renaissance.* Berkeley: U of California P, 1974.

———, ed. *A Short History of Writing Instruction from Ancient Greece to Twentieth-Century America.* Davis, CA: Hermagoras, 1990.

———. *Three Medieval Rhetorical Arts.* Berkeley: U of California P, 1971.

Odell, Lee, and Dixie Goswami, eds. *Writing in Nonacademic Settings.* New York: Guilford, 1985.

Olson, David R. *The World on Paper: The Conceptual and Cognitive Implications of Writing and Reading.* Cambridge: Cambridge UP, 1994.

Ong, Walter J. *Orality and Literacy: The Technologizing of the Word.* New York: Methuen, 1982.

Perelman, Les. "The Medieval Art of Letter Writing: Rhetoric as Institutional Expression." *Textual Dynamics of the Professions: Historical and Contemporary Studies of Writing in Professional Communities.* Ed. Charles Bazerman and James Paradis. Madison: U of Wisconsin P, 1991. 97–119.

Porter, Theodore. *Trust in Numbers: The Pursuit of Objectivity in Science and Public Life.* Princeton: Princeton UP, 1995.

Priestley, Joseph. *A Course of Lectures on Oratory and Criticism.* London: J. Johnson, 1777.

Prior, Paul. *Writing/Disciplinarity: A Sociohistoric Account of Literate Activity in the Academy.* Mahwah, NJ: Erlbaum, 1998.

Quintilian. *The Instituto Oratoria of Quintilian.* Trans. Harold E. Butler. 4 vols. Cambridge: Harvard UP, 1922.

Russell, David R. "Activity Theory and Its Implications for Writing Instruction." *Reconceiving Writing, Rethinking Writing Instruction.* Ed. Joseph Petraglia. Mahwah, NJ: Erlbaum, 1995. 51–77.

———. "Activity Theory and Process Approaches: Writing Power in School and Society." *Post-Process Theory: Beyond the Writing-Process Paradigm.* Ed. Thomas Kent. Carbondale: Southern Illinois UP, 1999. 80–95.

————. "Rethinking Genre in School and Society: An Activity Theory Analysis." *Written Communication* 14 (1997): 504–54.

————. "Writing and Genre in Higher Education and Workplaces: A Review of Studies That Use Cultural-Historical Activity Theory." *Mind, Culture and Activity* 4 (1997): 224–37.

Schudson, Michael. *The Power of News.* Cambridge: Harvard UP, 1995.

Scribner, Sylvia, and Michael Cole. *The Psychology of Literacy.* Cambridge: Harvard UP, 1981.

Selzer, Jack. "Intertextuality and the Writing Process." *Writing in the Workplace: New Research Perspectives.* Ed. Rachel Spilka. Carbondale: Southern Illinois UP, 1993. 171–80.

Shapin, Steven. *A Social History of Truth: Civility and Science in Seventeenth-Century England.* Chicago: U of Chicago P, 1994.

Spilka, Rachel, ed. *Writing in the Workplace: New Research Perspectives.* Carbondale: Southern Illinois UP, 1993.

Stratman, James. "Investigating Persuasive Processes in Legal Discourse in Real Time." *Discourse Processes* 17 (1994): 1–57.

Swales, John. *Genre Analysis: English in Academic and Research Settings.* Cambridge: Cambridge UP, 1990.

————. *Other Floors, Other Voices: A Textography of a Small University Building.* Mahwah, NJ: Erlbaum, 1998.

Tannen, Deborah, ed. *Coherence in Spoken and Written Discourse.* Norwood, NJ: Ablex, 1984.

van Nostrand, A. D. *Fundable Knowledge : The Marketing of Defense Technology.* Mahwah, NJ: Erlbaum, 1997.

Vygotsky, Lev. *Mind in Society: The Development of Higher Psychological Processes.* Cambridge: Harvard UP, 1978.

Yates, JoAnne. *Control through Communication: The Rise of System in American Management.* Baltimore: Johns Hopkins UP, 1989.

Young, Richard, Alton Becker, and Kenneth Pike. *Rhetoric: Discovery and Change.* New York: Harcourt, 1970.

CHAPTER TWO

Accounting for "Well-Worn Grooves": Composition as a Self-Reinforcing Mechanism

MAUREEN DALY GOGGIN
Arizona State University

STEVE BEATTY
Arizona State University

Toward the end of "'Tracing Round the Frame,'" Richard Young poses a question that serves as an impetus for this chapter, for it is a question that both of us as scholars and teachers of writing have pondered long and hard:

> [W]hy does our profession persist in relegating the study and teaching of writing to an inferior status despite what is by now more than a generation of serious theoretical, historical, and applied work in rhetorical studies in English Departments? One would think that the achievement and the potential it has revealed for valuable work in the future would have had a greater impact on attitudes and practices in the profession. We have swerved from well-worn grooves many times in the past for less reason. (150)

We, too, have wondered why, despite decades of dedicated efforts to unseat it, the compulsory first-year composition system established over a century ago remains impervious to any substantial change.

What makes this situation so puzzling is that since its inception as a response to perceived problems with student writing, college composition has been roundly and consistently criticized as inadequate. "If freshman composition really began in 1874," noted Leonard Greenbaum in "The Tradition of Complaint," "the first complaint was probably registered in 1875. But on record, in black print, the assault against freshman English began in 1911, and continued in 1928, 1929, 1931, 19 . . ." (175).[1] In the thirty years since Greenbaum's observation, the study of writing has received unprecedented scholarly attention. Yet, surprisingly, the substantial body of research we have accumulated on literate practices has had virtually no systemic effect on the teaching of writing. As Richard Marius rightly points out, "I can think of no book or article devoted to research or theory that has made a particle of difference in the general teaching of composition for the past twenty or thirty years—and I can think of a great many commonly held assumptions in the discipline that are supported by no major research at all" (466). Instead, we have the same old first-year composition and the same old complaints (Russell, "Vygotsky" 195; Crowley, "Personal"). That compulsory first-year composition programs continue, seemingly impervious to change, is a puzzle begging explanation.

In this chapter, we hope to contribute to that explanation. To do so, we draw on the powerful economic theory of the self-reinforcing mechanism (SRM), a theory that offers a robust explanation of how and why inferior technologies and systems succeed despite superior alternatives.[2] We then trace the emergence of first-year composition as a complex but suboptimal system. In so doing, we hope to explain how first-year composition emerged as a solution, how it became locked in as an SRM, and how we might "exit" lock-in to another alternative. In other words, we hope to explain how the "well-worn groove" Young speaks of was dug, why we remain stuck in it, and how we might swerve from it.

Why Inferior Systems Sometimes Succeed: The Story of QWERTY

Why was VHS able to corner the video market when Betamax, by all accounts a superior technological system, entered the market first? Why is the U.S. nuclear industry dominated by light-water reactors when safer and superior gas-cooled reactors have been available from the outset? Why did the auto industry end up producing only gasoline-powered engines when far safer, cleaner, and more efficient electric and steam-powered technologies were equally available? To explain how such inferior alternatives can prevail over superior ones, W. Brian Arthur turned to the physical sciences and the theory of self-reinforcing mechanism (SRM).

According to SRM theory, some dynamic systems in biology, physics, and chemical kinetics possess multiple "emergent structures." A system's initial starting point, combined with random events and fluctuations, can determine which of the possible emergent structures a system "locks into." Arthur effectively demonstrates how SRM theory can be applied to economics as well ("Competing," "Self-Reinforcing"). In his words, "in many economical systems, lock-in happens dynamically, as sequential decisions 'groove' out an advantage that the system finds hard to escape from" ("Self-Reinforcing" 13).

For example, if you look at your computer keyboard, chances are that the top row of letters spells out QWERTYUIOP. Although it has been long known that QWERTY is not the optimal keyboard arrangement, it remains the overwhelmingly dominant keyboard on the market today. In "Clio and the Economics of QWERTY," Paul A. David uses SRM theory to explain why.

Obviously, there are a number of possible emergent structures (that is, alternatives) for the arrangement of letters on a keyboard. To understand why the QWERTY keyboard prevailed, we must go back to October 1867, the month Christopher Latham Sholes, assisted by his two friends Carlos Glidden and Samuel W. Soule, filed a patent application for a primitive writing machine. As the fifty-second "inventor" of the typewriter, Sholes was by no means the first to create a writing machine, but he was the first to create a practical one. Earlier typewriters, originally invented for the visually impaired, were large (some as big as pianos), clumsy, and slow, far slower than writing by hand. Sholes designed a more efficient model, with keys that were arranged alphabetically in two rows. The letters were placed at the end of typebars that hung in a circle in the center of the machine. A roller, which held the paper in place, sat over the circle of typebars; when a key was pressed, the corresponding typebar swung up from underneath to strike the paper.

Unfortunately, Sholes's "Type Writer" had two major defects; its typebars tended to jam and its printing point was invisible to the typist. As a result, when typebars clashed and stuck together, the typist was unaware that succeeding strokes continued to hammer the impression of the bottom typebar—the same letter—onto the page. In an effort to minimize clashes and jams, Sholes drew on a study of letter-pair frequency conducted by educator Amos Densmore and rearranged the placement of keys to separate the most common pairs of letters, such as "TH." This rearrangement resulted in a four-row keyboard similar to the QWERTY arrangement we know today. In 1873, E. Remington and Sons purchased the manufacturing rights to Sholes's typewriter and switched the placement of the "R" with the period mark. Moving the "R" to the top row permitted Remington's sales force to rapidly type out its brand name—TYPE WRITER—and thus dazzle potential customers.

Thus a technological challenge—reducing clashing typebars—combined with a slick sales gimmick, determined the emergent structure of the QWERTY keyboard. Although the Remington TYPE WRITER with its QWERTY keyboard had the advantage of being the first system introduced in the United States, its position was tenuous as the typewriter boom of the 1880s exploded and multiple competitors with rival designs entered the market. Indeed, Remington's typewriter sales did not take off until after a second model, the Remington 2, was introduced in 1878. Unlike the TYPE WRITER, which contained only capital letters, the Remington 2 provided both upper- and lowercase letters through the only other major modification of the QWERTY keyboard, the Shift key.

Meanwhile, competitive machines were developed that eliminated both major defects of the Sholes typewriter. Not only did they offer a visible printing point but new designs such as Thomas Edison's electric print-wheel device (which eventually became the basis for the teletype machine) and Lucien Stephen Crandall's revolving cylindrical sleeve (a precursor to the revolutionary IBM 72/82's golf ball design) eliminated the need for typebars altogether. These alternative systems solved the technological glitches that had necessitated the design of the QWERTY keyboard. Freed from the restrictions of typebars and invisible printing points, competitors began offering new keyboard arrangements. In fact, no fewer than seven improvements on the QWERTY keyboard were patented in the United States and Great Britain by 1924. Most notable of the new arrangements was one featuring a DHIATENSOR home (middle) row. This arrangement, aptly termed the "Ideal" keyboard, enabled typists to compose over 70 percent of the words in the English language without leaving the home row.

Despite the introduction of more efficient keyboard designs and technological advances that made the QWERTY arrangement dispensable, the U.S. typewriter industry standardized the QWERTY keyboard, referring to it as "the Universal." Indeed, between 1895 and 1905 even nontypebar typewriter manufacturers began offering two versions of their machines, one with the Ideal keyboard and another with the Universal. Among these was Hammond, which in 1881 introduced a two-row, curved Ideal keyboard (the precursor to the ergonomically designed keyboards of today). But following the lead of other typewriter manufacturers, Hammond also soon made the Universal Hammond available.

In 1932 Professor August Dvorak of Washington State University took the principle underlying the Ideal keyboard even further. Placing the vowels AOEUI on one side of the home row and the consonants DHTNS on the other, Dvorak dramatically increased keyboard efficiency. His new arrangement meant that a typist could type about four hundred of the most common words in English without leaving the home row, compared to one hundred using the QWERTY arrangement. Yet even the invention of the Dvorak Simplified Keyboard—on which trained typists broke most of the world's records for speed typing and whose productivity was proven (in U.S. Navy experiments) to pay for the cost of retraining a group of typists within a mere ten days—was not enough to displace the dominance of the QWERTY design.[3]

Why did the QWERTY system prevail over superior alternatives? In an acronym, SRM. As Paul David explains, "[I]mportant influences upon the eventual outcome can be exerted by temporally remote events, including happenings dominated by chance elements rather than systematic forces" (332). In other words, seemingly incidental or even random events can set SRMs in motion and contribute to their staying power; or, as David puts it, competition in an imperfect market can drive an "industry prematurely into standardization *on the wrong system*" (336). What's more, according to Arthur, "once a solution is reached, it is difficult to exit from" ("Self-Reinforcing" 10).

In the case of the QWERTY system, it was the unforeseeable advent of touch typing (i.e., the method of assigning particular fingers to each key so that it is possible to type without looking) in the late 1880s that locked in the emergent structure of the keyboard to the QWERTY design. From its inception, touch typing was tied to the QWERTY design. Remington's introduction of the Shift key in 1878 favored touch typing because other manufacturers had doubled the number of keys, two for each letter, to add small-letter capability. Wed to the QWERTY keyboard, touch typing set in motion an SRM for the QWERTY system. And even when other manufacturers adopted the Shift key for alternative boards, QWERTY was on its way to lock-in.

Economic SRMs such as the QWERTY system, according to Arthur, derive from four sources: (1) large set-up or fixed costs; (2) learning effects; (3) coordination effects; and (4) adaptive expectations ("Self-Reinforcing" 10). The first of these four sources, large set-up or fixed costs, "give[s] the advantage of falling unit costs to increased output" (10). As more QWERTY systems were purchased (due in part to the popularity of touch typing), economies of scale came into play, and the cost of producing and selling QWERTY systems decreased in comparison to competitive systems. In addition, learning effects, which "act to improve products or lower their cost as their prevalence increases" (10), also promoted self-reinforcement. Once an increasing number of typists learned on QWERTY, businesses in turn were more likely to purchase QWERTY typewriters, and subsequent manufacturers had powerful incentives to produce QWERTY machines. The more these were produced, the lower the cost of manufacturing them. In addition, as more typists learned to type on QWERTY systems, the cost of QWERTY training decreased in comparison to training on less prevalent non-QWERTY systems. For example, if it costs $100 to train a typist and three of a firm's five typists are already QWERTY trained, it is less expensive to train the remaining two for $200 than to retrain the QWERTY three for $300.

Likewise, coordination effects "confer advantages to 'going along' with other economic agents taking similar action" (10). As more typists learned the QWERTY system, the likelihood increased that firms would purchase QWERTY machines since it would give them a larger labor pool to draw from; and, vice versa, as more firms purchased QWERTY machines, the likelihood increased that typists would choose to learn the QWERTY system since that would enlarge their pool of prospective employers. Finally, adaptive expectations hold that "increased prevalence on the market enhances beliefs of further prevalence" (10). The more consumers purchased and were trained on QWERTY keyboards, the more others (including competitive manufacturers) believed QWERTY systems would be purchased. Or to put it another way, as more people believed the QWERTY system would prevail, QWERTY dominance became a self-fulfilling prophecy. As a result, even the developers of the Ideal keyboard decided to offer the Universal in order to increase their market share.

In tracing the rise and eventual dominance of the inferior QWERTY keyboard arrangement, Paul David concludes, "I believe there are many more QWERTY worlds lying out there in the past" (336). So do we. Indeed, we believe first-year composition is just such a world.[4]

QWERTY-Nomics and First-Year Composition

An analogy can be drawn between the SRM of the QWERTY keyboard and that of first-year composition as a suboptimal system. The QWERTY keyboard has, of course, changed over the years since it was first introduced: circular metal keys have been replaced by square plastic ones, other keys have been added (e.g., the function keys on an extended computer keyboard), and, recently, more ergonomic keyboards have been designed. While these changes have admittedly improved functionality to a degree, they have not altered the basic QWERTY design. We argue that although first-year composition has undergone many changes in philosophy—current-traditional, neo-Romantic, expressivism, neoclassical, new rhetoric, social constructionism, and so on (Berlin, *Rhetoric*; Winterowd and Blum)—like the QWERTY keyboard, the system of composition as a universal, compulsory first-year requirement has remained essentially the same as when it first appeared at Harvard nearly 125 years ago. However, there is one major difference between the QWERTY keyboard and first-year composition. While the QWERTY keyboard may be inefficient, it still works. There is precious little evidence that compulsory first-year composition has ever worked (Crowley, "Personal"; Marius 467; Russell, "Vygotsky" 195).

To flesh out this analogy between QWERTY and first-year composition, we need to begin at the beginning, so to speak; we need to examine the nineteenth-century origins of first-year composition. Given the complexities of the emergence of composition, we might select any number of events as starting points and as particularly important chance happenings that contributed to the SRM of first-year composition. Given the limited space of this chapter, we focus primarily on three crucial events, all of which took place at Harvard: (1) the creation of an entrance examination in English composition, (2) the formation of English A, and (3) the report of the Harvard Committee on Composition and Rhetoric. To set the scene, we begin with the rise of the modern university.

In the nineteenth century, higher education was radically transformed as the modern university arose and eventually supplanted the classical college. Since the Middle Ages, the mission of the classical college had been to instill piety and morality and, above all, to *preserve knowledge*. Modern tertiary education, as Laurence Veysey has shown, sought three new goals—to create, use, and preserve knowledge; to eradicate ignorance; and to credential newly emerging professions. In the process, the four-year prescribed curriculum of the classical college was eventually displaced by an elective curriculum, and academic institutions were carved up into departments and disciplines. The emergence of new goals and pedagogical methods for higher education had an enormous impact on lower schools as they were forced to revise their curricula to prepare an ever growing new body of students for postsecondary education.

Historians of composition have examined how the study of rhetoric, which had dominated the curriculum in higher education for over 2,500 years, was displaced within U.S. educational institutions toward the end of the nineteenth century (Kitzhaber; Berlin, *Writing*; Crowley, *Methodical*; Johnson). In the classical college, the study of rhetoric commanded substantial curriculum space during all four years of academic study. However, as the focus of the modern university shifted, the number of courses in rhetoric dwindled to two, the now familiar first-year composition classes. Whereas once philosophies and theories of discourse were the core of rhetorical study, the composition course and the textbooks it gave rise to concentrated almost exclusively on the mechanical aspects (correctness and ease) of discourse. At the same time, literary studies, the new kid on the block, was inversely gaining in strength, numbers, and prestige. It was neither inevitable nor predictable that the study of rhetoric would dwindle into a state of such minor importance, nor that the study of literature would assume the central place in English studies. To understand this, we need to touch briefly on some of the forces underlying the rise of the modern university.

In the turmoil of defining disciplinary and departmental spaces in the newly emerging institutions of higher education, there were several viable paths open to those interested in the study and teaching of literate practices. Any of these might have secured a more prestigious and permanent space in academia than that which they eventually followed. First and foremost, those interested in literate *practices* had, but lost, an opportunity to secure a scholarly space rather than a marginalized service space. Had they established rhetoric and composition as an intellectual endeavor within departments of English, it would have found a legitimate place that would have led to undergraduate programs; in turn, primary and secondary education in English might have developed quite differently as well. Instead, rhetoric was conflated to rhetoric/composition, which was understood as a corrective to perceived deficiencies, and thus it assumed a marginal service position in English departments.

For a while in the beginning of the twentieth century, it appeared as though the study of literate practices might become the focus of serious scholarly attention. In one of several studies on questions concerning rhetoric and composition conducted by Fred Newton Scott, then president of the Pedagogical Section of MLA, English professors around the country were polled on whether they considered rhetoric to be an appropriate subject for graduate study.[5] The responses to Scott's survey, which were published in a report in *PMLA* in 1901, revealed that "a decided majority of the writers hold that the subject [rhetoric], as they define it, has a legitimate place as a graduate study" (Mead 188). Given this majority response, we cannot help but ask why rhetoric did not then become a subject of graduate study in departments of English and why it did not assume a scholarly place within the subject of English studies.

Part of the answer lies in the complex battles that took place as new departments and disciplines scrambled for limited space in the newly forming institutions of higher education. Although separate branches of knowledge had existed since classical times, with the trivium (rhetoric, logic, and grammar) and the quadrivium (arithmetic, music, geometry, and astronomy) being codified in the Middle Ages, modern disciplines emerged in the nineteenth century as a radically new concept and practice. Both the divisions of knowledge and the disciplinary organizations that were formed to support these divisions constituted a complete break with the past. To claim disciplinary status and, ultimately, secure departmental space for an academic subject, scholars had to demonstrate that their field was a *Wissenschaft* (science) rather than an art. The root *wissen* means knowledge. A *Wissenschaft* generated theory and knowing while an art was understood as a practice and a doing. Moreover, preference was given to those who could show that their field was a *naturwissenschaft* (a science dealing with that made by nature) rather than a *geisteswissenschaft* (a moral science dealing with that made by humans) since the former was understood to render universal truths while the latter was limited to contingent truths, those subject to human whim and thus deemed less reliable.

Unfortunately, there was little agreement among nineteenth-century rhetoricians on whether rhetoric could be best understood as a science or an art.[6] Henry Day, for example, declared, "*Rhetoric has been correctly defined to be the Art of Discourse.* This definition presents Rhetoric as an art, in distinction from a science" (864). Adam Sherman Hill likewise noted that rhetoric "is an *art*, not a science" (*Principles* 881). Speaking for the other side, David Hill argued that "as a *science*, [rhetoric] discovers and establishes these laws. Rhetoric is, therefore, the science of the laws of effective discourse" (880). This debate problematized the location and treatment of rhetoric within modern academia in general and within departments of English in particular. The picture drawn by respondents to Scott's poll was even more complicated.

Although the majority agreed that rhetoric was a fit subject for graduate study, the reasons given revealed vast disagreements about the nature, aim, and scope of rhetoric.[7] On the *Wissenschaft* side, there were those who argued that rhetoric was a theoretical enterprise and as such was deserving of advanced study. As one respondent put it, "it seems to me the value of Rhetoric as a subject for graduate work depends on whether it be regarded as an art or a science, if these distinctions be allowed. Rhetoric should be mastered in its practical aspects before the student completes his undergraduate study; but as a science I believe it is eminently suited for graduate work" (qtd. in Mead 198). On the other side were those who cast rhetoric as an art of production and argued that as such it was a fit subject for graduate work. As one person put it, "If regarded as an art, there would need to be a change in the interpretation of the advanced degrees. For the Oxford doctorate in music the candidate must present a musical composition as part of evidence of proficiency. I do not see why a rhetorical composition, an essay, a novel, a poem, or other literary kind should not count toward a degree in literature" (qtd. in Mead 198).[8] Still others eschewed both the theoretical and the practical, framing rhetoric as pedagogical. One wrote: "I believe that the strict aims of Rhetoric as a graduate study should be pedagogical in their nature" (qtd. in Mead 197).

In hindsight, it seems that what prevented rhetoric from assuming a legitimate place in English departments may not have been so much the multifaceted nature of rhetoric but the inability of those concerned to agree, if even temporarily, to a unified view (especially one that could accommodate multiple views of rhetoric as theory, practice, and pedagogy). Science, art, and pedagogy did eventually create spaces for themselves in higher education. Thus the study of literate practices might have fared better if those interested in it had followed the example of others who left departments of English to form their own disciplinary and departmental spaces.[9] For example, those framing rhetoric as a *Wissenschaft* might have argued that the study of discursive practices was a worthy theoretical enterprise and might have followed the lead of those in speech or linguistics who left English studies.[10] For those who claimed that rhetoric was an art—a *doing*—they might have argued the validity of studying rhetoric as a practice and followed the lead of journalism or drama, two other doings that withdrew from departments of English. Finally, for those who framed rhetoric as a pedagogical subject, they might have found space in the then newly emerging colleges and departments of education. Any of these routes would have secured the material space necessary for assuming a legitimate space.

Staking out a separate material space was certainly a viable option at the time, one that William Payne in his 1895 introduction to *English in American Universities* entertained. He was aware that divisions among rhetoric, linguistics, and literature might cause problems for future departments of English and thus considered the idea that perhaps there should be separate divisions:

> The questions may be raised whether it would not be well to set an official seal upon the separation of literature from its allied subjects by making it a separate department of university work. . . . The English scholars in our universities are, almost without exception, either literary critics or masters of linguistic science; they are rarely, if ever, both at once. Now this means that a department of English having a single head will almost inevitably become developed upon one side at the expense of the other. (27)

His prophecy, of course, came true. Literary studies developed at the expense of both rhetoric and linguistics.[11] It became another SRM, but that is another story for which we do not have the necessary space. (See, for example, Graff; Ohmann; Shumway.)

As a result, the teaching of writing but not the study of it became firmly entrenched within departments of English. Composition was not conceived of as an intellectual endeavor: it was not formed to *create*, *use*, or *preserve* knowledge. Rather, it was constructed as a marginal service enterprise, a temporary stopgap against alleged inadequacies of preparatory education, and positioned, often quite literally, in the basements of English departments.

The Birth of Composition

Just as the demise of rhetoric—or, more specifically, the study of literate practices within departments of English—was not inevitable, neither was the formation of English A as a prototypical dynamical system at Harvard. Nor was it inevitable that this system would eventually dominate writing programs across the country. At least two alternatives for dealing with the supposed "literacy problem" competed with the Harvard model of the two-semester first-year composition course.[12] The traditional classical course of rhetorical study, typically focusing on the theories of Blair, Campbell, Whately, and Cicero, had a strong hold on many colleges, especially in the East and South (Wozniak). At the other extreme, some schools such as Yale, Princeton, Stanford, the University of California, the University of Indiana, and the University of Nebraska offered no writing courses, relegating the responsibility to public and private preparatory schools. High entrance standards and a belief that students would absorb what they needed to know about writing from other courses in the college provided the rationale for not offering first-year composition. This latter alternative is, of course, what Harvard wanted to do, but it felt that its students' poor writing skills demanded immediate attention. First-year composition was developed to provide that attention; however, as we shall see later, it was never intended to be more than a temporary stopgap measure.

It is all the more surprising, then, that by the beginning of the twentieth century Harvard's two-semester, compulsory composition program had become firmly entrenched throughout the country. This is not to say that every school followed the Harvard model exactly; some focused on personal writing (a precursor to creative writing programs), others on writing about literature (what would become the ubiquitous Introduction to Literature course), and still others on an idea course (the precursor to the Great Books and general studies approaches). At many places, one or more of these approaches was blended with the Harvard expository approach. What is important for the purposes of our argument is that while there were various competing approaches to teaching composition, the basic structure was the same—one to two semesters of compulsory composition instruction.

Let us turn now to how the path was so deeply and unswervingly cut. Except for a series of chance events and what in retrospect we might term bad luck, composition might never have taken hold in the first year as a required course within departments of English. To explore these events, we need to consider briefly the history of Harvard University.

Emergence of the Entrance Exam at Harvard

In the two centuries leading up to 1865, students seeking admission to Harvard were required to demonstrate proficiency in Latin, Greek, and mathematics. Harvard had a classical four-year prescribed curriculum and conducted most of its instruction in Latin and Greek; its pedagogy was largely oral recitation. After Charles Eliot assumed the presidency, Harvard underwent enormous changes. Under Eliot an elective curriculum was developed, teaching in and about English assumed a strong position, and written work began to supersede oral recitation.[13] In 1865 the first entrance exam to test proficiency in English was administered. Between 1865 and 1872, students were tested in their ability to read English aloud. In the academic year 1872–73, for the very first time, students seeking admission were required to exhibit good written skills, namely, "correct spelling, punctuation, and expression, as well as legible handwriting" ("Three Harvard" 34). In June 1873, the first entrance examination in written composition was administered. The exam consisted of two parts: an essay based on a selection of English literature and the correction of poorly written, incorrect sentences.

The first written entrance exam was administered in the very year that Adam Sherman Hill was appointed as an assistant to Francis James Child, Boylston Professor of Rhetoric at Harvard.

Several years later, Hill replaced Child as Boylston Professor of Rhetoric, a position he held until 1904. Under the encouragement of then president Charles Eliot, Hill created the first composition program in 1874. Hill, who defined rhetoric as "an art not a science" (*Principles* 881), designed a two-semester, two-hour course based on his *Principles of Rhetoric*. His program was offered, alongside four years of rhetoric courses, at the sophomore level from 1874 until 1885, when it was moved, with much controversy, to the first year.

From just about the moment Hill's English A, as it was called, appeared on the schedule, Hill fought to have the hours increased to three hours per semester and to have it moved to the first year. His request caused ferocious battles. In 1879, Hill complained that "unfortunately, however, it has not been found possible to make room in the Freshman year for English, no one of the departments which now occupy the year being willing to give up any of its time, and each supporting the others in opposition to change" ("Answer" 52). The crux of the problem for the other departments was that the first year was a prime time to lure students into upper-division courses in their departments. The advent of the elective system meant that no one was guaranteed students; students' schedules were crowded and their interests did not always lie with these other departments. As Brown describes of those times, the other faculty "were engaged in a mad scramble to enlist recruits among the freshmen for their elective courses" (30). Nevertheless, Hill persevered. With the help of Le Baron Russell Briggs, who had become his assistant (along with Barrett Wendell and W. B. Shubrick Clymer) in the early 1880s, Hill won. In 1884 first-year college composition took its place firmly in the curriculum of the English department, where it became an SRM.

The course was intimately tied to yet another SRM, the entrance exam in English composition. The exam served, among other things, to secure the placement of composition squarely within the English department. Indeed, it can be argued that the entrance exam is to first-year composition what touch typing is to the QWERTY keyboard. What planted the composition course so firmly within the English department was the fact that the exam was tied to English literature (just as touch typing was tied to the QWERTY keyboard). For example, the subject for the 1879 composition entrance exam was drawn from "Shakspere's [sic] Macbeth, Richard II, and Midsummer Night's Dream; Scott's Guy Mannering; Byron's Prisoner of Chilton; Thackeray's Henry Esmond; Macaulay's Essay on Addison; the Sir Roger de Coverley Essays in the Spectator" (Hill, "Answer" 49). Prospective students were sternly warned: "Every candidate is expected to be familiar with *all* the books in this list" (emphasis in original, 49). Students could fail not only if their composition exhibited poor grammar and mechanics but also if they were not sufficiently familiar with the literary masterpiece they were to write about.

The test did not have to be tied to English literature. In fact, there were numerous proposals on the table to replace the literature-based entrance exam at Harvard with other content subjects. One proposal was to open the exam to any subject and "try the candidate's knowledge of English by all his examination books, considered, whatever their subjects, as English composition. This is an alluring plan, ideal in its excellence, and, alas," concluded Le Baron Russell Briggs, "ideal in its impracticability" (58). The problem was finding a variety of readers competent in the various subjects and then having the exams also read by those in the English department. Another plan was to tie the exam to history rather than literature—a proposal to which Briggs, Hill's successor as the Boylston Professor of Rhetoric, vehemently objected: "The proposal to substitute for the present test an examination in English History, and to mark each book twice, once for History and once for English, is open to like objections: it would double the time needed for handling the [examination] books, and it would require no knowledge of literature" (58). Other proposals included testing students on the *Primer of English Literature*, a philological text of historical and linguistic facts; replacing the section on correcting bad English with one on identifying good English; and abolishing the English entrance exam requirement altogether. Of the last, Briggs wrote, "They would suffer boys to come to college without a sense of literary form, and to 'dump' their knowledge promiscuously into their examination books" (58). At the center of the criticism of all these alternatives was the sentiment that "such an examination would not touch English literature" (58). Tied to literature, college English departments could retain a firm hold on the exam and composition programs. They could also control secondary education in English, not only by what they required for admission of *all* prospective students but also in how they trained prospective secondary English teachers. The college entrance exam on written composition quickly became a common practice at many colleges.

Every year the list of literary masterpieces for which students must be prepared changed. What made the situation even more problematic was the fact that other colleges following Harvard's lead issued their own lists of literature, which had the effect of multiplying exponentially the number of literary sources with which students needed to be familiar. Public and private preparatory schools were thus forced to prepare students on an ever increasing number of literary sources. English teachers at the secondary level had to focus greater and greater blocks of time on literature.[14] There was a certain irony at work here, for one of the primary purposes of the exam was to force lower schools to assume the burden of teaching students how to write in standard English—a point that is very clearly made in the Harvard Report on Composition and Rhetoric and one we discuss more fully in the following section. Yet this goal was undoubtedly undermined by the exam itself. It is reasonable to assume that lower-division English teachers would have been able to devote more time to the study, practice, and teaching of writing had they not been burdened by the enormous literary demands of the entrance exam. That the exam was maintained in large part to force lower schools to assume the burden of teaching writing had significant implications for the required first-year composition course.

Harvard Reports

Just six years after composition had been installed as a first-year requirement, the Harvard Board of Overseers assembled a committee to study the "problem" of composition and rhetoric. The problem, in brief, was that less than one-third of those applying to Harvard passed the entrance exam in English composition. Charles Francis Adams, Edwin Lawrence Godkin, and Josiah

Quincy (later replaced by George R. Nutter when Quincy became mayor of Boston) served on the committee for six years.
Between 1891 and 1897, the Harvard Committee on Composition and Rhetoric published four reports. Here we will concern
ourselves with the first. Payne drew attention to its importance
when he noted:

> [T]he Harvard Report may be said to have given the reform
> movement its strongest impulse, and made a burning "ques-
> tion of the day" out of a matter previously little more than
> academic in its interest. The subject was made to reach a larger
> public than it had ever reached before, and this new and wider
> public was fairly startled out of its self-complacency by the
> exhibit made of the sort of English written by young men and
> women supposed to have enjoyed the best preparatory educa-
> tional advantages. (12–13)

The reach of this report would have enormous repercussions for
the spread of first-year composition as a systemic response to
perceived problems in the writing of the typical first-year college
student, and for the public coming to firmly accept this response
as a solution. The fact that this solution was so widely embraced
is ironic given the arguments posed in the Harvard report.

Embedded but clear in the report is the sense that first-year
composition at Harvard was envisioned as a temporary stopgap,
existing only because it was believed that lower schools were not
doing an adequate job of preparing students to write English
clearly and correctly.[15] In the words of the committee members,
"At present a large corps of teachers have to be engaged and
paid from the College treasury to do that which should have
been done before the student presented himself for admission.
While teaching these so-called students to write their mother-
tongue, these instructors pass years correcting papers a mere
glance at which shows that the present preparatory training is
grossly inadequate" (Adams, Godkin, and Quincy 96). The committee therefore recommended:

> [T]he College should forthwith, as regards English Composi-
> tion, be put in its proper place as an institution of advanced
> education. The work of theme writing ought to be pronounced
> a part of the elementary training, and as such relegated to the

preparatory schools. The student who cannot write the English language with facility and correctness, should be sent back to the preparatory school to remain there until he can so write it. The College could then, as it should, relieve itself of one of the heaviest burdens now imposed upon it, while those admitted to College would be in a position to enter immediately on the studies to which they propose to devote themselves; and if, during the College course, they take English Composition as an elective they should pursue it in its higher branches, and not, as now, in its most elementary form. (96–97)

The report continued to "further recommend that steps be taken in relation to the standard of English Composition required for admission to our colleges which shall compel the preparatory schools to change their present systems, and raise the standard to the required point" (97). The message was clear. The entrance exam in English composition was meant to be as much a political tool for shaping the teaching of English in lower schools as it was a measure of incoming students. This agenda is stated most clearly in the opening of the report: "[T]he present report is intended to operate directly on the preparatory schools, with a view to elevating the standard, and, if possible, changing radically the methods of instruction in English Composition pursued in them" (78).[16]

The committee arrived at its recommendations after studying some 450 impromptu in-class essays written in 1891 by students enrolled in English A. For this essay, students were asked to describe "the methods of instruction in English Composition pursued in the school in which the writer of each paper had been prepared for college" (77). In all, the students came from 160 different preparatory institutions, and they described a wide range of experiences in studying English literature and composition, from no attention to a fairly hefty schedule during all four years of secondary education. The committee's conclusion presents a rather interesting paradox. Even as the writers of the report berated the quality of student prose and dismissed the essays, they relied on these same pieces of writing to provide quantitative and qualitative evidence for their report describing the kind and extent of prior training in English composition and literature students were then receiving. In other words, the student writings communicated well enough to yield evidence of the nature and degree of preparatory work, and yet still they were dismissed as being "no more creditable in form than they are in expression" (Adams, Godkin, and Quincy 92). What is most interesting in the diversity of responses, and what seems to have escaped the notice of the committee members, is that passing the Harvard entrance exam in English composition did not seem contingent on whether a student had had prior instruction in English composition and literature. That is, there did not seem to be a whit of difference between those who had had direct instruction and those who had had no instruction; just as many of the latter passed the exam as did the former (79–90).

Although this conundrum escaped the attention of the Harvard committee, it would fuel a debate published a few years later in *Century Magazine* under the title "Two Ways of Teaching English." It would also be taken up by William Lyon Phelps who, as Barrett Wendell's assistant, was teaching composition at Harvard during the same year the first Harvard committee report was undertaken. Two decades later Phelps would bluntly state, "On the subject of required English Composition, I am a stout, unabashed, and thorough skeptic" (287). While he had been at Harvard, between 1887 and 1891, he "then believed in the efficacy of the system" (288). However, based on his experience later at Yale, where there was no entrance exam in composition and no composition courses, Phelps's belief was shattered. At Yale he taught Introduction to Literature and required students to write "four or five rather long compositions" (288). In his words:

> When I took home the first batch, I said: "Now for trouble. These young men have never had instruction in English composition, and have never passed through the valuable drill in freshman year given in other colleges." But, to my unspeakable amazement, their compositions were just as good technically as those written by Harvard sophomores! It was a tremendous surprise, for the writers were not, as a class, one whit more advanced mentally than their Harvard brothers. (289)

Of course, Phelps was but one voice in a growing choir of voices that challenged Harvard's composition program on numerous grounds (see Brereton 236–312).

Despite full frontal attacks on the Harvard program,[17] despite Harvard's own apparent misgivings, and despite alternatives to the two-semester compulsory system of composition, first-year college composition became firmly entrenched not only in the ivy halls of Harvard but also throughout the rest of the country, where it had spread quickly. In just one generation, it became a fixed system on virtually every campus across the United States. The four sources of SRM—learning effects, large set-up and fixed costs, coordination effects, and adaptive expectations—help explain how and why this compulsory system locked in.

Digging the Groove: First-Year College Composition as an SRM

Of the four sources of self-reinforcing mechanisms, learning effects had perhaps the largest initial impact on college composition. As more individuals became trained through the system of first-year composition, both by taking courses and by teaching them, it quickly became the system of choice across the country. Learning effects were evident by the turn of this century, appearing with startling clarity in some of the responses to Fred Newton Scott's MLA survey of English professors on the question of whether rhetoric was an apt subject for graduate study. One of the participants in Scott's study distributed the survey to sixteen of his own English composition students. Eleven of these students already held college degrees from some fifteen other institutions, and some had taught English in secondary schools. Despite diverse educational backgrounds, "of these writers, every one discussed the main question as if Rhetoric were to be understood to mean English Composition as a whole or in part. Not one seriously considered the possibility of making rhetoric a study by itself" (qtd. in Mead 193). The remarkable similarity in the responses of this diverse group suggests that composition was quickly becoming the only system imaginable.

How could college composition become a fixed system so quickly? Rollo Walter Brown, a former student of Le Baron Russell Briggs (the man who helped Hill establish composition as a first-year requirement), offers a reasonable explanation for the wild-fire spread of Harvard's system of first-year composition:

> Harvard, with an honorable past, attracted many men who expected to do college teaching. These men, when they went to their posts all over the country carried with them, as every college graduate must, some memory of the way things were done by their Alma Mater. And when these newer institutions sought a means of preventing students from disgracing themselves every time they put pen to paper, they almost invariably made use of Harvard's experience and established prescribed freshman courses in writing. (30–31)

Just as touch typists who learned on a QWERTY keyboard spread quickly throughout the business world, thus encouraging the purchase of QWERTY typewriters, which in turn encouraged others to learn typing on QWERTY, those who had been trained under Harvard's composition system spread quickly to other colleges and there in turn taught others, reproducing the Harvard system.

Of course, the exponential growth of first-year college composition cannot be fully accounted for by these Harvard seed sowers. Learning effects were also spread quickly and efficiently via the newly emerging composition textbooks. These texts represented a radical departure in both scope and function from previous rhetorical textbooks. Whereas earlier textbooks were primarily philosophical and theoretical treatments of rhetoric, the new composition textbooks were prescriptive works, designed to help students avoid the kinds of writing errors that might mar clarity and grace. Production of these prescriptive books proliferated throughout the late nineteenth and early twentieth centuries. They became (and often still are) the first and only training in writing instruction that composition teachers received (Connors, "Textbooks," "Mechanical" 69). These teacher-proof textbooks thus helped perpetuate a mechanical view of literacy and validated the direct instruction of superficial features of discourse.[18]

Karen Schnakenberg, in this volume, provides an illuminating discussion of the influence of these texts. As she notes,

> When scholars such as [Richard] Hughes and [Edward P. J.]
> Corbett, strongly sympathetic to classical rhetoric and strongly
> interested in reviving it as a resource for contemporary theory
> and practice, attempt to translate their interests into instruc-
> tional texts, they are, I argue, more hampered by a combina-
> tion of their own knowledge and training and the characteristics
> of the source texts upon which they draw. . . . (166)

Composition textbooks became a strong vehicle for learning effects, developing an interdependent (dare we say *enabling*) relationship with the system of writing programs, each helping to
keep the other firmly in place.

Yet learning effects extended far beyond the profession and
its textual apparatus to the public at large. Once those inside the
academy came to believe that first-year composition was necessary, thus making it a universal requirement on almost every campus, those outside the academy came to believe it as well. That
belief became part of the fabric of our culture. As Donald
McQuade has rightly noted, "composition studies remains one
of the few academic disciplines in which outsiders insist on naming and authorizing its activities, without accepting the intellectual responsibility—and institutional consequences—of doing so"
(484). One of the most salient examples of this odd state of affairs can be found in the battle over, and ultimate rejection of,
the proposed reformation of the writing program at the University of Texas at Austin in the early 1990s. In describing the events
surrounding this battle, Linda Brodkey points out:

> For the most part, critics of the course seemed unaware that
> those who teach and study writing refer to and share a litera-
> ture on theory, research, and practice similar to that in other
> fields. In unabashedly reducing writing and the teaching of
> writing to rules—of grammar, punctuation, and spelling—these
> critics suggest that the entire field of composition is contained
> in the handbooks and style manuals published by the trade
> presses for undergraduates. (247)

The real problem, of course, is that so much of the profession of
teaching writing—the system of composition—is scripted in those
textbooks, the ones that teachers with little or no background in

the study of writing practices must depend on. The learning effects continue to run deep.

The second source of SRM, large set-up and fixed costs, also serves as a powerful influence on maintaining composition as a system. Once first-year composition became firmly entrenched in departments of English, it became increasingly inexpensive to run, and, in turn, it generated enormous profits. It is probably not an exaggeration to say that the system of composition has helped to keep English departments afloat economically. As Gerald Graff in his history of literary studies admits, "I deal only in passing with the teaching of composition [even though] . . . without that enterprise the teaching of literature could never have achieved its central status" (2). For English departments, composition is a cash cow.

Students pay the same tuition fees per credit hour for a first-year writing course as for any other course, yet the resulting profit margin per credit hour is typically much higher than that for any other class on campus. This is because first-year composition has been, and continues to be, taught primarily by low-paid adjunct faculty and teaching assistants, who not only receive a far smaller salary than faculty at any other rank but also generate far fewer overhead costs such as office space, telephones, computers, secretarial help, travel funds, sabbatical leave, and so on.[19] Given the large profit margin for composition, it pays to keep the course focused on mechanical literacy rather than on the study of literate practices. In other words, it pays to maintain it as a skills course rather than one aimed at the *creation, use,* or *preservation* of knowledge. In this way, it can be assumed that *anyone* can teach the course. And just about *anyone* does.

Finally, the last two sources of SRMs, coordination effects and adaptive expectations, are also evident in the system of first-year composition. Coordination effects—the advantages that accumulate from going along with what other agents are doing—are apparent on both inter- and intra-institutional levels. When first-year composition is a university- or collegewide requirement, all departments on a given campus are compelled to go along with that system. What department will or even can strike out on its own to abandon the requirement or offer something else in its place? Across institutions, the fact that first-year composition is in place at most colleges and universities becomes a self-evident argument for keeping it in place at any individual four-year school. This effect is perhaps most obvious in large integrated public or state systems of higher education (including universities, colleges, and community colleges) when compulsory university requirements become part of a further entrenched bureaucratic policy. That is, if compulsory composition is required at the university, then the other institutions must offer comparable first-year composition programs so that students can transfer those credits within the system. If they do not offer first-year composition, they risk losing students to other institutions that do. And so the question becomes: Which institution will dare to dismantle the system or offer an alternative to it when the vast majority of agents retain it?[20]

Coordination effects extend to the high schools as well. Secondary schools still prepare students for passing college entrance exams—ACTs and SATs. High school English still focuses largely on literature, and yet English teachers are also expected to prepare their students to write college essays. In short, high school English is still predicated upon preparing students for the Harvard system. A related problem is that secondary education English teachers are trained almost exclusively in literary studies; few English departments offer rhetoric and composition courses at the undergraduate level. Even though high school English teachers are responsible for teaching writing and continue to take the blame for students who are supposedly poorly prepared, they are given little training to equip them for that job.

Finally, adaptive expectations—the belief that the system will continue to be in place in the future—contribute to the tenacity of first-year composition. Those who believe that first-year composition is here to stay have no reason to question the system or to create alternative systems. Once the system of first-year composition became firmly entrenched, the belief that it was the only way to attack perceived literacy problems became more firmly implanted. In essence, the system came to be perceived as the subject matter. As a result, the response to the inadequacies of first-year composition has generally been to reform the system rather than to develop alternatives to it.

Today, the four sources of SRM continue to operate on first-year composition, keeping it a firmly entrenched system. The question is whether it is possible for the profession of teaching writing ever to exit from this locked-in path.

Swerving from the Groove: Exiting Lock-In

How likely is it that composition instruction can be changed systemically? In other words, how likely are we to swerve from the groove? Arthur notes, "[W]e can say that the particular equilibrium is *locked in* to a degree measurable by the minimum cost to effect changeover to an alternative equilibrium" ("Self-Reinforcing" 13). Exiting from lock-in is possible under certain circumstances, depending on which of the SRM sources is dominant.

According to Arthur's model, if coordinating effects and/or adaptive expectations are the primary sources of path dependence, the advantages of a new system can outweigh the familiarity of the old system, and thus wide-scale switching is more possible. Such was the case, for example, when Microsoft developed a graphical user interface (GUI) in the 1980s—similar to Apple's already successful GUI—to exit from the clumsier and, for some, more difficult command line interface of DOS. This kind of switch, however, can only take place if users believe that a particular technological system will be superior and if enough users switch. In the case of Microsoft, Apple's success with the user-friendly GUI set a precedent on which Microsoft could rely.

A switch is also possible by fiat: "a negotiated mandated changeover to a superior collective choice can provide exit into the new 'equilibrium' at a negligible cost" (Arthur, "Self-Reinforcing" 16). Typically, such moves require a central organization. Yet, even with its immense market power, Microsoft chose not to make the switch to GUI via fiat. Instead, it let users have the choice between Windows and DOS, while making it clear that Microsoft would focus its future product development on the Windows GUI platform. Windows has won out because, as Farrell and Solaner have shown, individual agents will decide to make the switch on their own as long as they believe others will prefer the new alternative ("Installed," "Standardization"). However, when individual agents cannot be certain how other agents will act, "excess inertia" can prevent exiting to a superior alternative. Put simply, without the expectation of coordinated action, individuals will not switch for fear of losing the benefits of coordinated effects. In the case of Microsoft Windows, third-party software developers had to believe that enough DOS users would switch to Windows to justify the cost of programming for Windows. Similarly, individual purchasers of Windows had to believe that enough software developers would create programs for the Windows platform to justify their own decision to purchase a Windows system. As Arthur points out, "as long as each user has certainty that the others also prefer the alternative, each will decide independently to 'switch'" ("Self-Reinforcing" 16). But where certainty does not exist, excess inertia will prevent exit from lock-in.

When learning effects and large set-up or fixed costs are the dominant sources of self-reinforcement, exiting lock-in is far more difficult. In this case, "usually advantages are not reversible and not transferable to an alternative equilibrium. Repositioning is then difficult" (Arthur, "Self-Reinforcing" 16). Here we can begin to understand why we are locked into a system that continues to keep instruction in and about literate practices marginalized, that remains impervious to the growing rich body of scholarship and research on literacy and rhetoric, and that is so ubiquitous. As a system, first-year composition appears far too profitable to risk changing. Moreover, redesigning the system and staffing it with professors who have a scholarly background in literacy would require prohibitively large initial set-up and fixed costs. Unlike the situation with Microsoft Windows in which a viable alternative interface system was already in place at Apple, there are as yet no alternatives to first-year composition, and the cost of developing and implementing a new system would be enormous.[21] Moreover, the pervasive learning effects within and beyond the walls of our profession and the institutions we serve are so strong that creating and selling an alternative system seems impossible.

Thus, at this point the possibility of swerving from the groove seems unlikely. In fact, it does not seem likely that first-year composition will be transformed in any significant way until, and unless, higher education itself undergoes a radical transformation, along the lines of which we have not seen since the rise of the modern university. Although we do not have a precise solution for this problem, we can envision three possible paths of action.

First, we can continue along the path we are on, struggling to reform the teaching of writing even though, as history has shown us, substantive change is highly unlikely because the system itself seems impervious to change. Perhaps there is value in continuing the struggle and in defining ourselves by that struggle. Disciplines define themselves in many different ways; struggling against the status quo is but one of them. Second, we might try simply to abolish the system. However, of all the options this is not only the least attractive but also the least viable. As Connors shows in tracing abolitionist calls throughout this century, these have not been successful ("New Abolitionism"). For one thing, abolishing composition without offering a viable alternative to deal with complex issues of student literacy seems not only irresponsible but also downright wrongheaded. In some ways, it may serve to further entrench the system. That is to say, calling to abolish the system means acknowledging the system, which further validates it. Despite the term Connors coined, the "new abolitionists," those in favor of dismantling the universal requirement are not suggesting that literacy not be taught but that it be taught under better systems (e.g., Crowley "Personal"; Fleming; Goggin; Jolliffe "Discourse," "Three"; Russell "Activity," "Vygotsky"; Trimbur). This debate brings us to our third option.

It seems clear to us that compulsory first-year composition is not going to change substantially and is not going away any time soon—no more than the QWERTY keyboard is likely to change. Rather than trying to reform the system (i.e., build a better keyboard) we might begin to develop a parallel alternative system that focuses on the study of literate practices. Within this alternative system, we could explore more fully the interrelationships between learning/studying about discursive practices and learning/studying the hows of multiple discursive practices. Just as there are those who are working on technologies other than keyboards for interfacing with computers (e.g., voice recognition systems), we might turn our energies toward creating theoretically grounded programs in literacy that can begin to run parallel to composition. Let others worry about the status of composition. Let us position ourselves to meet the needs of an educational system that might once again recognize discursive practices at the center of knowledge-making activities.[22]

In the meantime, as the QWERTY example demonstrates, technological breakthroughs do not necessarily provide exit from lock-in. After all, it has been well over a hundred years since technology has required a QWERTY keyboard. And yet, even though your computer probably employs a graphical user interface (e.g., Windows), it is even more likely that you are still using a QWERTY keyboard originally designed for a typewriter with no visible printing point. In English departments, we call that irony.

Notes

1. Greenbaum is not quite accurate here. His selection of 1911 to date the first appearance in print of the assault against first-year college English is reasonable when one considers that this marks the formation of the National Council of Teachers of English (NCTE), the first, and at that time only, legitimate professional and scholarly instrument for disseminating discourse on rhetoric and composition. But the record of complaints in print began much earlier. For example, *Century Magazine* printed such an assault in "Two Ways of Teaching English" in 1896. See Brereton (238–41) for a reprint of this article and Chapter 4, The Attack on the Harvard Program, 1890–1917.

2. Lest we be incorrectly accused of scientism—or in this case, "economicism"—the inappropriate, naive application of methods and frames from one intellectual area to that of another, let us quickly point out that economists themselves have argued the value and appropriateness of applying these frames to precisely the kind of problem we are entertaining here. David Colander, for example, who turns to an economic lens to analyze the current state of the discipline of economics, argues that "economic reasoning provides one with a powerful tool of analysis. It allows one to portray complicated systems in a relatively simple way" (4). He later explains that this powerful tool "is enormously strong; it extends beyond the sociological and rhetorical approaches to methodology, which simply look at what happens in science, and provides a theory of why what happens in science happens" (9). See Douglass North and David Wilsford for two additional arguments for using economic lenses as theoretical frames.

3. In the 1980s, Apple sold Apple IIC computers with a built-in switch which allowed users to convert instantly from the QWERTY to a Dvorak

keyboard (David 332). Even though Apple promoted Dvorak as a more efficient board, it made no impact on the monopoly of QWERTY.

4. Our selection of QWERTY to explain SRM is not an accident. We could have chosen any number of examples. A connection can be made between the rise of first-year composition and the emergence of new print technologies. Indeed, the ultimate spread of the QWERTY system needs to be understood as part of the rapidly changing practices of business at that time. Burton Bledstein reports that in 1870 there were about 154 stenographers and typists across the United States; by 1900 that number had risen exponentially to 112,364 (37). As Bledstein's figures suggest, by the end of the nineteenth century new business practices required an unprecedented number of literate workers. It also meant that a lot of QWERTY typewriters were flooding the marketplace to accommodate this growth. See Kaufer and Carley for a study of the impact of the rapid growth of print technology in the nineteenth century and its relation to the rise of the modern university and the university's shift from oral to written pedagogies.

5. The survey posed three questions: "1. Is Rhetoric, in your opinion, a proper study for graduate work? 2. If so, what is the proper aim, what is the scope, and what are the leading problems of Rhetoric as a graduate study? 3. If Rhetoric, in your opinion, should not be admitted to the list of graduate studies, what do you regard as the strongest reasons for excluding it?" (Mead 187).

6. Of course, this was not a new debate; it can be traced back at least as far as Plato, who in the *Gorgias* refused to give rhetoric the status of a theoretical practice, and Aristotle, whose *The "Art" of Rhetoric* set out to demonstrate that it was indeed a theoretical study. The difference is that in modern times the stakes had changed. The answer would determine whether rhetoric could gain a place in higher education and, by extension, in the lower schools.

7. The minority who argued against rhetoric as a fit subject for advanced study were equally divided about its scope and nature, some arguing against it as a science, others as an art. As noted in the report, those who denied it "maintained that there is no more reason for putting Rhetoric among the studies leading to a graduate degree than for putting arithmetic, political geography, or table etiquette there" (Mead 193).

8. Of course, it would take nearly half a century before creative writing pieces would count toward graduate degrees. See Myers on the rise of creative writing as a discipline.

9. A valuable model for just such a venture lay in Fred Newton Scott's graduate program in rhetoric at the University of Michigan. In 1903, Scott removed the program from the English department and formed a Department of Rhetoric. Three decades later, in 1930, Scott retired, and this department was dismantled; rhetoric, far more narrowly conceived than it had been under Scott, was brought back under the "wing" of the Department of English (Stewart). Had others followed Scott's lead, it might have been more difficult for those in the English department at Michigan to have co-opted the rhetoric department Scott had built.

10. See Andresen for a history of the formation of linguistics as a discipline and Cohen for a history of speech communication. Both trace early debates that revealed nascent scholars in each area arguing that their field was a *naturwissenschaft.*

11. Because linguistics was from the beginning defined as a science, it was saved from the kind of impoverishment and displacement suffered by rhetoric. This is not to say that it has not been marginalized within departments of English. It is often on the fringes of English departments. But it did avoid being created as an impoverished service enterprise.

12. John Brereton provides an excellent discussion of the various alternatives (14–16) and reprints many of the original documents that describe these. See also Berlin *Rhetoric, Writing*; Russell *Writing.*

13. In fact, Charles Eliot was the first to administer a written exam at Harvard. As a math instructor, he had to get special permission to give a written examination in place of the traditional oral exam (Kaufer and Carley 29).

14. For example, in the Harvard Committee on Composition and Rhetoric Report, the curriculum in English of one secondary school is described: "[T]he course of instruction is the usual one . . . during the first [year] three hours a week are devoted to reading prescribed English books, with one hour in two weeks spent in composition. During the second year, the time spent on English is reduced to two hours a week. During the third year, this time is further reduced to one hour a week, with about one hour in each two weeks passed in writing a composition, including the correction of sentences in bad English and the study of punctuation" (Adams, Godkin, and Quincy 79). Here it is clear that the greater portion of the limited time spent in studying English is given over to "reading English books."

15. Mike Rose demonstrates that this belief—namely, that "remedial efforts, while currently necessary, can be phased out once the literacy

crisis is solved in other segments of the educational system" (341)—continues to hold strong today. He calls this belief the Myth of Transience (355–57).

16. It is important to note that NCTE emerged in part to fight those postsecondary institutions that threatened to control the secondary curriculum of English studies. These institutions, largely private colleges and universities in the East, had proposed the Uniform College Entrance Requirements Committee as a body that would define uniform subjects and skills in English in order to make postsecondary admissions procedures more manageable. This legislative body threatened to dominate secondary English curricula by mandating specific literary works, skills, and topics that teachers would have to cover if their students were to be prepared for admission into higher education. In response, the Secondary Department of the National Education Association (NEA) called on J. F. Hosic, then head of the Department of English at Chicago Normal College, to lead a protest against the Uniform College Entrance Requirements. Hosic appointed a committee, which would later become known as the Committee of Thirty, and then called a conference for the Thanksgiving holiday vacation in 1911. This meeting resulted in the formation of the National Council of Teachers of English.

17. See Brereton, Chapter 4 (236–312), for a selection of articles published at the turn of this century that challenged Harvard's composition program in particular and first-year college composition in general. See also Connors's "The New Abolitionism."

18. As Robert Connors notes, "Bereft of a theoretical discipline and a professional tradition, teachers [at the end of the nineteenth century] had nothing to turn to for information about their subject—except their textbooks. After 1910, composition courses were increasingly staffed by graduate students and low-level instructors. Writing teachers became as a result the only college-level instructors who know no more of the discipline than is contained in the texts they assign their students—a sad pattern that still, alas, continues today at too many schools" ("Mechanical" 69).

19. The December 1997 MLA Committee on Professional Employment reported that "in Ph.D.-granting English departments . . . 96 per cent of the first-year writing classes are taught by graduate students, part-timers, or full-time, non-tenure track professors, compared with 64 per cent in departments that grant no more than master's degrees and 50 per cent in departments that grant only bachelor's degrees" (Schneider A15). Depending on the rank of the writing instructor, the profit for a composition course may run as high as $8,000 to $12,000 per class (Schneider A14).

20. Sharon Crowley has argued precisely this solution, that is, to abolish the requirement and make first-year composition an elective ("A Personal Essay"). At least one institution has done this. See Lil Brannon for her discussion of how compulsory first-year composition was abolished at the University at Albany, SUNY, in 1986, being replaced with a two-semester requirement of writing-intensive courses. Also see Bamberg; Graham, Birmingham, and Zachry; Chase; Gradin; and Kearns and Turner in the Fall 1997 issue of *WPA*, an issue devoted to exploring alternatives to first-year college composition.

21. Not only does first-year composition economically support literary studies within departments of English but the system has also created other economic webs that need to be considered. In responding to the volume *Reconceiving Writing, Rethinking Writing Instruction*, Charles Bazerman poses a series of questions to challenge those scholars in the volume who problematize and argue against first-year composition as a universal compulsory system. He asks:

> If there were no first-year writing programs to be taught and overseen, how many writing professionals would most English departments support? If there were no first-year writing course, how many of the now-autonomous writing programs could avoid being folded back into other units? If there were no strong first-year writing program, how many writing across the curriculum programs could resist the drift of loosely monitored writing-intensive requirements and the habit of disciplines to make their rhetoric invisible in the service of epistemic authority? If there were no highly visible writing program, how many institutions (other than technical universities) would recognize more advanced writing courses as appropriate college work and how many nominally advanced courses would reformulate to pick up the needs no longer served by the vanished first-year course? If the first-year course did not keep literacy on the university agenda, how much research into issues of literacy would be supported except in colleges of education, and what would happen then to research on the advanced literacy practices of disciplines, professions, and the workplace? (Bazerman, "Response" 259)

Bazerman poses important questions that we must confront as we try to reimagine the site of first-year writing programs. However, they also call our attention to the economics underlying the course. Dismantling the system would send devastating ripple effects through the ranks of those interested in literate practices. We are caught, then, in a web of costs.

22. A growing number of scholars and teachers in rhetoric and composition are calling for alternative models to do just this; see, for example, Fleming; Trimbur; the Fall 1997 issue of *Writing Program Administration*, and the collection of essays in Petraglia's *Reconceiving Writing, Rethinking Writing Instruction*.

Works Cited

Adams, Charles Francis, Edwin Lawrence Godkin, and Josiah Quincy. "Report of the Committee on Composition and Rhetoric (1892)." Brereton 73–98.

Andresen, Julie T. *Linguistics in America, 1769–1924: A Critical History*. London: Routledge, 1990.

Aristotle. *The "Art" of Rhetoric*. Trans. John Henry Freese. Cambridge: Harvard UP, 1994.

Arthur, W. Brian. "Competing Technologies, Increasing Returns, and Lock-In by Historical Events." *The Economic Journal* 99 (1989): 116–31.

———. "Self-Reinforcing Mechanisms in Economics." *The Economy as an Evolving Complex System*. Ed. Philip W. Anderson, Kenneth J. Arrow, and David Pines. Redwood City, CA: Addison, 1988. 9–31.

Bamberg, Betty. "Alternative Models of First-Year Composition: Possibilities and Problems." *Writing Program Administration* 21 (1997): 7–18.

Bazerman, Charles. "Response: Curricular Responsibilities and Professional Definition." Petraglia 249–59.

Berlin, James A. *Rhetoric and Reality: Writing Instruction in American Colleges, 1900–1985*. Carbondale: Southern Illinois UP, 1987.

———. *Writing Instruction in Nineteenth-Century American Colleges*. Carbondale: Southern Illinois UP, 1984.

Bizzell, Patricia, and Bruce Herzberg, eds. *The Rhetorical Tradition: Readings from Classical Times to the Present*. Boston: Bedford, 1990.

Bledstein, Burton J. *The Culture of Professionalism: The Middle Class and the Development of Higher Education in America*. New York: Norton, 1976.

Brannon, Lil. "(Dis)Missing Compulsory First-Year Composition." Petraglia 239–48.

Brereton, John C., ed. *The Origins of Composition Studies in the American College, 1875–1925: A Documentary History*. Pittsburgh: U of Pittsburgh P, 1995.

Briggs, Le Baron Russell. "The Harvard Admission Examination in English." *The Academy* (1888). Rpt. in *Twenty Years of School and College English*. Cambridge: Harvard U, 1896.

Brodkey, Linda. "Making a Federal Case Out of Difference: The Politics of Pedagogy, Publicity, and Postponement." *Writing Theory and Critical Theory*. Ed. John Clifford and John Schilb. New York: MLA, 1994. 236–61.

Brown, Rollo Walter. "Dean Briggs (1926)." Brereton 28–33.

Chase, Geoffrey. "Redefining Composition, Managing Change, and the Role of the WPA." *Writing Program Administration* 21 (1997): 46–54.

Cohen, Herman. *The History of Speech Communication: The Emergence of a Discipline, 1914–1945*. Annandale, VA: Speech Communication Association, 1994.

Colander, David. *Why Aren't Economists As Important As Garbagemen? Essays on the State of Economics*. Armonk, NY: Sharpe, 1991.

Connors, Robert J. "Mechanical Correctness as a Focus in Composition Instruction." *College Composition and Communication* 36 (1985): 61–72.

———. "The New Abolitionism: Toward a Historical Background." Petraglia 3–26.

———. "Textbooks and the Evolution of the Discipline." *College Composition and Communication* 37 (1986): 178–94.

Crowley, Sharon. *The Methodical Memory: Invention in Current-Traditional Rhetoric*. Carbondale: Southern Illinois UP, 1990.

———. "A Personal Essay on Freshman English." *PRE/TEXT* 12 (1991): 156–76.

David, Paul A. "Clio and the Economics of QWERTY." *American Economic Review* 75 (1985): 332–27.

Day, Henry. "From *The Art of Discourse*." Bizzell and Herzberg 864–73.

Farrell, Joseph, and Garth Saloner. "Installed Base and Compatibility: Innovation, Product Preannoucements, and Predation." *American Economic Review* 76 (1986): 940–55.

———. "Standardization, Compatibility, and Innovation." *Rand Journal of Economics* 16 (1985): 70–83.

Fleming, David. "Rhetoric as a Course of Study." *College English* 61 (1998): 169–91.

Goggin, Maureen Daly. "The Disciplinary Instability of Composition." Petraglia 27–48.

Gradin, Sherrie. "What Happens to the Writing Program Administrator When the Writing Requirements Go Away?" *Writing Program Administration* 21 (1997): 55–66.

Graff, Gerald. *Professing Literature: An Institutional History.* Chicago: U of Chicago P, 1987.

Graham, Margaret Baker, Elizabeth Birmingham, and Mark Zachry. "Reinventing First-Year Composition at the First Land-Grant University: A Cautionary Tale." *Writing Program Administration* 21 (1997): 19–30.

Greenbaum, Leonard. "The Tradition of Complaint." *College English* 31 (1969): 174–87.

Greenblatt, Stephen, and Giles Gunn, eds. *Redrawing the Boundaries: The Transformation of English and American Literary Studies.* New York: MLA, 1992.

Hill, Adams Sherman. "An Answer to the Cry for More English (1879)." Brereton 45–57.

———. "From *The Principles of Rhetoric.*" Bizzell and Herzberg 881–84.

Hill, David. "From *The Science of Rhetoric.*" Bizzell and Herzberg 877–80.

Johnson, Nan. *Nineteenth-Century Rhetoric in North America.* Carbondale: Southern Illinois UP, 1991.

Jolliffe, David. "Discourse, Interdiscursivity, and Composition Instruction." Petraglia 197–216.

———. "Three Arguments for Sophomore English." CCCC Annual Convention. Sheraton Harbor Island Hotel, San Diego. 2 Apr. 1993.

Kaufer, David S., and Kathleen Carley. *Communication at a Distance: The Influence of Print on Sociocultural Organization and Change.* Hillsdale, NJ: Erlbaum, 1993.

Kearns, Judith, and Brian Turner. "Negotiated Independence: How a Canadian Writing Program Became a Centre." *Writing Program Administration* 21 (1997): 31–45.

Kitzhaber, Albert R. *Rhetoric in American Colleges, 1850–1900.* 1953. Dallas: Southern Methodist UP, 1990.

Marius, Richard. "Composition Studies." Greenblatt and Gunn 466–81.

McQuade, Donald. "Composition and Literary Studies." Greenblatt and Gunn 482–519.

Mead, William Edward. "Report of the Pedagogical Section: The Graduate Study of Rhetoric." *PMLA* 16 (1901): xix–xxxii. Rpt. in Brereton 186–202.

Myers, David G. *The Elephants Teach: Creative Writing since 1880.* Englewood Cliffs, NJ: Prentice, 1996.

North, Douglass C. *Institutions, Institutional Change, and Economic Performance.* Cambridge: Cambridge UP, 1990.

Ohmann, Richard. *English in America: A Radical View of the Profession.* New York: Oxford UP, 1976.

Payne, William Morton, ed. Introduction. *English in American Universities by Professors in the English Departments of Twenty Representative Institutions.* Boston: Heath, 1895. 7–28.

Petraglia, Joseph, ed. *Reconceiving Writing, Rethinking Writing Instruction.* Mahwah, NJ: Erlbaum, 1995.

Phelps, William Lyon. "'English Composition' in *Teaching in School and College* (1912)." Brereton 287–91.

Plato. *Gorgias.* Trans. W. C. Helmbold. New York: Macmillan, 1952.

Rose, Mike. "The Language of Exclusion: Writing Instruction at the University." *College English* 47 (1985): 341–59.

Russell, David R. "Activity Theory and Its Implications for Writing Instruction." Petraglia 51–78.

———. "Vygotsky, Dewey, and Externalism: Beyond the Student/Discipline Dichotomy." *Journal of Advanced Composition* 13 (1993): 173–97.

———. *Writing in the Academic Disciplines, 1870–1990: A Curricular History*. Carbondale: Southern Illinois UP, 1991.

Schneider, Alison. "Bad Blood in the English Department: The Rift between Composition and Literature." *Chronicle of Higher Education* 13 Feb. 1998: A14–15.

Shumway, David R. *Creating American Civilization: A Genealogy of American Literature as an Academic Discipline*. Minneapolis: U of Minnesota P, 1994.

Stewart, Donald C. "Rediscovering Fred Newton Scott." *College English* 40 (1979): 539–47.

"Three Harvard Catalogue Course Descriptions from *Twenty Years of School and College English* (1896)." Brereton 33–44.

Trimbur, John. "The Problem of Freshman English (Only): Towards Programs of Study in Writing." *Writing Program Administration* 22 (1999): 9–30.

"Two Ways of Teaching English." *Century Magazine* 51 (1896): 793–94. Rpt. in Brereton 238–41.

Veysey, Laurence R. *The Emergence of the American University*. Chicago: U of Chicago P, 1965.

Wilsford, David. "Path Dependency, or Why History Makes It Difficult but Not Impossible to Reform Health Care Systems in a Big Way." *Journal of Public Policy* 14 (1994): 251–83.

Winterowd, W. Ross, and Jack Blum. *A Teacher's Introduction to Composition in the Rhetorical Tradition*. Urbana, IL: NCTE, 1994.

Wozniak, John Michael. *English Composition in Eastern Colleges, 1850–1940*. Washington: UP of America, 1978.

Young, Richard E. "'Tracing Round the Frame': Thinking about Writing in Departments of English." *Discourse Studies in Honor of James L. Kinneavy*. Ed. Rosalind J. Gabin. Potomac, MD: Scripta Humanistica, 1995. 149–67.

CHAPTER THREE

Cross-Disciplinarity in Rhetorical Scholarship?

JANICE M. LAUER
Purdue University

A decade ago in an opening talk to the Rhetoric Society of America Conference, Edward Corbett spoke of disappointment at the scarcity of interchange among rhetoricians in various disciplines in the previous twenty-five years ("Where Are the Snows"). This essay initiates an inquiry into some of the possible reasons for such lack of exchange in the past few decades. It asks to what extent rhetorical scholarship in rhetoric and composition, speech communication, and classics coheres and interrelates or whether these fields study different problems, are motivated by distinct issues, and are governed solely by their own guiding perspectives and interpretive practices. Finally, it explores whether this apparent lack of intertextuality still exists.

The separation of the Speech Communication Association (SCA) from the National Council of Teachers of English (NCTE) in the early twentieth century initiated divergent scholarly paths for these fields. Departments of English turned from rhetoric to the study of literature, a movement that has been amply documented by historians such as James Berlin (*Writing*). During the first part of the century, most of the historical work on rhetoric in the United States came from speech communication scholars. Richard Enos's 1985 essay, "The History of Rhetoric: The Reconstruction of Progress," catalogs the extensive list of studies on historical rhetoric by speech communication (hereafter referred to as communication) scholars in the first three quarters of the twentieth century. But since the midsixties, growing numbers of rhetoric and composition (hereafter referred to as composition) specialists have increased their investment in rhetorical theory and history, constructing an expanding body of scholarship, both traditional and revisionary. In classics departments over these years, rhetoric has been on the margins, claiming the attention of only a few scholars.

There are broad reasons to suggest why composition specialists in the sixties began to take directions in rhetorical scholarship different from the other two fields. Many of the first composition theorists received their training during the fifties, sixties, and seventies in literature. Their formal literary education introduced them to textual problems, issues, and interpretive strategies different from those in communication or from the philological orientation of classicists. With this background, composition specialists came to both primary and secondary rhetorical texts with their own disciplinary emphases, canonical preoccupations, and historiographical practices.

Another source of difference is the fact that composition specialists have had responsibility for teaching writing at all levels of education. This challenge has motivated them to reexamine canonical rhetorical texts for new accounts of how discourse, arts, and contexts have been linked in constructions of knowledge and exercises of power in cultural situations. The problems of literacy faced by composition specialists have, therefore, lent an urgency and consequential cast to their historical and contemporary inquiry in rhetoric. In contrast, Enos points out, although the early "development and direction of research in the history of rhetoric by speech communication scholars [w]as rooted in pedagogical and humanistic concerns," it gradually shifted from pedagogical issues to increasingly specialized historical research problems (28). These differences in background and motivation suggest that composition specialists have taken new turns in their study of rhetoric. But does their work bear this out? This essay will begin to tackle this broad question by sampling scholarly discussions on two topics in rhetorical theory and history: invention and writer/reader positioning in contexts. I will contrast selected composition studies in rhetorical history and theory with the work in communication and classics taken together.

Studies of Invention

In composition studies, invention, especially its epistemological functions and arts, has been a compelling area of inquiry for composition specialists since the sixties. Confronted with teaching students who needed help with generating ideas, judgments, and arguments, early theorists constructed new or revised sets of topoi and modern heuristics to guide exploration in the composing process, examining the relationship between knowledge and discourse. Richard E. Young, Alton Becker, and Kenneth Pike developed tagmemic rhetoric, including an epistemological guide sensitive to cultural difference. Edward Corbett resituated some of the classical topoi as flexible lines of reasoning rather than as discrete ways to develop essays, which they had become in the nineteenth century. Janice Lauer argued for rhetorical invention as heuristic rather than logical thinking. Linda Flower and John Hayes described students' planning processes, and later Flower studied collaborative inventional processes. Karen LeFevre outlined a theory of invention as a social construction of knowledge. Other theorists studied invention over the last three decades under such titles as writing as inquiry, writing as learning, writing as meaning making, writing as creative process, and writing as cultural critique. Composition researchers also examined the role of discourse in knowledge construction, extending inventional scholarship into different disciplines and the workplace.

Historians in composition studies also turned their attention to issues of invention. For example, Jasper Neel raised issues of Plato's logocentrism and exposed pedagogies such as *psophistry* that he maintained arose from Platonic influences. Sharon Crowley critiqued nineteenth- and early twentieth-century invention, pointing out the dangers of overformalizing rhetorical invention in textbooks. Susan Jarratt outlined a pedagogy as part of her revisionist study of sophistic epistemology. Janet Atwill argued that interpreting Aristotle's rhetoric as episteme rather than techne resulted in privileging elitist philosophical thought rather than probable reasoning and critique, denying rhetoric its power to enable "outsiders" to challenge current institutions and practices. Cheryl Glenn, Catherine Peaden, and Heping Zhao challenged gendered and Westernized conceptions of rhetorical knowing that posed problems for multicultural writing students in modern classrooms.

These studies have cohered within and contributed to the twentieth-century epistemological crisis in which language is being considered central to the construction of knowledge and student writing is viewed as a potent instrument of social and political change. Unlike conceptions of rhetoric (and written language) as a conduit or transmitter of knowledge, this composition scholarship has foregrounded invention as epistemic, guiding the writer in creating knowledge, new meanings. Motivated in part by conceptions of writing as a process which can be guided by arts or heuristics rather than as an entirely mysterious activity of creation, this work has introduced into composition theory and instruction conceptions of rhetoric as contextualized, strategic, social—a set of discursive practices with consequences for rhetorical practice in public life and for writing pedagogy.

Scholars in communication and classics have also given attention to invention during the last few decades. For instance, rhetorical theorists such as Robert Scott, Richard Cherwitz, and James Hikins have studied rhetoric as epistemic, participating in a debate categorized by Michael Leff as headed toward a perspective of epistemology as rhetorical. Historians have analyzed inventional arts in major texts, e.g., William Grimaldi's work on Aristotle's topics and enthymeme, Donovan Ochs's analyses of Aristotle and Cicero's systems of topics, Michael Leff's tracing of the topics from Cicero to Boethius, James McBurney's and Lloyd Bitzer's discussions of Aristotle's enthymeme, Martha Nussbaum's interpretations of Aristotle's and Plato's epistemologies, and Otto Dieter's and Ray Nadeau's studies of the continuity of stasis and status throughout major Greek and Roman rhetorics. These important studies appear to have as their primary thrust the establishment of preferable interpretations of the canonical texts under scrutiny, either by tracing influences or systematizing, as Carole Blair does, or in William Grimaldi's case, by constituting rhetoric as a philosophical discipline. Therefore, the consequences of these interpretations for current political practice and teaching communication are muted. Further, communication theorists tend to analyze epistemic positions in *already constructed* texts, while composition theorists stress the *construction* of knowledge through writing. Richard Enos underscores this point:

> In the history of rhetoric . . . relatively little attention has been paid to the relationship between the structuring of thought and the structuring of discourse. Consequently, the analysis of rhetorical theory is only rarely based upon a careful inquiry into the conceptual processes shaping discourse; instead explications of theory are predicated upon cognitive processes that are either assumed or ignored by the historian of rhetoric. (38)

Studies of Audience, Writers, Readers, and Contexts

A second issue of some urgency to composition theorists and historians has been the character of audiences for *written* discourse, the nature of writer and reader positions within rhetorical contexts. Scholarship here includes the conception of the audience of written texts as a constructed fiction (Ong); the notions of audience as addressed and invoked (Ede and Lunsford); theories of discourse community with the author and audience as co-creators of texts (Bizzell; Porter); critiques of the author as originary voice or autonomous subject (Clifford, "Subject"; Phelps; Jacobs); arguments for composition as cultural studies with writer and reader coded by the culture (Berlin, "Composition"; Trimbur); and research on writers and readers in electronic communities (Selfe and Wahlstrom; Sullivan; Howard). Other studies of writers and readers have been conducted in research on writing across the curriculum, writing in the disciplines, and workplace writing .

Composition historians have also found the relationship among writer, reader, and situation compelling to investigate. James Kinneavy has described *kairos* as the motivating and informing basis for a broad writing curriculum sensitive to situational and cultural context, rather than to sentence, paragraph, or error. Michael Carter has explained the theoretical and pedagogical consequences of interpreting kairos and stasis as artistic discursive practices in the social construction of knowledge. Historians have also examined the nature of writers and readers in different disciplinary communities, for example, Charles Bazerman's study of Darwin and James Zappen's work on Bacon, Newton, and Darwin. Other composition scholars have examined marginalized audiences, audiences in transitional periods from orality to literacy, and the economic and class status of readers in different periods and cultures, producing revisionary accounts of textual audiences and author formations. The majority of this work investigates the readers of written texts in a variety of previously unstudied discourse communities and social and political contexts. Further, it probes the participatory role of audience in the construction of meaning, reconfigures notions of author subjectivities, and incorporates discussions of the consequences for practicing and teaching discourse.

Scholars in communication and classics have also theorized rhetorical situations, such as the debate among Lloyd Bitzer, Richard Vatz, and Scott Consigny. Historians have focused on audiences of *oral* discourse, generally treating them as addressed, with the writer as agent, e.g., William Sattler's tracing of ethos through the works of major rhetorical theorists; Charles Willard's analysis of the auditor in Aristotle's rhetoric; Richard Enos and Jeanne L. McClaren's depiction of the crowds for Cicero's speeches; and William Fortenbaugh's discussion of Aristotle's idea of persuasion through character. While these studies have implicit consequences for the practice and teaching of discourse, most do not make explicit the "arts" of invention or audience positioning.

Directionality and Intertextuality

The preceding examples suggest that scholarship in composition has been motivated for the most part by different issues and consequences than scholarship in communication and classics even though the topics have often been similar. A perusal of their references also indicates a difference in scholarly direction. The works of the composition historians and theorists mentioned here cite some relevant scholarship in communication and classics. In contrast, studies in communication and classics referred to in this essay contain no references to scholarship in composition. Two recent works exhibit this same silence. Thomas Farrell's argument for norms for rhetorical culture shares an interest in praxis— the role of rhetoric in public life—and in ethics with such compositionists as Kinneavy and those working in cultural studies, but his text does not intersect with any composition studies. Likewise, Dilip Gaonkar's depiction of the contrast between classical rhetoric and modern rhetoric ignores the theories and practices of composition studies, citing only one composition theorist, Alan Gross, the editor of the interdisciplinary collection. These one-way citation practices suggest the kind of directionality described by John Clifford, who comments on the power relations among fields within English studies.

> Perhaps this is yet another representative anecdote about the continuing asymmetrical power arrangements within even sophisticated English departments where composition specialists are expected to be knowledgeable about the literary canon from Beowolf to Barth, from Plato to Fish, while avant-garde critics seem quite satisfied with being "a little old-fashioned" about writing theory. ("Toward a Productive Crisis" 259)

There are signs, however, that intertextuality is on the rise among communication scholars with interests in poststructuralism, postmodernism, and revisionist historiography, e.g., "critical rhetoricians" such as Michael McGee, Richard Hariman, and Ramie McKerrow, and postmodern historians such as John Poulakos, Jane Sutton, Carole Blair, and Barbara Biesecker, who argue for rhetoric, whether contemporary or historical, written or oral, as a critique of discourses of power with a view toward change. They challenge agent-centered views, seeing discourse as mediated and fragmented, rejecting Platonic and Kantian configurations of rhetoric, and instead situating it as doxastic and interpretive. These scholars ideologically agree with and are occasionally in textual conversation with a number of composition specialists, particularly those doing cultural studies such as James Berlin and Takis Poulakos, those informing composition with postmodern thought such as Lester Faigley, Patricia Harkin and John Schilb, or those applying poststructuralist perspectives to historical research such as Janet Atwill, Sharon Crowley, and Susan Jarratt.

This rising intertextuality is fostered by journals such as the *Rhetoric Society Quarterly* and *Rhetorica* as they encourage disciplinary diversity. Further, recent collections of essays have drawn together scholars from these fields in volumes such as *A Short History of Writing Instruction from Ancient Greece to Twentieth-Century America* (Ed. James Murphy); *Writing Histories of Rhetoric* (Ed. Victor Vitanza); *Rethinking the History of Rhetoric* (Ed. Takis Poulakos); *Defining the New Rhetorics* (Ed. Theresa Enos and Stuart Brown); and the *Encyclopedia of Rhetoric and Composition* (Ed. Theresa Enos). A more recent exchange has been occurring on the listserv H-Rhetor. Will this intertextuality increase? I hope so. If these disciplines take seriously the questions they pose about rhetorical theory, practice, and pedagogy, should they not welcome all cross-disciplinary research and scholarship that contributes to new understandings of these questions?

Works Cited

Atwill, Janet. "Instituting the Art of Rhetoric: Theory, Practice, and Productive Knowledge in Interpretations of Aristotle's *Rhetoric.*" *Rethinking the History of Rhetoric: Multidisciplinary Essays on the Rhetorical Tradition.* Ed. Takis Poulakos. Boulder: Westview, 1993. 91–117.

Bazerman, Charles. *Shaping Written Knowledge: The Genre and Activity of the Experimental Article in Science.* Madison: U of Wisconsin P, 1988.

Berlin, James. "Composition Studies and Cultural Studies: Collapsing Boundaries." *Into the Field: Sites of Composition Studies.* Ed. Anne Ruggles Gere. New York: MLA, 1993. 99–116.

———. *Writing Instruction in Nineteenth-Century American Colleges.* Carbondale: Southern Illinois UP, 1984.

Biesecker, Barbara. "Rethinking the Rhetorical Situation from within the Thematic of Difference." *Philosophy and Rhetoric* 22 (1989): 110–30.

Bitzer, Lloyd. "Aristotle's Enthymeme Revisited." *Quarterly Journal of Speech* 45 (1959): 399–408.

———. "The Rhetorical Situation." *Philosophy and Rhetoric* 1 (1968): 1–14.

Bizzell, Patricia. "College Composition: Initiation into the Academic Discourse Community. " *Curriculum Inquiry* 12 (1982): 191–207.

Blair, Carole. "Contested Histories of Rhetoric: The Politics of Preservation, Progress, and Change." *Quarterly Journal of Speech* 78 (1992): 403–28.

———. " 'Meta-Ideology,' Rhetoric and Social Theory: A Reenactment of the Wisdom-Eloquence Tension after the Linguistic Turn." *Rhetoric and Ideology: Compositions and Criticisms of Power*. Ed. Charles Kneupper. Arlington, TX: Rhet. Soc. of Amer., 1989. 21–29.

Carter, Michael. "*Stasis* and *Kairos*: Principles of Social Construction in Classical Rhetoric." *Rhetoric Review* 7 (1988): 97–112.

Cherwitz, Richard, and James Hikins. *Communication and Knowledge: An Investigation in Rhetorical Epistemology*. Columbia: U of South Carolina P, 1986.

Clifford, John. "The Subject in Discourse." Harkin and Schilb 38–51.

———. "Toward a Productive Crisis: A Response to Gayatri Spivak." *(Inter)views: Cross-Disciplinary Perspectives on Rhetoric and Literacy*. Ed. Gary A. Olson and Irene Gale. Carbondale: Southern Illinois UP, 1991. 255–60.

Consigny, Scott. "Rhetoric and Its Situations." *Philosophy and Rhetoric* 7 (1974): 175–86.

Corbett, Edward. *Classical Rhetoric for the Modern Student*. New York: Oxford UP, 1971.

———. "Where Are the Snows of Yesteryear? Has Rhetoric Come a Long Way in the Last Twenty-Five Years?" *Visions of Rhetoric: History, Theory, and Criticism*. Ed. Charles Kneupper. Arlington, TX: Rhet. Soc. of Amer., 1987.1–10.

Crowley, Sharon. *The Methodical Memory: Invention in Current-Traditional Rhetoric*. Carbondale: Southern Illinois UP, 1990.

Dieter, Otto. "On *Stasis*." *Communication Monographs* 17 (1950): 345–69.

Ede, Lisa, and Andrea Lunsford. "Audience Addressed/Audience Invoked: The Role of Audience in Composition Theory and Pedagogy." *College Composition and Communication* 35 (1984): 155–71.

Enos, Richard. "The History of Rhetoric: The Reconstruction of Progress." *Speech Communication in the 20th Century*. Ed. Thomas Benson. Carbondale: Southern Illinois UP, 1985. 28–40.

Enos, Richard, and Jeanne L. McClaren. "Audience and Image in Ciceronian Rome: Creation and Constraints of the *Vir Bonus* Personality." *Central States Speech Journal* 29 (1978): 98–106.

Faigley, Lester. *Fragments of Rationality: Postmodernity and the Subject of Composition*. Pittsburgh: U of Pittsburgh P, 1992.

Farrell, Thomas. *Norms of Rhetorical Culture*. New Haven: Yale UP, 1993.

Flower, Linda. *The Construction of Negotiated Meaning: A Social Cognitive Theory of Writing*. Carbondale: Southern Illinois UP, 1994.

Flower, Linda, and John Hayes. "Cognitive Process Theory of Writing." *College Composition and Communication* 32 (1981): 365–87.

Fortenbaugh, William W. *Aristotle on Emotion: A Contribution to Philosophical Psychology, Rhetoric, Poetics, Politics and Ethics*. New York: Barnes, 1975.

Glenn, Cheryl. "sex, lies, and manuscript: Refiguring Aspasia in the History of Rhetoric." *College Composition and Communication* 45 (1994): 180–99.

Gaonkar, Dilip. "The Idea of Rhetoric in the Rhetoric of Science." *Rhetorical Hermeneutics: Invention and Interpretation in the Age of Science*. Ed. Alan Gross and William Keith. Albany: SUNY P, 1997. 25–85.

Grimaldi, William. *Aristotle, Rhetoric I: A Commentary*. New York: Fordham UP, 1980.

———. *Aristotle, Rhetoric II: A Commentary*. New York: Fordham UP, 1988.

———. *Studies in the Philosophy of Aristotle's Rhetoric*. Wiesbaden: F. Steiner, 1972.

Hariman, Richard. "Critical Rhetoric and Postmodern Theory." *Quarterly Journal of Speech* 77 (1991): 67–70.

———. "Status, Marginality, and Rhetorical Theory." *Quarterly Journal of Speech* 72 (1986): 38–54.

Harkin, Patricia, and John Schilb, eds. *Contending with Words: Composition and Rhetoric in a Postmodern Age.* New York: MLA, 1991.

Howard, Tharon. *A Rhetoric of Electronic Communities.* Greenwich: Ablex, 1997.

Jacobs, Debra. "Voice in Writing." *Encyclopedia of English Studies and Language Arts.* Ed. Alan Purves. Vol. 2. New York: Scholastic, 1994. 1250–55.

Jarratt, Susan. *Rereading the Sophists: Classical Rhetoric Refigured.* Carbondale: Southern Illinois UP, 1991.

Kinneavy, James. "*Kairos*: A Neglected Concept in Classical Rhetoric." *Rhetoric and Praxis: The Contribution of Classical Rhetoric to Practical Reasoning.* Washington, DC: Catholic U of America P, 1986. 79–105.

Lauer, Janice. "Heuristics and Composition." *Contemporary Rhetoric: A Conceptual Background with Readings.* Ed. Ross Winterowd. New York: Harcourt, 1970. 79–90.

LeFevre, Karen. *Invention as a Social Act.* Carbondale: Southern Illinois UP, 1986.

Leff, Michael. "In Search of Ariadne's Thread: A Review of the Recent Literature on Rhetorical Theory." *Central States Speech Journal* 29 (1978): 73–91.

———. "The Topics of Argumentative Invention in Latin Rhetorics from Cicero to Boethius." *Rhetorica* 1 (1983): 23–44.

McBurney, James. "The Place of the Enthymeme in Rhetorical Theory." *Communication Monographs* 3 (1936): 49–74.

McGee, Michael. "'Ideograph:' A Link between Rhetoric and Ideology." *Quarterly Journal of Speech* 66 (1980): 1–16.

———. "Text, Context, and the Fragmentation of Contemporary Culture." *Western Journal of Speech Communication* 54 (1990): 274–89.

McKerrow, Ramie. "Critical Rhetoric: Theory and Praxis." *Communication Monographs* 56 (1989): 91–111.

Nadeau, Ray. "Hermogenes' *On Stasis*: A Translation with an Introduction and Notes." *Communication Monographs* 31 (1964): 361–424.

Neel, Jasper. *Plato, Derrida, and Writing*. Carbondale: Southern Illinois UP, 1988.

Nussbaum, Martha. *The Fragility of Goodness: Luck and Ethics in Greek Tragedy and Philosophy*. Cambridge: Cambridge UP, 1986.

Ochs, Donovan. "Aristotle's Concept of Formal Topics." *Communication Monographs* 36 (1969): 419–25.

———. "Cicero's Topica: A Process View of Invention." *Explorations in Rhetoric: Studies in Honor of Douglas Ehninger*. Ed. Ray E. McKerrow. Glenview, IL: Scott, 1982. 107–18.

Ong, Walter, S. J. "The Writer's Audience Is Always a Fiction." *PMLA* 90 (1975): 9–21.

Peaden, Catherine. "Feminist Theories, Historiographies, and the Histories of Rhetoric: The Role of Feminism in Historical Studies." *Rhetoric and Ideology: Compositions and Criticisms of Power*. Ed. Charles Kneupper. Arlington, TX: Rhet. Soc. of Amer., 1989. 116–25.

Phelps, Louise. "Audience and Authorship: The Disappearing Boundary." *A Sense of Audience in Written Communication*. Ed. Gesa Kirsch and Duane Roen. Newbury Park: Sage, 1991. 153–74.

Porter, James. "Intertextuality and the Discourse Community." *Rhetoric Review* 5 (1986): 34–47.

Poulakos, John. "Toward a Sophistic Definition of Rhetoric." *Philosophy and Rhetoric* 16 (1983): 35–48.

Poulakos, Takis. "Isocratean Rhetorical Education: A Structural Precedent for Cultural Studies." *Rhetoric in the Vortex of Cultural Studies: Proceedings of the Fifth Biennial Conference*. Ed. A. Walzer. Minneapolis: Rhet. Soc. of Amer., 1992. 42–50.

Sattler, William. "Conceptions of Ethos in Ancient Rhetoric." *Speech Monographs* 14 (1947): 55–65.

Scott, Robert. "On Viewing Rhetoric as Epistemic." *Central States Speech Journal* 18 (1967): 9–16.

———. "On Viewing Rhetoric as Epistemic Ten Years Later." *Central States Speech Journal* 27 (1976): 258–66.

Selfe, Cynthia, and Billie Wahlstrom. "An Emerging Rhetoric of Collaboration: Computers, Collaboration, and the Composing Process." *Collegiate Microcomputer* 4 (1986): 289–95.

Sullivan, Patricia. "Taking Control of the Page: Electronic Writing and Word Publishing." *Evolving Perspectives on Computers and Composition Studies: Questions for the 1990s.* Ed. Gail Hawisher and Cynthia Selfe. Urbana, IL : NCTE, 1991. 43–61.

Sutton, Jane. "The Death of Rhetoric and Its Rebirth in Philosophy." *Rhetorica* 4 (1986): 203–36.

Trimbur, John. "Cultural Studies and Teaching Writing." *Focuses* 1 (1988): 5–18.

Vatz, Richard. "The Myth of the Rhetorical Situation." *Philosophy and Rhetoric* 6 (1973): 154–61.

Willard, Charles Arthur. "The Conception of the Auditor in Aristotelian Rhetorical Theory." Diss. U of Illinois at Urbana-Champaign, 1972.

Young, Richard, Alton Becker, and Kenneth Pike. *Rhetoric: Discovery and Change.* New York: Harcourt, 1970.

Zappen, James. "Historical Perspectives on the Philosophy and History of the Rhetoric of Science: Sources for a Pluralistic Rhetoric." *PRE/TEXT* 6 (1985): 9–29.

Zhao, Heping. "Liu Xie and His *Wen Xin Diao Long*: An Early Chinese Rhetoric." Diss. Purdue U, 1990.

CHAPTER FOUR

Shaping Sophisticates: Implications of the Rhetorical Turn for Rhetoric Education

JOSEPH PETRAGLIA
Texas Christian University

T he editor has titled this anthology *Inventing a Discipline* in honor of Richard E. Young's long-standing contributions to both theories of rhetorical invention and the disciplinary status of rhetoric, especially as it has played out in the field of composition. Yet it may be that Young has contributed not only to a discipline but also to a professional space that presents rhetoric with a much wider academic beachhead—one that might be exploited more readily using the intellectual resources of a broad, rhetorical zeitgeist than from continued allegiance to impoverished pedagogical frameworks for rhetoric education such as general writing and speaking skills instruction. And so my purpose in this chapter is not to carp about composition's shortcomings (I've done that elsewhere) but to consider the great expectations for rhetoric education that Young has been instrumental in setting into motion.[1]

Not so very long ago, rhetoric educators' expectations were considerably lower. When I entered a rhetoric doctoral program in 1987, I knew that I would earn my keep in the academy by teaching students "to write" (whatever that meant). Rather quickly this prospect became less and less satisfying, for as I was preparing to teach composition, I was also learning of rhetoric's historic significance within the academy as well as its relevance to many contemporary knowledge-making enterprises. And so while composition is "what brung me" to the academic ball, I and many of my contemporaries have eagerly sought out more nimble dance partners. As part of this search, we teach courses in document design, the history of rhetoric, technical writing, the rhetoric of science, and, only occasionally, first-year writing (more often we leave this to the more junior, less empowered members of our department).[2] Rather than composition, then, many writing theorists and researchers see the role of shaping sophisticates—of instructing students in the practices of reading and responding to situations with a rhetoricized consciousness—as more reflective of our pedagogical mission. The greatest factor permitting this reconceptualization might be what is often referred to as the academy's "rhetorical turn."

A Space for Rhetorical Education[3]

By way of considering the implications of the rhetorical turn for rhetoric education, let me first propose that all curricular enterprises require a *space* and a *content,* the latter of which I discuss in the next section. By space, I mean that any new pedagogical enterprise that hopes to command the allegiance of others in the discipline and the understanding of others in the academy must conceptually take root within an existing educational climate. While particular historical events (the launch of Sputnik or the GI Bill, for example) may create such an exigency, I believe that the steady evolution of educational theory itself summons into existence a new space for rhetoric education.

The almost unchallenged dominance (in theory if not always in practice) of what might be called a *constructivist metatheory* explicitly places argument and negotiation at the heart of education. My use of the term *metatheory* is not intended to erase the considerable differences between Piaget and Vygotsky or Bartlett and Montessori but to blur them and to suggest that, given a sufficiently distant vantage point, we can comfortably speak of a sizable group of scholars and practitioners within the cognitive sciences and education who share with Dewey the premises that we construct our knowledge of the world based on prior knowledge and experience, and that knowledge and learning are derived from participation in activities that are distributed across social, cultural, and material dimensions. As with any metatheory,

constructivism has grown out of a century-long intellectual pro-
gression rather than from any single framework attributable to
any single movement or individual. It is the result of a widespread dissatisfaction with "transmission" models of learning,
"instructivist" models of teaching, and "information-processing"
theories of cognition that preclude context. For this reason, Carole
Bagley and Barbara Hunter are right, I believe, to identify
constructivism as the third pillar of educational reform in the
United States, alongside school restructuring and the integration
of technology.

A relatively recent manifestation of the constructivist
metatheory is the move to "situate" cognition, which suggests
that we need to understand thinking as *context-bound* rather
than as a fixed set of cognitive processes or heuristics that an
individual applies independently of the circumstances at hand.
As James Greeno puts it, situated cognition promotes the view
that "thinking is situated in physical and social contexts. Cognition, including thinking, knowing, and learning, can be considered as a relation involving an agent in a situation, rather than as
an activity in an individual's mind" (135). This approach is rooted
in the proposition that learning is a by-product of social and
cultural activity rather than the result of an individual's autonomous mastery of objective information. David Jonassen suggests
that because constructivism is based on the principle that learning is actively integrating new experience into existing schemas,
"learning environments should support that process by providing multiple perspectives or interpretations of reality and enable
knowledge construction in the learner through providing con-
text-rich, experience-based activities" (394).

The triumph of metatheoretical movements such as situated
cognition over traditional transmission theories of education
seems assured. As Roy Pea and John Seeley Brown have concluded:

> The situated nature of learning and remembering through ac-
> tivity is a central fact. It may appear obvious that human minds
> develop in social situations, and that they come to appropriate
> the tools that culture provides to support and extend their sphere
> of activity and communicative competencies. (ix)

So how does the constructivist metatheory present a space for rhetoric education? If we see knowledge making as the outcome of argumentative processes, we can then appreciate education as an essentially rhetorical enterprise, for rhetoric is, in its deepest and most fundamental sense, the advocacy of realities. As educational technologists Sack, Soloway, and Weingrad conclude, "activities of knowledge production (e.g., science) and reproduction (e.g., education) are about convincing, recruiting and enculturating others. In short a constructivist analysis of knowledge foregrounds rhetoric: the powers of persuasion and the difficulties of dispute" (381).

The idea that learning and rhetoric share a common framework has been put forward most explicitly and in most detail by Michael Billig. The title of one of his most cited works, *Arguing and Thinking: A Rhetorical Approach to Social Psychology,* hints at his generative premise: that the very nature of human learning is rhetorical and that argument works both intra- as well as interpersonally. Elsewhere, Billig quotes the Eleatic Stranger in Plato's *Sophist* (263E) as saying, "'[T]hought and speech are the same; only the former, which is a silent inner conversation of the soul with itself, has been given the special name of thought'" (qtd. in "Psychology" 120). In response, Billig notes that "[t]hinking is not merely the silent argument of the soul with itself, but, even more frequently, it is the noisier argument of one individual with another. And rhetoric, as the traditional study of the study and practice of argument, provides an entry to, and understanding of, thinking" ("Psychology" 121).

As the symbol-mediated process through which we build and shape understanding, representation is the site where rhetoric and education are conjoined. The most thoughtful strain of the rhetorical tradition has always been concerned with understanding and conviction based on a knower's representation of the world and the problems to be confronted in it—not on eternal verities or powers of objectivity. Although a detailed cognitivist concept of representation is largely a product of the twentieth century, rhetoricians have always been vitally concerned with the ways in which the mind creates an image of reality. The Sophist Gorgias would have been as comfortable as Allan Newell and Herbert

Simon in maintaining that "the behavior of the subject cannot depend on what the problem *really is*—neither he nor we know that—but only on what the stimulus is" (emphasis added, 64). Thus rhetoric and cognitivism share an essential focus on representation independent of objective reality. Cognitively speaking, one could say that the goal of every rhetor is to encourage a particular problem representation and a particular conception of reality in the mind of his or her audience.

Rhetoric's affinities with constructivism are further illustrated in the well-known disagreement between Lloyd Bitzer and Richard Vatz. Bitzer argues that a "rhetorical situation" is an external reality, or exigency, to which the rhetor responds. Exigencies for rhetorical behavior, according to Bitzer, "come into existence because of some specific condition or situation that invites utterance" ("Rhetorical Situation" 4). Conversely, Vatz argues much as a radical constructivist would by insisting that situations are not "out there," that "no situation can have a nature independent of the perception of its interpreter . . . ," and that the reality of a rhetorical situation is not objective but rather depends on the rhetor's desire and ability to create it (154). The debate is later joined by Scott Consigny who, I think, successfully puts the issue in perspective by distinguishing between those situational constraints which are preexisting and those which must be constructed by the rhetor before he or she conveys them to the audience, echoing Aristotle's distinction between artistic and inartistic types of "proofs." Like Billig, Consigny argues that rhetoric is a constructive process but that it is not wholly constructed by the individual rhetor; it must draw its material from a reality that exists prior to the rhetor's awareness of it (though all agree, of course, that at a prior level an understanding of this shared reality is also socially constructed).

Within both rhetorical and constructivist educational theory, then, knowledge is produced by systems erected to serve human needs and curiosities that are in line with the social and scientific practices validated by given communities at given times. As such, knowledge and information rely heavily on interaction among knowledge producers and knowledge consumers, consumers who reproduce that knowledge for others' consumption. This interaction is largely discursive, and knowledge is "brought about" through language by means of activities in which knowers participate. As Vygotskian theories of activity suggest, language is the most important tool we have at our disposal, for it is the paramount means by which we come to know things and transform knowledge into actions, objects, and other symbol systems. It is the means by which knowledge is created as well as the process by which knowledge is inculcated in others. Thus both constructivism and rhetoric put forward the view that learning entails a deliberate and ongoing reordering of information that comes to us from every corner of our experience. Rhetoric and constructivism "happen" both within individuals and among them. For the rhetorician as well as the constructivist educator, the real world is always in play. It is always subject to negotiation, and its construction is an end in itself as well as means to other ends. A rhetorical view of education is therefore inextricably bound up in questions of intersubjectivity, and thus, like the constructivist view of education, the rhetorical view posits that "learning" is the name we give the argumentative processes that transpire among teachers, students, and their real worlds. For the contemporary educator, then, the idea that we argue for knowledge is a statement of fact rather than a recommendation. It is not our prerogative to *permit* alternative constructions of the way the world works. Instead, we must first acknowledge them as the logical consequence of a constructivist view of learning and then engage these constructions in a manner we find beneficial to the learner.

With the advent of constructivism in educational psychology and the resurgence of what we now call the New Rhetoric, the frameworks of rhetoric and education have become less distinguishable. Both have emphasized thinking and argumentation as the result of experience, actions, prior understandings, and the individual's cultural, economic, and social situation. Both are premised upon the individual's active construction of knowledge and his or her perceptions of the world. Although rhetoric remains the study of argument and persuasion, we now appreciate that education is equally rooted in social interaction and the individual's capacity for drawing on evidence to impose coherence on a jumble of perceptions that have no direct relationship to the external world.[4] We are reminded of Donald Bryant's oft-cited explanation that rhetoric serves the function "of adapting ideas to people and of people to ideas" (19). I propose that constructivism provides us with good reasons for conceiving of education in precisely the same manner, and therefore I would argue that the entire enterprise of education, as articulated by its modern theorists, has consolidated a space that is more welcoming of a new sort of rhetoric education than ever before.

A Content for Rhetoric Education

Constructivism's metatheoretical mélange of Piagetian theory, Vygotskian sociohistoricism, and Deweyan progressivism, along with new movements such as situated cognition, is giving rhetoric a higher profile in education circles, but it has surely escaped no reader's notice that the rhetorical turn has pervaded education in other ways as well. Throughout the academy, the turn is reflected in notions and movements ranging from the rise of ethnographic and narrative methodology in the social sciences to the growth of identitarian projects (e.g., women's studies) and a renewed interest in the ways that technologies mediate understanding. At the same time, the traditional curricular spaces for rhetoric education (that is to say, speech and writing) have escaped their narrow confines and have grown more intellectually ambitious. Within the discipline of rhetoric itself, the "rhetoric of inquiry" movement has served as a chronicle of and clearinghouse for the rhetorical turns taken throughout the academy.

There are at least three excellent accounts of the rhetoric of inquiry's genealogy available, [5] so I will present only the briefest of thumbnail sketches here. The rhetoric of inquiry can be seen as an offshoot of the discipline's continuing rehabilitation of the Sophists (Mailloux; Jarratt), which is in turn only the most recent manifestation of our recovery of rhetoric's relationship to epistemology. The recognition of rhetoric as epistemic suggests that knowledge is created, maintained, and altered through an individual's interaction with and within his or her "discourse community." Knowledge resides in consensus rather than in any transcendent or objective relationship between a knower and that which is to be known.

Michael Leff offers a number of variations on this theme. He classifies views of the knowledge-generating potential of rhetoric into four major perspectives. The first acknowledges rhetoric's weakest claim to knowledge generation: its ability to create a place in an already accepted paradigm for a new particular (cf. Chaim Perelman and L. Olbrecht-Tyteca's notion of basing arguments on the structure of reality). The second argues a stronger case for rhetoric's knowledge-making capability by noting its role in establishing consensus in order to create a social knowledge which complements personal knowledge (cf. Bitzer's conception of "public knowledge"). The third perspective views rhetoric as establishing the knowledge necessary to mediate the limitations of formal logic, and the fourth notion—of rhetoric as epistemic— suggests that knowledge *is* rhetorical. Through the rhetoric-as-epistemic movement, rhetoric is becoming increasingly associated with the study of how claims to knowledge are constructed, expressed, maintained, and challenged. Robert Scott, in his seminal "On Viewing Rhetoric as Epistemic," concludes that "insofar as we can say that there is truth in human affairs, it is in time; it can be the result of a process of interaction at a given moment. Thus rhetoric may be viewed not as a matter of giving effectiveness to truth but of creating truth" (16). By reclaiming rhetoric's philosophical and epistemological tradition, an understanding of rhetoric is made synonymous with understanding the rational structure of knowledge in any discipline. This is a logical result of the claim that, as James Crosswhite puts it, "all reasonable discourse, including advanced research, is both rhetorical and aimed at realizing certain social aims" (15).

Herbert Simons credits philosopher Richard Rorty with instigating the founding of the rhetoric of inquiry movement (vii). Rorty heightened rhetoric's profile by declaring philosophy dead and anointing the give and take of consensus building as its successor. Conversely, Randy Allen Harris attributes the first stirrings of the movement to Thomas Kuhn and the publication of the *Structure of Scientific Revolutions.* Kuhn first drew attention to the fact that while science is generally carried out in a "normal" mode, it proceeds more rapidly by means of the paradigm shift, a favorite buzz term of the last quarter century. He and others subsequently highlighted the highly discursive character of shifting and thus signaled a central role for language practices in scientific progress. Both Harris and Simons credit John Nelson with giving the rhetoric of inquiry movement its name and for the suggestion that not only the physical sciences but also every sort of academic undertaking is shaped by the language practices of its members.

The rhetoric of inquiry has slopped over into so many arenas and across so many methodological and epistemological boundaries that many of its best-known proponents have little or no training in rhetorical theory. Yet when a rhetorician might wish to quarrel with any presumption of the movement's cogency, or when the nonrhetorician succumbs to rhetoric's worst connotations (see Harris's example on p. x), the idea that academic inquiry proceeds along essentially rhetorical paths is one with which many in the sciences and social sciences are becoming acquainted, some are becoming enamored, and a few are becoming fearful. In Crosswhite's summary of the situation, "For skeptics, this realization is grounds for despair. For rhetoricians, this is not the end of philosophy, but the beginning of a new metaphilosophy, a rhetoric of reason and inquiry" (21).

Currently, scholars from various backgrounds are producing a voluminous body of work that is providing a de facto delimitation of content for a new rhetorical education, even though the rhetoric of inquiry has largely remained a loose confederation of academic researchers who share primary questions rather than a strong disciplinary identity. Perhaps the best way of getting a feel for the common denominator is simply to list the sorts of questions posed by rhetoricians of inquiry: In what ways can we speak of knowledge as rhetorical? Who are the principal "constructors" of knowledge in a given field? What role does academic collaboration play in knowledge construction? Who (and what) serve as "gatekeepers" in various fields? Are there genres of discourse that are discipline specific? If so, how do these genres form and how stable are they? How do jargon, numeric expression, metaphor, narrative, and other specialized vocabularies affect the knowledge that various disciplines produce? Are there any discipline-specific standards of validity? How does language promote and constrain commensurability in the physical and social sciences? What role does Burke's notion of recalcitrance play in the various fields (i.e., how much room is there in various disciplines for "play")? What are the epistemological consequences of writing conventions that have developed within disciplines over time? What are the consequences of methods?

Closer to home than the rhetoric of inquiry movement for many readers is the rhetorical turn's impact on the traditional pedagogic fora of writing and speech classrooms. The field of composition of which I have been so critical has nonetheless a great body of sophisticated scholarship on the cognitive, technological, and social implications of inscription. Theories of authorship, argument, invention, and organizational discourse have been developed by rhetoricians working under the umbrella of the fields of composition and speech communication. Just as rhetoric's epistemic significance has prompted widespread attention to the discursive practices in fields across the academy, it has worked within the traditional fields to create a parallel universe of knowledge bearing scant resemblance to the pedagogical "lore" generated in English and speech departments in the first three-quarters of this century. Within the writing field, for instance, writing across the curriculum (WAC) and technical writing have contributed to a new rhetorical content by detailing the discursive practices of academicians and other professionals. Arguably the pedagogical arm of the rhetoric of inquiry movement, WAC and technical writing have done much to illuminate disciplinary knowledge construction as well as the role that writing genres, formats, and technologies play in various fields. And since the 1970s, speech departments have become the principal generators of rhetorical theory and its application to the spheres of public policy and address. In sum, the rhetorical turn has provided, in a variety of ways, a space and a content for a new rhetoric education both within and outside the traditional academic homes of rhetoric.

Loose Ends / Loose Cannons

Strictly speaking, my thesis thus far has been more of an observation than an argument: the convergence of twentieth-century theories of education, learning, and disciplinary practice offers the rhetoric educator a well-equipped atelier in which to fashion a new conception of rhetoric education. With such an enormous space and content at our disposal, one might assume that the way we teach rhetoric at the end of the twentieth century could scarcely resemble the way we taught it before the academy took the rhetorical turn—but one would be wrong. Energizing this space and employing its resources in service of a new pedagogical framework has been difficult. I believe this is due to two central theoretical issues. First is the question of whether any notion of rhetoric education can overcome the technical tradition with which it has become almost synonymous—that is, whether rhetoric is inextricably bound to techne. Related to this question are subsequent and perennial questions of rhetoric's theoretical structure and scope. A second, and still related, issue that a new framework for rhetoric education confronts when attempting to link its pedagogical mission more closely with the rhetorical turn entails the difficulty a nontechnical conception of rhetoric education has walking the line between the academy's fear of antifoundationalism on the one hand and rhetoric's own latent potential for antiscientism on the other.

The Tether to Techne

Rhetoric's future as a pedagogical endeavor is hobbled by its recent past, one in which a particular conception of rhetoric education has dominated. Central to this conception has been the field's pedagogical link to techne, or the belief that rhetoric is the practicable and perfectible art that enables one to be eloquent and persuasive. Though we may be more circumspect in making overt claims, the modern teaching of writing and public speaking still presumes that students can be taught to communicate effectively irrespective of the actual situations in which rhetoric is used. The techne-centric classroom in its present shape is thus the footing for rhetoric education that I currently find inadequate. While one could provide a strong rationale for the continuance of rhetoric's technical mission, my own reading of the writing field's history leads me to believe that the current technical shape of rhetoric education is reactionary; no good-man-speaking-well stuff, but a fairly bald and pragmatic fear that American youth was (and is) losing its ability to communicate in an educated manner. This fear, rather than any positive sense of opportunity, continues to propel the enterprises of composition and public speaking and is the reason that a highly reductive conception of what George Kennedy labeled "technical rhetoric" has won out over "philosophical rhetoric."

Of course, technical rhetoric has uses apart from supporting graduate students working on degrees in literature and speech; and who can argue that the sought-after democratization of higher education in the United States will necessarily produce a college population that requires remediation in basic writing and speaking skills? The technical rhetoric embodied in first-year writing courses can teach undergraduates many things worth knowing about mechanical skills and academic conventions. It does not, however, provide the robust basis for rhetorical education that our new rhetorical space and content would encourage. For this reason, mine is not a live-and-let-live attitude; composition and public speaking courses *as mainstays* are the enemy of a new rhetoric education. So long as these courses are a palliative, a richer rhetorical curriculum cannot take their place. In short, then, keeping rhetoric education limited to techne is problematic for two reasons: most tautologically, because rhetoric may not be technical in nature and its teaching as a productive art is doomed to failure or trivial success, but also (as I am arguing in this chapter), even if one accepts that rhetoric has a technical dimension, a new rhetoric education cannot be limited to that, for the new rhetorical content is not.

Is Bigger Better?

The status of rhetoric as a limited techne plays out in another forum: in the age-old debate over rhetoric's scope. The recent book *Rhetorical Hermeneutics: Invention and Interpretation in the Age of Science,* edited by Alan Gross and William Keith, is devoted almost exclusively to the careful examination of this issue. *Rhetorical Hermeneutics* is comprised of a number of responses written by widely known rhetoric scholars arrayed around the central "provocation" provided by Dilip Gaonkar, a long-standing critic of rhetoric's revived hegemonic tendencies. Deirdre

McCloskey frames the debate as one pitting Big against Little conceptions of rhetoric. Big Rhetoric is a hermeneutic (and, some would say, hegemonic) stance—a metadiscursive dimension of all knowledge-producing activities including, but not limited to, overt persuasion and argumentation. Little Rhetoric, on the other hand, is an outgrowth of the classical study that gave birth to the technical rhetoric that, in time, produced our current disciplines of composition and public speaking. Gaonkar and others wonder if Big Rhetoric has any disciplinary boundaries. If it forms part of every discipline, can it be said to have any independent status?

Since Alan Gross and William Keith's introduction to the volume nicely frames what is at stake, permit me to quote them at length:

> Can this *productive* tradition be transformed without significant distortion into the enterprise that is before us, one that is essentially *critical* and *theoretical*? If it can, what is its legitimate scope and reason for being? Must rhetoric observe its traditional limits—restriction to strategic, agent-centered discourse in the public realm? Or is rhetoric to extend its analysis to all discourse, and beyond discourse, to nondiscursive means of persuasion—e.g., civil disobedience in the public realm, the authority of the crucial experiment in science? And what is the goal of rhetorical analysis? Is it empirical—the investigation of practice for its own sake? Or is it normative—the government of practice? In other words, is rhetoric a tool essential to democracy, and are its critics its caretakers? Has rhetoric now become the new Master Trope, an immense body of theory that draws virtually all the humanities into its irresistible gravitational orbit? (2)

Critics of the Master Tropism perspective point to the possibility that such a rhetoric, far from being aggrandized and recognized as architectonic, becomes just another body of ignorable humanist speculation. Furthermore, if it is a dimension of every discipline, can it offer any particular hermeneutic force to justify its disciplinary worth? And as David Kaufer (another contributor to the anthology) points out, smallness is not to be confused with modesty—advocates of a more traditionally technical rhetoric view its strength as lying in its smallness and precision—within bigness lies the fast track to oblivion.

David Fleming points out that the issue of Big versus Little rhetoric has clear implications for education.

> When construed as either anthropological fact or supplemental art, a discipline of rhetoric—one that knows its limits and strengths, that has a certain autonomy vis-à-vis other studies, that attracts students, serves widely shared goals, and still allows for internal debate and exchange—is difficult to locate and sustain. "Little" rhetoric, for example, is easily defined but also easily marginalized or assimilated into other disciplines . . . . "Big" rhetoric, on the other hand, is inclusive and flexible, but also radically unstable. (171–72)

Obviously, the question of rhetoric's scope cannot be "resolved"; it is not that sort of question. Douglas Ehninger showed us long ago that any notion of rhetoric serves particular needs which are, in turn, formed by disciplinary and social constraints. Even longer ago, among the Sophists, the object of rhetorical study was roundly yet inconclusively debated, and we have less reason than ever to think that any answer is going to satisfy many observers for any length of time.

Thus, as articulating a scope for rhetorical theory has proven so difficult, we can anticipate that definitional issues will dog any efforts to create a new notion of rhetoric education. Given the rhetoric field's enthusiasm for debating its own domain, and even its own existence, it is only prudent to assume that, as Gaonkar acknowledges, "however frustrated a traditionalist might feel about the promiscuous deployment of *rhetoric* as an interpretative term, a program to bridle its uses is unlikely to succeed," and rhetoric's promiscuity will continue to complicate its classroom application (47).

The Epistemological Stakes

As noted earlier, the rhetorical turn generally and the speech and writing fields' more contemporary aspirations have been driven by their excursion into the realm of epistemology. Ironically, this reconnaissance has created two diametrically opposed dangers for the renovation of rhetoric education: fear of antifoundationalism on the one hand, and the uncritical embrace of antifoundationalism on the other.

Edward Said gives voice to our fears of antifoundationalism when he notes that "no one finds it easy to live uncomplainingly and fearlessly with the thesis that human reality is constantly being made and unmade, and that anything like a stable essence is constantly under threat. . . . We need some foundation upon which to stand" (333). And as the metatheory which has provided rhetoric education with a new space, constructivism undermines foundations. In the conclusion of his essay "The Good, the Bad, and the Ugly: The Many Faces of Constructivism," Phillips identifies constructivism's good face as "the emphasis that various constructivist sects place on the necessity for active participation by the learner, together with the recognition (by most of these groups) of the social nature of learning" (11). The bad, according to Phillips, is

> the tendency within many forms of constructivist epistemology (despite occasional protestations to the contrary) towards relativism, or towards treating the justification of our knowledge as being entirely a matter of sociopolitical processes or consensus, or towards the jettisoning of any substantial rational justification or warrant at all. (11)

In a similar vein, as Yvonne Lincoln and Egon Guba contend, "When naive realism is replaced by the assumption of multiple constructed realities, there is no ultimate benchmark to which one can turn for justification—whether in principle or by a technical adjustment via the falsification principle. 'Reality' is now a multiple set of mental constructions" (295). In short, many fear that the rhetorical turn in education will usher in the demons of relativism. A rhetoricized theory of learning implies that each individual knows the world in a different way, that there is neither a shared world about which we can teach nor any means by which to assess the effectiveness of any particular pedagogical intervention. As William Winn puts it, "if knowledge is constructed entirely by students, there being no objective reality to teach them, there is nothing that . . . [teachers] . . . can do to affect student understanding and behavior" (189).

The very nature of disciplinarity requires that fields of study delimit, classify, isolate, and pick apart otherwise amalgamated constructs in order to make sense of the phenomenon they study. Even if our disciplinary interests lie in areas such as, say, accounting or fine arts, or even if we choose to excuse ourselves from "social scientific" conversations about our practices, most educators at least tacitly base their beliefs on evidence gathered from empirically based methods. And science, social or otherwise, provides an arena in which questions of the status of knowledge are most commonly fought, at least publicly. As educators, we are deeply indebted to scientific method even when we fail to acknowledge that debt. And so Gregory Cizek no doubt speaks for many educators across the academy when he complains that "if one accepts the notion that all understanding is contextualized, if all experience is embedded in culture, and if all knowledge is a personalized construction, and so on . . . then we are not only poststructuralist, postconstructivist, and postmodernist, but probably postscientific as well" (27).

Crosswhite notes that most academics have come to divorce their content-generating practices from pedagogy, even though the problems of knowing, reasoning, and arguing are the central problems in both (14). Ironically, even in the humanities, which presumably focus on the human crafting of knowledge, many teachers still view their role as the largely passive transmitter of information rather than the shaper of it. Perhaps for this reason, although the constructivist metatheory has stealthily pervaded the world of educational theory, it has been less successful at influencing practice. Therefore, pedagogy is not undertaken as rhetorical action in any epistemic sense, but as a means of simply facilitating the flow of information from expert to novice. Just as George Levine suggests that being a scientist means not being a rhetorician, being an educator has traditionally meant foregoing warranted belief in favor of Truth. And so a new rhetorical education might not be appealing to those in the academy who wonder if, by setting out to shape sophisticates, we are tacitly proclaiming that the knowledge bazaar is open. Rhetoricians, of course, have ready rebuttals to the charges of crude relativism (e.g., McGuire and Melia), which we will not examine here, but we must be prepared to confront such charges if educators choose to take on a more challenging and less innocuous rhetorical content.

The Siren's Song of Antiscience

The recognition that disciplinary content areas across the academy are the product of a social and cultural process is neither new nor necessarily politically motivated. Yet many in the field of cultural studies (another avatar of the rhetorical turn) are primarily interested in how the scientific tradition has been deployed to reify hierarchies and used to promote or justify sexism, racism, and inequitable economic relations. Of course, even science-sympathetic cultural theorists from Max Weber to Ernest Gellner have tied scientism to ideology, but more recently a narrower interest in debunking science or reducing science to the politically motivated apparatus by which dominant groups have perpetuated their power over others has been given a higher profile. It is this politicized stance toward the scientific enterprise that is sometimes labeled "antiscientism." In fact, antiscience is all that seems to bind diverse strands of cultural critique, for as Steven Fuller has noted, cultural theorists of science have had an uneasy relationship with Marxists and feminists, who "have been united more in terms of a common foe—the scientific establishment—than a common methodological and axiological orientation" (53).

The way in which antiscience poses a danger to a new rhetoric education may be illustrated in the recent controversy surrounding the publication of "Transgressing the Boundaries: Towards a Transformative Hermeneutics of Quantum Gravity" in the Spring/Summer 1996 issue of *Social Text*. For readers unfamiliar with the Sokal parody (or hoax, depending on one's point of view), Alan Sokal is a physicist at New York University who, disturbed by what he considered to be some cultural theorists' irresponsibility, conducted a little "experiment." In collaboration with sympathetic cultural studies colleagues, Sokal concocted a jargon-dense tour de force that defied both common sense and any known standard for rational argument. After the article was printed, Sokal revealed its true intent in an issue of *Lingua Franca* ("Physicist"). The experiment, he claimed, was designed to test two hypotheses: "Would a leading journal of cultural studies publish an article liberally salted with nonsense if (a) it sounded good and (b) it flattered the editors' ideological preconceptions?" (62). One of the parody's more memorable bits of cant insisted that the physical world "is, at bottom, a social and linguistic construct." This presumably came as news to people suffering from what they mistakenly thought were physical illnesses, material injustices, and natural disasters.

But perhaps more disturbing than the prank's success has been the antiscience movement's reaction to having been caught out. Exemplifying the view that the best defense is an offense, Stanley Fish, Andrew Ross, and other prominent antiscientists took to circling the wagons, ignoring what was plain to practically everyone: the gatekeeping mechanisms intended to ensure responsible scholarship had failed spectacularly. Further, this failure did not appear to be a fluke but, in fact, reflected a deeper, more systemic malaise in the cultural studies of science project rather than an indictment of the project itself. As Sokal points out in *Tikkun*, "Science and technology are legitimate, indeed crucial, subjects of public critique and democratic debate" and "the funding of scientific research by private corporations poses grave dangers to scientific objectivity" ("Truth" 58). He makes clear that his "objection is not to cultural analysis per se, but to a social constructivist and anti-realist philosophy run amok" (58).

Many cultural theorists of science have strategically cast Sokal's parody as a right-wing attack on the whole of cultural studies of science. Indeed, by fighting off the "Gingrich Congress" and the current "congressional war against public interest" (Ross 1), antiscientism is framed not so much as an intellectual position as a political and ethical stance. The purported political incorrectness of Sokal's experiment has subsequently become a central focus in the parody's postmortem (Sokal himself being careful to trot out his own leftist credentials as a teacher in Sandinista Nicaragua). The enormous irony in this, as numerous commentators have pointed out, is that the antiscientism evinced in some radical left circles is mirrored in the fundamentalist right (e.g., Nanda). Christian, Hindu, or Jewish fundamentalists; Sharia advocates in the Islamic world; or practically any theocratic or antidemocratic movement is given succor by the stance that science is culturally hegemonic when practiced outside the West and inherently a tool of oppression here at home. Antiscientism, it seems, like scientism, lends itself to many agendas, not all of them progressive.

But to return to the topic at hand, antiscience poses a concern for those of us seeking a new basis for rhetoric education, for if a potent conception of rhetoric is to retain some sort of status as a core requirement within the university, it must be seen as a useful and constructive study that furthers student understanding of disciplinary practices throughout the academy. In a familiar quote, Larry Laudan laments that "[t]he displacement of the idea that facts and evidence matter by the idea that everything boils down to subjective interests and perspectives is—second only to American political campaigns—the most prominent and pernicious manifestation of anti-intellectualism in our time" (x). The Sokal debacle has been a public relations nightmare for the cultural studies of science and, by extension, any future movement to create a new conception of rhetoric education. As Harold Fromm rightly noted, the parody and reaction to the parody provided ammunition to those who never thought much of cultural studies in any form. For them it confirms the image of a pseudointelligentsia more interested in posturing, in essentialisms complicated only by obfuscation, and in the appearance of political correctness than in any genuinely academic enterprise. The affair illustrated several points: the ease with which cultural studies of science (including the rhetoric of inquiry) can be tarred with facile caricatures, the contempt that is elicited from those relatively few scientists who take enough interest to be annoyed, and, most worryingly, the inability of some cultural theorists of science to distance themselves from the sillier fringes of antiscience excess.

Given that the rhetorical turn in a variety of disciplines will provide most of the content for any new version of rhetoric education, this education cannot and should not avoid political critique. When we consider issues of popular science or of science and public policy in particular, the political impact, motivation, and construction of knowledge making is a clearly significant aspect of its rhetoricality. As a corollary, rhetoric educators should also expect that some in the academy will be unwelcoming of rhetorical scrutiny and will bridle at any suggestion that science is a cultural practice; if this seems an occupational hazard, so be it. But even if we accept the knowledge/power equation, that is not all there is to say about the rhetorical production of knowledge—it is not even a particularly interesting thing to say in many cases. The Sokal affair has provoked a number of responses from across the academy that point to some of the battles a new rhetoric education will have to fight in the academy. Part of winning this war, to continue the martial analogy, will depend on choosing one's allies carefully. With friends like the antiscience wing of cultural studies, a new rhetoric education would need no enemies.

Conclusion

Fleming has commented on the odd phenomenon whereby

> rhetorical training (where it exists at all) is typically limited to the two extremes of higher education: a 15-week course on "writing" for incoming freshmen and a 5- to 7-year program of advanced study for Ph.D. students. The rhetoric of the first is often reduced and trivial. . . . The rhetoric of the second is devoted to highly specialized scholarship in historical, philosophical and empirical topics, work that is often tied to the 15-week course but out of all intellectual proportion to it. (173)

For several years now, I have been a proponent of the view that rhetoric research from the latter extreme is growing increasingly irrelevant to the pedagogic job at the former. I have suggested that in the writing field this has largely encouraged a move away from the composition-boundedness of the profession. In this chapter, I have tried to further that argument by suggesting that the rhetorical turn within the academy may enable us to act on this disjuncture and that it has laid the ground for a new footing for rhetoric education. Constructivism in educational theory has provided a pedagogical space. The rhetoric of inquiry, as well as more local movements in the fields of speech and composition, such as WAC, have provided a broader and deeper subject matter than we might have imagined possible when Richard Young first began exploring the world of rhetorical invention.

But in setting out a space and a content, I have conveniently ignored a third essential component a new rhetoric education will require: a curriculum—the pedagogic apparatus that transforms space and content into a workable and academically legitimate undertaking. As practicing academicians know, the space and the content are the relatively easy parts. The issue of a new rhetoric curriculum presents us with difficult questions, such as, What classes should be taught? In what department(s) should rhetoric instruction be housed? and most important, How can a new rhetoric education enrich traditional, technical training in writing and speaking? The ability to concoct a curriculum requires enormous diplomatic skill, political will, and singularity of purpose that, as a body of researchers and educators, we may yet lack.

Those of us in rhetoric-based fields are unaccustomed to genuine opportunity in the academy and have had little incentive, or occasion, to recuperate the richness of a rhetorical tradition that was first overwhelmed by techne, and then by philosophy and the sciences, and most recently by the literary tradition that dominates English departments. So what compels us to formulate a new vision of rhetoric education? Very little. But if nature abhors a vacuum, the rhetoric field might slowly come to perceive an intellectual vacuum in its present curricular vehicles that demands filling. The compulsion, then, may not be a powerful, purposeful act of a field to take charge of its destiny, but a sheepish acknowledgment that composition and public speaking classes are pale reflections of what we know about rhetoric and the demands for rhetorical training emanating from elsewhere in the academy as a result of the rhetorical turn.

Notes

1. Briefly, my arguments against the "compositionist" cast of rhetoric and writing generally center on the observation that rhetorical action is vitally situated and that teaching writing as a compendium of all-purpose "general writing skills" misses the point completely. Most compo-

sition courses, I argue, generally require a kind of pseudotransactionality that only pretends to engage rhetorical constraints and are thus incapable of providing a true education in rhetorical performance. My elaboration of this position, along with similar arguments from colleagues in the field, are collected in the anthology *Reconceiving Writing, Rethinking Writing Instruction*.

2. The October 1998 *PMLA* contains statistics that verify this: at Ph.D.-granting universities, 63 percent of first-year writing courses are taught by graduate students, 19 percent by part-timers, 14 percent by non-tenure-track (but full-time) instructors, leaving a mere 4 percent of first-year courses taught by tenure-track faculty.

3. Many of the arguments in this section are taken from, and more widely elaborated in, my monograph *Reality by Design: The Rhetoric and Technology of Authenticity in Education*.

4. Although the topic lies outside the scope of this chapter, technologies of education, informed by the constructivist metatheory, not only open up a space for a new rhetoric education but perhaps also demand its construction. Part hype but increasingly a part of every educator's reality, the advances in technologies of learning pose serious, and often unpleasant, challenges to education. As a modern enterprise, education has always been essentially textual and tied to print literacy. But as a variation of the "where there's muck there's money" credo, the problems hypertextualization and hypermediation raise create the kind of crisis in which both constructivist educational practices and rhetoric can flourish.

5. See Nelson, Megill, and McCloskey; Simons; and Randy Allen Harris's introduction to *Landmark Essays in the Rhetoric of Science*.

Works Cited

Bagley, Carole, and Barbara Hunter. "Restructuring Constructivism and Technology: Forging a New Relationship." *Educational Technology* (July 1992): 22–28.

Billig, Michael. *Arguing and Thinking: A Rhetorical Approach to Social Psychology*. Cambridge: Cambridge UP, 1987.

———. "Psychology, Rhetoric and Cognition." *The Recovery of Rhetoric: Persuasive Discourse and Disciplinarity in the Human Sciences*. Ed. R. H. Roberts and J. M. Good. London: Bristol Classical, 1993. 119–36.

Bitzer, Lloyd. "Rhetoric and Public Knowledge." *Rhetoric, Philosophy, and Literature: An Exploration.* Ed. Don M. Burks. West Lafayette: Purdue UP, 1978. 67–93.

———. "The Rhetorical Situation." *Philosophy and Rhetoric* 1(1968): 1–14.

Bryant, Donald C. "Rhetoric: Its Function and Scope." *The Province of Rhetoric.* Ed. Joseph Schwartz and John A. Rycenga. New York: Ronald, 1965. 3–36.

Cizek, Gregory. J. "Crunchy Granola and the Hegemony of the Narrative." *Educational Researcher* 24 (1995): 26–28.

Consigny, Scott. "Rhetoric and Its Situations." *Philosophy and Rhetoric* 7 (1974): 175–86.

Crosswhite, James. *The Rhetoric of Reason: Writing and the Attractions of Argument.* Madison: U of Wisconsin P, 1996.

Ehninger, Douglas. "On Systems of Rhetoric." *Philosophy and Rhetoric* 1 (1968): 131–44.

Fleming, David. "Rhetoric as a Course of Study." *College English* 61 (1998): 169–91.

Fromm, Harold. "My Science Wars." *The Hudson Review* 49 (1997): 599–609.

Fuller, Steven. "Does Science Put an End to History or History to Science? Or Why Being Pro-Science Is Harder Than You Think." *Science Wars.* Ed. Andrew Ross. Durham: Duke UP, 1996. 29–60.

Gaonkar, Dilip. "The Idea of Rhetoric in the Rhetoric of Science." Gross and Keith 25–85.

Greeno, James G. "A Perspective on Thinking." *American Psychologist* 44 (1989): 134–41.

Gross, Alan, and William Keith. Introduction. Gross and Keith 1–22.

———, eds. *Rhetorical Hermeneutics: Invention and Interpretation in the Age of Science.* Albany: SUNY P, 1997.

Harris, Randy Allen, ed. *Landmark Essays on Rhetoric of Science.* Mahwah, NJ: Erlbaum, 1997.

Jarratt, Susan C. "In Excess: Radical Extensions of Neopragmatism." *Rhetoric, Sophistry, Pragmatism.* Ed. Steven Mailloux. Cambridge: Cambridge UP, 1995. 206–27.

Jonassen, David H. "Cognitive Flexibility Theory and Its Implications for Designing CBI." *Instructional Models in Computer-Based Learning Environments*. Ed. Sanne Dijkstra, Hein P. M. Krammer, and Jeroen J. G. van Merriënboer. Berlin: Springer, 1992. 385–403.

Kaufer, David. "From Tekhne to Technique: Rhetoric as a Design Art." Gross and Keith 247–78.

Kennedy, George. *Classical Rhetoric and Its Christian and Secular Traditions from Ancient to Modern Times*. Chapel Hill: U of North Carolina P, 1980.

Kuhn, Thomas S. *The Structure of Scientific Revolutions*. 2nd ed. Chicago: U of Chicago P, 1970.

Laudan, Larry. *Science and Relativism: Some Key Controversies in the Philosophy of Science*. Chicago: U of Chicago P, 1990.

Leff, Michael. "In Search of Ariadne's Thread: A Review of the Literature on Rhetorical Theory." *Central States Speech Journal* 29 (1978): 73–91.

Levine, George. "Why Literature Isn't Science." *Rethinking Objectivity*. Ed. Allan Megill. Durham: Duke UP, 1994. 65–79.

Lincoln, Yvonna, and Egon Guba. *Naturalistic Inquiry*. Newbury Park: Sage, 1985.

Mailloux, Steven. "Introduction: Sophistry and Rhetorical Pragmatism." *Rhetoric, Sophistry, Pragmatism*. Ed. Steven Mailloux. Cambridge: Cambridge UP, 1995. 1–31.

McCloskey, Deirdre. "Big Rhetoric, Little Rhetoric: Gaonkar on the Rhetoric of Science." Gross and Keith 101–12.

McGuire, J. E., and Trevor Melia. "The Rhetoric of the Radical Rhetoric of Science." *Rhetorica* 9 (1991): 301–16.

Nanda, Meera. "The Science Wars in India." *Dissent* 44 (1997): 78–83.

Nelson, John S., Allan Megill, and Deirdre N. McCloskey, eds. *The Rhetoric of the Human Sciences: Language and Argument in Scholarship and Public Affairs*. Madison: U of Wisconsin P, 1987.

Newell, Allen, and Herbert A. Simon. *Human Problem Solving*. Englewood Cliffs, NJ: Prentice, 1972.

Pea, Roy D., and J. S. Brown. Series Foreword. *Distributed Cognitions: Psychological and Educational Considerations*. Ed. Gavriel Salomon. Cambridge: Cambridge UP, 1993. iv–xxi.

Perelman, Chaïm, and L. Olbrechts-Tyteca. *The New Rhetoric: A Treatise on Argumentation.* Notre Dame: U of Notre Dame P, 1969.

Petraglia, Joseph. *Reality by Design: The Rhetoric and Technology of Authenticity in Education.* Mahwah, NJ: Erlbaum, 1998.

———, ed. *Reconceiving Writing, Rethinking Writing Instruction.* Mahwah, NJ: Erlbaum, 1995.

Phillips, Denis C. "The Good, the Bad, and the Ugly: The Many Faces of Constructivism." *Educational Researcher* 24 (1995): 5–12.

Ross, Andrew. Introduction. *Science Wars.* Ed. Andrew Ross. Durham: Duke UP, 1996. 1–15.

Sack, Warren, Elliot Soloway, and Peri Weingrad. "Re-Writing Cartesian Student Models." *Journal of Artificial Intelligence in Education* 3 (1992): 381–402.

Said, Edward. *Orientalism.* 2nd ed. New York: Vintage, 1994.

Scott, Robert. "On Viewing Rhetoric as Epistemic." *Central States Speech Journal* 18 (1967): 9–16.

Simons, Herbert W. "Introduction: The Rhetoric of Inquiry as an Intellectual Movement." *The Rhetorical Turn: Invention and Persuasion in the Conduct of Inquiry.* Ed. Herbert W. Simons. Chicago: U of Chicago P, 1990. 1–31.

Sokal, Alan. "A Physicist Experiments with Cultural Studies." *Lingua Franca* (May/June 1996): 62–64.

———. "Transgressing the Boundaries: Toward a Transformative Hermeneutics of Quantum Gravity." *Social Text* 14 (1996): 217–52.

———. "Truth or Consequences: A Response to Bruce Robbins." *Tikkun* 11, 1 Nov. 1996: 58-61.

Vatz, Richard. "The Myth of the Rhetorical Situation." *Philosophy and Rhetoric* 6 (1973): 154–61.

Winn, William. "A Constructivist Critique of the Assumptions of Instructional Design." *Designing Environments for Constructive Learning.* Ed. Thomas Duffy, J. Lowyck, and David Jonassen. Berlin: Springer, 1993. 189–212.

II

WAVE: TEMPORAL AND SPATIAL EXPLORATIONS OF RHETORICAL THEORY AND PRACTICE

The wave view recognizes some dynamic feature of the unit, noting flow or movement in time, in space, or in a conceptual framework.

YOUNG, BECKER, AND PIKE, *Rhetoric: Discovery and Change*

Young, Becker, and Pike explain that "viewed as a wave, a unit interacts with other units in a larger context that can itself be considered a higher-level wave unit in a still larger dynamic context" (124). The essays in this section offer theoretical, historical, and empirical investigations of specific rhetorical theories and practices that may be understood as dynamic systems operating within larger dynamic spatial and temporal contexts.

In the first essay in this section, Robert Inkster argues that rhetoric is best understood as epistemic; truth is discursively constructed. In his words, "[o]ur grasp on the truth is always tenuous. It is always limited by our language, the underlying assumptions we bring from our time, place, and culture, and by our personal interests and ambitions." For Inkster, "if all knowledge is rhetorical, then all rhetoric is *noetical*." His essay thus provides a valuable frame for understanding the power of rhetoric, a frame within and against which the other essays in this section may be read.

Eugene Garver's essay prompts us to ask, Why study Aristotle, or any rhetorician, for that matter? Garver offers a cautionary but provocative discussion, arguing that Aristotle's "art of rhetoric makes no promises to improve practice or make us more persuasive." Indeed, he contends that Aristotle's "art of rhetoric will not improve practice, any more than his competitors' will," nor will it make us more ethical, virtuous, or wise. Yet Garver's exploration of the "modesty" of Aristotle's rhetoric provides compelling reasons for why we do indeed need to study Aristotelian and other rhetorics. Garver's essay serves as a foil to the subsequent essay by Karen Schnakenberg.

Through an extensive analysis of the relationship among representations of classical, and primarily Aristotelian, rhetoric in scholarship and those appearing concurrently in four landmark textbooks, Schnakenberg explores the question of why classical rhetoric had (and continues to have) so little impact on writing instruction. Her essay reveals how a powerful confluence of forces (e.g., past scholarly perspectives and textbook writers' own prior training, tacit assumptions, and interests) operates to construct rhetorical theory, practice, and pedagogy.

Winifred Bryan Horner then poses a forceful argument for reviving the last two of the five canons of rhetoric: memory and delivery. Her historical tracing of rhetoric reveals how rhetorical systems themselves are contingent on the context in which they operate, so that rhetoric is best understood as rhetorics. She argues that since new digital literacies are emerging, we are again uniquely posed to construct new rhetorics and to turn renewed attention to canons that have been largely neglected under print literacies.

Victor Vitanza's essay also responds to the emerging digital literacies, in which he sees a space for reimagining invention. In particular, he argues for exploring aleatory procedures, those more open and "apparently rather mysterious approaches to invention." These are chance and accidental procedures. As he explains, his intention "is only to begin to discuss at the level of theory and practice and beyond the immanent conditions for the possibilities of returning to the third terms and practices known as *aleatory* procedures with their general economy of excess. These conditions are re-presenting themselves to us by way of a shift from literacy to 'electracy' (which is Ulmer's word for electronic discourse or hyperrhetoric)."

Lee Odell and Karen McGrane argue in the next essay that since teachers and students are "already immersed in a world in which visual elements are central to communication," we need to find "principled ways to help students integrate visual elements into their composing." Yet, as they note, most of the work in visual rhetoric has taken place in the field of technical communication, with very little attention given to it in rhetoric and composition. They call for bridging the gap between verbal and visual rhetoric by explicating several integrative principles and by applying those principles to several social scientific and scientific texts to demonstrate how they work.

The following two essays address the relationship between the sciences and rhetoric. Danette Paul and Ann Blakeslee examine the rise of science as a discipline in nineteenth-century North America as a unique formation, distinguishable from that of Great Britain. Their history demonstrates that science "rhetorically positioned itself in American culture by playing up its connection to middle-class capitalist values of practicality, progress, and individuality while also appealing to a pure science ideal." Paul and Blakeslee's essay provides a significant context in which to understand multiple discursive practices of the sciences today.

Carol Berkenkotter's essay addresses a series of important questions concerning the complex relationship between scientific thinking and writing. Berkenkotter's exploration of these interdependent activities calls attention to the need for teaching multiple literate practices in a variety of fields. As she concludes, "every discipline has its own *doxa*: as teachers of language, we must learn to see beyond ours."

The essays in this next section present situated explorations of complex literate practices and their relationship to disciplinarity that not only exemplify Berkenkotter's conclusion but also help to realize it.

Work Cited

Young, Richard E., Alton L. Becker, and Kenneth L. Pike. *Rhetoric: Discovery and Change*. New York: Harcourt, 1970.

CHAPTER FIVE

Rhetoric and the Ecology of the Noosphere

ROBERT INKSTER

St. Cloud State University

In *The Philosophy of Literary Form*, Kenneth Burke lays out the following scene:

> Imagine that you enter a parlor. You come late. When you arrive, others have long preceded you, and they are engaged in a heated discussion, a discussion too heated for them to pause and tell you exactly what it is about. In fact, the discussion had already begun long before any of them got there, so that no one present is qualified to retrace for you all the steps that had gone before. You listen for a while, until you decide that you have caught the tenor of the argument; then you put in your oar. Someone answers; you answer him; another comes to your defense; another aligns himself against you, to either the embarrassment or gratification of your opponent, depending upon the quality of your ally's assistance. However, the discussion is interminable. The hour grows late, you must depart. And you do depart, with the discussion still vigorously in progress. (94–96)

Burke himself refers to this as the "unending conversation," and I have come to think of this scene as the Great Conversation metaphor. Two things, I think, are especially striking about this scene and what it suggests metaphorically. First, without the voices of individual speakers or rhetors, there would be silence—a void. Without the words through which their individual worlds are made manifest and through which they contend with the words and the worlds of the other individual speakers, there would be no conversation.

But, while the conversation is utterly dependent on the words of individual speakers, it transcends the words of any one of them. In Burke's scene, the conversation was going on long before you entered the parlor, and it is still going on—vigorously—when you depart. Before you speak, you listen, and you catch the tenor of the argument before you speak. Otherwise, you simply indulge in a solipsistic babble.

We sometimes say that a discussion took on a life of its own. And this vernacular expression is literally true, both when we are talking about the microcosm of a single colloquy at a particular time and a particular place—my Tuesday evening writing class, for example—and when we are talking about the grand global colloquy, the amalgamated colloquies of humankind. This essay is an exploration of the nature of the grand global colloquy, of its relation to our own voices and words as individual rhetors, and of its relation to that about which our voices and words contend: the truth.

The conversation has a life of its own. In *The Phenomenon of Man* (*Le Phenomene Humain*), Father Pierre Teilhard de Chardin calls it the *noosphere*. In the evolution of our planet from the beginning to the present day, Teilhard sees three momentous creative phenomena, each of which brought about the emergence of a new sphere of being. The first is the phenomenon that created the planet in the first place, resulting in the geosphere. The second was the emergence of life on the planet, chemistry and physics achieving an organic synthesis resulting in life—biology—and hence the biosphere. And, as this second sphere has flourished, diversified, and ramified throughout the geosphere, there has emerged consciousness, sentience, finally thought, language, *shared* thought, and then the emergence of the third sphere of being, the noosphere. Like the second and the first, this third sphere of being is dynamic and evolving. Indeed, it is, for us who inhabit it, even more obviously dynamic and evolving than the other two spheres. Individually and collectively, we make up our minds and change our minds constantly. And as we do, we create and sustain this third sphere of being, this ultrabiological sphere that transcends the biological existence of any one of us in a miraculous ontological leap. This leap, then, is an exact analog of the antecedent leap whereby biotic existence, while grounded in the physics and chemistry of the geosphere and absolutely dependent on these physical and chemical processes, nonetheless achieves an utterly new level of existence. The noosphere—our noosphere—is an organic, dynamic, living entity, an achievement in which we may justifiably take a certain anthropocentric pride. In fact, we may point to it as our grand synthesis, the ultimate social construction that is the consummation of all our other social constructions. And to call the noosphere a social construction is not to denigrate it in the least. The noosphere is not an epiphenomenon. It is real, as real as the biosphere.

If Teilhard's analogy between the noosphere and the biosphere is true, then two other propositions would seem to follow. First, the noosphere is a milieu, an environment, an atmosphere, a whole ecosystem that makes our existence as human beings possible and without which we could not survive as human beings. Second, this noetic ecosystem, like the physical ecosystem, is finite and fragile. If the toxic effluent of industrial and municipal waste is threatening the biotic ecosystem, the toxic flow of much of our economic and civic discourse is surely stressing the noosphere. If we breathe ideas and language as we breathe the air, then we need to be as solicitous about the ecology of the noosphere as we are about the ecology of the biosphere.

This argument is clearly conservationist—and I would say conservative. But it is not an argument that favors, for example, censorship aimed at preserving an established orthodoxy. Indeed, precisely the opposite is true. A rich and diverse noetic gene pool is as vital as a rich and diverse biotic gene pool. If the language that embodies an idea or set of ideas is silenced so that the idea dies, the loss is analogous to the extinction of a biological species. The full ramifications of that loss are impossible to project, but they are potentially catastrophic. On the other hand, this qualification is not a call to relativism. It is not an assertion that an idea is an idea is an idea and that all ideas have equal merit. A crucial argument in this essay is that there is real truth, not simply socially constructed "truths," qualified by their enclosing quotation marks.

These tensions highlight the complexity of the very nature of the noosphere, of how it contributes to our individual discourse and knowing, and of how our individual discourse and knowing contribute, in turn, to it. This complexity and tension are manifest in the two preceding paragraphs. First, I argued that the noosphere is our grand global social construction. Next, I distinguished truth from socially constructed "truths." As a social construction, comprising what we know collectively, the noosphere is not precisely congruent with the truth. Rather, it is our shared speculative instrument (à la I. A. Richards) for probing the truth and for synthesizing insights that approach truth and that serve as truths.

In order to argue that this process is true at more than a metaphorical level, I will shift perspective from the global, systemwide view—what Young, Becker, and Pike call a field view—of the noosphere to the structure and the dynamic of an individual act of knowing by a single knower as this structure and dynamic have been explained by Michael Polanyi. Polanyi took his cue from the insights of Gestalt psychology when he developed his theory of personal knowledge. All knowledge, he argued, is a dynamic act, an achievement, with three essential elements. First, there is the knower; second, there is a complex of clues, assumptions, values, interpretative strategies, sensations, specific data points, and vague, general senses that collectively make up what Polanyi calls tacit knowledge; and third, there is the focal meaning that the knower generates out of the tacit knowledge.

For purposes of illustration, imagine you have two volunteers who have agreed to sit at the front of a room and be blindfolded. You hand them each a dowel and ask them to describe what they feel. The reports you get will probably be something like this: "I feel a long, thin, cylindrical object. It's hard. It's smooth on the sides but more roughly textured on the ends. I can feel it bend if I stress it slightly."

You now bring two more volunteers into the room, sit them at the front blindfolded, and hand them each a dowel. But you ask these people to find their way to the back of the room using what you have just handed them as a probe, and you ask them to describe what they are feeling while doing this exercise. These reports will probably sound something like this: "I feel the leg of the chair I'm starting from. Now I feel the edge of the carpet. Now here's the leg of another chair. Here's the back of the chair.

Here's . . . oops, here's somebody's foot. Excuse me. I feel the leg of another chair."

These are two radically different sets of reports from the two different sets of people. And yet perhaps the most interesting thing about these differences is that all four people are basing their reports on almost exactly the same physical sensation—the physical sensation of holding a dowel in their hand. The dowel disappeared for the people who used it as a probe because they made it a part of their tacit knowledge, and they focused their effort at meaning making just beyond the dowel. But for the first two people, the dowel was the focus of their attention, the target of their effort to generate meaning.

Of the several conclusions that can be drawn from this demonstration, four are of particular interest here. First, this is a demonstration of Polanyi's proposition that all knowledge is either tacit knowledge or is grounded in tacit knowledge. Any focal meaning that we comprehend is grounded in experiences, sensations, memories, assumptions, purposes, goals, and values that are, at that moment, tacit and unquestioned by us. We achieve meaning through an act of interpretation, through selecting and organizing a stream of sensations into a coherent pattern using what Polanyi calls an interpretative frame. We in turn gain our memories, assumptions, purposes, goals, and values by living in them, by ingesting them and inhaling them from our noetic ecology. In this sense, we are inescapably the creatures or products of our particular time, place, and culture—even of our own individual, uniquely lived experience. And our unique dwelling place within the noosphere means that our individual understanding is necessarily limited, parochial, even often tendentious. It means, among other things, that our arguments are always subject to ad hominem attack. Yet the only way to insulate ourselves from this uniquely lived, parochial experience is to insulate ourselves from all experience. If we attempt to cut ourselves off from these parochial roots in the name of objectivity, we create the risk of destroying comprehension by cutting off the grounds of our knowing in the first place.

Second, the dowel exercise is a demonstration of the proposition that all knowledge is indeed personal knowledge—in other words, without the intelligent interpretive effort of the knower, there are only subjective sensations on the one hand and objective data points on the other hand, all equally meaningless. So we are ultimately responsible for our own knowing. We must, in the words of the common idiom, make up our own minds.

Third, it is a demonstration of how malleable knowledge is in the hands—or the mind—of the knower. Knowledge that is tacit in one context and under one set of conditions becomes focal knowledge in another. Suppose the second pair of people in the dowel experiment stopped halfway to the back of the room and asked what was this thing they were using as a probe. At that moment, the dowel, which they had been using as an extension of their own bodies, relying on it tacitly to relay data about the world beyond, would be instantly transformed in their experience. It would no longer be tacit, but it would be the explicit, focal object of their attention. And, as long as it remained the explicit, focal object of their attention, it would be useless as a probe for understanding some other phenomenon.

Even members of our own body are subject to this kind of transformation. Suppose I am one of the subjects in the dowel exercise. Suppose that, in the course of the exercise, I get a cramp in the hand that is holding the dowel. Now my attention is drawn back still further. My hand is now the point of focal attention, and, because it is, it no longer functions as an instrument for examining the dowel.

In the same way, the ideas, values, prior experience, and assumptions that provide the interpretative frame we rely on for making sense of an experience at one moment may, at some other time, be the focal object we investigate using some other set of experiences, values, and assumptions as a tacit probe. What is tacit knowledge in one situation may be the object of our explicit, focal effort to understand in another situation. So, notwithstanding that we are inescapably the creatures of our own time, place, culture, and individual experience, this conclusion calls us to examine the unexamined assumptions, values, and experience that we bring to our knowing. And yet, there are limits, too. We cannot "use our own spectacles to examine our spectacles." We cannot examine the dowel and use it as a probe at the same time. As long as we hold something at a distance and examine it, we cannot indwell it uncritically and use it as tacit knowledge.

The fourth conclusion is that there exists in all our sentient activities an impulse, an attraction, an inclination toward the truth. While the link here may be more subtle than the other three, I think the dowel exercise calls for this conclusion just as compellingly as it calls for the other three. Both activities—describing the dowel and finding one's way back to one's chair—are trivial activities, but even here we can see at work what Polanyi calls the heuristic gradient. Even here, people are moved by a heuristic impulse toward discovery, toward knowing, toward the truth. This is the crucial conclusion that ultimately distinguishes this concept of personal knowledge from the idiosyncratic or the subjective.

This same heuristic impulse, this hunger for meaning and for a true understanding, is also the crucial force that links us as individual knowers to one another and to the noosphere. Conclusion 1 tells us that our knowledge is always bounded by and grounded in the local particularities of our own lives. Conclusion 4 shows us that in spite of this local grounding, we are aiming at insights that are universal. In other words, we are striving for the truth when we commit these acts of knowing. Furthermore, this is not some qualified or ironic "truth" that we feel constrained to put in quotation marks, but it is the actual truth that we yearn for.

We can all document this impulse in ourselves by recalling some insight that we have achieved. We can reflect on the range of emotional experiences associated with that insight, including the sense of satisfaction that accompanied our discovery in the first place. In particular, we can consider the emotions we have experienced when someone has challenged an insight we have achieved. Our common reactions include a sense of surprise, perhaps shock, perhaps even betrayal, and almost certainly a sense of disdain for our challenger, who appears to be incapable of seeing the truth in what we see. If we do not dismiss this person out of hand, our next impulse is likely to be a desire to educate our challenger, to help this person toward a true understanding, a sharing of the insight we have achieved. Again it is Polanyi's language that expresses this idea most aptly. He says that the heuristic passion, as soon as it achieves an insight, becomes a persuasive passion. We want to share our vision, to persuade the world to see things as we have come to see them. Where competing insights contend with one another, "our vision must conquer or die" (150).

This process whereby our insights contend with one another is, of course, rhetoric. And this interplay of conclusions 1 through 4 leads to two additional conclusions. Conclusion 5 is that all knowledge, both personal and communal, is rhetorical. Indeed, theories of rhetoric and theories of knowledge have mirrored each other and have resonated with each other for as far back as we can trace the two. Plato's condemnation of rhetoric was as much a condemnation of the Sophists' epistemological and ethical relativism that is reflected in their rhetoric as it was a condemnation of their rhetoric itself. Plato's protégé, Aristotle, then delimited the role of rhetoric, pointing out that there are issues in which the empirical evidence is compelling, and he observed that it makes no sense to argue about things that are subject to empirical demonstration. Some two thousand years later, with the triumph of an empiricist/objectivist epistemology, rhetoric shrank to the study of clear and concise exposition of the observed data. Rhetoric had little reason even for being if the truth lay in the data. Given this epistemology, one must conclude that if two people argue about the truth, it simply means that one or both of them are not paying attention.

For more than a century now there has been a progressive erosion of this objectivist epistemology. And, as one would expect, rhetorical theory continues to mirror epistemological theory. Consider, for example, how the structure of argument that unfolds in Stephen Toulmin's *The Uses of Argument* resonates with the structure of knowledge in Polanyi's epistemological theory. Toulmin rejects the traditional analysis of effective argument as inadequate for any real-world contingency. He argues that it is only in the rarefied atmosphere of pure mathematics or symbolic logic that the structure of major premise, minor premise, and conclusion can actually make sense. The contingencies, complications, and conflicted interests of the real world require that we see argument as having a more complex, subtle, flexible structure, Toulmin says, and he proposes the following nomenclature: claim, data, warrant, backing, qualification, reservation. In this nomenclature, Toulmin's claim corresponds exactly to Polanyi's

focal knowledge. When we are confident that we know something, we claim it is true. We may, in making the claim, mention
some of the grounding for the claim, but the bare claim alone is
the root element of the expressed argument. If there is no challenge or other query in response to the claim, the argument or
discussion of the argument may be over as soon as the claim is
made. But this situation can hardly be called rhetorical. Rather,
it smacks of the objectivist's ideal, in which argument consists
essentially of demonstration, of pointing at facts that speak for
themselves. Except in situations that are trivial or in which the
facts and their meaning are understood in the same way by all
parties present, some challenge or query in reply is likely. And if
there is a challenge or question in response to the claim, then we
consider the question, and we answer by making explicit—both
for ourselves and for our interlocutor—some of the tacit grounding for the claim. This grounding may be data that support the
claim, or it may be a warrant, a heretofore unstated principle or
assumption or value that informs our perspective on the issue
and constitutes our rationale for making our claim.

Here's an illustration, adapted from Ross Winterowd's discussion of Toulmin in *The Contemporary Writer*. First, I make
the claim that the coach should be fired. Someone challenges my
claim: why would I ever think that, this someone wonders. I can
reply with either data or a warrant—or both, for that matter. If I
respond with data, I might say that the coach's record this year is
one win and fourteen losses, and I might then repeat my claim.
The warrant in this case is still unspoken. If I respond with a
warrant, I might say that coaches are supposed to win ball games,
and I might leave unspoken the data. If I do leave either the data
or the warrant unspoken, I may be challenged to supply the element that I have left unspoken.

This process is equivalent to someone stopping to check the
dowel in the dowel exercise. The challenge to the explicit claim
forces me to stop and begin to examine the tacit elements that
inform that claim. And Toulmin's structure here is precisely congruent with Polanyi's. In fact, he goes beyond Polanyi in identifying, by their functions, different elements within the tacit structure
of knowledge as they are transformed in an argument. If my
warrant (Coaches should win) is challenged with a competing

warrant (e.g., Coaches should be exemplars of virtuous behavior), I may reply with another warrant that serves as backing for my original warrant (To be credible exemplars of virtuous behavior, coaches must first win). Or, if I am persuaded that the challenge to my warrant does in fact point out an area where my warrant does not hold true, then I may either qualify my original claim (e.g., The coach should be fired if he doesn't win at least half of the remaining games) or I state a reservation to my warrant (e.g., unless in this situation it really isn't important to anyone that the team loses all the time).

Conclusion 6 is the converse of 5. If all knowledge is rhetorical, then all rhetoric is noetical. All rhetoric aims at the truth in the same sense that all our efforts to understand and know our world aim at the truth. It is no accident that theories of knowledge and theories of rhetoric go hand in hand.

I have rejected the devaluing of the concept of truth and the signifying of that devaluation by putting the word *truth* in quotation marks to indicate an ironic or qualified use of the word. At the same time, though, I have been careful in my use of the word. At no time have I claimed for anyone an absolute possession of the truth. The structure of knowledge—of personal knowledge grounded in one's tacit knowledge and held by a committed, passionate heuristic effort to achieve a coherent, meaningful insight into one's world—precludes any such absolute claim. Our grasp on the truth is always tenuous. It is always limited by our language, by the underlying assumptions we bring from our time, place, and culture, and by our personal interests and ambitions. Yet none of us willingly deceive ourselves. For me to willfully lead myself astray would be perverse madness. In fact, this kind of disorientation *is* madness. Of course, we may mislead ourselves with unrealistic hopes and expectations or unrealistically low or high self-esteem, but we always do so in good faith.

Likewise, the presumption operates almost all the time that we will act in good faith with one another. A deceitful rhetor may prevaricate, may bluff, may engage in a variety of deceptions. But even the deceitful rhetor is at pains to create at least the *illusion* of truth, and if he or she is successful in the deception, even that deceit is dependent on the shared expectation that the rhetor will not lie.

Why is this expectation, this presumption, so strong, and why does it matter anyway? The triumph of Newtonian physics that gave such force and credibility to objectivist theories of knowledge has been overtaken in this century by concepts in physics that have names like the theory of relativity and the uncertainty principle. The Sophists against whom Plato argued are now thriving in academic departments all across the land. If our grip on the truth is always tenuous and provisional, why not just put it in quotation marks and figure we will use rhetoric as a weapon to get as many toys for ourselves as we can? I think we decide this question the same way we decide not to use chlorofluorocarbons. I cannot see the ozone layer any better than I can see the truth, but I believe they are both there. And what I know about the structure of the biosphere and the structure of the noosphere convinces me that my life, the lives of my neighbors, and the lives of our children depend on both of them.

I make mistakes all the time. I misread texts, people, situations. Sometimes my misreadings are a product of my own self-interested blind spots. Sometimes I am misled by people who wish to deceive me. Sometimes I draw conclusions and make claims based on evidence that is incomplete and that later turns out to have been inadequate. Some of these times I should have withheld judgment. I should have waited for more complete data or for a better grounding in the appropriate values and assumptions for the situation. But other times I did not act inappropriately even though I was in error. I cannot wait for a complete, utterly confident understanding of the truth before I act, because, if I wait for an absolute hold on the absolute truth, I will remain paralyzed in a self-induced stupor of indecision. This stuporous state of avoiding deception by refusing to decide is no better than the alternative at the other extreme, the madness of deliberate self-deception. So I must decide, and I must act, even though I am always risking error.

And if I propagate that error, if I persuade my friends and neighbors to decide as I have decided, I degrade the noosphere. So the risk compounds and the stakes rise. Fortunately, however, neither I nor my friends and neighbors are bent on deliberate self-deception. Our errors, both individual and collective, are corrigible. We have the Burkean conversation to sustain us. Despite the fact that the scene plays out in an imaginary parlor, the conversation is not a mere parlor game. Burke notes that, depending on the quality of your ally's assistance, your opponent may be either embarrassed or gratified, and this ego investment in the argument is always present. But we may also presume that your opponent is not inclined to perverse self-deception, and if your ally, while creating momentary embarrassment for your opponent, has shifted the grounds of your opponent's knowing and thereby achieved ever so slight a correction in the noosphere, then your opponent may be *both* embarrassed and gratified.

The crucial element, without which rhetoric cannot serve this creative, corrective, nourishing, and sustaining dialectic between our own individual acts of knowing and the noetic ecology in which we dwell, is simple conviviality: a predilection for the conversation and a willingness to resist the temptation of treating any part of the conversation as the last word. We may, for any number of reasons, find it useful to take snapshots of the noosphere at particular points. We may wish to treat some area of the noosphere as a fixed particle for purposes of defining it, understanding it, or contrasting it with some other part at some other time. For example, if we wish to understand the genius of Galen and his contribution to the understanding of physiology and wellness and to our theories of disease and treatment, we might focus on Galen as if his were the last words on anatomy and the etiology and treatment of disease. But if we were to allow our respect for his genius to ossify into a craven orthodoxy, as happened in the Middle Ages, we would have to await our own Paracelsus and Vesalius to revivify the conversation.

The noosphere, like the ozone layer, is remarkably resilient. The example of Galen is one of an endless number illustrating how the collected global wisdom of the ages is chock full of error and contradiction, of hypotheses that are near misses and hypotheses that are distant misses of the truth. Yet those misses, both near and distant, are with few exceptions made with a single aim: the truth. That Galen was wrong in some fundamental ways about anatomy and disease is not grounds for a censorious excision of his work. He got some important things right, including his empirical methodology, which was ignored for centuries while many of his errors were dogmatically propagated. Similarly, the

Copernican cosmology can be read as an extension, elaboration, and correction of the Ptolemaic system rather than as a rejection of Ptolemy, in the same sense that successors to Copernicus can be read as extending, refining, and correcting his work and elaborating the questions he left unanswered (and in many cases unasked).

Burke's conversation metaphor rides atop a lengthy footnote to his discussion of the United States Constitution as dramatic act within a historical scene. He notes two antecedent documents, the Magna Carta and the British Bill of Rights, and he describes each of the three documents, like all historic documents, as "a strategy for encompassing a situation" (93). Each document entered the "unending conversation" at a particular time, and each is to be understood first in the context of the conversation of its own time. Each is, like the work and words of Galen, Ptolemy, Copernicus, Paracelsus, and Vesalius, a dipping in of an oar, an assertion made—an assertion grounded in and bounded by the particularities of its time and place but accredited by its aiming at a truth transcending time and place. And that common aim, sustained by conviviality—an ethic that respects both dissent and that which is the object of dissent—enables the conversation to go on when we have passed from the scene.

Works Cited

Burke, Kenneth. *The Philosophy of Literary Form: Studies in Symbolic Action*. 1941. New York: Vintage, 1957.

Polanyi, Michael. *Personal Knowledge: Towards a Post-Critical Philosophy*. 1958. Chicago: U of Chicago P, 1962.

Richards, Ivor Armstrong. *Speculative Instruments*. Chicago: U Chicago P, 1955.

Teilhard de Chardin, Pierre. *The Phenomenon of Man*. Trans. Bernard Wall. New York: Harper, 1959.

Toulmin, Stephen. *The Uses of Argument*. Cambridge: Cambridge UP, 1958.

Winterowd, W. Ross. *The Contemporary Writer: A Practical Rhetoric*. 2nd ed. New York: Harcourt, 1981.

Young, Richard E., Alton L. Becker, and Kenneth L. Pike. *Rhetoric: Discovery and Change*. New York: Harcourt, 1970.

CHAPTER SIX

The Modesty of
Aristotle's Rhetoric

EUGENE GARVER
St. John's University

When in doubt, tell the truth.
RICHARD YOUNG

Twenty years ago I spent a summer studying theories of composition with Richard Young. I went to the NEH seminar in part because I realized that I was a terrible writer, and, good academic that I was, I thought I could learn how to write by learning how people teach writing. Ever since, I have periodically worried about the same problem that took me to Ann Arbor: Why is writing so hard? Why do so many otherwise intelligent and accomplished people have so much trouble communicating their thoughts to others? One of the reasons I have been attracted to Aristotle's *Rhetoric* is that he thinks that rhetoric—effective public speaking, not writing—is easy. It is a universal art. Although some do it better than others, there is nothing very important to know, and there is no reason to think it is difficult to be an effective rhetorician, and no reason to think that one can become more persuasive through studying with someone who understands the principles of the art. Since this attitude seems so contrary to my own personal experience as a writer, and so contrary to the opinions of almost every college teacher about her students, I have studied the *Rhetoric* for the last twenty years hoping for enlightenment.

My rabbi recently informed me that in the world to come there will be no faculty meetings. Whether or not the world of

Aristotle's *Rhetoric* is paradise, I can confidently attest that there are no composition teachers there. No departments of communication either. The enterprise of the *Rhetoric* is organized by a principle of modesty. His art of rhetoric makes no promises to improve practice or make us more persuasive. Its competition claims to improve practice, but Aristotle thinks those claims are false. His judgment against claims to improve practice is not a purely empirical one and cannot be refuted by empirical studies of the effects of public speaking and writing courses. He is willing to believe that the Sophists' customers might get what they pay for and become, by their own lights, more successful. But when these other "arts" improve practice, they do so only because the speaker or writer is trying to persuade corrupt audiences and persuade them by corrupting them further. Such projects are not arts, and they do not, except by their own circular criteria, improve practice either.

Aristotle's art of rhetoric will not improve practice any more than his competitors' will, and I will soon try to explain why not. But first I want to list further aspects of the modesty of the *Rhetoric*. According to Aristotle, the practice of his art of rhetoric will make no one wiser about anything (I.2.1355b32–34). Rhetoric is modestly confined to argument, not knowledge of real things. These practical and cognitive dimensions of modesty are matched by an ethical modesty. The *Rhetoric* is perhaps the only art of rhetoric which makes no claim to teach virtue. If philosophy cannot teach virtue, as Aristotle maintains in the *Ethics* (e.g., II.5.1105b12–18, X.9), certainly rhetoric cannot. Aristotle's ethical modesty is a true modesty, in contrast to those rhetorics which advertise themselves as mere amoral technique. While such a claim sounds ethically modest, making no promises at all, it always turns out that this amorality is actually a robust moral claim.[1]

Cicero says that the decline of the golden age started with Socrates. Before Socrates, wisdom and eloquence, philosophy and rhetoric, were one. But Socrates made each so difficult that people had to choose and specialize in either one or the other, either a barbarous, precise, esoteric, and unintelligible philosophy or an empty, superficial, and immoral rhetoric. Although Cicero does not put it this way, one could say that Socrates divided *logos* into *ratio* and *oratio*. Some teachers of communication have accepted the Socratic division of labor and held that their job has nothing to do with wisdom. Hirsch, at least in *The Philosophy of Composition*, sees it as the goal of composition to minimize the effort the reader has to exert to understand a given message. The content of the message is of no concern to the composition teacher. Aristotle would consider this a rhetoric of style that neglects argument. Other teachers of eloquence have followed Cicero and tried to reunite wisdom and eloquence. Those who associate composition with critical thinking or problem solving aim at this reunion of wisdom and eloquence, extending the reach of rhetoric to things and not just words, and I would place Richard Young as a successor to Cicero in this aspiration. Because of the modesty of his conception of the art of rhetoric, Aristotle is not a participant in this enterprise.

While Aristotle's art is a modest one in the three ways I have outlined, he is aware that there are other versions of the art that pretend to greater ambitions. Various pressures and factors make his modesty precarious and liable to be undermined. Aristotle does not propose a border patrol to keep rhetoric from becoming specialized, either as wisdom or as eloquence. Nor does he propose censoring all claims by rhetoricians to improve their audiences morally. Good laws can prevent speakers from getting off the subject. To the extent that speakers stay on the issues, and audiences, either voluntarily or because of the coercion of the laws, respond only to the issues, eloquence—as opposed to the attention to argument Aristotle recommends—will be ineffective. But good laws can do only so much.

On the side of wisdom, the faculty of rhetoric sometimes hits on principles of sciences, but this is an accident, neither to be encouraged nor discouraged, neither praised nor blamed. It is worth quoting Aristotle's words at some length:

> A very great difference between enthymemes [and other syllogisms] has escaped the notice of nearly everyone, although it also exists in the dialectical method of syllogisms. For some of them belong to rhetoric, some syllogisms only to dialectic, and others to other arts and faculties. . . . Hence it is that this escapes the notice of the speakers, and the more they specialize in a subject, the more they transgress the limits of rhetoric and dialectic. . . .

I mean by dialectical and rhetorical syllogisms those which are concerned with what we call topics. . . . *Idia* on the other hand are derived from propositions which are peculiar to each species or genus of things. . . . The first kind [of syllogisms] will not make a man practically wise about any particular class of things, because they do not deal with any particular subject matter; but as to the latter kind, the happier a man is in his choice of propositions, the more he will unconsciously produce a science quite different from dialectic and rhetoric. For if once he hits upon principles, it will no longer be dialectic or rhetoric but that science whose principles he has arrived at. (I.2.1358a1–28)[2]

It is possible for the rhetorician to stray outside Aristotelian borders, but Aristotle's attitude in this case is not pejorative. "In proportion as anyone endeavors to make of dialectic and rhetoric, not what they are, faculties, but sciences, to that extent he will, without knowing it, destroy their real character, by crossing over into the domain of sciences, whose subjects are certain definite things, not merely arguments (*logoi*)" (I.4.1359b12–17). The rhetorician can suddenly find himself knowing what he is talking about. For this to be at all possible, rhetoric cannot ever be purely verbal or formal, even when it is about *logoi* and not the facts or "certain definite things," *ta pragmata*. Rhetoric is about argument, and sometimes arguments reach scientific truths.

The boundaries of rhetoric can cross into wisdom or knowledge in another way. The doctor persuading the patient to take his medicine *uses* rhetoric. Because of the ignorance of her audience or because of time pressure, the doctor cannot teach what she knows and so has to persuade the patient. At times, rhetorical practice *should* behave less modestly than its art prescribes.

But toward specialized eloquence, as opposed to specialized wisdom, Aristotle's attitude is different: he morally condemns the enterprise. Philosophers are allowed in Aristotle's world but not writing or public speaking teachers. He condemns the idea of making eloquence into a specialty on both moral and intellectual grounds. Such so-called arts are both impossible and undesirable. Where others, starting with the Sophists, see professional rhetoric as a democratizing force, substituting a reason and eloquence available to all for a more restricted source of power in wealth or ancestry, Aristotle sees professional rhetoric as undermining both political relations and individual character.[3] Advocates of professional rhetoric see it as advancing democracy by providing a common power for individual assertion, whereas Aristotle sees it as antidemocratic since it introduces its own form of expertise. Because writing teachers have good reason to view their work as advancing the cause of democracy, I would like to use the *Rhetoric* as a caution against believing in those aspirations too confidently. Those who talk about the delights and motives of eloquence, such as Kenneth Burke and Richard Lanham, might think that eloquence for its own sake develops from pleasures specific to enjoying language itself. Aristotle traces a different genealogy. The impulse to specialization and professionalization is always a motive extraneous to the arts themselves and is therefore subject to condemnation. Here is what he says about the analogous problem in music:

> It is evident that the learning [of music] should neither be an impediment with a view to later activities, nor make the body vulgar and useless with a view to military and political training. . . . This would result in connection with the learning [of music] if they did exert themselves to learn either what contributes to contests involving expertise in the art or those works that are difficult and extraordinary (which have now come into the contests, and from the contests into education). (*Politics* VIII.6.1341a6–14)

Professionalized musical proficiency is always impelled by an external motive and for that reason should be condemned. Analogous criticisms of rhetoric are apposite. To the extent that rhetoric becomes a matter of competition and performance, rhetorical proficiency is educationally suspect since it is "an impediment with a view to later activities," including, I believe, activities of a civic and democratic persuasion. It is practically suspect, too, since it draws attention to these performance values and away from the subjects under consideration and the arguments made about them. The pleasures of eloquence are corrupt pleasures. Eloquence makes for bad citizens.

I have mentioned three distinct violations of rhetoric's borders: first, the rhetorician who inadvertently presents scientifically grounded arguments about reality, or who has scientific knowledge about which he must be persuasive; second, the rhetorician who claims to benefit the audience, or bystanders or students, ethically; and finally, the rhetorician as stylist; and I have given examples of Aristotle's attention to the first and third of these. Aristotle does not show the connections among these three, but I think it is worth drawing them. When rhetoric persuades through charm and through style, it is being sophistical. When rhetoric acts as though it knows something, it is being sophistical. What is fundamentally wrong with sophistic rhetoric is not its intellectual emptiness nor its stylistic excesses but its external motive. Because it aims at victory rather than the more limited rhetorical aim of finding in a given case the available means of persuasion, it *must* pretend to expert knowledge. "Rhetoric dresses itself up in the form of politics, as do those who pretend to a knowledge of it, partly from lack of education, partly from boastfulness, and other human causes" (*Rhetoric* I.2.1356a27–30).

"Sophistry is not a matter of ability (*dynamis*) but of deliberate choice (*prohairesis*) [of specious arguments]" (I.1.1355b18).[4] This does not mean that the true rhetorician does not try to win. It only means that he tries to win through argument and does not separate winning from arguing. When my wife studied landscape architecture, she learned how to make presentations that would sell her projects at first glance. This is winning distinct from argument. At my university, there was recently a quasi-judicial hearing concerning a charge of sexual harassment. Advocates trying to prove that sexual harassment had taken place cleverly trapped the defendants into exhibiting what they considered sexism in front of the judicial panel. But the advocates' tactic was seen as clever, not as proof. Their zeal to win made them neglect argument. This is a rhetoric of style and delivery rather than argument. All three border violations—cognitive, eloquent, and ethical—often occur together. Aristotle condemns border violations which claim that rhetoric teaches virtue and which valorize style over argument, while he neither condemns nor encourages the intrusion of wisdom into eloquence. Audiences are suspicious of both wisdom and eloquence, and Aristotle thinks they are right to be suspicious. The difference is that claims to wisdom are sometimes suspect, while eloquence always is.

The border violation about which Aristotle is neutral, which happens when the rhetorician knows what she is talking about, is the subject of innumerable books and articles about whether expertise destroys the public or the political, or whether techne destroys praxis. Aristotle's ethical distinction between rhetoric and sophistry is easily interpreted as reductive moralizing: I use rhetoric because my motives are pure, while you are a sophist because of your disreputable ends. This reasoning is like Socrates' distinction in the *Gorgias* between rhetors who speak in the interest of the audience and those who speak for their own interest (502e). Aristotle's talk of ulterior motives and his distinction between choice and the art itself become commodity fetishism, taking something that should be a means and treating it as an end, as he does in his criticism of professionalized music. The increase in expertise is frequently discussed as the domination of the scientific world picture. Enough has been written about these two corruptions, or successes, of rhetoric that I can safely leave them out of my discussion here.

I want to look not at these cognitive or moral violations but at the practical and stylistic one. In *Aristotle's Rhetoric: An Art of Character*, I tried to show how Aristotle's distinction between rhetoric and sophistry—the difference between acting according to art and acting according to an ulterior motive—is actually a way to avoid moralizing. Here I want to look at what happens to eloquence when it becomes a matter for specialists. The fact that Aristotle's three border violations often occur together points to a neglected dimension of the problem: threats to the public from specialized eloquence. Eloquence becomes art for art's sake, and I see such specialized eloquence as a threat to audiences and their civic responsibilities because I deny the autonomous origins of artful eloquence and instead see it as a function of expertise and ulterior motives. Rousseau makes more eloquently and laconically the same point that Aristotle makes about professionalized music when he says that so-called progress in the arts and sciences "adorns our wit and corrupts our judgment" (81).

As a paradigm of the way the interconnection of wisdom and eloquence creates mistrust, I want to offer Ernest Gellner's striking report of a civilization and culture apparently different from ours, as well as from Aristotle's. I think the reader will see strong parallels between the people of the High Atlas and all rhetorical and political situations.

> Specialists *as such,* of any kind, are morally suspect. I was told in the central High Atlas that any clan which acquires the reputation of special wisdom is *therefore* deprived of the vote in tribal elections. Excellence of any kind is a form of specialization and that precludes full citizenship. The unspecialized human being constitutes the moral norm. It is he who can lose himself in a solitary unity, and gladly accept collective responsibility. By contrast, the specialists of the towns, for whom specialization is of the essence, are politically castrated and incapable of cohesion, and hence of self-government. Consequently they are also incapable of governing others. (148)

Aristotle gives no directions for border maintenance to keep either eloquence or wisdom from becoming professionalized. He also gives no directions, and no hint that there can be directions, for getting (back) to such a world. Unlike Cicero, he is not trying to reunite wisdom and eloquence. The *Rhetoric* seems to me to present an alternative both to philosophers becoming more rhetorical and to rhetoricians becoming wiser. We can dispense with philosophers trying to become relevant by becoming conversationalists and critics of culture rather than abstruse specialists. And we can do better than rhetoricians restoring the dignity of their subject by transforming rhetorical invention into inquiry into matters of substance, so that once again the good speaker has to know what he's talking about and become a universal expert. Aristotle offers a different way of thinking about problems which concern us. The *Rhetoric* is an alternative to programs of nostalgia for the less specialized days when wisdom and eloquence were united. It is also a response to the separation of wisdom and eloquence that declares such a separation a victory rather than a crisis and proclaims the autonomy of rhetoric as an art of style.

The *Rhetoric* reunites philosophy and rhetoric in a way quite different from Cicero's more familiar strategy. Rhetoric, like dialectic, is a universal art, not the property of specialists. For that reason, those who claim to be specialists in teaching eloquence are frauds, a judgment that would put many of us out of business. Additionally, there are no such specialists because, as I said earlier, understanding the art of rhetoric is no guarantee that one's practice will get any better. Aristotle thinks that his dismissal of teachers of rhetoric has empirical backing. For purposes of action, experience is just as good as art: "With a view to action experience seems in no respect inferior to art, and men of experience succeed even better than those who have theory without experience" (*Metaphysics* I.1.981a13–15). Aristotle never promises that knowing his art of rhetoric will improve practice. When discussing style in III.10, he says that "it is possible to create [urbanities and well-liked expressions] by natural talent or practice, but to show what they are belongs to this study" (*Rhetoric* 1410b7–8). By art, we can know what stylistic virtues are, but Aristotle does not imply that we will be any better at them because of this art. And what is true for style is true for the whole art of rhetoric. Aristotle reflects on the common experience of being able to understand why one speech or one piece of writing succeeds and another fails without being able oneself to speak or write effectively. His rhetoric is, like dialectic, a universal art. The difficult challenge of the *Rhetoric* is to see how such capacities, which make no one wiser, yet are not empty verbal arts— how an art of argument is neither empty nor scientifically substantive.[5]

Again, I want to look more closely at the relations among the three dimensions of modesty—practical, cognitive, and ethical—and expertise to suggest that eloquence poses at least as much threat as expertise and that the pursuit of eloquence is a neglected part of the modern problem of techne replacing praxis. The delights and powers of eloquence are part of the problems typically discussed in relation to other forms of expertise. Recall that when rhetoric hits on scientific principles, it stops being rhetoric and becomes science. This is the one border crossing that Aristotle does not condemn, but even it leads to the ethical and stylistic violations of sophistry, which he does condemn. Sometimes speakers step outside the bounds of rhetorical modesty because they really do know what they are talking about, and sometimes, as quoted before, "rhetoric dresses itself up in the form of politics, as do those who pretend to a knowledge of it, partly from lack of education, partly from boastfulness" (I.2.1356a27–30).

The audience cannot initially tell which border violation they are experiencing, and often the speaker cannot either. The relation of speaker and listener is transformed when the speaker possesses scientific knowledge. Since the speaker knows something the audience does not, at least in that respect she cannot approach them as an equal. Therefore, why not fool them into believing something that is for their own good? If I have esoteric knowledge which I cannot quickly teach to the audience, why not resort to esoteric, nonargumentative means of persuasion that focus on the virtues of presentation and style? If I have scientific knowledge, it will not help to pretend that I do not and that I am really just plain folks. This is how violation of the border with respect to wisdom can lead quite innocently to violations with respect to eloquence, and thus to moral violations. When the object of deliberation becomes a set of objects for technical manipulation rather than for deliberation and praxis, so too is the audience liable to be seen as ripe for technical manipulation. Expertise leads to the division of labor and therefore to inequality. Knowing what one is talking about seems, and is, innocent, yet it can have seriously destructive consequences.

For example, when my students and I deliberate about the meaning of a passage in Plato, I know more than they do. Otherwise I would not be teaching. But there can still be a form of equality between speaker and listener if I try to present the relevant evidence and grounds for our judgment and decision. In Aristotle's terms, I am using technical rather than extratechnical means of persuasion. I am inventing arguments rather than presenting evidence that removes the need for argument. Once I present those arguments, we stand as equals. In any rhetorical situation, the speaker has to reconcile the following two values: the orator must be someone worth listening to, and to that extent must be distinct from the audience, and he must also be someone who shares the values and opinions of the audience, and to that extent must be one with the audience. When I talk to a student whose opinions place us in two different communities—communities constituted by the opinions we argue from and act on—things are very different.[6] I cannot engage in common deliberation with the creationist, the fundamentalist, or the rather charmingly benighted students who wear purple buttons that ask, "What's Your Truth?" Without a community of opinion, certain rhetorical options are closed. Therefore, ominously, others open. Creationists are not interested in argument anyway; why not overwhelm them with eloquence, which they might mistake for wisdom?

Thus Aristotle's *Rhetoric* is not only modest in the claims it makes for an art of rhetoric, but it enjoins a practice of rhetoric that is itself modest. The purpose of rhetoric is not to persuade but to find available means of persuasion. It is up to the audience to be persuaded, and so the audience is not a passive element in the persuasive transaction. The rhetorician "has no function except to show that something is or is not true or has happened or has not happened; whether it is important or trivial or just or unjust, in so far as the lawmaker has not provided a definition, the juryman should somehow decide himself and not learn from" the rhetorician (I.1.1354a26–30). The rhetorician can usurp the power of judgment Aristotle vests in the audience, and can do so through the imposition of wisdom, through the magic of style, or through a putative moral superiority. The sophist cannot rest with finding the available means of persuasion but must try to persuade. If I have knowledge that the audience lacks, or stylistic powers, or moral superiority, why leave the judgment up to the audience?

The three kinds of immodesty go together. Professional, specialized rhetoric which focuses on eloquence rather than on argument is generally correlated with claims to wisdom and with sophistic rhetoric which aims at winning rather than finding in a given case the available means of persuasion. That seems to me an important, and far from obvious, thesis. This discovery gives us resources that go beyond moralizing for fortifying the autonomous borders of rhetoric. Writing teachers may have grounds for hope after all. Partisans of style rather than of invention and argument can be aware of how easy it is for professional eloquence to lead to cognitive and moral pretensions that they would like to resist. I take it that this is the moral of the *Gorgias*. Gorgias is right to be embarrassed by the inferences Polus and Callicles draw, but they are right to draw those inferences. Community of opinion, in which Aristotle's modest rhetoric operates, can be destroyed by superior knowledge or be an ulterior motive. Either can be the source of a demand for specialized eloquence.[7]

Let me give a more extended example of how Aristotle's modest rhetoric works. For the past three years I have been engaged in processes of persuading and being persuaded on my university's Rank and Tenure Committee, and I found that the experience wonderfully exemplified Aristotelian rhetoric at its best. It succeeded because it denied specialized wisdom, eloquence, and ulterior motives, Aristotle's three border violations. Of course I entered deliberations wanting my view of the candidate to be the one the committee adopted, but I wanted to win through argument. In that sense, I did not have an ulterior motive distinct from rendering the best decision we as a committee could. The lack of ulterior motive is not some grand moral test. It is simply a commitment to be bound by argument. Therefore, members of the committee engaged with each other in rhetoric, not sophistry. Our deliberations were exercises in invention and persuasion, and they employed all three kinds of proof: ethos, pathos, and logos. Each of the trio can be at work in an argument from precedent, so looking at arguments from precedent helps to clarify the three sources of proof and see in a bit more detail what the modesty of Aristotle's rhetoric means.

When I try to persuade a colleague to vote for candidate X by a reminder of the reasons previously given for supporting candidate Y, I could be using any of the three modes of proof: (1) My appeal to precedent could be a logical argument of consistency. (2) It could be an emotional appeal if I try to get my colleague to see herself as committed to something she would otherwise resist. She should be shamed by the tacit implication that she was not really committed to the reasons she proffered for candidate Y but was instead really motivated by envy or resentment or party loyalty. She will vote my way so that she can feel the emotions she would like to feel. (3) I can appeal to those same reasons ethically if I take her commitments and principles seriously and join with her in reasoning from them. Here the goal is not consistency, as in the logical appeal, but reliability. My appeal to a specific audience in this case is not a concession to its weakness or an occasion for manipulation. I join her in exploring the implications of her principles. I display ethos in tracing the implications of another's beliefs.

My example has a moral. The modest Aristotelian rhetoric is obviously not able to do certain things that the less restrained professional rhetorician can. There can be no appeals to irrelevant emotions, no distractions or winning an audience through humor, no use of vivid language and images to cloud the judgment. So Aristotelian rhetoric always looks as if it prescribes that the rhetor "fight" with one hand tied behind his back. Part of the appeal of specialized eloquence is the freedom to fight fire with fire, working from the assumption that if someone else is not bound by ethical considerations, you are at a disadvantage. But while the sophist has certain tools not available to the rhetorician, Aristotle's modest rhetoric reveals powers not available to more ambitious brands of rhetoric, complicating the calculations of whether common decency will triumph over specialized powers. Convincing an audience through ethos, as opposed to logos and pathos, requires a community of argument not available to the sophistical rhetorician who possesses superior knowledge, stylistic abilities, or ulterior motives. Both Aristotle's artful rhetorician and the sophist can deploy emotional and logical arguments, but only the civic rhetorician can use ethical argument. In discussions of the contest between the good rhetorician and the sophist, the advantage always seems to be with the latter. My example, however, shows gain and loss on both sides. Earlier I said that without a community of opinion, certain rhetorical options are closed and therefore others open. This is the principle at work here.

As mentioned earlier, the lack of ulterior motive is not a moral test but simply a commitment to be bound by argument. This dimension of moral modesty recalls my statement that the *Rhetoric* may be the only art of rhetoric which makes no claim to teach virtue. A situation like my experience with the Rank and Tenure Committee can demand and inspire virtuous behavior, but the experience does not *teach* virtue. There may be no carryover to the rest of our lives. Virtue consists of doing good things for their own sake and not for an ulterior motive. Vicious action has an ulterior motive apart from the action itself. So while I am deliberating in that committee, I am not only performing virtuous—in this case, just—actions but also doing them justly and as the just person would do them. No doubt such experiences *can* help someone develop habits of doing things for their own sake. But there is also no reason to think that by themselves such experiences will develop such a habit. Aristotle's polis is full of occasions like my Rank and Tenure Committee experience, and so virtue develops into second nature there. But outside the polis, all we have are discrete circumstances and experiences which might or might not unify into a good life. The point remains: a commitment to be bound to and by argument *is* doing good for its own sake. It would be immodest for rhetoric to demand more.

We work hard on our Rank and Tenure Committee to deny expertise because expertise can destroy community. When a colleague of mine from the Philosophy Department is being considered for tenure, I do not appeal to things I "know" about him that are not present in the file, or to my superior experience in reading philosophy files, just as I do not persuade an undergraduate class about the meaning of a passage in Plato by referring to some piece of esoteric knowledge not available to students—"I've read Vlastos, and you haven't." If a candidate alleges that her unfavorable student evaluations were due to gender discrimination, we deliberate about the evidence in front of us and do not call in experts on how to interpret student evaluation forms, even though we have available many experts who urgently offer their services. Expertise, since it is immodest, makes deliberation impossible.[8]

The difference between civic and professional rhetoric can be seen in what happens to the rhetorician's ability to argue both sides of a question and think from the opponent's point of view. Professionally, one has to argue both sides of a question because one might be employed by either side, and one has to think from the opponent's point of view in order to anticipate objections. The civic and ethical rhetorician argues both sides of a question and thinks from the opponent's point of view in order to form a community of inquiry. These two approaches are not equivalent. Free debate and the open clash of opinions do not by themselves always lead to truth or progress in inquiry. They can lead to a contest of rhetorical skill, a rhetorical race to the bottom. We are all familiar with both processes, rhetorical contests that lead to truth and those that lead to competitors aiming at victory by appealing to the worst aspects of their audiences. Aristotle's *Rhetoric* and its principles of modesty invite us to see why rhetorical debate sometimes leads to truth and sometimes to corruption.[9]

For example, to decide for myself which way to vote on the Rank and Tenure Committee, I often try writing letters to the candidate giving the grounds for both favorable and unfavorable recommendations. I usually find that I cannot write one of the letters and thereby discover where the preponderance of evidence lies. But "can" here is an ethical, not a logical, term. I could write a letter on either side, where "could" means the ability to assemble arguments and make a persuasive case. Anyone who has ever been on a faculty committee has copious experience with defending the indefensible. But if my purpose is to arrive at the best judgment I can, then I should be able to write one letter and not the other. "One should be able to argue persuasively on either side of a question . . . not that we may actually do both (for one should not persuade what is debased) but in order that it may not escape our notice what the real state of the case is and that we ourselves may be able to refute if another person uses speech unjustly" (I.1.1355a29–32).

I want to juxtapose this picture of modest rhetoric with the more expansive senses of rhetoric that rely on specialized knowledge or eloquence. The demand for professional eloquence, and so for writing teachers, can have three sources, according to my analysis. First, sometimes someone has specialized knowledge, such as a doctor. The doctor has to persuade me to take my medicine, and neither of us has the time for me to learn physiology. That's why I'm paying her. Technical communication is not a universal art like rhetoric and dialectic. It *uses* rhetoric but does not simply engage in it. To me, the ignorant patient, my doctor's wisdom is an *atechnos*—something like the laws, contracts, and witnesses that Aristotle lists—that the audience must either accept or not but about which it cannot reason. Second, the demand for professional eloquence can come from an ulterior motive. For example, there are no significant differences between brands of soap or make of automobile, and so advertising cannot be the argumentative presentation of evidence. Advertising must succeed through style and delivery, since argument is not available. This is why I think that advertising and other content-free persuasions supply a bad model for rhetoric. Rhetoric is tied to deliberation, where one's choice makes a difference. Stylistic appeals are appropriately central when the decision does not matter. Finally, the demand for professional eloquence can come from eloquence itself. This is what Burke calls "pure persuasion," and it is connected to the delights of language that Lanham has stressed more recently. These are the competitive pleasures that Aristotle censures with regard to music. Here too is room for specialized teaching and performance, rather than a universal art like Aristotle's. But, to repeat, Aristotle thinks that pure persuasion always comes from competition and always makes us unfit for more modest, more ethical, occupations.

We do not live in heaven or in Aristotle's world, so it is silly to condemn specialized eloquence and the teaching of it. We do not always find ourselves in situations in which modesty can be a principle or a virtue. The three sources of specialized eloquence listed all seem to be at least sometimes legitimate, or at least unavoidable. But immodesty always has a cost. The challenge in each case—a challenge which is often successfully met—is to develop specialized eloquence in a way that avoids the moral dangers Aristotle cautions against. The three sorts of border violations often occur together, but they are not connected by chains of necessity. We must draw connections between the border violations—be they wisdom, or eloquence, or ulterior motive—and argument and ethos.

As one gesture toward this complication of my thesis, I want to return again to the fact that Aristotle regarded border violations of wisdom differently than those of eloquence. Artful eloquence destroys deliberation. Learned eloquence is out of place in our deliberations on the Rank and Tenure Committee that I presented as the practice of ideal Aristotelian modest rhetoric. Someone who tried to persuade his colleagues through the pleasures of style would be ridiculous, whether in oral deliberation or when we write memos to each other. My colleagues who represent the natural sciences on the committee seem to regard the lack of eloquence as proof of wisdom, and so their ethos contains a studied (I hope) inarticulateness; the fact that they would fail a first-year composition course does not relegate them to a reduced place in our deliberations, since persuasiveness is tied to argument, not eloquence. But, as Aristotle indicated, the entrance of wisdom into deliberation is more complicated than that of eloquence. It would be silly to say that self-denying ordinances should always be followed and that expertise is always out of place because it destroys deliberation. Moral condemnations of sophistic rhetoric are cheap. What if I have specialized knowledge and have to persuade an uneducated audience to do something I know is right, whether taking their medicine or accepting higher taxes? What if I am debating an opponent who is using dishonest tactics in a cause which I know to be a bad one? Eloquence by itself is not much of a danger, but the eloquence naturally engendered by appropriate border violations concerning knowledge and ulterior motives is a serious danger.

Recently I was a member of a search committee to find a new dean. After reading his file, I had questions and suspicions about one applicant. I telephoned someone at his former university and learned that the candidate had been found double billing his travel so that his wife could accompany him on business trips. This information, of course, was not in his file. I reported it to my colleagues on the committee. Our deliberations were then very short. My colleagues relied on my putative expertise. They trusted me, and my injection of specialized knowledge did not destroy community or permanently change the rhetorical situation. Such introductions of specialized knowledge may not be ideal, but sometimes they are necessary for successful deliberation. But what if I, and I alone, continued to introduce such evidence about each candidate? In that case, we would no longer have an Aristotelian rhetorical situation in which audiences judged arguments, because they would be relying on what Aristotle called *atechnoi*, extra-argumentative grounds for persuasion. Aristotle's examples in *Rhetoric* I.15 are contracts, written laws, oaths, and the results of torture, but my back-channel telephone conversations qualify as well. I would be an expert, and the committee would become quite a different kind of community.

I conclude that in any particular case it is a matter for individual judgment whether to rely on expert knowledge and professional eloquence. This is the traditional rhetorical topos of how to argue against an unjust opponent, the topos of the conflict between playing by the rules and trying to win. Generally, it is best to stick to common opinion, common values, and publicly accessible modes of argument, but in some cases the stakes are too high, and the importance of winning outweighs the value of staying with civil methods of argument. Assume that I am right to try to defeat this candidate for the dean's job rather than take the attitude that the best argument should triumph in our deliberative process. His file was good enough that many of my colleagues had placed him first on their list. If I argue to win, based on expertise and an ulterior motive, there is still a cost. The cost is the loss of the ethical kind of proof available only in a community. Even so, community is not destroyed by every violation of these terms, by every appeal to expert knowledge. One can try to ensure through argument that the community remains intact despite a necessary violation. While my evidence supplanted deliberation in this instance, I had to present it in such a way that it did not threaten the deliberative structure of our rhetorical community.

Why is the appeal to esoteric knowledge, hitting on a scientific principle, not only a rhetorical but also an ethical loss? In a true rhetorical situation, such as the Rank and Tenure Committee, I, the speaker trying to persuade, think that there is room for dispute, and I also think that one alternative is best. I can therefore argue with members of an audience who also face a situation that can go either way and who are called upon to make a decision. The audience and I both face rhetorical situations, situations in which we must choose the best available alternative. But in arguing with the creationist, the fundamentalist, or the postmodern relativist, or in arguing with colleagues who cannot know the crucial facts about double billing that I know, I do not consider myself in a rhetorical situation. I do not think there are two sides to the question. It would be dishonest to act as though there were. On the other hand, although it would not be dishonest, it would be most unpersuasive to act as though the case is settled in front of people for whom my arguments are at best persuasive, not compulsive. This is what Aristotle means when he says that arguments that are "too logical" drive out the emotional and the ethical. "Nor should you seek an enthymeme when the speech (*logos*) is being 'ethical' (*ethikos*); for logical demonstration has neither *ethos* nor moral purpose (*prohairesis*)" (III.17.1418a17).

We can see this driving out in action in a specific form of immodesty Aristotle discusses, namely excessive precision. Excessive precision is a character flaw, not just the mistake in argument we are warned against elsewhere in Aristotle. Precision is not a logical property but an ethical one. The overly precise speaker is not persuasive, because excessive accuracy is a sign of vice, not virtue. "It is more fitting that a virtuous man should show himself good than that his speech should be painfully exact" (III.17.1418b1–3). Aristotle condemns the man who stands on his rights for demanding an ethically excessive sort of precision concerning the subject of justice and the distribution of goods (V.10.1137b34–1138a3). To argue on the basis of reason alone is a character flaw, a failure of ethos, and therefore a failure to persuade. Excessive precision is in both cases unethical because it takes something which should be within the range of praxis and judgment and makes it into a subject for more precise, scientific determination.

For the individual speaker, the conflict between engaging in civic rhetoric and winning a particular case is a matter for judgment. In any particular case, the individual must decide whether to rely on expert knowledge or professional eloquence. But there is another point of view from which to examine these things— the systemic point of view. Not all border transgressions are bad. Wisdom and science are good, as we have seen. But the loss of the ethical is a loss usually worth preventing. One further lesson of Aristotle's *Rhetoric* is that the individual rhetorician's point of view, or that of the individual moral agent making an ethical decision, is not the point of view from which to think about these things. Instead, the goal is to develop a community perspective, to create a community which enables argumentative rhetoric.

Worries about the domination of expert knowledge are common enough today to constitute their own genre. By tying together Aristotle's three kinds of boundary maintenance for rhetoric, I have emphasized the connections between expertise and professional rhetoric. But, unlike Cicero's hopes for reuniting wisdom and eloquence, Aristotle offers something more interesting than nostalgia for a simpler age. Aristotelian modesty prescribes not a plain style but plain argument. Expertise exists. Aristotle never condemns "hitting on a principle" and moving from rhetoric to a science. To the extent that esoteric knowledge is the motivation for professional rhetoric, though, Aristotle's criticisms of his competitors, who, like rhetoricians today, emphasize affecting the emotions as the manner of presentation, are worth taking seriously. Concentration on the emotions and on affecting the audience, Aristotle says, leads to setting up judicial rhetoric as the paradigm for rhetoric in general. Concentration on style and delivery makes epideictic rhetoric the paradigm. Each is more competitive and professional than the deliberative rhetoric which Aristotle sets as the central form of rhetoric. The challenge to rhetoric today is to restore the primacy of the deliberative in circumstances that make this priority much more difficult than it was for Aristotle.

I said earlier that in any rhetorical situation the speaker has to reconcile the following two values: the orator must be someone worth listening to, and to that extent must be distinct from the audience, although not always superior in knowledge, and the orator must also be someone who shares the values and opinions of the audience, and to that extent must be one with the audience. That conflict is present not only in every rhetorical practitioner but also in everyone who tries to theorize about rhetoric and to teach rhetoric in a way inspired by Aristotle. To teach is to know and to know the causes of success and failure. Such knowledge is not universally possessed. On the other hand, rhetoric, like dialectic, is a universal faculty. Everyone can and does practice it, often with greater success through experience or talent than through learning. Understanding the principles of persuasion—Aristotle's sense of an art of rhetoric—helps us judge the moral dimensions of rhetorical situations and thus the costs and advantages of relying on a universal faculty and on expertise. Maybe there is room for composition teachers after all. There are worthwhile things to worry about other than improving practice.

Notes

1. In "The 'Q' Question," Lanham outlines answers both for and against the proposition that virtue can be taught by rhetorical training. But it is instructive how his exemplars of those who deny moral benefits of rhetoric, such as Ramus, are in fact making very strong moral claims.

2. I have offered an analysis of this passage from the *Rhetoric* in Garver, "Aristotle's." See also *Theaetetus* 172d.

3. The recent attempts by feminism to appropriate the Sophists are only the latest manifestation of this association of artful eloquence with extensions of democracy. For one example, see Jarratt.

4. I analyze Aristotle's distinction between the art of rhetoric and external motives in more detail in *Aristotle's Rhetoric: An Art of Character*. That book also contains a detailed explication of the distinction between aiming at winning and aiming at finding in any particular case the available means of persuasion. I hope that all other assertions about the *Rhetoric* for which there is no time for adequate argument in this chapter can be found to be convincingly proven in that book.

5. In denying that Aristotle's *Rhetoric* can improve a student's ability to write or speak, I realize that I am dismissing several contemporary attempts to use Aristotle to do just that, e.g., Horner; Gage; and Crowley. These works seem to me testimony to the talents of their authors and the richness of Aristotle's text. No law dictates that Aristotle's text can be understood only in the way I claim it is meant to be taken, and much intellectual progress is occasionally made by appropriating texts for purposes quite foreign to their intentions.

6. "*Homonoia* is not merely sharing a belief, since this might happen among people who do not know each other. Nor are people said to be in concord (*homonoia*) when they agree about just anything, e.g., on astronomical questions, since concord on these questions is not a feature of friendship. Rather a city is said to be in concord when [its citizens] agree about what is advantageous, make the same decision, and act on their common resolution" (*Ethics* IX.6.1167a22–30). See also IX.6.1167b3–4: "Concord, then, is apparently political friendship (*philia*) . . . for it is concerned with advantage and with what affects life."

7. It is beyond the scope of this paper but worth noting that the modesty of Aristotle's *Rhetoric* is matched by a corresponding modesty of the *Ethics* and *Politics*. Often what I call modesty is read as Aristotle's dispute with Plato, but I prefer to see it as internally motivated.

8. Sometimes the purpose of the invocation of expertise is precisely to destroy community and substitute domination, often justified by moral superiority—thus the expert who wants to interpret student evaluation forms for us to detect gender discrimination. Thus the politician who pronounces on the metaphysics of homosexuality—whether it is innate or acquired—in order to license discrimination, or on the metaphysics of personhood in order to remove questions about abortion from deliberation. On the homosexuality example, see Garver, "Philosophy." For an argument against esoteric biology as opposed to common knowledge in moral deliberation about abortion, see Hursthouse: "One cannot have the right or correct attitude to something if the attitude is based on or involves false beliefs. And this suggests that if the status of the foetus is relevant to the rightness or wrongness of abortion, its status must be known, as a truth, to the fully wise and virtuous person. . . . But the sort of wisdom that the fully virtuous person has is not supposed to be recondite; it does not call for fancy philosophical sophistication" (235).

9. For a different version of the way both rhetoricians and dialecticians argue both sides of a question, see Plato's *Phaedrus* 261c–d.

Works Cited

Aristotle. *Aristotelis Ars Rhetorica*. Trans. D. Rudolph Kassel. Berlin: De Gruyter, 1971.

———. *Aristotle's Eudemian Ethics*. Trans. Michael Woods. Oxford: Clarendon P, 1982.

———. *Metaphysics*. Trans. Hippocrates G. Apostle. Bloomington: Indiana UP, 1966.

———. *Nicomachean Ethics*. Trans. Terence C. Irwin. Indianapolis: Hackett, 1985.

———. *The Politics*. Trans. Carnes Lord. Chicago: U of Chicago P, 1984.

Burke, Kenneth. *Language as Symbolic Action: Essays on Life, Literature, and Method*. Berkeley: U of California P, 1966.

Cicero. *Cicero on Oratory and Orators*. Trans. J. S. Watson. Carbondale: Southern Illinois UP, 1970.

Crowley, Sharon. *Ancient Rhetorics for Contemporary Students*. New York: Macmillan, 1994.

Gage, John. *The Shape of Reason: Argumentative Writing in College*. New York: Macmillan, 1991.

Garver, Eugene. *Aristotle's Rhetoric: An Art of Character*. Chicago: U of Chicago P, 1994.

———. "Aristotle's *Rhetoric* on Unintentionally Hitting the Principles of the Sciences." *Rhetorica* 6 (1989): 381–93.

———. "Philosophy, Rhetoric and Pluralism." *Rhetoric and Hermeneutics in Our Time: A Reader*. Ed. Walter Jost and Michael Hyde. New Haven: Yale UP, 1996. 171–95.

Gellner, Ernest. "Trust, Cohesion, and the Social Order." *Trust: Making and Breaking Cooperative Relations*. Ed. Diego Gambetta. Cambridge, MA: Blackwell, 1988. 142–57.

Hirsch, E. D., Jr. *The Philosophy of Composition*. Chicago: U of Chicago P, 1977.

Horner, Winifred Bryan. *Rhetoric in the Classical Tradition*. New York: St. Martin's, 1988.

Hursthouse, Rosalind. "Virtue Theory and Abortion." *Virtue Ethics*. Ed. Daniel Statman. Washington, DC: Georgetown UP, 1997. 227–44.

Jarratt, Susan. *Rereading the Sophists: Classical Rhetoric Refigured*. Carbondale: Southern Illinois UP, 1991.

Lanham, Richard A. *The Electronic Word: Democracy, Technology, and the Arts*. Chicago: U of Chicago P, 1993.

Plato. *Gorgias*. Trans. W. C. Helmbold. New York: Macmillan, 1952.

———. *Plato's* Phaedrus. Trans. R. Hackforth. Cambridge: Cambridge UP, 1952.

———. *Theaetetus*. Trans. John McDowell. Oxford: Clarendon P, 1973.

Rousseau, Jean-Jacques. *The Social Contract and Discourses*. Ed. G. D. H. Cole. New York: Dutton, 1906.

CHAPTER SEVEN

Classical Rhetoric in American Writing Textbooks, 1950–1965

KAREN ROSSI SCHNAKENBERG
Carnegie Mellon University

The question that gave rise to the research presented here began with the kind of intellectual unease that Richard Young frequently refers to as a "felt difficulty." In this case, the difficulty involved a puzzlement I felt as I studied both classical rhetoric and the history of writing instruction within English departments. The difficulty gradually formalized into this question: Why did classical rhetoric, which has so much to offer writing instruction, have such a negligible impact on composition studies and writing instruction in the 1950s and early 1960s, a period generally characterized in our accounts of the period as one of renewed interest in rhetoric within English departments in U.S. colleges and universities?

The search for answers resulted in a broad study (Schnakenberg) that examined the social and disciplinary contexts within which the revival of interest in rhetoric in English departments took place, along with twentieth-century American scholarship on classical and Aristotelian rhetoric related to that revival, including histories of rhetoric, writing textbooks featuring classical rhetoric, and journal articles focusing on classical and Aristotelian rhetoric published in major journals in English and speech communication (*PMLA, College Composition and Communication, College English,* and the *Quarterly Journal of Speech*). That work demonstrates in detail both the broad range of sources and interpretations of classical rhetoric that were actually available to scholars seeking to explore classical rhetoric, and the very narrow subset of those sources that made their way into the journal articles and writing textbooks most frequently read by scholars with an interest in writing instruction. Among the study's many conclusions are several directly relevant to the topic of this chapter, the representations of classical and Aristotelian rhetoric in writing textbooks and the ways in which those representations enabled or discouraged the use and adaptation of classical rhetoric as a foundation for writing pedagogy.

The first of these findings was that advocacy for classical rhetoric within English departments was narrower and more scattered than prominent commentaries on the period have suggested (Berlin, *Rhetoric*, "Writing Instruction"; Russell; Connors, Ede, and Lunsford). Of the very small number of articles linking classical rhetoric and writing instruction published in *College English, College Composition and Communication*, and *PMLA* during the period,[1] only a small subset represented classical rhetoric positively or called for its direct revival and use. Far more common were characterizations that rejected classical rhetoric as hopelessly outdated (Keniston; Ohmann) or called for a limited revival under which classical rhetoric would be made available as a legitimating foundation for writing instruction but not used directly in any substantive way (Francis; Kitzhaber, "Freshman English," "New Perspectives"; Bailey; Booth, "Rhetorical," "Revival"; Burke; Christensen; Gorrell). Virginia Burke, for example, in a 1965 article titled "The Composition-Rhetoric Pyramid," nicely summarizes the limited revival view when she simultaneously calls for the revival of knowledge of classical rhetoric as a general framework and legitimating predecessor for writing instruction, advocates the development of a modern rhetoric "designed for the twentieth century milieu" (7), and warns against attempts to revive classical rhetoric that involve "gathering up unexamined scraps from the banquet of the ancients" (4). Like Burke, most who espouse this position are more concerned with developing what Kitzhaber describes as "a new and intellectually respectable curriculum" than with reviving or using any particular aspect of classical rhetoric ("4C" 129). Those very few articles that advocated a broad and specific revival of classical rhetoric—Bilsky et al.; Congleton; Corbett, "Usefulness"; and Hughes—constitute a small minority within a minority.

A second relevant finding was that those scholars who advocated a revival of classical rhetoric were linked in some substantive way to one of two widely different interpretive traditions, both of which featured narrow views of classical and Aristotelian rhetoric that limited its potential applicability to writing instruction: the philosophical but strongly logic-centered view of rhetoric associated with scholars at the University of Chicago, and the analytic and literary view of rhetoric associated with the Cornell school of rhetoric that emphasized the use of rhetorical concepts as a framework for the close reading of finished texts. Neither tradition emphasized rhetoric as a techne or art of production. In sum, even the very limited number of positive representations of classical rhetoric presented a truncated and therefore inadequate view of the complexity and range of both classical and Aristotelian rhetoric. In addition, these representations provided little in the way of the specific discussion of pedagogy that would have been needed to make the tenets of classical rhetoric a viable foundation for writing instruction.

The failure to provide both an adequate and accessible explanation of classical rhetoric and a related pedagogy takes on particular significance against the background of widespread ignorance of classical rhetoric within English departments and the common concerns underlying efforts to improve writing instruction during the period. The single most important factor in the resurgence of interest in classical rhetoric was a strong agreement both within and beyond academia that there was a crisis in writing instruction and, more specifically, that the prevailing method of instruction, now commonly referred to as the current-traditional approach, was ineffective. This perception of a crisis led to a broad search for new ideas and methods for teaching writing. In this search, scholars interested in improving writing instruction were concerned with identifying both a legitimating foundation for writing instruction and a related and specific pedagogy that could be widely and effectively adopted. While the concern for identifying a legitimating foundation has received attention in recent scholarship and even been characterized as the driving force behind representations of classical rhetoric (Berlin, "Revisionary"; Atwill), my close examination of the issues under debate in the 1950s indicates that scholars in English seeking to improve writing instruction were initially more concerned with identifying and implementing effective pedagogy. The search for a legitimating foundation, and related efforts to secure disciplinary status and institutional respect for writing instruction, did become more prominent in the early to mid-1960s, but even in that period the concern for effective writing instruction carried at least equal weight (Schnakenberg).

In the search for both a foundational grounding and a related method for writing instruction, classical rhetoric was put forward as a potential candidate by a very small number of individuals and competed, largely unsuccessfully, with several other candidates, including literature, communication theory, structural linguistics, and current-traditional rhetoric (Young and Goggin 1993). In the intense competition and jockeying for position that the multiplicity of candidates produced, classical rhetoric began with a distinct disadvantage for two prominent reasons. First, it was virtually unknown to all but a handful of scholars within English departments. Second, it faced the double stigma of being linked negatively to propaganda and manipulation in the postwar period and of being generally perceived as "old" and "outdated" in a period when "new" and "modern" were highly valorized concepts.

Disciplinary Role and Status of Writing Textbooks

The representations of classical, and most commonly Aristotelian, rhetoric presented in writing textbooks published between 1950 and 1965 are of particular significance to the question at issue here because of the unusual relationship between textbooks and scholarship in writing instruction. While scholarship is conventionally viewed as the main avenue through which new knowledge and theory are developed within a discipline, textbooks tend to be seen as vehicles for reflecting and transmitting the established facts, theories, and procedures that have been determined and modified through scholarship (Kuhn; Rothman; Olsen; Connors, "Textbooks"). What this traditional view overlooks, however, is that the relationship between scholarship and textbooks is not consistent across or even within disciplines. Within disciplines such as the hard sciences that Kuhn, for example, uses as his paradigm cases, textbooks and scholarship do frequently share a "coevolutionary socioculture" in which scholarship constantly works to advance the state of knowledge preserved in the texts, and textbooks change mainly in response to perceived gaps between their representation of the field and current knowledge as represented in the scholarship (Connors, "Textbooks" 190). Textbooks change, in effect, when they need to "catch up" to developments in the field.

This relationship is somewhat different, however, in fields such as writing instruction in which there is neither a single agreed-upon disciplinary foundation nor an accepted body of precepts and procedures. Under these conditions, textbooks tend to define rather than reflect accepted theory, subject matter, and method (Woods; Connors, "Rise"). As Welch has succinctly noted, "The power of the printed word dominates change in the teaching of writing" ("Reply" 367). Under these conditions, textbooks tend to structure both classroom instruction and teachers' knowledge of the field.

The potential for textbooks to define a field does not, however, necessarily imply that fields such as writing instruction undergo constant change. In periods when there is little scholarship to prompt change from within and no external impetus to encourage change from without, new textbooks will tend to resemble their predecessors. A clear example here is the dominance of the four-modes approach through the first half of this century (Connors, "Rise"; Fogarty). In periods when internal or external circumstances prompt change, scholars, unconstrained by strong linkage to an underlying discipline, have the opportunity to use textbooks as vehicles to introduce radically different approaches or to graft new approaches onto the old. Although both responses are possible, a combination of training, habit, and market forces will tend to encourage grafting.

According to Connors, the conditions just described influenced writing-textbook production and reception in the 1950s and early 1960s when postwar demands for practical literacy prompted strong calls for change in writing instruction ("Rise," "Textbooks"). Connors documents something of a shift during this period away from textbooks based on the four modes of discourse and toward texts that featured literary study or were based on a variety of approaches related to the communications and general semantics movements. A similar change occurred in the late 1960s and into the 1970s, but in this period the new approaches tended to draw more on linguistics, transformational grammar, theories of artistic expression, and developmental, social, and cognitive psychology (Berlin, *Rhetoric*). The textbooks written under these conditions do introduce new material, but they tend, more often than not, to blend the new material with an ample measure of content and approaches drawn from prior textbooks (Connors, "Textbooks").

The tendency for the old to dominate, or at least provide a situating context for, the new has at least three powerful sources. First, because textbooks are primarily commercial products, a combination of old and new will often be encouraged and perhaps even required by publishers, who both seek a reasonable profit and recognize the often conservative tendencies of textbook adoption committees. This conservative impulse is more than understandable given the potential for fragmentation in the textbook market and the fact that a familiar and widely adopted composition text such as McCrimmon's *Writing with a Purpose*, a modal text first introduced in the mid-1950s, can sell between forty and fifty thousand copies a year (Winterowd). A second, somewhat subtler but probably more important source of conservatism is that authors of writing textbooks have, at least until quite recently, learned most of what they know about writing instruction through exposure to existing textbooks rather than through training or research in a foundational discipline. Thus, even when they draw from other disciplines and seek to introduce new knowledge and methods in their texts, their own perceptions and approaches are strongly influenced by prior textbooks as well as their own experience and training. A third and closely related factor is that writing textbooks frequently serve as primers for both teachers and their students (Applebee; Welch, "Ideology"). Authors facing the daunting task of introducing new material to subject-matter novices may find it necessary to situate new concepts and procedures within a context of familiar ones. Given these conditions, it is not surprising that the process of introducing and institutionalizing change in writing textbooks and methods of instruction is quite slow, even when new and relevant knowledge and methods are available in preceding scholarship and when the textbooks are written by scholars who themselves participate in that scholarship (Stewart; Rose; Woods; Johnson).

Four composition textbooks seeking to introduce elements of classical rhetoric into writing instruction in the 1950s and early 1960s—Richard Weaver's *Composition: A Course in Writing and Rhetoric*, Manuel Bilsky's *Logic and Effective Argument*, Richard Hughes and Albert Duhamel's *Rhetoric: Principles and Usage*, and Edward P. J. Corbett's *Classical Rhetoric for the Modern Student*—illustrate the difficulties of introducing change into writing instruction, of translating disciplinary knowledge into effective pedagogy, and of producing permanent change in a field with no agreed-upon disciplinary foundation. They also illustrate the essential conservatism of textbooks within such a discipline and the ways in which this conservatism affected early efforts to introduce elements of classical and Aristotelian rhetoric into writing instruction.

1950s Writing Textbooks Introducing Elements of Classical Rhetoric

Two composition textbooks published during the 1950s by scholars affiliated with the University of Chicago are notable for both their introduction of terms and concepts from classical rhetoric and their restricted representation of rhetoric as an art of logical argument. Richard Weaver's 1957 *Composition: A Course in Writing and Rhetoric*, like the majority of comprehensive writing textbooks prominent in the period, is structured around the four modes of discourse—exposition, description, narration, and argument. Within this traditional framework, the text emphasizes the specific characteristics of each mode and distinctions among them. The modal approach emphasizes the final form of a discourse and gives little attention to rhetorical concerns such as purpose, audience, and context. Weaver's text also resembles other texts of the period in including a handbook, a set of readings, and extensive discussions of paragraph and sentence structure. Despite its resemblance to other modal texts, however, it was considered unusual at the time because of its stress on rhetoric and argument and its inclusion of a section on "the now almost totally neglected 'topics' of persuasion" ("Among the New Texts" 253).

Bilsky's 1956 text, although much shorter than Weaver's (104 pages in the 1963 revised edition compared to 670 pages for Weaver's 1967 second edition), discusses argument—its sole focus—in more detail and gives it significantly more prominence. Both texts, however, strongly emphasize the logical elements of argument. Weaver, in his section on Deduction, focuses exclusively on logical argument that is patterned on the syllogism and evaluated according to the rules of formal logic. In fact, Weaver's focus on logic is unrelenting. He never mentions ethical or pathetic appeals, does not distinguish between probable and absolute premises in syllogisms, and defines the enthymeme as a syllogism or "deductive argument with one of its propositions . . . missing" (133). Bilsky also emphasizes logical argument but in a less unrelenting manner. Bilsky defines argument as the central task and genre of composition rather than simply one of four modes, but he closely associates argument with logic and "informative" language and pointedly directs students to avoid "expressive" terms which convey feelings and emotions (13). Bilsky does differ from Weaver in alluding to the power of expressive language but takes pains to link such language negatively to advertising, drama, and political speeches. Students are directed to keep to the "neutral" territory of informative language and clear logic.[2]

Unlike Weaver, Bilsky does allow for probability in inductive argument and plausibility in what he refers to as "practical arguments," but he focuses mainly on deductive arguments governed by the rules of formal logic. His strong preference for formal logic is evident in his early statement that "[n]o degrees of validity are possible; the argument is either valid or invalid" (22), and in his strong focus on the rules of syllogistic reasoning (37–39) and the "form" rather than the content of argument (26). Like Weaver, he refers almost exclusively to syllogistic rather than enthymematic reasoning and defines the enthymeme as a syllogism with one or more missing parts (43). The majority of Bilsky's text is devoted to "empirical patterns" (87) of deduction and induction, with the final fourteen pages reserved for "Practical Patterns," i.e., arguments that involve judgments or values. Bilsky notes that such arguments are "extremely pervasive" and cover "a vast area" in which the empirical patterns "are neither directly available nor immediately appropriate except in a highly attenuated form" (87). Although he touches on the relation of practical arguments to judgments and values and concedes that their effectiveness "depends partly on situation" (91), he seeks to ground them as much as possible in "rational, logical arguments" (89) by focusing on "the relevance of the reasons offered" (90) as a primary measure of effectiveness.

Thus, in both Weaver's and Bilsky's texts we see rhetoric defined primarily in terms of patterns of argument, and argument defined primarily in terms of deductive reasoning carried out by means of syllogisms. Ethical and pathetic appeals are either ignored or strongly discouraged. One possible explanation, supported by statements in Weaver's preface, is that ethical and pathetic appeals are considered so odious, inappropriate, and thoroughly linked to emotional manipulation that it seems best to ignore them. Rather than present logic as an antidote to emotional appeals, they present it as a substitute. For Weaver, a second explanation grows out of his Platonic view of rhetoric and dialectic as related but "distinguishable stages of argumentation" (*Ethics of Rhetoric* 27). Dialectic is said to precede rhetoric and to secure the "truth," which rhetoric then presents. In this view, logical argument and formal logic are considered the appropriate means of conveying established truth, and all other types of appeals or forms of arguments are either extraneous or detrimental.

Bilsky explicitly claims an Aristotelian framework, but his emphasis on logical argument suggests more affinity with the *Organon* and the interpretive tradition in philosophy that views Aristotelian rhetoric as primarily logical than with the *Rhetoric* itself. In sum, both texts reflect the valorization of logic over rhetoric and the absolute over the contingent (Florescu). From the perspective of the late 1990s, both texts are notable for what is missing: context, contingency, audience, emotion, and forms of argument other than the syllogism.

Hughes and Duhamel's *Rhetoric: Principles and Usage*

I turned to Hughes and Duhamel's 1962 *Rhetoric: Principles and Usage* with high expectations because of the distinctive and promising view of Aristotelian rhetoric as a "generative" and "creative" art that Hughes presented in his 1965 article on "The Contemporaneity of Classical Rhetoric." In that article, in a position that foreshadows later discussions of what is frequently referred to as "the rhetorical turn," Hughes presents argument as the dominant form of discourse that subsumes exposition, narration, and description. The last three are presented as forms or shapes that a particular argument may take (158). Additionally, Hughes argues that the creation of an argument is not a straightforward process that begins with the writer knowing what she wants to say and then finding a form in which to say it, but rather is the end result of a "gradual evolution of a judgment out of disparate and embryonic evidence, the formulation of the realized judgment in the rhetor's own mind" (158).

Hughes's view of the role of the topics as inventional strategies is similarly distinctive. While many in the period, including Corbett, viewed the topics as a system for determining how best to present a previously established judgment, Hughes's article presents the rhetor as one who, using the resources of rhetorical invention, most notably the topics, "discovers a judgment in an area where experience is still flexible enough to take many shapes" (158). Both rhetoric and the topics deal with "the area of probabilities . . . where separate items of experience have not yet evolved into a reality" (158). In other words, something new, something which did not previously exist, comes into being through the creative inquiry initiated by the rhetor.

Unfortunately, the conception of rhetoric instantiated in the 1962 text that Hughes co-authored with Albert Duhamel owes more to current-traditional rhetoric and literary criticism than to either the *Rhetoric* itself or to the rich conception of classical and Aristotelian rhetoric presented in Hughes's article. Although Hughes and Duhamel label their approach as essentially Aristotelian, they organize their text according to the four modes. This organization is not immediately apparent because the text is nominally arranged in three main sections that suggest a break from the modes approach: Organization, Invention, and Style. The link to the modes approach becomes clear, however, in Section I, Organization, which includes chapters on three of the four traditional modes—description, narration, and exposition. The fourth mode, argumentation, is discussed in Section II, under Invention. Although even considering invention is certainly an innovation, Hughes and Duhamel limit invention to argument and restrict argument primarily to logical reasoning, thus reflecting prior textbook approaches more closely than the classical or Aristotelian rhetoric they claim as their framework.

Hughes and Duhamel's text nicely illustrates how adoption (and adaptation) of classical rhetoric was influenced by a confluence of often disparate assumptions. The interpretations of rhetoric presented in the text show strong influence from formal logic, literary study, preceding writing textbooks and composition practice, psychological research on image and motivation, and preceding interpretations of classical rhetoric. Like Weaver's and Bilsky's earlier textbooks, Hughes and Duhamel's illustrates an often uneasy alliance of classical and contemporary assumptions. The Aristotelian tradition provides the nominal framework, but classical rhetoric often seems less important than the literary, logical, and social science influences.

The strong literary and current-traditional influence is evident in a number of features in addition to the modal framework, most notably the pervasive focus on text and text features, a strong emphasis on close reading as the first step in learning to write, and the use of literary texts for a substantial portion of the model texts to be analyzed and imitated. The influence of work in logic and prior scholarship on the *Rhetoric* is similarly evident. Enthymemes, for example, are treated as truncated syllogisms and restricted to logical appeals (228). The section on invention does discuss ethical and emotional appeals in addition to logical ones, but the authors' preference for the logical is clear in both the amount and type of attention given to logic. Logical appeals are treated first, presented as the essence of argument and proof, and given more text space and detail than other types. Appeals based on "image" and "emotion" are labeled as "extralogical" (353), and emotional appeals are associated with "the irrational in human behavior" (338) and the "prejudices" of the audience (340). Drawing on social science research and Vance Packard's *The Hidden Persuaders*, Hughes and Duhamel reluctantly acknowledge that Aristotle was correct in understanding that the ethical appeal "is, indeed, the strongest argument for or against a proposition" (351), but they present the audience's tendency to accept extralogical appeals as a regrettable weakness. That the emphasis on logic is influenced by Cold War concerns is evident in their inclusion of a 1937 article on "How to Detect Propaganda" as part of the text. The obvious concern with countering propaganda, coupled with the strong associations between propaganda, manipulative emotionalism, and non-logical appeals, creates a situation in which a strong emphasis on logic seems to be both appropriate and necessary.

Like the earlier texts written by Bilsky and Weaver, Hughes and Duhamel's text is notable for the amount of attention it gives to argument, but it is still ultimately a modal text with modifications in the argument section drawn primarily from prior work in logic. In this text, invention and the topics are presented as methods for discovering preexisting evidence, and argument and logic are methods for presenting and testing, rather than creating, positions.

Corbett's *Classical Rhetoric for the Modern Student*

Corbett's *Classical Rhetoric for the Modern Student* was both the first and the most widely adopted modern rhetoric textbook to be based primarily on classical rhetoric. First published in 1965, the text was issued in a third printing by 1966 and a second edition by 1971, although its popularity as a composition text had already waned somewhat by that time (Corbett, *Classical*). At least as important as its use as a writing text, however, was its influence as one of the main sources through which many scholars active in rhetorical studies in English today first encountered the classical tradition and its history.[3] The 1990 publication of its third edition, identical to the original in all significant interpretive and pedagogical aspects, attests to its continuing importance, as does the recent publication of composition texts grounded in classical rhetoric—notably Horner's *Rhetoric in the*

Classical Tradition and Crowley's *Ancient Rhetorics for Contemporary Students*—that pay explicit homage to Corbett and would most likely not have existed without Corbett's pioneering work.

Two elements of the text deserve particular attention in terms of this investigation of the revival of interest in classical and Aristotelian rhetoric and its influence on writing instruction: Corbett's specific interpretation of classical rhetoric and his pedagogy based on that rhetoric.

Classical Rhetoric from Corbett's Perspective

Corbett's distinctive interpretation of classical rhetoric is presented in both the thirty-three-page "A Survey of Rhetoric" at the end of the text and the detailed explications of classical rhetoric presented throughout the text. Although the title and Corbett's consistent references to "classical rhetoric" imply that the work draws on a broad tradition, the conception of rhetoric he presents is based primarily on ideas drawn from Aristotle's *Rhetoric* and the interpretive scholarship on it. The survey covers the 2,500-year span from 500 B.C. through the nineteenth century. Classical rhetoric is covered in nine pages, of which two are specifically devoted to Aristotle. The most important point about this historical survey is that Corbett, like Donald Clark and Thonssen and Baird, on whom he explicitly relies, tends to simplify and overextend the role of Aristotle and the *Rhetoric* in rhetorical history. Using an influence-tracing approach as his framework, Corbett presents Aristotle as the central figure whose seminal ideas are influenced, extended, contracted, and challenged by other theorists.[4] As Carole Blair and others have recently noted, this approach distorts the history of rhetorical theory and practice by concealing the variety and particularity of the broad range of approaches covered under the general heading of classical rhetoric.

Although the section of the survey that focuses directly on classical rhetoric is quite short, it is important because it emphasizes elements of Aristotelian rhetoric that had little exposure or currency within works directly addressed to scholars in English at the time. In a section that strongly echoes Warner Jaeger and quotes directly from Lane Cooper's commentary on the *Rhetoric*, Corbett argues that Aristotle developed his treatise as a counter to Plato's negative views of rhetoric, and that it was the philosophical nature of Aristotle's treatise that influenced not only Cicero and Quintilian, but also the rhetoric of the Middle Ages, of the Renaissance, and of modern times, all of which, in their "best elements," have been and are "essentially Aristotelian" (540).[5] More specifically, Corbett works to counter contemporary criticisms of the *Rhetoric* as an overly narrow and pragmatic handbook focusing primarily on logical argument. Corbett stresses that Aristotle emphasized the substance rather than the language of discourse and developed a set of abstract first principles to demonstrate that rhetoric is an "art" or "a teachable and systematic discipline" rather than a mere "knack" (539). As Richard Young's influential work on invention has demonstrated, this conception of rhetoric as a teachable "art" is critically important because it provides both a rationale for viewing rhetoric as a disciplinary foundation for a broad range of inquiry and the specific key to developing writing pedagogy grounded in a rhetorical perspective.

For Corbett, the key to Aristotle's approach to rhetoric is a combination of this philosophical emphasis and Aristotle's recognition "that *probability* is the basis of the persuasive art" (emphasis in original). For Corbett, as for Aristotle, rhetoric's dependence on probability is not, as Plato had insisted, a defect; it is instead a significant and defining characteristic of rhetoric (540). And it is precisely this emphasis on probability that allows Corbett to make the important move away from the prevailing emphasis on logical appeals and toward an approach that stresses the necessary interrelationship of ethical, pathetic, and logical appeals.

The conception of classical rhetoric featured in the survey is echoed throughout the textbook. Distinctive features include a clear move away from the four-modes approach, a stress on the probable and contingent nature of rhetorical argument, a detailed discussion of invention, and an integrated presentation of the three types of appeals. Unlike Hughes and Duhamel, Bilsky, or Weaver, all of whom valorize logical appeals and either ignore or strongly criticize ethical and pathetic ones, Corbett clearly argues for the existence, importance, and interdependence of all three. Corbett's text does show a preference for logical appeals as the mainstay of any argument (20), does argue that it would be preferable if all persuasion took place through appeals to reason (80), and does devote significantly more text space to appeals to reason than to the other two.[6] Nevertheless, as Berlin has noted, Corbett is alone in the period in consistently emphasizing the necessary reliance of all argument on all three types of appeals and thus providing "a holistic response to experience" (*Rhetoric* 157).

Corbett's treatment of logical and ethical appeals nicely illustrates the way in which his text both reflects preceding work and begins to move beyond it. Corbett's extensive treatment of logical appeals, and several explicit statements that he prefers them, firmly position the text within the context and tradition of prior work. At the same time, Corbett's discussions of ethos, pathos, and logos are strikingly different from related discussions in prior texts and scholarship and much more closely reflective of Aristotle's presentation of the three types of appeals in the *Rhetoric*. In the American scholarship focusing on the *Rhetoric* that preceded Corbett's text, only McBurney ("Some Recent," "Place"), Bryant, and Grimaldi had presented similar characterizations. In the discussion of the ethical appeal, Corbett parallels Aristotle on a number of points: the assertion that ethical appeals "can be the most effective" type, especially with regard to "matters about which absolute certainty is impossible and opinions are divided"; the importance of ethical appeals in deliberative rhetoric; the insistence that ethical appeals should have their effect "through the speech itself" rather than through prior knowledge of the speakers or their reputations; and discussions of the ethical appeals in relation to both arrangement and style.

The discussion of emotional appeals is somewhat less dependent on Aristotle and relies more heavily on ideas drawn from Campbell and Whately. To the Aristotelian perspective that emotional appeals are integral and necessary parts of all persuasion, Corbett adds the faculty psychology view that emotional appeals influence the will, logical appeals influence reason, and the two act in tandem to produce both reasoned assent and emotional willingness to act in accordance with that assent. Corbett's approach is particularly noteworthy for its calm insistence that "[t]here is nothing necessarily reprehensible about being moved to action through our emotions; in fact, it is perfectly normal" (86). Like Aristotle, Campbell, and Whately, and unlike much of the preceding work that valorized logic, Corbett accepts and even champions the ethical and emotional as necessary parts of human nature and thus of all discourse.

Corbett's treatment of enthymemes and syllogisms shows a similarly distinct mixture of reliance on prior scholarship and a return to specifically Aristotelian concepts. Corbett presents the enthymeme as both an "abbreviated syllogism" (7, 62) in the tradition of prior texts and as "a deductive argument based on probable premises" defined as both "what usually or generally happens but also . . . what people believe to be true" (63). He clearly distinguishes between syllogisms and enthymemes on the basis of the nature of their premises (absolute vs. contingent) and conclusions (necessary vs. probable) but, significantly, presents both syllogisms and enthymemes as working on the same general pattern and principles.

In sum, Corbett's presentation of classical rhetoric is both strongly dependent on a range of preceding scholarship on Aristotle's *Rhetoric* and distinct from the logic-centered view of classical rhetoric presented in other composition texts of the period that drew on classical rhetoric for at least part of their framework.

Corbett's Pedagogy

While Corbett's representation of classical rhetoric breaks with prior work in significant ways, his pedagogy is squarely in the tradition of preceding textbooks on both composition and rhetorical criticism. The relationship is particularly marked in Corbett's approach to invention and his very narrow and limited treatment of purpose, audience, and context as factors affecting discourse. The most striking resemblances involve Corbett's consistent focus on texts as products that package what a writer has previously determined to say and his cursory treatment of both the situations in which texts function and the relationships between writers and their audiences (McNally).

In view of both Corbett's comments on audience and context in "The Usefulness of Classical Rhetoric" and his strong statement in the textbook itself that rhetoric concerns "a specific kind of discourse directed to a definite audience for a particular purpose" (32), his treatment of purpose, context, and audience is puzzlingly limited. Although Corbett refers approvingly to Aristotle's "stress on the audience as the chief informing principle in persuasive discourse" (540), the text actually includes little specific discussion of audience or audience differences and how these might affect a writer's options and choices. Corbett's virtual silence on this point leads to an inference that all audiences are basically alike, an inference supported by his comment that "rhetoric is the practical art by which we learn how to manipulate all the available means of persuading a large, heterogeneous, perhaps uneducated audience" (39). Throughout the text, Corbett assumes that all rhetorical audiences are equivalent and that the choice of approach is governed more by the subject matter and the writer's point of view than by audience or purpose. The approach is ultimately audience- or writer-centered rather than reader-centered.

Purpose is addressed only broadly in terms of the writer's general aim of gaining acceptance for a given thesis or proposal. One explanation for this broad treatment may lie in Corbett's adoption of Aristotle's three types of persuasive discourse—deliberative, forensic, and epideictic—as a "well-nigh exhaustive" (28) classification of the purposes of discourse and thus presumably a sufficient definition of purpose. Corbett's limited approach to purpose is typified in the section on the special topics, which Corbett argues are valuable to composition because "once the student has determined which of the three kinds of rhetorical discourse he is committed to, he knows immediately what his general objective is and also the more or less special kinds of arguments that he must pursue to attain his objective" (133). A similarly broad treatment of purpose is obvious in the analyses of sample readings provided as exemplars for students to follow. In these analyses, purpose is handled simply by labeling the type of rhetoric involved in a manner that closely resembles the techniques of neo-Aristotelian rhetorical criticism. The first edition of Corbett's text surprisingly did not even include explanatory headnotes on the authors or contexts for each reading.[7] A final telling point is that the index includes no listings for "purpose," "aim," "context," "situation," or related terms.

Throughout the text, Corbett focuses on the activity of the rhetor and very specifically on the activity of a student writer. This emphasis might lead one to expect at least some emphasis on invention, but such discussion is oddly limited. Nowhere is this more marked than in the five-page section on discovery of arguments that begins with a section on formulating a thesis. This section is the closest Corbett comes to outlining any procedures for beginning a composition, but his inventional focus is clearly limited by the precedent of current-traditional pedagogy. The student writer, who is assumed to have a "subject" in mind, is directed to use status theory as a quick method for defining a specific thesis about that subject in one declarative sentence. There is no discussion of how the writer is to come to the conclusion or how it may be developed or modified in the process of developing an argument to support it. Further, neither purpose nor context nor audience is mentioned as a factor that might influence the formulation of a thesis and its development or potential effectiveness.

Berlin attributes Corbett's limited view of invention to an underlying positivist philosophy ("Contemporary," *Rhetoric*). Lauer, I suspect, comes closer to the mark when she notes the strong influence of the current-traditional approach on Corbett's text. Corbett, Lauer argues, follows current-traditional precedent, which "sees the exploratory act of invention as coming into play after the writer has a judgment" (132). This approach "leaves the discovery of the thesis to other arts like dialectic or to the writer's unaided talents" and thus focuses on developing material to support an already determined conclusion. Although the current-traditional approach is, as Berlin has effectively argued, strongly grounded in a positivist philosophy, I suspect, along with Lauer, that it is the influence of precedents provided by current-traditional pedagogy rather than a strong acceptance of a positivist philosophy that is responsible for Corbett's approach. I see this as a defensible position because Corbett so strongly embraces Aristotle's grounding distinction that rhetoric is a necessary art distinct from logic and dialectic precisely because so many aspects of human experience fall within the realm of the contingent rather than that of the absolutely provable.

From the perspective of the new millennium, one can easily find problems in both Corbett's pedagogy and his representation of classical rhetoric, but it is important to view Corbett's text from the standpoint of its distinctiveness and importance in 1965 and within English studies. Quite simply, Corbett provided the fullest explanation of classical and Aristotelian rhetoric directed to scholars and teachers in English studies at the time and one which stressed important features of classical rhetoric that had been obscured or distorted in preceding work. Corbett's text is particularly notable for its strong assertions that rhetoric is a learnable and teachable "art," that it involves situations in which probable rather than certain knowledge is all that is possible, and that this dependency on probability is a defining characteristic of rhetoric rather than a lamentable flaw. Additionally, Corbett's conception of classical rhetoric is important for its insistence that logical, ethical, and emotional appeals are mutually necessary and interdependent components of all persuasive discourse. Finally, it must be noted that Corbett's text, in conjunction with related scholarship, introduced students and scholars within English who had little prior exposure to classical rhetoric to a conceptual vocabulary that provided a lingua franca, allowing detailed and technical discussion of discourse to develop.

Of the small group of scholars in English discussing classical rhetoric in any detail in the period under examination, Corbett comes closest to providing a useful combination of theory and method. Even he ultimately falls short, however, because he presents classical rhetoric as a closed system applicable to a relatively narrow range of discourse and provides a severely limited view of invention. An additional shortcoming is that his pedagogy emphasizes analysis rather than production. Corbett provides little to no guidance on how to use rhetoric productively, an obviously crucial need in writing instruction. A final, and perhaps critical, problem is that Corbett's text pays only passing attention to situational factors that give rise to discourse and thus tends to present rhetoric as an arhetorical, presentational art rather than a purpose-directed use of language within specific situations. Corbett has surely done the most to introduce classical rhetoric to a generation of scholars through his teaching, text, and publications, but his textbook serves ultimately more as an introduction to the features of Aristotelian rhetoric as filtered through neo-Aristotelian rhetorical criticism and current-traditional rhetoric than as either a full explanation of classical or Aristotelian rhetoric or a text on writing instruction. In short, if we look at the situation of the 1950s and early 1960s in English as one of a problem looking for a solution, it is quite clear why classical rhetoric as presented in the writing textbooks of the period would not have been seen as providing a usable or appropriate solution.

Observations on Textbooks and the Revival of Classical Rhetoric

Both Berlin ("Revisionary") and Atwill have recently argued that the failure of scholars in English to produce a usable combination of rhetorical theory and practical pedagogy in the 1960s was the direct result of their preoccupation with establishing a disciplinary grounding for writing instruction. Berlin makes the general argument that this search for disciplinary grounding led to a treatment of rhetoric as intellectual history and theory rather than as a situated use of language arising from specific material and social practices ("Revisionary" 135–36). Atwill argues a similar point with specific reference to Grimaldi's interpretation of Aristotle's *Rhetoric*. According to Atwill, Aristotle presented rhetoric primarily as a productive rather than a theoretical art, but a hegemonic push for disciplinarity, coupled with disciplinary disdain for mere practice and production, led scholars such as Grimaldi to represent the *Rhetoric* as strongly philosophical so that it might be claimed as an appropriate theoretical basis for a discipline.

While disciplinary concerns were evident features of the revival of interest in rhetoric in the early 1960s, I doubt that Atwill is correct in her judgment that the theoretical "bias" she observes in Grimaldi's work is broadly responsible for a deliberate neglect of method and pedagogy, especially in works such as the textbooks examined in this study. In view of the nature of the preceding scholarship, it seems more likely that a plausible reason for the lack of specific attention to production was quite simply a combination of the influence of the preceding scholarship that was Corbett's and other scholars' main source of information on classical rhetoric and the textbook writers' own prior training and interests. The speech communication scholarship on which Corbett strongly relies, for example, tends to use Aristotelian rhetoric as a framework for critical analysis of existing texts rather than as a guide to the invention and production of new discourse. Thus it provides few precedents for a useful writing pedagogy. When scholars such as Hughes and Corbett, strongly sympathetic to classical rhetoric and strongly interested in reviving it as a resource for contemporary theory and practice, attempt to translate their interest into instructional texts, they are, I would argue, more hampered by a combination of their own knowledge and training and the characteristics of the source texts upon which they draw than by specific intent to promote disciplinary interests.

Finally, however, it is important to emphasize that neither Bilsky nor Weaver nor Hughes and Duhamel nor Corbett succeeded in providing the necessary combination of a full and relevant theory and a specific method or pedagogy that would have been needed to make classical rhetoric a viable foundation for writing instruction. Despite this lack, the texts are important for what they do introduce to composition studies. The texts are also important for what they illustrate about the essential conservatism of textbooks and the ways in which this conservatism affected early efforts to reintroduce classical rhetoric into writing instruction. This conservatism is important because, as Applebee succinctly argues, "textbooks are in charge of training writing teachers before they teach the students" (127). Thus the representations of classical rhetoric instantiated in textbooks have the potential to be immediately and perhaps ultimately more influential than the theories upon which they are based.

Notes

1. In the period from 1950 to 1965, *PMLA* published only three relevant articles: Wayne Booth's 1965 "The Revival of Rhetoric," a transcript of a talk Booth delivered at the MLA convention in 1964, and articles by Keniston and Wimsatt that draw on Highet's strong rejection of the classical tradition and offer similar rejections of Aristotelian rhetoric as overly narrow, logical, and outdated. Of the 612 articles with a focus on rhetoric or composition published in *CCC* and *CE* from 1950 to 1965, only 40 (roughly 7 percent) included content in what Virginia Burke (1965) disparagingly referred to as the "hucksterism" of using concepts related to classical rhetoric (Young and Goggin). Further, more than a few of these 40 articles engage the term *rhetoric* as an enticement to potential readers rather than as an accurate description of the content of the article. When I examined these 40 items (along with all other articles published in these journals in the period) with the goal of locating articles with a substantive focus on classical rhetoric, whether positive or negative, the set of relevant articles shrank to 16. Further detail and analysis can be found in Schnakenberg.

2. In making this point, Bilsky discusses making a choice between the words *nigger* and *Negro*. He recommends avoiding *nigger* because "the connotations—the feelings it would arouse" would be more likely to incite action rather than convey information. *Negro* is defined as "the more neutral term" and recommended as more appropriate because it conveys information without provoking feeling.

3. Current scholars explicitly acknowledging Corbett as their introduction to classical rhetoric include, as one might expect, many who studied with him: Sharon Crowley, Robert Connors, Andrea Lunsford, Lisa Ede, and Winifred Horner. Given that one of the reasons the second edition was published in 1971 was a recognition that the text was being used in graduate level courses in rhetoric (Corbett, *Classical*), it seems likely that Connors in *Selected Essays* and Berlin in *Rhetoric* are accurate in their similar assessments that Corbett was the most influential spokesperson for the revival of classical rhetoric writing in the 1960s.

4. The characterization of Aristotle as the center of classical rhetoric is not unique to this item in Corbett's impressive list of scholarship but appears consistently throughout his works. At various times, Corbett refers to Aristotle as, for example, the "fountainhead" ("Usefulness"), the "originator" ("Rhetoric"), and the "underpinning" ("Changing") of classical rhetoric.

5. Corbett is quoting the first page (xvii) of the introduction to Cooper's translation. Corbett acknowledges Cooper as the source but does not supply the specific reference.

6. Corbett's preference for logical argument is evident in a number of features of his text, beginning with the discussion of ethos, pathos, and logos in relation to a passage from the *Iliad* in the first chapter. In this discussion, Corbett argues that logical arguments are generally tried first, but if these fail, we then attempt to move our audiences by appealing to their emotions or by relying on the strength of our character as presented in the discourse (20). This preference for logical argument is carried throughout the text. The main section on the appeal to reason covers forty text pages, for example, while only six pages are devoted to the ethical appeal and eight to the emotional appeal. Additionally, the bulk of the forty-eight-page section on the common and special topics focuses on using the topics in logical argument. Exceptions here include the eight-page section on testimony, including a discussion of authority, testimonial, statistics, and maxim, all of which rely wholly or partly on ethical appeals, and scattered comments on the emotional appeal in relation to the topics. It is important to note, however, that Corbett does define the topics as a method "to aid the speaker in discovering matter for the three modes of appeal" (24).

7. Headnotes providing some contextual information for each reading were added to the 1971 second edition.

Works Cited

"Among the New Texts." *College Composition and Communication* 8 (1957): 253.

Applebee, Arthur N. *Tradition and Reform in the Teaching of English: A History.* Urbana, IL: NCTE, 1974.

Atwill, Janet. "Instituting the Art of Rhetoric: Theory, Practice, and Productive Knowledge in Interpretations of Aristotle's *Rhetoric.*" *Rethinking the History of Rhetoric: Multidisciplinary Essays on the Rhetorical Tradition.* Ed. Takis Poulakos. Boulder: Westview, 1993. 91–118.

Bailey, Dudley. "A Plea for a Modern Set of Topoi." *College English* 26 (1964): 111–17.

Berlin, James A. "Contemporary Composition: The Major Pedagogical Theories." *College English* 44 (1982): 765–77.

————. "Revisionary History: The Dialectical Method." *Rethinking the History of Rhetoric: Multidisciplinary Essays on the Rhetorical Tradition.* Ed. Takis Poulakos. Boulder: Westview, 1993. 135–51.

————. *Rhetoric and Reality: Writing Instruction in American Colleges, 1900–1985.* Carbondale: Southern Illinois UP, 1987.

————. "Writing Instruction in School and College English, 1890–1985." *A Short History of Writing Instruction from Ancient Greece to Twentieth-Century America.* Ed. James J. Murphy. Davis, CA: Hermagoras, 1990. 183–220.

Bilsky, Manuel. *Logic and Effective Argument.* New York: Holt, 1956.

Bilsky, Manuel, M. Hazlett, R. Streeter, and R. Weaver. "Looking for an Argument." *College English* 14 (1953): 210–16.

Blair, Carole. "Contested Histories of Rhetoric: The Politics of Presentation, Progress, and Change." *Quarterly Journal of Speech* 78 (1992): 403–28.

Booth, Wayne. "The Revival of Rhetoric." *PMLA* 80 (1965): 8–12. Rpt. in *New Rhetorics.* Ed. Martin Steinmann. New York: Scribner, 1967. 1–15.

————. "The Rhetorical Stance." *College Composition and Communication* 14 (1963): 139–45.

Bryant, Donald C. "Aspects of the Rhetorical Tradition—I: The Intellectual Foundation." *Quarterly Journal of Speech* 36 (1950): 169–76.

Burke, Virginia M. "The Composition-Rhetoric Pyramid." *College Composition and Communication* 16 (1965): 3–7.

Christensen, Francis. "A Generative Rhetoric of the Paragraph." *College Composition and Communication* 16 (1965): 144–56.

Clark, Donald. *Rhetoric in Greco-Roman Education.* New York: Columbia UP, 1957.

Congleton, J. E. "Historical Development of the Concept of Rhetorical Properties." *College Composition and Communication* 5 (1954): 140–45.

Connors, Robert J. "The Rise and Fall of the Modes of Discourse." *College Composition and Communication* 32 (1981): 444–55.

————, ed. *Selected Essays of Edward P. J. Corbett.* Dallas: Southern Methodist UP, 1989.

———. "Textbooks and the Evolution of the Discipline." *College Composition and Communication* 37 (1986): 178–94.

Connors, Robert J., Lisa Ede, and Andrea Lunsford. "The Revival of Rhetoric in America." *Essays on Classical Rhetoric and Modern Discourse.* Ed. Robert J. Connors, Lisa S. Ede, and Andrea A. Lunsford. Carbondale: Southern Illinois UP, 1984. 1–15.

Cooper, Lane, trans. *The* Rhetoric *of Aristotle: An Expanded Translation with Supplementary Examples for Students of Composition and Public Speaking.* New York: Appleton, 1932.

Corbett, Edward P. J. "The Changing Strategies of Argumentation from Ancient to Modern Times." *Practical Reasoning in Human Affairs: Studies in Honor of Chaim Perelman.* Ed. James L. Golden, and Joseph J. Pilotta. Dordrecht, Neth.: Reidel, 1986. 21–35. Rpt. in *Selected Essays of Edward P. J. Corbett.* Ed. Robert J. Connors. Dallas: Southern Methodist UP, 1989. 322–40.

———. *Classical Rhetoric for the Modern Student.* New York: Oxford UP, 1965.

———. "The Rhetoric of the Open Hand and the Rhetoric of the Closed Fist." *College Composition and Communication* 20 (1969): 288–96.

———. "The Usefulness of Classical Rhetoric." *College Composition and Communication* 14 (1963): 162–64.

Crowley, Sharon. *Ancient Rhetorics for Contemporary Students.* New York: Macmillan, 1994.

Florescu, Valery. "Rhetoric and Its Rehabilitation in Contemporary Philosophy." *Philosophy and Rhetoric* 3 (1970): 193–224.

Fogarty, Daniel. *Roots for a New Rhetoric.* New York: Columbia UP, 1959.

Francis, W. Nelson. "Modern Rhetorical Doctrine and Recent Developments in Linguistics." *College Composition and Communication* 5 (1954): 155–61.

Gorrell, Robert. "Very Like a Whale: A Report on Rhetoric." *College Composition and Communication* 16 (1965): 138–43.

Grimaldi, William M.A., S.J. "A Note on the *Pisteis* in Aristotle's *Rhetoric.*" *American Journal of Philology* 78 (1957): 188–92.

Highet, Gilbert. *The Classical Tradition: Greek and Roman Influences on Western Literature.* New York: Oxford UP, 1949.

Horner, Winifred Bryan. *Rhetoric in the Classical Tradition*. New York: St. Martin's, 1988.

Hughes, Richard. "The Contemporaneity of Classical Rhetoric." *College Composition and Communication* 16 (1965): 157–59.

Hughes, Richard, and P. Albert Duhamel. *Rhetoric: Principles and Usage*. Englewood Cliffs, NJ: Prentice, 1962.

Jaeger, Werner. *Aristotle: Fundamentals of the History of His Development*. Trans. Richard Robinson. Oxford: Clarendon, 1934.

Johnson, Nan. "Origin and Artifact: Classical Rhetoric in Modern Composition Texts." *English Quarterly* 19 (1986): 207–15.

Keniston, Hugh. "Champions of the Great Tradition." *PMLA* 69 (1954): 3–11.

Kitzhaber, Albert R. "4C, Freshman English, and the Future." *College Composition and Communication* 14 (1963): 129–38.

———. "Freshman English: A Prognosis." *College English* 23 (1962): 476–83.

———. "New Perspectives on Teaching Composition." *College English* 23 (1962): 440–44.

Kuhn, Thomas. *The Structure of Scientific Revolutions*. Chicago: U of Chicago P, 1970.

Lauer, Janice M. "Issues in Rhetorical Invention." *Essays on Classical Rhetoric and Modern Discourse*. Ed. Robert J. Connors, Lisa S. Ede, and Andrea A. Lunsford. Carbondale: Southern Illinois UP, 1984. 127–39.

McBurney, James A. "The Place of Enthymeme in Rhetorical Theory." *Speech Monographs* 3 (1936): 49–74.

———. "Some Recent Interpretations of Aristotelian Enthymeme." *Papers of the Michigan Academy of Science, Arts and Letters* 21 (1936): 489–500.

McNally, J. R. "Review of Classical Rhetoric for the Modern Student, 2nd. ed." *Philosophy and Rhetoric* 6 (1973): 125–26.

Ohmann, Richard. "In Lieu of a New Rhetoric." *College English* 26 (1964): 17–22.

Olsen, David R. "On the Language and Authority of Textbooks." *Journal of Communication* 30 (1980): 186–96.

Packard, Vance. *The Hidden Persuaders*. New York: McKay, 1957.

Rose, Mike. "Sophisticated, Ineffective Books: The Dismantling of Process in Composition Texts." *College Composition and Communication* 32 (1980): 65–74.

Rothman, R. A. "Textbooks and the Certification of Knowledge." *American Sociologist* 6 (1971): 125–27.

Russell, David R. *Writing in the Academic Disciplines, 1870–1990*. Carbondale: Southern Illinois UP, 1991.

Schnakenberg, Karen Rossi. "Aristotle's Rhetoric in American Rhetorical Scholarship, 1950–1965." Diss. Carnegie Mellon U, 1996.

Stewart, Donald C. "Composition Textbooks and the Assault on Tradition." *College Composition and Communication* 29 (1978): 171–76.

Thonssen, Lester, and Albert C. Baird. *Speech Criticism: The Development of Standards for Rhetorical Appraisal*. New York: Ronald, 1948.

Weaver, Richard M. *Composition: A Course in Writing and Rhetoric*. New York: Holt, 1957.

———. *The Ethics of Rhetoric*. 1953. Davis, CA: Hermagoras, 1985.

Welch, Kathleen E. "Ideology and Freshman Textbooks: Publisher-Author Relationships." *College Composition and Communication* 38 (1987): 139–51.

———. "Reply." *College Composition and Communication* 39 (1988): 367–68.

Wimsatt, W. K. "Verbal Style: Logical and Counter Logical." *PMLA* 65 (1950): 20.

Winterowd, W. Ross. "Composition Textbooks: Publisher-Author Relationships." *College Composition and Communication* 40 (1989): 139–51.

Woods, W. F. "Composition Texts and Pedagogical Theory 1960–80." *College English* 43 (1981): 393–409.

Young, Richard E., and Maureen Daly Goggin. "Some Issues in Dating the Birth of the New Rhetoric in Departments of English." *Defining the New Rhetorics*. Ed. Theresa Enos and Stuart Brown. Newbury Park: Sage, 1993. 22–43.

CHAPTER EIGHT

Reinventing Memory and Delivery

WINIFRED BRYAN HORNER

Radford Chair Emerita of Rhetoric and Composition
Texas Christian University

Professor Emerita, University of Missouri–Columbia

In 1970, Richard Young described rhetoric as a "need in search of a discipline" (8). The book *Rhetoric: Discovery and Change,* which he wrote with Alton L. Becker and Kenneth L. Pike and from which that quotation comes, marked a turning point not only in the profession but in my own life as well. I did not have a doctorate at that time, and I was acutely conscious of my need to know more. I knew from my background in teaching composition that I was vitally interested in language—how we use language and how we are used by language—but how I might fulfill this need was still vague—until I read *Rhetoric: Discovery and Change.* The book literally changed my life. The authors visualized the domain of rhetoric as a "study embracing phonetics, grammar, the process of cognition, language acquisition, perception, social relations, stylistics and logic," and they concluded this comprehensive list with "and so on" (1). To that book they brought their combined knowledge of rhetoric, philosophy, and linguistics. They criticized the old rhetoric as representing "the control of one human being by another"(7). Finally, they called for a new rhetoric that "has as its goal not skillful verbal coercion but discussion and exchange of ideas" (8). That phrase is double underlined in my copy. I subsequently entered the graduate program at the University of Michigan and worked with all three authors. That book and their teaching molded my ideas, my studies, and my future research and writing.

In that program, I received a thorough grounding in classical rhetorics, and I early learned to shape my thinking about the processes of speaking/writing and reading/listening within the boundaries of an expanding rhetoric. I felt then that my ideas on language were not only not confined by the parameters of rhetoric but were in fact enlarged and amplified by the precepts. Kathleen Welch argues that classical rhetoric is "the most complete critical system for the analysis and production of discourse" (3). Throughout my studies, I have found this to be true. The five offices of the ancient system—sometimes termed faculties, functions, or parts of rhetoric—were invention, arrangement, style, memory, and delivery.[1] Through the centuries, rhetoric has shifted its emphasis from one office to another in response to its cultural milieu. Always sensitive to popular needs, rhetoric in the classical world was embedded in the politics of the day and served as instruction in the art of persuasive speech making. There were two roads to power in that world. One was military prowess; the other was eloquence. Training in rhetoric was the key to the second. Both were embodied in the life and works of Cicero. In the medieval world, rhetoric was revived by St. Augustine as a persuasive vehicle for the sermon. As rhetoric shifted its emphasis to the analysis of texts in the English Renaissance, style, with its endless figures of speech, became dominant, and in the eighteenth century, when proper speech became a rung on the ladder of upward mobility in a society that allowed such movement, style, renamed elocution, rose to dominance. Finally, in the late eighteenth century and early nineteenth century, in what many scholars term the period of the demise of rhetoric, the five offices were reduced to style and arrangement, and their connection with an ancient comprehensive system was obscured through new terminology and a desire on the part of scholars to divorce themselves from the increasingly trivial study of elocution. Rhetoric went underground and was lost to serious scholars until the middle of the twentieth century when language researchers, especially composition scholars, began to explore their roots. Richard Young was preeminent among those twentieth-century pioneers.

In conversations with Young while we were designing my program, he told me of his interest in invention, the first office of rhetoric, which he felt had been unduly ignored in modern composition. He argued for the revival of invention as an aid to writers. The ancient art of invention was the discovery of arguments through the examination of topics best known to composition instructors today as the familiar comparison/contrast, definition, cause and effect—methods newly employed to organize paragraphs or whole papers. Invention also included the familiar set of questions developed by Hermagoras and enlarged by Cicero of who, where, what, why, and how—questions familiar to modern journalists and fundamental to stasis theory.[2] In subsequent articles and conference papers, Young developed the idea of invention. It began to surface in composition texts as "prewriting"— and later in a number of forms with such names as freewriting, journaling, listing, and questioning.[3] Today, invention, under its altered nomenclature, has its place in every modern composition text. But while reinventing invention, Young continued to minimize memory and delivery. He devotes one short paragraph to both in his 1970 book with Becker and Pike.

> Memory, the art of committing the speech to memory by various mnemonic devices, and delivery, an art akin to acting, were essential to rhetoric as a spoken art. As the importance of the written word increased . . . the importance of memory and delivery as rhetorical disciplines diminished. (5)

This represents for me an uncharacteristic closed-mindedness about the expansiveness of rhetoric. In the twenty-first century, it is necessary to think of rhetoric as the production and analysis of discourse—both spoken and written—and as the broad discourse of the computer that produces a mixture of images, sounds, and print in a rapidly developing new technology that has only begun to unfold. As the possibilities for communication continue to increase, our rhetorical concepts need also to expand. If our concepts begin to cramp our thinking and fail to fit around the expanding technology, time then to discard them like outdated clothes that no longer fit the growing child. My argument in this article is that memory and delivery are two offices of rhetoric that need to be revived and enlarged to serve the rhetoric of the twenty-first century. Following in the intellectual tradition of Richard Young, who reinvented invention for the twentieth century, it is time for scholars to reinvent memory and delivery for the twenty-first.[4]

As we consider memory and delivery in the light of modern technology, we need to remind ourselves of Walter Ong's insistence that writing was the first technology and that computers are only a new step that follows in the tradition of that first technology. In 1982 he wrote:

> Plato was thinking of writing as an external, alien technology as many people today think of the computer. Because we have today so deeply interiorized writing, made it so much a part of ourselves . . . we find it difficult to consider writing to be a technology as we commonly assume printing and the computer to be. (81)

Writing—the encoding of ideas in a second symbol set—is only five thousand years old—a comparatively short span in the history of the world. In classical times, knowing how to read and write was knowing a technology that did not necessarily ensure literacy since reading aloud was common and most writing was dictated to a scribe—again aloud. Cicero apologized to a friend for not having answered his letter sooner and gave as his excuse a persistent case of laryngitis. So a person might participate in literacy without understanding the details of the technology of writing. The scribe understood the technology, but Cicero was literate. The early churchmen made a clear distinction between *legere* as reading and *intellegere* as understanding. Reading, like writing, was the mastery of a technology, but understanding was the mark of the literate man, usually a member of the clergy.

Through the Middle Ages, writing was dictation, and the *ars dictaminis* was the art that governed the skill. The scribe or clerk was only the medium between the individual and the written word. In much the same way, the twentieth-century executive who dictated to a skilled secretary may have had little knowledge of spelling and sentence structure and even less of typing and word processing and was in some ways, though literate, still divorced from the technologies of writing and the computer. Writing was the medium as the computer is the medium today.

The printing press more than any other factor facilitated the development of this early technology, but Gutenberg, credited with the invention of print, found his public loath to abandon medieval manuscripts, and his early printing efforts were hampered by attempts to imitate the cursive writing of medieval manuscripts. In the same way, computer operators eschew justifying margins in an effort to cling to the old typewriter style that was technologically unable to achieve such margins.

Writing, like computers, was distrusted from the beginning, first by Plato who, ironically, framed his objections in writing. The early church fathers guarded access to the Bible and insisted on the need for scriptural interpretation through church "lessons" and "homiletics." The common person was denied access to the technology through which they might gain access to the scriptures, and the protestant movement was largely a protest of this fact. John Wycliffe, a member of the Lollards and the first translator of the Bible into English, was hanged in the fourteenth century. His chief crime was translating the Bible into the vernacular language of the people, thus making it accessible.

Like all technologies, writing was regarded with grave suspicion from the beginning—a suspicion that continues to the present day in the widespread distrust of signing documents and the fear of "putting it in writing." Many slave owners in the nineteenth-century United States evidenced the same attitude in forbidding their slaves access to instruction in reading and writing. A number of religions regard writing as an inappropriate medium for the word of God. In Paul's letter to the Corinthians, he warned that "the letter killeth, but the spirit giveth life," and the word is written "not in ink, but with the spirit of the living God; not in tablets of stone, but in fleshy tables of the heart" (2 Cor. 3.3). In the first half of the nineteenth century, the same sentiment is expressed by Chief Cobb of the Choctaw tribe: "The Great Spirit talks. We hear him in the thunder, in the sound of the wind, and in the water. He never writes" (qtd. in Pattison 37).

Writing did not in fact become deeply interiorized until the nineteenth or twentieth century. For centuries after the advent of writing and the invention of print, Western culture was still basically oral, and as late as the seventeenth century most of the population was illiterate. When scholars wrote and read, they did it aloud—hence the word *carrel*—from the Latin for "chorus"—for the library study. Accounts were audited—literally read aloud—not scanned visually as they are today. The skill of writing was limited to only a small proportion of society. Today there is a gray area between the oral and the written in computer technology. What has happened to letter writing with e-mail? Some scholars argue that it marks a revival of writing; others see it as closer to the spontaneity of speaking. How do we handle the written words that the computer turns into sound? Stephen Hawking is able to lecture at Cambridge University only because of the new technology. How will we handle the voice-activated technology that will turn the sound of our voices into written language, a development promised for the near future?

Certainly, the difficulties connected with writing slowed its acceptance. Writers using clay bricks and animal skin with hair still clinging to the edges and working with horns, quills, or brushes were not inclined to be prolific. The process was tedious and laborious and best entrusted to scribes. Today, as the use of the computer spreads in Western cultures, the technology of the computer is being interiorized in the same way that writing was interiorized but at a much faster rate. Already many colleges are using the Internet for research, finding it cheaper than maintaining large library holdings, while students find it far more accessible than print books and journals. Children with their agile minds are interiorizing computer technology at a speed that often leaves adults far behind. A program in Missouri uses elementary school children to teach adults how to use the Internet. Many of us regard these innovations with suspicion and fear, and our feelings are sometimes expressed on the computer, as Plato's objections to writing were expressed in print. But as the interiorization of the new technology moves ahead, how ought we as scholars to approach it? What questions should we ask? How finally do we expand our concept of rhetoric, and particularly of memory and delivery, to consider the ramifications of the new technology?

In the ancient texts, memory was an important part of rhetoric. Frances Yates, in her comprehensive work on memory, attests to the importance that Plato, Aristotle, Cicero, and Quintilian all attributed to memory. It was regarded as "the noblest of the canons, the basis for the rest" (Carruthers 9). It was also regarded as a mental exercise that could and should be cultivated. Memory was internal, contained within the mind. Long orations had to be memorized, and orators, who had no teleprompters, needed to have information ready to insert when necessary, in the same way that debators today have card files carefully prepared. In the *De Oratore*, Cicero tells the story of Simonides of Ceos who, after reciting a poem at a banquet, was called outside. While Simonides was outside, the roof of the banquet hall collapsed, killing the guests, who were mangled beyond recognition. The mythical story states that Simonides was able to identify the bodies by recalling who had been sitting where at the banquet. Thus the ancient art of memory developed as *loci* or "places" that were used as mnemonic devices. Yates cites the methods outlined in the *Ad Herennium* and suggests that these methods might well "belong to a world which is impossible for us to understand" (12).

> According to the early writers retention and retrieval are stimulated best by visual means, and the visual form of sense perception is what gives stability and permanence to memory storage. They do not talk of "auditory memory" or "tactile memory" as distinct from "visual memory" as the moderns do. (17)

The ancient rhetoricians speak consistently of images that can be "seen" and "scanned" by the "eye of the mind" (17). Mary Carruthers cites the 1968 study of A. R. Luria, a neuropsychologist who reports on a professional "Mnemonist," a performing memory artist, whom he studied over a thirty-year period. The memory artist relied on visual images that in his mind he placed on a familiar street or in a room and held them "in precise detail in his memory" (75). The mnemonist had no professional training and no knowledge of the rhetorician's complex memory systems, but he relied entirely on visual images and "places" on which to superimpose the images, a method familiar to the ancient and medieval rhetoricians. Memory was a cultivated internal art.

Today memory has become external as we rely on the cultural memory outside of our own minds stored in books and more and more commonly on the Internet. We refer to these electronic places as "sites," and they are often marked with images or icons. Rather than storing memories in our minds, we store them on Internet sites enhanced with visual, auditory, and written images. Today we do not train our minds to remember but instead enhance our skills in retrieving and evaluating the huge storehouse of electronic memory. So the fourth office of rhetoric is revived today through the modern technology that is increasingly available to us.

Plato was the first to connect writing with memory—an idea that was ignored through the centuries of orality. He objected to writing on the grounds that it would "produce forgetfulness" and that those who learn it "will not need to exercise their memories, being able to rely on what is written" (275). Hieronimo Squarciafico criticized print in much the same way in 1477 when he argued "that the abundance of books makes men less studious; it destroys memory and enfeebles the mind by relieving it of too much work" (qtd. in Ong 80). These same sentiments are echoed today in criticisms of pocket calculators and computers. But Plato could not have envisioned that human memories would be replaced by powerful technological external memories in books, libraries, and finally in the huge computer databases that can store the memory of a culture. With the first technology, history—the cultural memory—began, and memory in the limited internal sense was permanently altered.

Just as Plato recognized the first technology as altering the rhetorical memory, he also foresaw the effect of writing on the fifth canon, delivery.

> Writing, you know, Phaedrus, has this strange quality about it, which makes it really like painting; the painter's products stand before us quite as though they were alive; but if you question them, they maintain a solemn silence. So, too, with written words; you might think they spoke as though they made sense, but if you ask them anything about what they are saying, if you wish an explanation, they go on telling you the same thing, over and over forever. Once a thing is put in writing, it rolls about all over the place, falling into the hands of those who have no concern with it just as easily as under the notice of those who comprehend. (275)

The importance of these prophetic words has still to be fully understood. In Plato's day, a scroll "rolled." Today we have words, images, and sounds traveling into outer space, bouncing off of satellites and back again—separated from the speaker or the writer. Whereas Quintilian worried about the drape of the toga during delivery, whereas elocutionists worried about the timbre of the voice or the facial expression, words and sounds come to us today via the Internet—disembodied and anonymous.

Plato compares written words to the seed of the farmer who fails to care where he plants his crop or to take pleasure in his harvest. Plato's misgivings have proved prophetic in ways he could never have imagined with the spread of writing, the advent of print, the interiorization of reading and writing, and the modern development of other technologies to record and preserve the auditory message, the visual image, and the written word. Other scholars have considered the effects of writing on cultures and on the human consciousness, but few have given thought to the serious and far-reaching consequences of technology on delivery. A number of scholars have treated computer delivery in terms of graphics, desktop publishing, and print fonts, rendering the fifth canon trivial and unimportant. But they have missed the big picture by ignoring the messenger behind the message.

What Plato could not foresee is that technology would introduce a new dimension to human communication in this divorce of the speaker from the text. This separation began with the introduction of writing, continued to have even more widespread effects with printing, and continues into the modern age of computer technology. Modern technology is not revolutionizing language; it is merely continuing the revolution begun many centuries ago by writing.

In ancient oral societies, before writing, speakers were physically attached to their words, and the audience consisted of those people within reach of the orators' voices. Speakers and orators could not be separated from what they said. They had to stand behind their utterances—quite literally. The speaker was always present in the rhetorical act, and the orator's character and reputation all added to the credence of the words—or not, as the case might be.

Today we appear to be completely comfortable with reading a text in a book or on a computer screen or hearing a recording of a text that was written or spoken by a person separated from us by many years and thousands of miles. The voices of dead writers speak with great eloquence in their disembodied texts. Our computer screen speaks to us, and we are becoming more and more comfortable with only the voice of the computer or the Internet to deliver the message.

This separation of speakers from their texts became well established in the eighteenth and nineteenth centuries, resulting in the copyright laws that developed during this period. As soon as the text became a permanent thing distinct from its author—transmitted to paper, bound between covers, and widely disseminated through print, a thing that can be picked up, put on a shelf, or given to a friend—as soon as this happened, the text became a piece of property, and legal matters came into question. Who owned this property, this collection of sounds? The person who held it in her hand? The person who has it on his shelf? The person who wrote it? Copyright laws are the author's way of trying to keep control over this text now contained in a book, an article, a tape, a computer disk, or a Web page. In Plato's metaphor, it is the farmer trying to keep control of his harvest. In the Middle Ages, stories and songs were borrowed freely—often with no acknowledgment; the oral tradition belonged to everyone. But by the eighteenth and nineteenth centuries, written and recorded language, separated from its author, became a valuable property protected by complex copyright laws.

Copyright laws are still in the making, as authors and publishers struggle to retain control of their texts as computers make them instantly available to anyone with access to the Internet. The laws are still struggling with the complexities of the new technology as words, sounds, and images escape their authors and as information on computers becomes something that can be shared, borrowed, or stolen, moving around at a far greater speed than Plato's scrolls.

In the twenty-first century, delivery is far more than the draping of the toga; it is far more than voice and gestures; it is far more than graphics—finally, delivery is concerned with the messenger behind the message. Who or what is speaking? How can I judge the message until I know the messenger? This is the concern for those of us teaching delivery in the twenty-first century.

In the complexities of modern technology, the external memory becomes blended with invention, the exploration of a subject, while delivery becomes mixed with ethos, the character of the speaker, as we search in vain for the messenger behind the message. In rethinking the canons of memory and delivery, there are no answers—only questions. But these are questions we need to ask as we try to keep up with the pace of technology. We need to explore the new discourse of the twenty-first century. Today we have an opportunity through modern technology to create and participate in the enlarged rhetoric that Richard Young visualized over twenty-five years ago—a true rhetoric for the "discussion and exchange of ideas" (Young, Becker, and Pike 8). But before we can reclaim this rhetoric, we need to be aware of how to use the vast resources of modern technology and not be used by its endless possibilities for manipulation.

Notes

1. The Greek names for these parts are eloquent testimony to the status of rhetoric in popular culture today. Known in Greek as *heurisis, taxis, lexis, mneme,* and *hypocrisis,* we have the modern English derivatives of heuristics, taxonomy, lexicon, mnemonics, and hypocrisy. So delivery becomes hypocrisy, and rhetoric itself, in the dictionary definition, becomes "empty and insincere speech."

2. In my book *Rhetoric in the Classical Tradition,* a textbook for students, I extended the stasis theory as a method of exploring a subject, drawing on the work of Professor Katherine Raign, a former student.

3. D. Gordon Rohman probably first coined the term *prewriting* in his 1965 article in *College Composition and Communication.*

4. Frederick Reynolds edited a 1993 collection of articles on memory and delivery that was the first treatment of the subject in the context of twentieth-century rhetoric.

Works Cited

Carruthers, Mary J. *The Book of Memory: A Study of Memory in Medieval Culture.* Cambridge: Cambridge UP, 1990.

Cicero, Marcus. *Cicero on Oratory and Orators*. Trans. John S. Watson. Carbondale: Southern Illinois UP, 1970.

Horner, Winifred Bryan. *Rhetoric in the Classical Tradition*. New York: St. Martin's, 1988.

Ong, Walter J. *Orality and Literacy: The Technologizing of the Word*. London: Methuen, 1982.

Pattison, Robert. *On Literacy: The Politics of the Word from Homer to the Age of Rock*. New York: Oxford UP, 1982.

Plato. *Phaedrus*. Trans. W. C. Helmbold and W. G. Rabinowitz. Indianapolis: Bobbs, 1956.

Reynolds, John Frederick, ed. *Rhetorical Memory and Delivery: Classical Concepts for Contemporary Composition and Communication*. Hillsdale, NJ: Erlbaum, 1993.

Rohman, D. Gordon. "Pre-Writing: The Stage of Discovery in the Writing Process." *College Composition and Communication* 16 (1965): 106–12.

Welch, Kathleen E. *The Contemporary Reception of Classical Rhetoric: Appropriations of Ancient Discourse*. Hillsdale, NJ: Erlbaum, 1990.

Yates, Frances A. *The Art of Memory*. Chicago: U of Chicago P, 1966.

Young, Richard E., Alton L. Becker, and Kenneth L. Pike. *Rhetoric: Discovery and Change*. New York: Harcourt, 1970.

CHAPTER NINE

From Heuristic to Aleatory Procedures; or, Toward "Writing the Accident"

VICTOR J. VITANZA
University of Texas at Arlington

When I was an NEH Fellow (1978–79) studying rhetorical invention with Richard Young, I inquired one day about the differences between a heuristic procedure and an aleatory procedure and specifically asked for examples of the latter. Richard made the distinction very clear and gave me a couple of examples of aleatory procedures. He also directed me to his colleague Herbert Simon, the cognitive psychologist and economist.

At the time, there was really little information in rhetoric and composition on aleatory procedures. Every attempt in relation to the new rhetoric was to break away from algorithmic (rule-governed) procedures in favor of heuristics that were being developed by and borrowed from cognitive psychologists. Rhetorical invention was being returned to the canon of composition studies, and its reinclusion was touted as part of the paradigm shift from product to process theory and pedagogy (Young, "Paradigms"). To be sure, there were clashes of opinion about borrowing from cognitive psychology (e.g., between Lauer and Berthoff[1]), but it appeared at the time that the most systematic new approach would have more followers than would a return to the considerations of the value of metaphor or acts of the imagination. Heuristics based on the social sciences, in fact, had their day in the composition journals, while the less systematic approaches were set aside either as unclear or too literary, or as vitalist and therefore unteachable.[2] Even today, a move toward establishing composition studies as a discipline has favored topoi over tropoi or has favored the means of establishing probable arguments over those of chance or accidental para-arguments. Members of composition studies generally view the latter as foreign, poststructuralist, or too ludic and therefore as having less value to a field that aspires to be a discipline. Since that time and even more so today, I have continued in my attempts to understand both the conditions and possibilities of this apparently rather mysterious approach to invention called aleatory procedures, or as it is sometimes referred to, "a throw of the dice."

It became clear to me in the early 1980s that much of what poststructuralism was attempting was a new economy of writing based not on exclusion or on the semiotics of the negative (or positive), but on a radical inclusion or a new semiotics of the "nonpositive affirmation" (Foucault 36).

◆ While the former is predicated on a binary (negative/positive), the latter searches for third terms (nonpositive affirmation) that signify limitlessness. (See Eco and Sebeok 1–10; Deleuze, *Cinema*, 98–101, 197–205; Vitanza, "Threes," *Negation*.)

◆ While the former is based on a "restricted" economy, the latter is baseless on an economy of "excess." (See Bataille; Derrida, "Restricted.")

◆ While the former discovers or invents meaning by way of defining (i.e., limiting), and therefore while it is indebted to the basic principles of formal logic (identity, noncontradiction, and the excluded middle), the latter is not indebted to these principles and instead makes meanings by recalling to mind what heretofore had been excluded by the principle of the excluded middle. (The latter would embrace all the excluded so-called monsters of thought.)

◆ While the former searches for meaning by establishing a species in a genus (a human being is a featherless biped that is either male or female), the latter forgoes such logical categorization and seeks out the conditions for the possibilities of recalling what has been excluded (a human being is both a feathered and a featherless biped, triped, and so forth, that is either male or female or both, as in a hermaphrodite, or different yet paradoxically similar, as in what some geneticists call a *merm* or *ferm*, and whatever else had been excluded because it was thought monstrous). In the animal kingdom, a platypus makes biological categorization problematic; in the human-animal kingdom, a hermaphrodite and other forms of sexuality make for similar difficulties.

The differences between heuristics (the old economy) and aleatory procedures (the ever new economy) are not to be found in the binary of actuality/fiction or reality/fantasy, which serves only as a means of, or alibi for, deflecting what wants to be re-called to thought by way of the newer economy of third terms (or excluded thirds). The actual/fiction or reality/fantasy dichoto-mies have become the hyperreal, giving us new conditions: alea-tory procedures are chance procedures. But chance means unaccountable hazard, not accountable probability. Chance means accidental. For Aristotle it was *tuche*. For the hyperreal "us," it means *crash* (Ballard; Baudrillard, *Simulacra*, 111–19).

We will not be dealing forever with "fictions" or "fantasies," for my alternative—perhaps comic—definition of a human be-ing is not a product of fiction or fantasy but a so-called fact re-cently established by geneticists such as Anne Fausto-Sterling. The next important step, after genetics has been nonpositively affirmatively deconstructed, is to break the binary differences between nonhuman and human, or lower and higher animals. The exploding of this binary is presently under way by Donna Haraway. Yet another important step is to break the binary dif-ferences between organic and inorganic, or carbon- and silicon-based life forms. The exploding of this binary is likewise under way in relation to Creutzfeldt-Jakob disease (CJD), specifically in its bovine form (BSE), known as mad cow disease. David Walton writes that this disease is "not a bacterium, not a virus, not anything with nucleic acid. It's a crystal, a rogue seed crystal like the apocalyptic Ice 9 in Kurt Vonnegut's 1963 novel *Cat's Cradle*" (9).

While fact and fiction merge and implode, what effect will this implosion have had on rhetorical invention? The political and ideological ramifications are plentiful in this rethinking of invention and discovery and *thought*. It has been bad enough that the second sex (females) has been excluded ethically, mor-ally, and politically; now we are realizing the exclusion of the third+ sexes. And, yes, their possible reinclusion. As Baudrillard points out, we are favoring the nonrational moves of reversibility and indetermination, which is a shift—a paradigm shift?—from stasis to metastasis. Hence, not only are the conditions of rhetorical invention changing, but the very foundations of invention—stasis theory—are being changed and, if not imploded, then dispersed.

In the history of the West, "thinking" has been done in terms of the ideal (Plato) or the actual (Aristotle), with the third term generally excluded or suppressed or unfavored. Exclusion purchases stability (i.e., a point of stasis). That third term is the possible, which is a topos admitted by Plato and Aristotle but only admitted, as I have stressed, under the sign of the negative (Vitanza, *Negation*). Poulakos rethinks the possible in terms of Heidegger, which means a condition of the possible still practiced under the sign of the negative. All inventing has been done semiotically across these three conceptual starting places. Or the possible has been practiced for *the most part* across the negative, for there are always rogue thinkers who would think the unthought and thereby be tempted to follow unorthodox or heretical paths of thinking.

There is what might be called an incipient history of these paths of thinking. Gilles Deleuze has recorded much from his readings of early modern thinkers such as Spinoza and Leibniz (*Fold*) and modern thinkers such as Henri Bergson. Indeed, when describing these and other thinkers, Deleuze makes them sound like the Sophists as we have come to "think" of them (see Crowley; Poulakos; Consigny; Vitanza, *Negation*).

The third term, when not excluded or suppressed by way of the negative, can be called the *compossible* (forming many *incompossibilities*, as Deleuze points out that Liebniz describes them). In the fictions of Jorge Luis Borges, we find compossible worlds at play, with none considered by him to be the best of all incompossible worlds. In Deleuze the term is *thirdness* or the *virtual*, which he takes from Peirce and Bergson respectively.

Is this thirdness limited to outlaw philosophers only? No, for it can be found in many ethico-political writers such as Hélène Cixous, Jacques Derrida, Luce Irigaray, Julia Kristeva, Jean-François Lyotard, Andrea Nye, and E. C. White. This thirdness has for some time now been making its way into the disciplines. For example, in the ethnographies or theory-fictions of Stephen

Pfohl we find compossible worlds and para-objects at play. The same holds true for other writing practices in other disciplines as well. Yes, writing in the disciplines is changing. (Or should I have written, Writing in the disciplines will have changed? I do not think so, for disciplines are presently eroding, though not recognized as eroding. Something new is never recognized in its beginning. The change can only be intuited.) All of this slipping out of the binary into a third place is happening at the very moment composition studies is announcing to the world that it is a new discipline and therefore wants to be taken seriously! Yes, it takes but one mad-Artaud-like writer to bring dis-ease to a discipline, shaking and tumbling and opening it to all that had heretofore been excluded. And there is more than one mad-Artaud-like writer loose now in composition studies. However, setting the madlike authors aside, we can say that this movement toward thirdness is happening because of the inclusion of computer technology into the field of composition studies. Computers paradoxically are entirely suitable for the introduction of randomness. Though computer programming is done in binary fashion, it is on the brink of changing to third-level programming. And already languages such as Java can easily be used to introduce randomness and aleatory procedures into composing.

My intent in this article is only to begin to discuss, at the levels of theory and practice and beyond, the immanent conditions for the possibilities of returning to the third terms and practices known as aleatory procedures, with their general economy of excess. These conditions are re-presenting themselves to us by way of a shift from literacy to *electracy* (Ulmer's word for electronic discourse or hyperrhetoric [*Heuretics*]). The so-called paradigm shift that Young ("Paradigms") and then Hairston spoke of in terms of moving from style to invention or from product to process was not *the* shift but only a prejudgment and misunderstanding of what was to come—the shift to, not "secondary orality" as Walter Ong would have it, but to chance as hazard or to the monstrous. Or in a less prejudgmental term, the shift to a new reordering of what now will count as and for thinking. The question forever is, What is thinking? Propositional and/or nonpropositional? I am not asking the question as an ontogenetic question or as a negative-essential one, which is normally how such a question does get asked, answered, and canonized in composition studies.

As Deleuze would say, thinking can be the compossibility that lies on the plane of immanence (or wills to power) and all along the surface of immanence (what could easily have been and will have been), but for the most part lying there as unthinking still unthought (*Fold* 59–75). While only a few poetical thinkers have been able to spell out what nibbles on the rind of their consciousnesses, computer scripts written to tease out the permutations and combinations of, say, hidden anagrams will continue to disspell mystery as a mere vitalism and romantic fancy, will continue to present the hidden paracodes of the logos. The simplest, plainest text can be passed through aleatory procedures to read like messages similar to St. John the Divine's Revelation.

I will discuss specifically two aleatory procedures in terms of electracy, two general procedures that will express the unthought:

- one procedure developed by Greg Ulmer, such as his *heuretics* (heuristics + heretics)

- another procedure (over)developed by the Object (which will go by the entitlement of an Anagram Maker) and readily available now as a search engine on the World Wide Web

Rather than giving the dialectics of good versus bad, both procedures tend to move on progressively to a third term or place, or what Baudrillard would call the ecstasy of communication (*Fatal* 41, 67). They tend to move on to a scene unseen that moves in a devolutionary manner, again as Baudrillard would describe it, "from forms of expression and competition toward aleatory and vertiginous forms that are no longer games of scene, mirror, challenge, duel games, but rather ecstatic, solitary and narcissistic games, where pleasure is no longer a dramatic and esthetic matter of meaning, but an aleatory, psychotropic one of pure fascination" (68). My intent—Does this "I" have an intent that it can call its own?—is not only to discuss the theoretical principles but also to demonstrate in passing how these paramethods might be applied in the un/learning of writing. But the latter will be performed indirectly.

While Ulmer takes simple phrases or names and searches for similar happy accidents that are often paralogical in their connections, the Object (anagram search engine) takes simple phrases or names and searches for anagrams written within them and then writes inventively from these discoveries. Both paramethods bring to the surface information and connections that the so-called new rhetoric, with its commitment to formal and informal logic, would have to discard as nonsense or as illegitimate, thereby deflecting what desires to be said. Or written. The new rhetoric would have to construct the strongest of alibis for an ignorance of what desires to be expressed. However, with our use of Ulmer's approach and the Object's approaches, we will be able to create whole new worlds of writing that heretofore have been forbidden or hidden from us. And though, paradoxically, we will "write" them, they will remain hidden. Disciplined writing will have become another "writing" that I would call a "writing of the accident." The C/Rash.

Ulmer's Heretical Heuristic

Gregory Ulmer has progressively been developing a theory of invention that would be appropriate and productive for those cultural theorists who have an interest in electronic media. In his *Applied Grammatology*, he moves from Derridean deconstruction (a mode of analysis) to grammatology (a mode of composition), that is, to exploring "the nondiscursive levels—images and puns, or models and homophones—as an alternative mode of composition and thought applicable to academic work, or rather, play" (xi). Ulmer focuses primarily on a theory of invention in terms of these images and puns, which would lay bare associational thinking, coincidences, and accidents, yet produce nondisciplinary meaning. Ulmer's discussion indirectly furthers and complicates Winston Weathers's Grammar B.

In *Teletheory*, Ulmer rethinks a theory of genre that would complement his grammatological theory of invention. Ulmer does for cultural theorists what Hayden White in *Tropics of Discourse* and elsewhere does for historians, namely, invites cultural theorists and historians to reinvent "doing" cultural theory and history while they are "doing" it. One of the genres that Ulmer develops is "mystory" or "mystoriography" (with variations such as history, herstory, maistrie, mystery, my story), which he sees as a post(e)-pedagogy. Freud, for example, wrote a kind of mystory when he developed self-analysis, psychoanalysis, not knowing what it was while he was doing it. Ulmer's discussion indirectly furthers and complicates Elbow's expressive writing.

If I may give a quick example from the middle of Mystory: If we take my name, Victor Vitanza, examine it carefully, etymologically, and punningly, etc., we might get the following heuretic (grammatological) reading. *Victor* generally means "conqueror." *Vita* signifies "life." *Anza* signifies (in Italia) "against." When thus disclosed, my family name, Vitanza (the sub-stance of my Being), and its possible meaning were rather disconcerting. The very idea that my heritage was *against life!* However, when I recalled that my first name signified conqueror and put the full name together into "conqueror of death," I begin to feel much better. My name is, as Derrida would say, *paregonial*, both *contra to* and *alongside* (*Truth*). Does it all stop here? No. It only ever rebegins. (This form of composition goes beyond mere deconstructive textual analysis, for it is grammatological in its emphasis.) When looking at *Finnegans Wake*, which is against death, I discovered that Joyce had invented mystory before I was even born—as "Victa Nyanza" (558.28). 'Tis a name that is echoed throughout the wake, signifying the origins of the Nile and the two great bodies of water from which the Nile arises: Victoria and Albert Nyanza (558.27, 598.5–6). Freud has his Nile; V.V. has his. You have yours. And yet, there is the pun on "Nyanza" as No Answer (89.27) in disrespect to origins and in respect to proleptic (perverse, reversed) thinking. The Nil/e is "soorcelessness" (23.19). The connections continue to resonate.

Ulmer's third book, *Heuretics,* is the one I am most concerned with here. This book more than the others carefully defines in terms of a theory of invention how "to play" on the road to Serendip(ity), while confessing ignorance of the rules of the game. Ulmer's discussion indirectly furthers Lyotard's discussion of "just gaming."

Heuretics calls for a return of "a rhetoric/poetics leading to the production of a new work" (94). But as an antimethodology, heuretics is not concerned with critique or with the meaning of a particular text but with "a generative experiment: Based on a given theory, how might *another* text be composed?" (4–5). In other words, heuretics does not critique ludic discourses for not being political but calls for them to invent a (nonreactionary) politics (5). The principle of invention, then, is not by way of negation but by way of nonpositive affirmations. (This principle of invention is an economy of thinking without reserve, which would be a leap out of Oneness and binaries.)

From Plato to the present, one of the invidious tests for whether a notion or a practice has any value is to determine whether it can be generalized (is generic) and whether it is transferable (codifiable, teachable). If not, usually the assumption is that there is no method but merely a knack, an irrationality, and thus it is left to the forces of chance (Young, "Arts"). Often, the choice here is based on the differences between thinking by way of rhetorical invention and thinking by way of style. Or between topoi and tropoi. Not all knowledge is determined by *physis* or *nomos* or, more important here, *logos-as-rational;* knowledge is also determined by *kairos*, which, as Eric C. White reminds us, is a principle of "spontaneity and risk" (20).

Ulmer, as I suggested, situates himself in the paradox of saying Yes twice to the text of his problem: to having a method and not having a method. (This is his heretical act of negating the principle of noncontradiction and thereby allowing for the return of the excluded third.) He gives us what he calls CATTt. The acronym stands for the following:

C = Contrast (opposition, inversion, differentiation)
A = Analogy (figuration, displacement)
T = Theory (repetition, literalization)
T = Target (application, purpose)
t = Tale (secondary elaboration, representability)

Ulmer boldly opens his book with the unfolding of this antimethod. Although there is no way to summarize Ulmer's particular rationalization, I can make a few generalizations about the heuristic. *Contrast* is intended in a sophistic sense; that is, it functions as the second part of *dissoi logoi*, initially arguing both sides of the case. When the dominant discourse becomes a Cartesian *Discourse on Method*, then someone like an André Breton can develop an anti- or counter-Cartesianism, or surrealism, a "false discourse on method that would be not just contrary to Descartes but completely different" (*Heuretics* 14). It is this pressing of the antimethod that can remove us from the simple opposite, or binary, out and beyond to something novel. Ulmer explains:

> The strategy is heuristic, employing several ad hoc rules that require continuous decisions and selections (there is no "algorithm" for this exercise). The chief such rule is to read the *Discourse* at the level of its particulars—its examples, analogies, and evidence—rather than at the level of its arguments. The antimethod will break the link between the exposition and the abstract arguments that proved the coherence of the piece. . . . Accept Descartes's particulars, that is, but offer a different (for my exercise, an *opposite*) generalization at each point, to carry the examples elsewhere, to displace them. The idea is to strip off the level of argument and replace it with an opposite argument that should in turn be made similarly coherent (secondary elaboration). (12)

In this way, Ulmer is able to say Yes to the text twice (to both Descartes and Breton). The *dissoi logoi* approach, however, is not limited to arguing, for what CATTt stresses is poetizing. Again, while Freud was developing (collaboratively) his notions of psychoanalysis with, say, Dora, he on occasion spoke of being "hysterical" himself. Confused, he found himself writing fiction, poetizing (his guesses, his filling in the *mise-en-abyme*) along with the so-called scientific protocol that his colleagues demanded he follow. Freud said Yes to the text twice (262).

By itself, the acronym of five conceptual starting places, CATTt, looks as if it overlaps with a number of other rather conventional sets of topoi, for example, Aristotle's twenty-eight, Cicero's sixteen, Kenneth Burke's Pentad (perhaps his four master tropes, which Hayden White uses), or Young's tagmemic nine-celled matrix or any variation of it. However, Ulmer's intention for its usage is very different. Whereas heuristics, or inventional procedures, focus more on topoi as arguments rather than as tropes, Ulmer stresses the latter over the former. (As Ulmer progresses in his discussion, he introduces the third term *Chora* to better suggest what the word *tropes* cannot since they are caught in the binary of topos/trope.)

Ulmer introduces CATTt as a "modest proposal" in support of many methodologies, but especially those outside the dominant discourse, "to invent an electronic academic writing the way Breton invented surrealism, or the way Plato invented dialectics: to do with 'Jacques Derrida' (and this name marks a slot, a *passepartout* open to infinite substitution) what Breton did with Freud (or—why not?—what Plato did with Socrates)" (*Heuretics* 15). Such a proposal stands diametrically opposed to the academic protocol of writing (linear, hierarchical, cause/effect writing), which is bolstered by traditional heuristics. And such a proposal would achieve its ends without a traditional concern for memory.

Ulmer's is not, therefore, a conventional argumentative thinking and writing; his is a grammatological approach to thinking and writing that emphasizes picto-ideogrammatic, aesthetic representations—writing intuitively. The CATTt is the perverse side of Aristotle and perhaps should be seen also as an extension of Aristotle's *Poetics*, but with the perverse addition of comedy over tragedy, so as perhaps to reach for a tragicomedy, or joyful pessimism. Like a sophist, Ulmer supports the weaker argument or the supplementary notion (negative deconstruction), but with the purpose of passing out of the binary (affirmative deconstruction).

Ulmer's proposal looks toward "the logic of cyberspace" (hypermedia). The movement from orality to literacy is now rushing on to a third place, which Ulmer refers to as *electracy*. And academic writing will have changed. In the midst of this change, Ulmer is inventing practices that will invite us all to disengage in an unkind of writing practice that we are "inventing while [we are] inventing it" (17). Again, he presents the paradox and the avant-garde. Ulmer would have us practice "hyperrhetoric . . . which is assumed to have something in common with the dream logic of surrealism" (*Heuretics* 17). It is "a new rhetoric . . . that does not argue but that replaces the logic governing argumentative writing with associational networks" (18). Yes, we can say there is nothing new about this kind of writing. Such an assessment, however, would miss the shifts in medium that are occurring. Electronic media have changed the very conditions for the possibilities of lexical (play)fields. Those of us familiar with writing in the new media can easily understand that Ulmer is talking about hypertext (extended texts) the way that George P. Landow, Jay David Bolter, and Richard A. Lanham have most recently. And yet Ulmer would go beyond. And has. Ulmer speaks of "chorography (the name of the method that I will have invented)" (26). Ulmer's notion of topos (the where?) is "the thing" that has been systematically excluded. He, like Kristeva and Derrida before him, returns to Plato's *Timeaus* and specifically the discussion of the three kinds of nature: being, chora, and becoming. The excluded is the chora. The excluded third, or middle (muddle), is the chora.

The chora is neither male nor female but third genders. It is the twisting, turning, folding of cyberspace in multimedia. And it has a totally new reconception of memory. The chora is the impossible. CATTt can only be a stand-in for this impossibility. Ulmer writes, "My problem, in inventing an electronic rhetoric by replacing topos with chora in the practice of invention, is to devise a 'discourse on method' for that which, similarly, is the other of method" (*Heuretics* 66). Hence, my earlier reference to the CATTt as Ulmer's "rationalization."

While there is always already a need to methodize nature, no need can express the desires of nature (*physis*) denegated. Ulmer's antimethod is at present the best rationalization that the fields of philosophy, rhetoric, and composition have for glimpsing the power that lies in what they have dubbed "vitalism." Or what I would rather call, borrowing another term from Bergson, the *Virtual*. What I am insisting on as the difference between the old new rhetoric and the newest new rhetoric or rationalized thinking about composing is that to understand the often misunderstood, each of us must set aside classical, Aristotelian logic informed by the terministic screens of *dynamis* (power, potential for what is possible) and *energeia* (the act that actualizes the possible or probable). When I read Ulmer, I hear him attempting to rationalize a new screen (or monitor) with terms such as *chora* that would be a Derridian-Deleuzean paralogic, making visible the Virtual, or the unthought, that lies on the plane of immanence.

The key to Ulmer's heuretics in great part is the new concept of memory. Ulmer explains that chorography as a practice corresponds to recent developments in computing such as "connectionism." Opposed to the classical concept of memory as storing information in some specific locale from which it may be retrieved, connectionism designs memory as not stored at any specific locus (topos, lines of argument determined by negation) but in the myriad relationships among various loci, topoi-cum-chora (atopoi, nonlinear lines of para-arguments undetermined by nonpositive affirmations). It's worth repeating: Not *in* loci but *among*. Entitlement has gone to the computer, the newest medium, if the word *entitlement* can still be used in this context. And connectionism entitles while it perpetually dis-entitles. The bits and bytes, though systematically numbered, are *not,* as we keep touting in commonsensical ways, predetermined according to algorithmic connections. At least, they are not in hypertext and hypermedia. But I need not back off from this argument, for "bits and bytes" themselves (b/b)—in my rationalization—are ever desiring the new "border logics" (M. Bricken; W. Bricken) that totally reconstitute computer programming *from* on/off, +/–, in/out *to* what lies in the virgule (/), lies in the middle, muddle of what Joyce calls the "sounddance" (378.29–30). The binary machines are becoming-desiring machines! The scattered possible readings or con-fusions I gave in terms of my entitled, proper name are possible—virtually future-perfect possible—in multimedia environments. Joyce only suggests them in the breakup (accident, crash) of literacy called *Finnegans Wake,* while linguists and critics attempt to fix them again as actual across the semiotic axis of arrangement and substitution. However, Yes is the answer to every question—or heretofore possible con-fusions—concerning every connection in my perpetual dis-entitlements. Living in the immanence of the breakup (accident, crash), I-cum-we have arrived to find ourselves (now or later, however long it may take) in Borges's Chinese Encyclopedia or in the labyrinth of the forking paths or in other incompossible worlds yet to have made themselves thought.

Space has changed. "In short," Ulmer says, "the change in thinking from linear indexical to network association—a shift often used to summarize the difference between alphabetic and electronic cognitive styles . . . —is happening at the level of technology itself" (*Heuretics* 36). As hardware and software change, so institutions and disciplines change. So do the thinking and writing generated by them. And yet, how is one to write by way of the chora, when apparently there is no way? Ulmer muses:

> An important aspect of chorography is learning how to *write* an intuition, and this writing is what distinguishes electronic logic (conduction) from the abductive (Baker Street) reasoning of the detective. In conjunction the intuitions are not left in the thinker's body but simulated in a machine, augmented by a prosthesis (whether electronic or paper). This (indispensable) augmentation of ideological categories in a machine is known in chorography as "artificial stupidity," which is the term used to indicate that a database includes a computerized unconscious. (*Heuretics* 37–38)

And yet again, there is a way: "Here is a principle of chorography: do not choose between the different meanings of key terms, but compose by using *all* the meanings (write the paradigm)" (48; emphasis added). And I would casuistically stretch Ulmer as adding, "and all the ways previously found illegitimate as making meanings." And while doing so, write, unbeknownst to yourself and others, new paradigms that might generate still other para-digms, saying Yes to everything and No to only the negative. To approach, as incompossibles, the worlds other than that One we have from *the* mode of production of the real world.

What follows from this discussion of the first fifty pages of *Heuretics* are two hundred pages of brilliant performances that begin with Ulmer's mother sending him "some clippings from my hometown newspaper about preparations for the centennial celebration of Montana's statehood" (49). In themselves, these pages function as paradigm after paradigm of writing the accident, from which colleagues and students might work—that is, play. Ulmer begins practicing connectionisms among Parc de la Villette, the Columbian Exposition, Disneyland (Epcot Center), Ziegfield Follies, an excursion on the etymology of *folly,* Miles

City, saloon/salon (this is more of the Paris–Miles City axis that would not be allowed under the rules of standard logic), Poe's "The Black Cat," CATTt, and on into the next chapter, which begins with Atlantis and desires to move rhizomatically *beyond*. Ulmer (or "Ulmer" [a.k.a. "Glue"], the proper-improper name) connects the dots and in unexpected ways. In my estimation, Glue gives—the chora gives—us (without entitlement) a dreamwork that suggests, as Peter Sloterdijk might phrase it, that "the dying tree of philosophy [and rhetoric might just] bloom once again . . . with bizarre thought-flowers, red, blue, and white" (xxxviii).

Anagrammatic Writing

> There is today a possibility that the object will say something to us, but there is also above all the possibility that it will take its revenge!
>
> BAUDRILLARD, "The Revenge of the Crystal"

> Anything that was once constituted as an object by a subject represents for the latter a virtual death threat. No more than the slave accepts his servitude does the object accept its compulsory objectivity. The subject can attain only an imaginary mastery of it, ephemeral at all events, but will not escape this insurrection of the object—a silent revolution, but the only one left now.
>
> BAUDRILLARD, *Fatal Strategies*

In discussing Ulmer's *Heuretics*, I have been especially heretical in insisting and perhaps inciting that we—the various WES (Can one even address a "WE" anymore?)—think the unthought, or illegitimate notion—that *things can think. Can do. Can have their revenge.* We think the unthought: that matter has a memory (Bergson) and can make things happen. There is, to be sure, a history of this kind of "silly" thinking within the dominant thinking of philosophy. And of poetics. Often such thinking is disregarded as "magical thinking" and considered, in specific contexts, to be dangerous thinking. So be it! I would agree that it is dangerous thinking and that there is good cause for showing just how dangerous it can be, since, in my estimation, it is overthrowing the present dominant, more dangerous grammatical paradigm. *Nothing*, however, can(not) stop this unkind of thinking. Let's just explain it, without a wide range of justifications accepted by logic, to be, as Baudrillard would call and characterize it, "the revenge of the crystal" or "the object." Too much subjectivity or mastering of the object creates the conditions for the object to talk back to us. And always accidentally.

Baudrillard writes:

> By the beginning of the twentieth century science recognized that any means of microscopic observation provokes such an alteration in the object that knowledge of it becomes imperiled. . . . The hypothesis is never entertained, beyond an object's being distorted, of its active reply to the fact of being questioned, solicited, violated.
>
> Perhaps unhappy with being alienated by observation, the object is fooling us? Perhaps it's inverting its own answers, and not only those that are solicited? Possibly it has no desire at all to be analyzed and observed, and taking this process for a challenge . . . it's answering with a challenge. . . . Today the analyzed object triumphs everywhere, by its very position as object, over the subject of analysis. It escapes the analyst everywhere, pushing him back to his indeterminable position of subject. By its complexity it not only overflows, but also annuls the questions that the other can ask of it. (*Fatal* 81–82)

The object or crystal, as I would discover it here, is (in) language (or rather in language as alogoi). Language (logos) is our mad cow dis-ease (alogoi), turning itself into a crystal, growing in crystal form, and making an indiscriminate sponge of our gray matter and its memories. A sponge that would soak up everything in its violation of Platonic-Aristotelian rules of reasoning.

By way of furthering a preface (*praefatio*) to our monstration of the aleatory, let us recall poor Ferdinand de Saussure, who as a philologist studied Latin hymns and poetry, the *Rig Veda*, the *Niebelungen*, and found in them, far beyond what anyone might expect, anagram after anagram. Saussure found anagram dedications to God and to gods and even found cryptograms (signs) uttered by the gods in pagan poetry and prose. As Jean-Jacques Lecercle points out, Saussure kept his distance, maintained his objectivity, in his search for proof or substantiation of what he but glimpsed. Finding no proof, allegedly, Saussure never made public what could only be a monster, or what Lecercle and so many other commentators saw as a condition that would invite the philologist to drift into the ecstasy of madness (2–4). Lecercle concludes, or rebegins, by saying, "Language [logos] loses its capacity to communicate. But it can also, at the same time, increase its power: it ceases to be controlled by the subject but on the contrary rules over him" (7). I am not sure I agree that logos loses its capacity to communicate. I guess it depends on what constitutes a communicative act. Should ideal or pragmatic speech-act theory determine what constitutes a communicative act? I think other/wise, which leads me—drives my desire—to the following pronouncement:

I have discovered a wonderful Invention-Discovery (Difference) Machine on the Web. It is Internet Anagram Server/I, Rearrangement Servant. Anyone using this difference machine will quickly come to the conclusion that language is thoroughly anagrammatic. If it were not for grammars, we would easily drift into psychotic episodes. Or if it were not for the presence of anagrammaticisms, we, and you and I, would drift into thinking that we were "subjects," that is, that we say what we mean and mean what we say. And everything else is not what "we say."

Inventio: For fun one morning I typed my name into the difference machine and I could not believe what it generated, and yet the pull toward believing it all was remarkably powerful. Seductive over productive. As Baudrillard writes, "We were all once produced, we must all be seduced. That is the only true 'liberation,' that which opens beyond the Oedipus complex and the Law, and which delivers us from a stern psychological calvary as well as from the biological fatality of having been sexually engendered" (*Fatal* 138). Later, in the evening, I typed "rhetorical invention."

When visiting the site *to help me complete this article* by searching for my name, your name, and our names in "rhetorical invention," you will read the onslaught of returns. Yes, I am asking you—dear reader—to complete this article with a metaphorical throw of the dice. I am asking you to light out for the digital territory. However, be sure to keep, as Lecercle says, your distance! (Is it not remarkable how incipient Paranoia—meaning, too many meanings, coincidences—becomes Theory? And yet, simultaneously, threatens another sense of Theory?) Visit Internet Anagram Server/I, Rearrangement Servant (formerly known as Inert Net Grave Near Mars) at http://www.wordsmith.org/anagram/.

Coda: Baudrillard writes:

> The work of reason is not at all to invent connections, relations, meaning. There's too much of that already. On the contrary, reason seeks to manufacture the neutered, to create the indifferent, to demagnetize inseparable constellations and configurations, to make them erratic elements sworn finally to finding their cause or to wandering at random. Reason seeks to break the incessant cycle of appearances. Chance—the possibility of indeterminate elements, their respective indifference, and, in a word, their freedom—results from this dismantling. (*Fatal* 151–52)

This will have been our fatal strategy in para-inventions and hyperinventions. If by chance we meet, let us not bore each other. For, if so, this will have been our banal strategy. Virtually, I do not think that we can bore each other IF we but attend to the writing of the accident(s) and the accident(s) of writing. No longer will we *clash* in arguments instead we will *crash* in accidents. Baudrillard writes:

> It is no longer a question, in [J. G. Ballard's] *Crash*, of accidental signs that would only appear at the margins of the system [as the waste or byproduct of communication]. . . . It is no longer at the margins, it is at the heart. It is no longer the *exception to* a triumphal rationality, it has become the Rule, it has devoured the Rule. . . . It is the Accident that gives form to life, it is the Accident, the insane, that is the sex [production] of life. (*Simulacra* 112–13; emphasis added)

Notes

1. Winterowd has collected and reprinted the exchanges that passed between Berthoff and Lauer. See pages 79–103.

2. Lest there be a misunderstanding, Young does not argue for an exclusive use of heuristic-tagmemic invention: "A tagmemic rhetoric stands somewhere between the rigorous theories of science and the almost purely intuitive theories of the humanities. We see no reason to reject the insights of either the former or the latter, believing that all new knowledge—like the process of writing itself—involves both intuitive analogy and formal precision" (Young and Becker, 468).

Works Cited

Ballard, J. G. *Crash*. New York: Farrar, 1973.

Bataille, Georges. *The Accursed Share: An Essay on General Economy*. Trans. Robert Hurley. Vol. 1. New York: Zone, 1988.

Baudrillard, Jean. *Fatal Strategies*. Trans. Philip Beitchman and W. G. J. Niesluchowski. Ed. Jim Fleming. New York: Semiotext(e), 1990.

———. "The Revenge of the Crystal." Interview with Guy Bellavance. *Baudrillard Live: Selected Interviews*. Ed. Mike Gane. New York: Routledge, 1993. 50–66.

———. *Simulacra and Simulation*. Trans. Scheila Faria Glaser. Ann Arbor: U of Michigan P, 1994.

Bergson, Henri. *Matter and Memory*. Trans. Nancy Margaret Paul and W. Scott Palmer. London: Allen, 1911.

Bolter, J. David. *Writing Space: The Computer, Hypertext, and the History of Writing*. Hillsdale, NJ: Erlbaum, 1991.

Bricken, Meredith. *A Calculus of Creation*. Tech. Pub. No. HITL-P-91-3. Seattle: Human Interface Technology Laboratory of the Washington Technology Center, 1991.

Bricken, William. *An Introduction to Boundary Logic with the Losp Deductive Engine*. Tech. Rep. No. HITL-R-89-1. Seattle: Human Interface Technology Laboratory of the Washington Technology Center, 1989.

Consigny, Scott. "Sophistic Freedom: Gorgias and the Subversion of Logic." *PRE/TEXT* 12.3–4 (1991): 225–35.

Crowley, Sharon. "Of Gorgias and Grammatology." *College Composition and Communication* 30.3 (1979): 279–83.

Deleuze, Gilles. *Cinema 1: The Movement-Image*. Minneapolis: U of Minnesota P, 1986.

———. *The Fold: Leibniz and the Baroque*. Trans. Tom Conley. Minneapolis: U of Minnesota P, 1993.

Derrida, Jacques. "From Restricted to General Economy: A Hegelianism without Reserve." *Writing and Difference*. Trans. Alan Bass. Chicago: U of Chicago P, 1978.

———. *The Truth in Painting*. Trans. Geoff Bennington and Ian McLeod. Chicago: U of Chicago P, 1987.

Eco, Umberto, and Thomas A. Sebeok, eds. *The Sign of Three: Dupin, Holmes, Peirce*. Bloomington: Indiana UP, 1983.

Fausto-Sterling, Anne. "The Five Sexes: Why Male and Female Are Not Enough." *The Sciences* (March/April 1993): 20–25.

Foucault, Michel. *Language, Counter-Memory, Practice: Selected Essays and Interviews*. Trans. Donald F. Bouchard and Sherry Simon. Ithaca: Cornell UP, 1977.

Freud, Sigmund. *The Standard Edition of the Complete Psychological Works of Sigmund Freud*. Vol. 1. Trans. James Strachey. London: Hogarth, 1962. 24 vols.

Hairston, Maxine. "The Winds of Change." *College Composition and Communication* 33 (1982): 76–88.

Haraway, Donna J. *Modest_Witness@Second_Millennium.FemaleMan_Meets_OncoMouse$^{(TM)}$: Feminism and Technoscience*. New York: Routledge, 1997.

Joyce, James. *Finnegans Wake*. New York: Penguin, 1976.

Landow, George P. *Hypertext 2.0*. Rev. ed. Baltimore: Johns Hopkins UP, 1997.

Lanham, Richard A. *The Electronic Word: Democracy, Technology, and the Arts*. Chicago: U of Chicago P, 1993.

Lecercle, Jean-Jacques. *Philosphy through the Looking Glass: Language, Nonsense, Desire*. LaSalle, IL: Open Court, 1985.

Lyotard, Jean-François. *The Postmodern Condition: A Report on Knowledge*. Trans. Geoff Bennington and Brian Massumi. Minneapolis: U of Minnesota P, 1984.

Ong, Walter. *Interfaces of the Word: Studies in the Evolution of Consciousness and Culture.* Ithaca: Cornell UP, 1977.

Pfohl, Stephen. *Death at the Parasite Cafe: Social Science (Fictions) and the Postmodern.* New York: St. Martin's, 1992.

Poulakos, John. "Rhetoric, the Sophists, and the Possible." *Communication Monographs* 51 (1984): 215–26.

Sloterdijk, Peter. *Critique of Cynical Reason.* Trans. Michael Eldred. Minneapolis: U of Minnesota P, 1987.

Ulmer, Gregory L. *Applied Grammatology: Post(e)-Pedagogy from Jacques Derrida to Joseph Beuys.* Baltimore: Johns Hopkins UP, 1985.

———. *Heuretics: The Logic of Invention.* Baltimore: Johns Hopkins UP, 1994.

———. *Teletheory: Grammatology in the Age of Video.* New York: Routledge, 1989.

Vitanza, Victor J. *Negation, Subjectivity, and the History of Rhetoric.* Albany: SUNY P, 1997.

———. "Threes." *Composition in Context: Essays in Honor of Donald C. Stewart.* Ed. W. Ross Winterowd and Vincent Gillespie. Carbondale: Southern Illinois UP, 1994: 196–218.

Walton, David. "Author Hears Time Bomb Ticking in Mom's Meatloaf." Rev. of *Deadly Feasts: Tracking the Secrets of a Terrifying New Plague,* by Richard Rhodes. *Dallas Morning News* 16 Mar. 1997: 8–9J.

Weathers, Winston. *An Alternate Style: Options in Composition.* Rochelle Park, NJ: Hayden, 1980.

———. "Grammar B." *Freshman English News* 4.3 (1976): 1–18.

White, Eric Charles. *Kaironomia: On the Will-to-Invent: Essays in Cultural Criticism.* Ithaca: Cornell UP, 1987.

Winterowd, W. Ross. *Contemporary Rhetoric: A Conceptual Background with Readings.* New York: Harcourt, 1975.

White, Hayden. *Tropics of Discourse.* Baltimore: Johns Hopkins UP, 1978.

Young, Richard E. "Arts, Crafts, Gifts and Knacks: Some Disharmonies in the New Rhetoric." *Reinventing the Rhetorical Tradition.* Ed. Aviva Freedman and Ian Pringle. Conway: U of Central Arkansas, 1980. 53–60.

———. "Paradigms and Problems: Needed Research in Rhetorical Invention." *Research on Composing: Points of Departure.* Ed. Charles R. Cooper and Lee Odell. Urbana: NCTE, 1978. 29–48.

Young, Richard E., and Alton L. Becker. "Toward a Modern Theory of Rhetoric: A Tagmemic Contribution." *Harvard Eduational Review* 35 (1965): 450–68.

CHAPTER TEN

Bridging the Gap: Integrating Visual and Verbal Rhetoric

LEE ODELL
Rensselaer Polytechnic Institute

KAREN MCGRANE
Rensselaer Polytechnic Institute

For more than a decade now there has been increasing interest in what Ben Barton and Marthalee Barton once referred to as the "rhetoric of the visual." In this rhetoric, visual elements such as layout, typography, color, and pictures are not viewed as mere ornaments, devices to keep a text from looking too dull and gray. Instead, visual elements are seen as contributing substantially to the messages readers derive from a text. And they are recognized as powerful influences on the reading process, guiding readers' attention (Redish), helping them recognize related information (Keyes), and even influencing their sense of the voice or persona reflected in a text (Schriver).

Much of the interest in visual rhetoric has come from the field of technical communication, where textbooks routinely incorporate findings from current research on effective illustration and page design. The field of rhetoric and composition, by contrast, has had little to say about visual rhetoric, preferring to cling to a tradition that Alton Becker has appropriately labeled "graphocentric." For decades this tradition has emphasized the power of the written word, giving little attention to oral communication and none at all to visual communication. Even today the most widely used textbooks in rhetoric and composition provide almost no discussion about how the look of a text relates to the message(s) readers derive from that text.

LEE ODELL AND KAREN MCGRANE

For a long time, this graphocentrism may have seemed justified for purely pragmatic, technological reasons. As recently as fifteen years ago, we and our students were composing almost exclusively in longhand or on typewriters. We might analyze some medium that integrated visual and textual information (e.g., an ad, a movie), but when it came time to compose, we had few visual options. We couldn't do anything with color unless we wanted to type on the red portion of our typewriter ribbon. We couldn't do much with format other than shift from single to double spacing. Nor could we include pictures or graphs unless we were dealing with a commercial publisher or we wanted to paste in a picture and then photocopy the page it was on.

Now, however, such pragmatic justifications for ignoring visual rhetoric no longer exist. Thanks to recent developments in word-processing programs, even the most technologically challenged among us have access to visual resources that a few years ago were available only to graphic artists. We now have the means to insert pictures, use a two- or three-column format, play with typography and color, and create (hyper)texts that bear little resemblance to conventional essays.

Such resources are, of course, a mixed blessing. They provide us with opportunities to change our teaching and expand our notion of what it means to compose (Odell and Prell). But these visual resources also lead us into the realm of graphic designers, a discourse community with its own unique language and concepts. Even when graphic designers talk about a familiar topic, they do so in language that, perhaps to understate the case, will strike most rhetoric and composition specialists as esoteric. In discussing the structure of a text, for example, graphic designers may talk about *accessibility, eye path,* or *navigation,* while we teachers of writing are more likely to talk about *organization, transitional phrases,* or *forecasting.* Even more intimidating, graphic designers consider issues that simply lie outside the ken of most specialists in rhetoric and composition. How many of us, for example, are comfortable talking about such matters as *leading, kerning, screen density,* or *modular grid?* (For discussion of these and other elements of visual communication, see, for example, Schriver.) Given these differences, any effort to bridge the gap between visual rhetoric and verbal rhetoric immediately forces us to confront fundamental questions: Will we be able to function when we move into what may seem for most of us like foreign, even hostile, territory? Is there anything we can bring with us, anything we already know that might be helpful, that might let us move freely between our turf and that of the graphic designer? And even if we *can* do so, *should* we?

For us, the answer to all of these questions is Yes. Despite the many differences between the two fields, we have access to a set of integrative principles that describe both the visual and the verbal elements of a text and, consequently, let us argue that what we *can* do as specialists in rhetoric and composition is, in fact, what we *ought* to be doing.

Integrative Principles

Much of the basis for integrating visual and verbal rhetoric originates in discussions of the relationships between readers and writers. Some years ago, Linda Flower argued that if people are to function effectively as writers, they will have to understand how readers go about constructing meaning from a written text. More recently, this argument has been picked up by scholars such as Janice Redish and Karen Schriver, who have expanded not only our understanding of the meaning-making processes readers engage in, but also of the term *reading* itself. Because Redish and Schriver are concerned with written texts that rely heavily on such visual elements as typography, format, pictures, and graphs, they have found themselves discussing ways readers construct meaning by using both visual and verbal elements of a text.

Accepting the premise that reading entails making full use of all the cues a page presents to us, and relying heavily on the example of Flower, Redish, and Schriver, we propose the chart in Table 10.1 as an expansion of Redish's 1993 article "Understanding Readers."

Two important words in this chart are *likely* and *probably*. We leave it to others to identify fixed, invariant operations that always guide the meaning-making processes of all readers and writers in all contexts. But the reading processes mentioned in

TABLE 10.1. A Guide to Understanding Readers

Because readers are likely to:	Writers should probably:
• Integrate new information with what they already know, feel, understand, etc.	• *Move from "given to new"* information, establishing common ground before moving to unfamiliar or uncongenial material
• Decide whether to read a text	• Motivate readers, usually by *creating dissonance*
• Sample the text rather than read every word	• *Make the text accessible,* structuring it so that readers can - Find what they are looking for - Determine what the author(s) think(s) is important - Develop appropriate expectations about tone and content
• Depend on the text for information and/or insight	• *Explore the topic thoroughly,* demonstrating their credibility by, for example, defining terms, anticipating a reader's questions, seeing relationships, asking who, what, when, and so forth
• Respond to ethos or voice	• Make astute decisions (about diction, syntax, organization, content) that will *indicate a credible and appropriate stance toward audience and subject*
• Respond to visual elements	• Use visual elements to help with all of the above

the left-hand column are well documented (see, for example, Redish). The emphasized phrases in the right-hand column are drawn from work in rhetoric, linguistics, composition, and technical communication. They represent a set of perspectives or "terministic screens" through which one might examine both visual and verbal elements of a text.

Given/New. The phrase "given/new" comes from discussions of syntax in which scholars argue that sentences are more easily comprehended if they move from "given" or "old" information at the beginning of a sentence to "new" or unfamiliar information at the end of the sentence. (See, for example, Joseph Williams.) Underlying this view of syntax is a principle that applies not only to sentence structure but to larger chunks of text as well. If readers are to make the leap from what they currently understand (believe, feel, value . . .) to some new insight, they have to be able to plug the writer's statements into the world that already exists in their minds (Flower). If genuine communication is to take place, it must do so, to use a phrase of Richard Young's, over a "bridge of shared features" (Young, Becker, and Pike 172–80).

Sometimes readers can assimilate new material with relatively little help from a writer, especially when they are close to the writer, sharing a lot of the writer's prior experiences, assumptions, and values. But often a writer has to work hard to help readers make the leap from given to new by providing background information, appealing to readers' values or prior knowledge, or locating the message in the context of a matter (intellectual, emotional, aesthetic) that readers care about. Much of the time, writers have to help readers move from given to new by constructing the bridge across which communication can take place.

Dissonance. In composition studies, this principle may have found its strongest advocate in Linda Flower's discussions of problem solving and writing. The premise here is that all human activity begins with what Jean Piaget referred to as "disequilibrium" or what Leon Festinger termed "cognitive dissonance." People read, act, write, speak in large part because they feel some gap in their understanding, some inconsistency in their own or others' thoughts or feelings, some disparity between what is and what might be or between their thoughts/feelings and their words/actions. If we want others to attend to what we write or say, we need to make sure our readers see how our words pertain to some dissonance they care about.

Dissonance may take the form of an issue or exigency, reflecting some outright conflict. In many scholarly articles, for example, writers often begin with this line of reasoning: Many people think X is true. However, in this article I will show that X is wrong and Y is true. When people discuss public policy, they often try to show that one plan of action is better than plans advanced by opponents. Sometimes, however, the dissonance may be more subtle and personal, arising, for example, from one's efforts to come to terms with the feelings, perceptions, and reactions that are part of one's own experiences. Whether the dissonance is public and explicit or personal and implicit, audiences are most likely to attend carefully to what we say if they can feel the dissonance(s) that prompted us to speak or write.

Accessibility. This term is often used in discussions of technical communication and reflects two assumptions: (1) that users of technical documents attend only to those parts of a document that immediately concern them; and, consequently, (2) authors of a document must make it easy for users to find passages they need and ignore those they do not need. Underlying these two pragmatic assumptions is a more profound and more widely applicable premise from Kenneth Burke: form (or organization) consists of creating and fulfilling expectations (Burke uses the term "appetites," 31) in the audience. That is, even if an audience is willing to read every word of a text, that audience needs to have some sense of where the author is heading and of what the author is going to say next and how the author is going to say it. In more technical or specialized documents, some of these expectations may be created through the use of abstracts, headings, or subtitles. In any text, expectations may be created through the use of what Rise Axelrod and Charles R. Cooper call "forecasting statements" (466–67), as well as by sentence structure, format, or organizational pattern.

Topic. The importance of exploring a topic thoroughly has long been recognized, whether one uses the phrase to mean finding all the available means of persuasion, using appropriate claims and warrants, determining empirical "facts," or engaging in the process medieval scholars called "sic et non" and Peter Elbow has labeled "doubting and believing" (*Writing*). To this long history we want to add two closely related premises: (1) visual elements may constitute arguments, implicitly or explicitly making claims and/or providing evidence and warrants; and (2) these visual elements have epistemic value, influencing the ways an audience understands a document's message(s) and even an author's exploration of the subject.

Voice. This is another term that has a long history, one that occasionally involves other terms: *persona* and *ethos*. In recent years, some scholars have questioned the usefulness of this analytic category, arguing that it is impossible to determine whether a text reflects a writer's "true" or "honest" voice or whether it reflects the discourse practices of larger groups rather than the work of an individual "author." (See Elbow, "Introduction," for a discussion of some of these issues.) For us, these criticisms are beside the point. Whatever the source of voice, whether or not we can determine if a voice is "true," it is still useful to accept Walker Gibson's premise (1969) that a text can reflect an attitude toward an audience and toward a subject. Readers' perceptions of this attitude will influence their willingness to accept or act upon the message(s) conveyed through a text.

Visual Information. Of all the principles mentioned above, this may seem the most counterintuitive. Most discussions of rhetorical theory focus on verbal arguments rather than visual elements of a text. And certainly the most widely used composition texts have little or nothing to say about the use of images, format, or typography. But in the remainder of this chapter, we will try to show that visual elements are fundamental to observing all the previously mentioned rhetorical principles, moving from given to new, creating dissonance, and so forth.

Texts and Analysis

To show how the preceding principles apply to both visual and verbal information, we analyze a series of texts, beginning with a student's response to a type of assignment that is often done in composition classes. The student text "Schizophrenia: What It Looks Like, and How It Feels" is reprinted in the chapter "Explaining a Concept" in Axelrod and Cooper's *St. Martin's Guide to Writing* (5th ed.). In an attempt to match the basic purpose and type of subject matter of "Schizophrenia," we selected two additional texts that sought to explain a concept related to mental health. One of these additional texts is a student-written brochure titled "What, Me Depressed?" The other is an article from *Science*, "Linking Mind and Brain in the Study of Mental Illnesses: A Project for a Scientific Psychopathology."

All of these texts exemplify characteristics that Axelrod and Cooper ascribe to explanatory discourse. The texts speak authoritatively, drawing information from well-established sources and providing the kinds of details that should be both engaging and informative to an audience that knows less about the subjects than the authors do. Both the organization and the content of these texts enable readers to understand the topics under discussion "without too much uncertainty or frustration" (168). In short, all of these texts accomplish the fundamental goal of explanatory discourse—"educating" readers (157) in ways that will "interest and inform" them (168).

In working toward this common goal, however, these texts vary widely in their use of visual information. The essay "Schizophrenia" has the standard look of a college essay—long passages of text interrupted only by paragraph indentations. The brochure "What, Me Depressed?" has a very different appearance, making extensive use of visual elements such as headings, bulleted lists, photos, and variations in typeface. The magazine article "Linking Mind and Brain" lies somewhere between the extremes represented by the student essay and the brochure, although it has more in common with the brochure than one might initially think. By discussing the "Schizophrenia" text first, we follow our own advice and move from the familiar or given to the new, that is, from familiar-looking college essays to texts whose appearance may be quite different from the student work that college instructors often see. Throughout this analysis, we use boldface and italics to highlight strategies writers use in enacting key integrative principles.

"Schizophrenia: What It Looks Like, How It Feels"

Although the audience for this essay is never explicitly identified, Axelrod and Cooper tell us that the student author, Veronica Murayama, composed the piece "as a first year college student" (173). Presumably, her audience consisted of her instructor and, perhaps, her classmates—an audience that might have many of the characteristics Axelrod and Cooper attribute to readers of explanatory discourse. These readers

- Have relatively little detailed information about the topic and, hence, depend on the writer for a thorough, fair discussion of the topic;

- Are not especially interested in the writer's personal opinions or feelings;

- Value information that is "novel or surprising" (191);

- May become impatient when they cannot readily see what the author is getting at or where the discussion is headed.

In trying to reach this audience, Murayama makes skillful use of all the integrative principles mentioned earlier. She does this primarily through her written text, although visual elements contribute in several ways to the overall effect of the piece and further

SCHIZOPHRENIA: WHAT IT LOOKS LIKE, HOW IT FEELS
Veronica Murayama

Some mental illnesses, like depression, are more common than schizophrenia, but few are more severe. A schizophrenic has delusions and hallucinations, behaves in bizarre ways, talks incoherently, expresses little feeling or else feelings inappropriate to the situation, and is incapable of normal social interactions. Because these symptoms are so severe, about half the hospitalized mentally ill in America are schizophrenics. Only 1 percent of Americans (between 2 and 3 million) are schizophrenic, and yet they occupy about one-fourth of the available beds in our hospitals ("Schizophrenic," 1987, p. 1533). Up to 40 percent of the homeless may be schizophrenic (King, 1989, p. 97).

Schizophrenia has been recognized for centuries, and as early as the seventeenth century its main symptoms, course of development, and outcome were described. The term *schizophrenia*, first used in 1908, refers to the disconnection or splitting of the mind that seems basic to all the various forms of the disease. It strikes both men and women, usually during adolescence or early adulthood, and is found all over the world. Treatment may include chemotherapy, electroconvulsive therapy, psychotherapy, and counseling. Hospitalization is ordinarily required, but usually not for more than a few months. It seems that about a third of patients recover completely and the rest can eventually have "a reasonable life adjustment," but some effect of the illness nearly always remains, most commonly lack of feeling and reduced drive or ambition ("Schizophrenic," 1987, pp. 1533, 1537–1539). Schizophrenia hits adolescents especially hard, and the effect on their families can be disastrous.

Though much is known about schizophrenia and treatment is reasonably effective, specialists still argue about its causes. For example, various researchers blame an unsatisfactory family life in which one or both parents suffer from some form of mental illness (Lidz, 1973), some aspects of genetic inheritance and family life ("Schizophrenic," 1987, p. 1534; "Schizophrenia," 1987, p. 192), or "an early developmental neuropathological process" that results in reduced size of certain brain areas (Suddath, Cristison, Torrey, Casanova, & Weinberger, 1990, p. 793). What is known and agreed on, however, is what schizophrenia looks like to an observer and what it feels like to a sufferer, and these are what I want to focus on in this essay. I have always believed that when people have knowledge about any type of human suffering, they are more likely to be sympathetic with the sufferer. Schizophrenic symptoms are not attractive, but they are easy to understand. The medical manuals classify them approximately as follows: bizarre delusions, prominent hallucinations, confusion about identity, unconnected speech, inappropriate affect, disturbances in psychomotor behavior, impaired interpersonal functioning, and reduced drive.

Schizophrenics themselves experience the disease to a large extent as delusional thinking. For example, one woman said, "If I use a phone, I can talk on it without picking it up, immediately, anywhere in the world. But I don't abuse it. I'm authorized by AT&T. In the Yukon. And RCA" (Shane, 1987). It is common for schizophrenics to have delusions that they are being persecuted—that people are spying on them, spreading false stories about them, or planning to harm them. Events, objects, or people may be given special threatening significance, as when a patient believes a television commentator is making fun of him. Other delusions are very likely: "the belief or experience that one's thoughts, as they occur, are broadcast from one's head to the external world so that others can hear them; that thoughts that are not one's own are inserted into one's mind; that thoughts have been removed from one's head; or that one's feelings, impulses, thoughts, or actions are not one's own, but are imposed by some external force" ("Schizophrenia," 1987, p. 188). Sometimes delusions are grandiose, as when a patient thinks that he is the Messiah and will save the world or that she is the center of a conspiracy. A woman patient wrote, "I want a revolution, a great uprising to spread over the entire world and overthrow the whole social order. . . . Not for the love of adventure! No, no! Call it unsatisfied urge to action, if you like, indomitable ambition" (cited in Lidz, 1973, p. 134).

FIGURE **10.1.** *Page 1 of Veronica Murayama's college paper, "Schizophrenia: What It Looks Like, How It Feels."*

illustrate the integrative principles. Figure 10.1 is a reproduction of the opening portion of Murayama's essay.

GIVEN/NEW

Throughout the text, Murayama does a fine job of using visual and textual information to establish common ground with her readers before moving them on to new insights. Although the visual appearance of her essay is not as dramatic as that of the brochure "What, Me Depressed?", this appearance is not trivial. The very look of Murayama's essay will seem familiar and reassuring to many college faculty. She avoids flamboyant or dramatic visual information, choosing instead to rely on more subdued visual qualities that her readers are likely to value. Her essay has the appearance many teachers associate with carefully done college writing—long stretches of text interrupted by paragraph indentations rather than by headings or bulleted lists. Type style and format vary only in the references section, where these variations are dictated by scholarly custom rather than an individual writer's preferences. Granted, these visual appearances will get students only so far; they will not compensate for a discussion that is superficial, disorganized, or unclear. But they can begin establishing common ground before the reader actually reads a word of the text, in effect saying to the reader, "You and I have some things in common; we both know what a careful, rational explanation should look like, and we value the conventions that contribute to this appearance."

In her written text, Murayama continues to develop common bonds with her readers. She explores the topic (see the Topics section below) in ways that suggest a rational, dispassionate approach to a topic that could have been treated in a highly emotional, even sensationalized, manner. In addition, the introductory section of her piece includes references to concepts, experiences, or values that her audience should be able to relate to. Murayama includes terminology that almost any reader might associate with mental illness ("delusions and hallucinations," "bizarre" behavior, "psychotherapy"). She refers to sights the reader is likely to have seen, such as homeless people on city streets. And she asserts an attitude her readers might be able to share: "I have always believed that when people have knowledge about any type of human suffering, they are more likely to be sympathetic with the sufferer."

At the paragraph and sentence level, Murayama routinely establishes common ground and then leads the reader to new and often surprising information. As a rule, her paragraphs move from a concept the reader may be familiar with to specific examples that are likely to be new to the reader. In her fourth paragraph, for example, she illustrates the familiar phrase "delusional thinking" with details that go well beyond what readers are likely to mean when they casually refer to someone deluding him- or herself. At the sentence level, she generally structures her sentences so that they move from old information to new, referring at the beginning of one sentence to information that has been introduced in a previous sentence. (See, for example, the first two sentences of her essay.)

DISSONANCE

Murayama does not go to great lengths to create dissonance in either the visual or the verbal elements of this piece. There is nothing about the look of the piece that would startle readers or grab their attention. Similarly, the introductory section of the text presents no dramatic conflicts. She makes no direct challenges to a reader's (mis)perceptions, nor does she locate her discussion in the context of a scholarly argument (Some people think X is true, but really Y is true.).

Given her audience and purpose, none of this is really necessary. Because Murayama can assume that her readers are predisposed to learn about this topic, she does not have to create powerful dissonances in order to gain their attention. Although she must create enough dissonance to keep her discussion engaging as well as informative, she needs to stop well short of the sensational. Murayama effectively balances these two needs by (1) mentioning facts that her readers are likely to find disturbing but not personally threatening (e. g., that about 40 percent of the homeless are schizophrenic), and (2) using elaboration that gives new, surprising meaning to concepts that already exist in her readers' minds. (See, for example, the previous discussion of delusional thinking.)

ORGANIZATION/ACCESSIBILITY

In her effort to help readers see what to expect or find what they are looking for, Murayama uses only two types of visual cues—paragraph indentation and the traditional format for references. As noted earlier, she avoids other visual cues such as headings, bulleted lists, variations in typeface—a wise decision, most likely, since such cues may strike some of her readers as less appropriate for college essays than for journalism or technical communication.

Although she limits her use of visual cues, Murayama makes extensive and effective use of verbal cues that keep readers from becoming confused or frustrated as they try to follow her discussion. Throughout her essay, she uses forecasting words, phrases, and clauses. In the third paragraph, for example, she sets up the entire piece with the following phrases (the critical words have been underlined): "what schizophrenia *looks like to an observer* and what it *feels like to a sufferer*"; "manuals classify [symptoms] approximately as follows: *bizarre delusions, prominent hallucinations . . .* "). In subsequent paragraphs, she discusses each of these symptoms and shows how each symptom is experienced by both an observer and a schizophrenic.

She also does a good job of putting key points at the beginning of paragraphs and linking those points to forecasting words. For example, in the last paragraph of the excerpt presented in Figure 10.1, Murayama asserts, "Schizophrenics themselves experience the disease to a large extent as delusional thinking." These underlined phrases clearly echo forecasting phrases mentioned in the preceding paragraph of her essay.

Murayama is also skillful in creating and fulfilling expectations at the sentence level. She does this by elaborating on points she puts in the emphatic part of the sentence (that is, at the end). For instance, she ends one sentence ("Schizophrenics also present themselves in inappropriate ways, referred to as 'inappropriate affect'") by putting the phrase "inappropriate affect" in the emphatic position. By placing this emphasis on a term that may well be unfamiliar to a nonspecialist, she creates the expectation that she will elaborate on it, which she does in the next sentence, noting that "Their *voices are often monotonous* and *their faces expressionless."*

TOPIC

On the face of it, visual elements may seem to have no connection with Murayama's exploration of her topic. Certainly these elements have less influence here than they do in the brochure and scholarly article. Yet Murayama is working within a format—that of the classroom essay—that both enables and constrains her exploration of her topic in ways that seem highly appropriate, given her apparent audience. As will become apparent in the subsequent discussion of the brochure "What, Me Depressed?," this essay format allows her more space—literally the opportunity to use more words—than does a brochure. Furthermore, the essay format helps free Murayama from the obligation to present information in the short, easily digestible blocks of text that typically appear in brochures.

On the other hand, the classroom essay—at least for most composition classes—usually allows a writer less space than a scholarly article. "Choose a *manageable* topic," we often tell students, a topic they can cover thoroughly in the relatively brief space (usually well under ten pages) we can read carefully. Especially in dealing with student writing, some limitation on page length is a good idea. More is not always better. But the space limitations we usually impose do influence the scope of students' topics and the extent to which they can elaborate and pursue finer points of their topic.

Just as the format of Murayama's work should seem familiar and congenial to her intended readers, her written text shows her using strategies that are consistent with what readers might expect to find in a rational, authoritative explanation of a concept. She draws on multiple sources, ranging from a newspaper and a popular magazine to research and theory from the field of mental health. She relates her topic, schizophrenia, to another topic (depression) with which her readers may be more familiar. She uses quotes and examples that vividly dramatize the nature of the disease (in effect, she follows the admonition "show, don't tell"). And she makes good use of classification, not only mentioning different types of symptoms (e. g., delusional thinking) but also setting up subcategories (e. g., different types of delusions).

VOICE

By this point in the analysis of Murayama's essay, her voice or stance toward audience and subject seems clear. Throughout the piece, she keeps a certain distance from her subject and remains solicitous of her readers. She does not talk about her own opinions, feelings, or experiences, choosing instead to introduce us to concepts that have been thoroughly studied and agreed upon by authorities in the field. Yet she does not seem unfeeling. In discussing delusional behavior, Murayama cites this remark from one patient: "If I see a phone, I can talk on it without picking it up, immediately, anywhere in the world." Had Murayama stopped with this information, the patient would have been little more than a curiosity, a bizarre example. But Murayama includes a further, more humanizing comment from the patient: "But I don't abuse it [her power]. I'm authorized by AT&T." By including this additional comment, Murayama attributes to the patient an admirable trait (a reluctance to take advantage of others), thereby suggesting that Murayama may have a degree of sympathy for people who suffer from schizophrenia.

Her solicitous stance toward her readers manifests itself in a number of ways. We have already seen how she accommodates her readers' expectations and values in her choice of format and in her exploration of the topic. Further, she defines specialized terms that may be peculiar to this topic, yet she avoids insulting her readers' intelligence by omitting definitions of terms that are likely to be familiar to people whose backgrounds and interests would lead them to read about this topic in this format. Finally, her solicitous attitude seems apparent in the fact that she makes the essay accessible and by creating and fulfilling clear expectations.

"What, Me Depressed?"

In some respects, the audience for this brochure by Heather Saddler (reprinted with permission) is similar to the audience Murayama is addressing. Saddler's audience is not interested in Saddler's personal feelings or experiences; instead, her readers need an authoritative, reliable discussion of a topic they may know little about. Yet even with these similarities, Saddler's readers seem different from Murayama's in that they

- ◆ Are harried almost to the point of distraction, beset by a number of day-to-day obligations that compete with Saddler's text for their attention;
- ◆ Do not seem especially concerned with scholarly documentation for claims;
- ◆ Appear to have neither time nor inclination to reflect dispassionately on topics that are unrelated to their day-to-day lives;
- ◆ May be assuming that their day-to-day lives are untouched by depression or, indeed, by any form of mental illness;
- ◆ May need to use this information as a basis for deciding whether they should consult a doctor about depression as a possible cause of symptoms they are experiencing.

In light of this audience, Saddler's rhetorical task is different from and in some ways more difficult than Murayama's. Like Murayama, Saddler must inform and engage her readers. But these readers may have no inclination to read about depression, and they are likely to encounter the brochure in a context in which they are highly distracted—they may be dealing with a child running amok in a doctor's waiting room or writing a check while standing at the receptionist's counter where several brochures may be displayed. Consequently, the task of gaining and holding their attention seems formidable indeed. See Figure 10.2 for the first several pages of Saddler's brochure.

What, Me Depressed?

You visited your primary healthcare physician because you haven't quite been yourself lately. Perhaps you're experiencing fatigue or loss of energy, constant muscle pain or an inability to sleep. After a full examination and a series of questions, your primary care provider has just presented you with some startling news. You may be suffering from depression. Her recommendation is for Zoloft, an anti-depressant drug. You're thinking, "Who, me?!"

Many of us think of "the depressed" as individuals who spend much of their time sleeping or crying, seldom leaving their homes, paralyzed by despair and unable to function. You're thinking, "That's certainly not me! I lead a very busy life, balancing a career with family, managing a household, working hard to make ends meet, maintaining important relationships, maybe raising children, maybe going to school, and dealing with countless sources of stress." In fact, so many of us are careening through our days, weeks and months at such break-neck speeds that we are clearly pushing the limits of mind and body. And guess what? Eighteen million Americans, (2/3 of them women) suffer from depression today.

So what is depression?

Although we all get the blues once in a while, clinical depression is much more serious than a case of the blues. In short, depression is the result of certain biologic and social forces that, in a complex setting, act detrimentally on a person's nervous system function. Depression is not a sign of personal weakness. Many people think they ought to "handle it" or "tough it out" but it is as impossible to "snap out of" as a case of pneumonia. It requires proper treatment.

Most people don't know they are suffering from depression until they see their primary care physician with complaints of physical ailments or changes in their usual functioning. These symptoms include:

- Fatigue or energy loss
- Noticeable change in sleeping patterns, such as inability to sleep or sleeping too much
- Noticeable change in eating patterns, with either significant weight gain or weight loss not attributable to dieting
- Feeling irritable or over-whelmed, as if "everything is too much"
- Inability to concentrate, make decisions or remember details
- Aches and pains, constipation or other physical ailments that cannot be explained.
- Loss of interest and pleasure in activities previously enjoyed, including sex
- Persistent anxious feelings

Anyone experiencing a combination of these symptoms for more than two weeks or whose everyday functioning is impaired by these symptoms may be suffering from depression.

Do I really need an anti-depressant?

Your health care provider can help you make that decision. For most people, the best way to combat depression is to combine an anti-depressant with therapy and some of nature's anti-depressants, such as relaxation, exercise, a healthy diet and plenty of sleep. Anti-depressants work to relieve painful or disruptive symptoms relatively quickly so that you can get on with your life and learn how to deal with stress over the long haul.

Here's how anti-depressants work:

Many of the symptoms of depression may result from lowered levels of serotonin in the brain. Serotonin is a neurotransmitter (conveying messages from cell to cell throughout the central nervous system). Serotonin neurons set the overall tone or activity level of other regulatory systems, in a slow rhythmic pattern. Serotonin is also a stress-adaptation mechanism. By inhibiting the intensity of signals, especially those from outside sources, serotonin ensures that the signals that get through are the important ones. When serotonin is deficient, a person may become overwhelmed by too many signals. Serotonin-boosting drugs improve people's stress tolerance.

The SSRI (serotonin reuptake inhibitor) Zoloft has increased in popularity with its less objectionable side affects (than Prozac). Zoloft works to eliminate your symptoms and does not "make you act differently". Many Zoloft takers praise the drug for simply "taking off the edge" as it reduces anxiety.

FIGURE 10.2. *Several pages of Heather Saddler's brochure, "What, Me Depressed?"*

GIVEN/NEW

In light of the audience and context mentioned earlier, Saddler has to work doubly hard to find common ground with her readers, convincing them that an abstract, esoteric topic may have direct bearing on their immediate situation. To do this, she relies heavily on both visual and verbal cues to establish rapport with her readers and, subsequently, move them beyond their "given," their understanding of their own situation and the disease that is depression.

She begins establishing this rapport by including a photograph that ostensibly has nothing to do with the topic at hand but that actually reflects personal relationships the reader is likely to value. People in the photograph appear to be family members who are happy and comfortable with each other; at least during the moment the picture was taken, they are physically close, the adults smiling and holding their children. Further, Saddler uses a familiar, unintimidating format, one that typically presents technical information in relatively short chunks, makes key facts or points easy to find through the use of bulleted lists, and uses headings that anticipate a reader's likely questions. In effect, this format lets Saddler say, "I am not coming from the world of scientific research. I am coming from your world; I understand your harried lifestyle. Although I have access to specialized information, I am not a medical expert who will insist that you enter my discourse community in order to find out what I have to say. To the contrary, I am on your side, eager to present specialized information in ways that will be readily comprehensible and useful to you."

To continue to develop this personal rapport, Saddler uses many of the same verbal strategies that appear in Murayama's essay. She refers to things her readers are likely to have experienced—everyday complaints such as fatigue, muscle pain, even the occasional sleepless night, all of which are familiar to people who are not suffering from depression. She also refers to an assumption her readers are likely to share: that the clinical term *depression* applies only to people who are unable to function, spending most of their time sleeping or crying; everyone else just has a case of the "blues." Given this assumption, Saddler anticipates her readers' likely reaction to her brochure: "That's certainly not me!" In general, her sentences move from given information to new, and in the introductory scenario under the family photo, she sequences her sentences so they lead from a familiar, mundane experience ("you haven't quite been yourself lately") to a novel interpretation of that experience (the "startling news" that the reader "may be suffering from depression").

DISSONANCE

Because of her readers and the physical context in which they are likely to encounter this text, Saddler, like Murayama, has to work hard to create a sense of dissonance that will impel her readers to pick up the brochure and read it carefully. Thus it is not surprising that Saddler combines both visual and verbal information to challenge the reader's personal feelings, values, and understandings.

As noted earlier, the photograph of the family creates common ground with her readers. But when Saddler juxtaposes that picture against written text (the title of the brochure, "What, Me Depressed?"), she implies a threat to the feelings of warmth and security suggested by the picture. This family's situation may not be quite as pleasant and comforting as it seems. Further, she uses visual cues to emphasize aspects of the written text that may heighten readers' sense of dissonance. She uses large, boldface type to emphasize questions she hopes the reader will consider, and she poses those questions as headings—using white space as well as typeface to highlight those questions—for different sections of text. This is apparent in the heading **"So, what is depression?"** in the second column and in such subsequent headings as **"Do I really need an anti-depressant?"** and **"Are there any side effects?"** Finally, she uses bullets to highlight phenomena (the symptoms of depression) that she wants readers to consider in a new light.

To further her readers' personal sense of dissonance, Saddler begins with a scenario that sounds familiar (a visit to a doctor's office for minor complaints) and then gives that scenario a startling twist, presenting a new interpretation of familiar experiences. Other dissonances are explicit and directly related to the readers. For example, Saddler mentions disparities or conflicts between readers' likely misconceptions and the actual nature of depression. Contrary to what readers may think, depression is not an example of personal weakness that can be handled by simply trying to "snap out of it."

ACCESSIBILITY

As does Murayama, Saddler makes it easy for readers to see what she is getting at. In several respects, this "seeing" is quite literal. She structures her discussion around questions the reader is likely to ask, and she makes it easy for readers to find those questions, marking them in ways that have already been mentioned. This structure makes it easy for her harried readers to focus directly on issues that concern them and ignore the rest. And, again as already noted, she highlights key information about the symptoms of depression by placing them in a bulleted list, thereby enabling readers to find out quickly whether they may be suffering from depression. Saddler also uses different type styles to indicate different kinds of information: her introductory scenario is in italics; most of the immediately pertinent technical information appears in regular type; and on a subsequent page of the brochure, she marks background information by printing it in a shaded box.

In the text itself, she uses several strategies that should make it easy for her distracted audience to see what she is getting at and what they should expect in subsequent passages of text. She gets right to the point (e.g., "clinical depression is much more serious than a case of the blues"). And she follows through on expectations created by material appearing in the emphatic part of the sentence (e.g., having ended one sentence with an assertion about the seriousness of depression, she goes on in the next to elaborate on that seriousness: "In short, depression is the result of certain biologic and social forces . . . ").

TOPIC

As does Murayama, Saddler presents a good bit of authoritative-sounding factual information. Although she does not cite scholarly sources for her claims, she does appear quite knowledge-able, not only mentioning details readers are familiar with but also linking them with authoritative statistics (e.g., the number of women who suffer from depression). Like Murayama, Sad-dler defines specialized terms (e.g., *depression, seratonin*) and provides quotes (albeit hypothetical) and examples.

But in many respects, Saddler's exploration of her topic is much more personal than Murayama's. This personal quality is apparent in her selection of the photograph with which the bro-chure opens. People in this photograph are *regular* looking—reasonably attractive but not fashion models, the sort of middle-class people one might see working in a front yard or at a church or neighborhood meeting. Their very typicality readily enables a middle-class reader to identify with them personally.

This photograph and the scenario that follows it clearly ground the discussion in the realm of daily life rather than in that of scientific inquiry. Many of her sentences focus on human be-ings doing something rather than on abstract concepts. And even when she narrates a scientific process—e.g., her explanation of "how anti-depressants work"—she does so in anthropomorphic terms (e.g., "Seratonin neurons set the overall or activity level of other regulatory systems"). When she defines a specialized term, she does so to correct a misperception a lay person might have.

VOICE

As is the case in other texts analyzed in this chapter, much of what there is to say about voice in this brochure is already im-plied in earlier discussions. To use Walker Gibson's term, Saddler seems "close" to both reader and subject. She uses personal pro-nouns and conversational diction ("haven't quite been yourself"; "we all get the blues"), and talks in terms of what the reader may be experiencing or may need to do to combat depression. She is even more solicitous of her readers' time and energy than is Murayama, giving visual cues (indentation, white space, differ-ent typefaces, bullets) that help a busy reader find key points easily. She presents her explanation in a brochure format, thereby obligating herself to present information in relatively brief chunks of text that can be readily absorbed by readers with multiple demands on their time and attention.

"Linking Mind and Brain in the Study of Mental Illnesses: A Project for a Scientific Psychopathology"

This article, which appeared in the magazine *Science*, seems addressed to an audience having more in common with Murayama's readers than with Saddler's. (Figure 10.3 is the first page of this article.) Author Nancy Andreasen appears to assume that her readers

- ◆ Have both time and inclination to follow a detailed, complicated discussion;

- ◆ Value scholarship for its intrinsic interest rather than for its immediate applications;

- ◆ May know relatively little about the specific topic at hand but know a good bit about related fields and about scientific methodology.

GIVEN/NEW

In many ways, Nancy Andreasen's article contrasts dramatically with Saddler's brochure, differing not only in content and tone but also in visual appearance. Yet, as does Saddler's brochure, Andreasen's piece combines both textual and visual features to develop common ground with readers, saying, in effect, "I am one of you. We share many assumptions, values, and background knowledge. I differ from you in my expertise on this specific topic. But otherwise, you and I are peers, perhaps even colleagues; we are all comfortable in the world of scientific research and are ready to take a long, careful look at an esoteric subject."

Much of this common ground is established in the way Andreasen explores her topic (discussed below). However, a good bit of common ground comes from the values implicit in both the words and visual appearance of the article. Frequently, Andreasen alludes to values that are likely to be shared by her readers. She assumes, for example, that her readers will appreci-

Linking Mind and Brain in the Study of Mental Illnesses: A Project for a Scientific Psychopathology

Nancy C. Andreasen

Brain research on mental illnesses has made substantial advances in recent years, supported by conceptual and technological developments in cognitive neuroscience. Brain-based cognitive models of illnesses such as schizophrenia and depression have been tested with a variety of techniques, including the lesion method, tract tracing, neuroimaging, animal modeling, single-cell recording, electrophysiology, neuropsychology, and experimental cognitive psychology. A relatively sophisticated picture is emerging that conceptualizes mental illnesses as disorders of mind arising in the brain. Convergent data using multiple neuroscience techniques indicate that the neural mechanisms of mental illnesses can be understood as dysfunctions in specific neural circuits and that their functions and dysfunctions can be influenced or altered by a variety of cognitive and pharmacological factors.

In 1895, a little-known Viennese neuropsychiatrist named Sigmund Freud wrote a largely unnoticed work entitled *A Project for a Scientific Psychology*, in which he proposed that the cognitive mechanisms of normal and abnormal mental phenomena could be explained through orderly and rigorous study of brain systems. Freud began his career researching pharmacology (the therapeutic effects of cocaine), neurology (aphasia in children), and basic neuroscience (staining techniques for visualizing neurons), but he ultimately abandoned both the project and neuropsychiatry. During the *fin de siècle* 1900s, however, Freud's project is slowly being achieved. This fruition reflects the maturity of the techniques of neuroscience, as well as the convergence of efforts from multiple domains: psychiatry, cognitive psychology and neuropsychology, and clinical and basic neuroscience. Models of illness mechanisms have been developed through the use of clinical observation, experimental paradigms developed in psychology, animal and human lesion studies, anatomic studies of neural circuits, neuroimaging, and behavioral neuropharmacology. The long-term goal is to achieve a "scientific psychopathology": to identify the neural mechanisms of normal cognitive processes and to understand how they are injured in mental illnesses.

This overview provides a summary of some of the fundamental conceptual issues that are being addressed in pursuit of this long-term goal. The work of neuroscientists studying two common mental illnesses—

schizophrenia and depression—illustrates the consensus that is developing among investigators who begin with different strategies originating from different disciplines in the broad field of cognitive neuroscience.

Fundamental Conceptual Issues

The relationship between mind and brain. Mental illnesses have historically been distinguished from other medical illnesses because they affect the higher cognitive processes that are referred to as "mind." The relationship between mind and brain has been extensively discussed in contemporary philosophy and psychology, without any decisive resolution (1). One heuristic solution, therefore, is to adopt the position that the mind is the expression of the activity of the brain and that these two are separable for purposes of analysis and discussion but inseparable in actuality. That is, mental illnesses arise from the brain, but mental experience also affects the brain, as is demonstrated by the many examples of environmental influences on brain plasticity (2). The aberrations of mental illnesses reflect abnormalities in the brain/mind's interaction with its surrounding world; they are diseases of a psyche (or mind) that resides in that region of the soma (or body) that is the brain.

Mind and brain can be studied as if they are separate entities, however, and this is reflected in the multiple and separate disciplines that examine them. Each uses a different language and methodology to study the same quiddity. The challenge in developing a scientific psychopathology in the 1990s is to use the power of multiple disciplines. The study of mind has been the prov-

ince of cognitive psychology, which has divided mind into component domains of investigation (such as memory, language, and attention), created theoretical systems to explain the workings of those domains (constructs such as memory encoding versus retrieval), and designed experimental paradigms to test the hypotheses in human beings and animals (3). The study of brain has been the province of several disciplines. Neuropsychology has used the lesion method to determine localization by observing absence of function after injury, whereas neuroanatomy and neurobiology have mapped neural development and connectivity and studied functionality in animal models (4). The boundaries between all these disciplines have become increasingly less distinct, however, creating the broad discipline of cognitive neuroscience. The term "cognitive" has definitions that range from broad to narrow; its usage here is broad as it covers all activities of mind, including emotion, perception, and regulation of behavior.

Contemporary psychiatry studies mental illnesses as diseases that manifest as mind and arise from brain. It is the discipline within cognitive neuroscience that integrates information from all these related disciplines in order to develop models that explain the cognitive dysfunctions of psychiatric patients based on knowledge of normal brain/mind function.

Using the phenomenotype to find the biotype. There are at present no known biological diagnostic markers for any mental illnesses except dementias such as Alzheimer's disease. The to-be-discovered lesions that define the remainder of mental illnesses are likely to be occurring at complex or small-scale levels that are difficult to visualize and measure, such as the connectivity of neural circuits, neuronal signaling and signal transduction, and abnormalities in genes or gene expression. Despite their lack of a defining objective index such as glucosuria is for diabetes, however, these illnesses are very real. Not only do they produce substantial morbidity and mortality, but advances in psychiatric nosology have produced objective, criterion-based, assessment techniques that produce reliable and precise diagnoses (5). In the absence of a pathological marker, the current definitions of mental illnesses are syndromal and are

The author is at the Mental Health Clinical Research Center, The University of Iowa Hospitals and Clinics and College of Medicine, 200 Hawkins Drive, Iowa City, IA 52242, USA.

FIGURE 10.3. *Page 1 of Nancy Andreasen's* Science *article, "Linking Mind and Brain in the Study of Mental Illnesses: A Project for a Scientific Psychopathology."*

ate the need for "a defining objective index" or for an adequate "model" of a phenomenon that cannot be observed directly. She refers to such matters without explaining or justifying them. They are simply givens in the discourse community she and her readers inhabit.

– 228 –

The serious, thoughtful nature of this community is further reflected in the visual elements of the article. As with Saddler's brochure, the article's format itself becomes a given, in this case creating the visual impression of a scholarly journal, one whose contents would be taken seriously by Andreasen's audience. Although the heading "Abstract" is not used, the piece begins with what is clearly an abstract, a single paragraph set apart from the text by its two-column line length and bold, sans serif typeface, not to mention the black bar that appears just below the paragraph. At the bottom of the first column, again set off by a black bar and sans serif typeface, is a brief note indicating the author's scholarly affiliation.

The scholarly nature of the piece is further emphasized by the columns of text that give the piece a "gray" look typical of scholarly articles; headings and subheadings are relatively few, and the visual images that do appear (toward the end of the article) seem designed to convey highly technical information about the subject rather than to promote, say, human-interest aspects of the topic. Overall, the visual appearance of the page conspires with the written text to suggest that both writer and readers have the discipline and focus to persist in understanding a complex, technical subject with little in the way of entertainment or diversion.

DISSONANCE

As one might expect in a scholarly looking journal such as *Science*, dissonances are muted. This is not a sensationalizing journal—it is not *Parade* or *Psychology Today*, in which readers have to be drawn into complicated topics with startling images or dramatic challenges to what someone (the reader, other authorities) mistakenly believes to be true. There is virtually no dissonance in the visual appearance of the piece; the page design looks conventional, designed to appeal to, even reassure, a scholarly, thoughtful audience that there are still places where complex subjects will be examined in a dispassionate way. The only possible source of dissonance created through graphics comes late in the article, where Andreasen presents a series of photographs that show subtle differences between the neural circuits of two healthy people and those of two schizophrenics. These visual differences are, at least to the untrained eye, so subtle as to be unrecognizable without the text that accompanies them. (The photographs are too small to reproduce in this chapter.)

Dissonances in the written text are similarly understated. These dissonances are subtle, often implicit, requiring the reader to pay close attention and perhaps to bring a good bit of background knowledge to the text in order to appreciate various conflicts or incongruities. Some of this background knowledge is widely shared. Most readers, for example, would appreciate the incongruity of referring to Sigmund Freud as a "little-known Viennese neuropsychologist"—an accurate characterization of Freud at one stage of his career, but hardly consistent with his current status in the history of treatment of mental illness.

Other dissonances arise from still more specialized knowledge that only certain readers could bring to the text. For example, at the end of the introductory section Andreasen remarks on "the consensus that is developing among investigators who begin with different strategies originating from different disciplines. . . ." Consensus sounds reassuring enough, but anyone who has attempted cross-disciplinary work understands that such consensus is usually achieved only after prolonged struggle—to understand another discipline's concepts, to protect the turf of one's own discipline, or even to soothe the ego of researchers who find that scholars in other fields may treat them with less deference than they have grown accustomed to from members of their own field. For the insider, then, this article may evoke a good bit of dissonance not readily accessible to outsiders. The insider quality of dissonance here serves, perhaps ironically, to heighten the bonds of the "given" or common ground.

ACCESSIBILITY/ORGANIZATION

Superficially, Andreasen's article appears to have much more in common with Murayama's than with Saddler's. Although printed in three-column format, it is clearly a scholarly article, not a brochure, and some pages consist of lines of written text uninterrupted by bullets, pictures, or headings set in a large, dramatic typeface. Furthermore, Andreasen makes use of the same verbal strategies Murayama uses in creating and fulfilling expectations. She includes a number of forecasting phrases that are clearly linked to subsequent sections of the text. For example, the second paragraph includes a phrase ("fundamental conceptual issues") that is echoed at the beginning of the first major section of the article. She routinely puts her claims at the beginning of a section of text (see, for example, the first sentence of paragraph 4). And she usually fulfills the expectations created by the material she situates in the emphatic position at the end of a sentence. In paragraph 3, for instance, she notes that "mind" and "brain" are "separable for purposes of analysis and discussion but inseparable in actuality." This apparent paradox creates the expectation that she will explain her statement, which she does in the next sentence, "That is, ..."

Despite these similarities to Murayama's essay, some of the accessibility of Andreasen's text comes from her use of the same kinds of visual cues that Saddler uses. Andreasen's article incorporates headings and subheadings that are given visual emphasis: slightly larger boldface type for the first level headings and italics for the second level headings. Further, the article uses various visual cues to mark different types of information. The abstract is printed in dark, sans serif type, with lines extending across two columns. Legends for the photographs included toward the end of the article are also presented in sans serif type with some lines extending across more than one column. Although visual cues in the Andreasen essay are less dramatic than in the Saddler brochure, they are present and they help readers see what the author is getting at and what kind of information a reader can expect to find in a given section.

TOPIC

As with Murayama's essay, the visual appearance of this piece is so familiar that we could overlook its significance in the exploration of the topic. In contrast to the constraints imposed by a brochure format, Andreasen has plenty of space to explore her topic fully, with no need to break it into discrete, easily digestible chunks. She is able to use several graphics which reflect the impersonal, dispassionate exploration of subject matter apparent in the written text.

In developing this sort of explanation, Andreasen does all of the things one would expect a writer to do in discussing "fundamental conceptual issues" concerning an area of scientific inquiry. Although she cites some of her own research in this area, she rarely asserts her own opinion and provides no cues regarding her feelings about the prospects for "linking mind and brain." She draws on a wide range of authoritative-looking sources, many of them published recently enough to suggest that she is up to date on work in this area. She categorizes scholarly work (e.g., that which treats mind and brain as though they can be studied separately and that which assumes they cannot). She defines some terms that may have specialized meaning in this field (e.g., *pharmacology*, in paragraph 1) and leaves undefined those terms (e.g., *lesion method, memory encoding*) whose meaning might either be inferred from context or be clear to someone who routinely reads medical research.

Voice

All of the preceding analysis suggests the voice of someone who is highly knowledgeable about the subject but not emotionally engaged with the topic. This detachment is suggested not only in ways already mentioned but also in the relative abstractness of Andreasen's discussion. Following principles articulated by Joseph Williams and others, she gives most of her sentences an agent-action structure, but the agents are almost invariably abstractions or concepts. Consider, for example, the grammatical subjects of clauses in the second paragraph; actions are being performed, but the agents are "this overview" and "the work of neuroscientists." A human agent, Freud, appears only briefly in the early sentences of paragraph 1. This detachment is echoed in visual features that have already been mentioned: long, virtually uninterrupted stretches of "gray" text and the highly detailed photographs of neural circuits that remove any sense of "human interest" in the topic.

What We *Can* Do, What We *Should* Do

Running throughout this discussion has been one fundamental assumption about our work as composition/rhetoric specialists: we need some principled way to help students integrate visual elements into their composing. In effect, it is no longer possible or desirable to think of ourselves strictly as "writing" teachers; we need to move away from the graphocentrism that currently dominates much of our teaching and almost all of our popular composition textbooks.

This point of view, of course, invites a number of objections or at least caveats. For one thing, as Steve Doheny-Farina has pointed out, visual images can have such emotional power that they do not always invite careful reflection; indeed, they can subvert such reflection. This is certainly true of video or multimedia presentations, and it can also be true of images included in print. Furthermore, technologically sophisticated writers can produce visually attractive texts that have little substance, a situation giving new meaning to the request for "More matter with less art." And finally, there is the fact that many (most? all?) of the sophisticated graphics we see in popular media are created not by writers but by graphic designers. It seems unlikely, for example, that Nancy Andreasen had much to do with the page design and typography of her article "Linking Mind and Brain."

Doheny-Farina's point about visual information is undoubtedly true. But it also applies to features of written text: careful reflection can be thwarted by the use of emotionally loaded language, by the selection and manipulation of "facts," or by the unacknowledged use of dubious assumptions. As is the case with every other communicative practice, students need to learn to use visual elements ethically as well as effectively.

As for the prospect of students' using visuals to give their written work an attractive appearance in order to mask superficiality or disorganization, that prospect is already a reality. Students who do not have access to a computer often do have access to a local typing service, where computer operators can manipulate line length and typeface, even managing to stretch a two-page paper so that it appears to satisfy a minimum requirement of a three-page paper. One way or another, students have access to all sorts of visual devices. And even students who have a great deal to say—students such as Veronica Murayama—make effective use of these devices. The look of her essay may not have been a conscious choice. That is, she may not have considered turning in a brochure or a hypermedia text instead of creating a conventional college essay. But the visual appearance of her work represents a set of choices, not a set of constraints that must govern all the writing people do in college or in life. Surely our responsibility as teachers of rhetoric and composition is to help students understand what their options are in a given situation and make full use of all the communicative resources that exist in our culture.

Important as these options are, it is true that writers may have little to say about how their work appears on the printed page of a magazine. Yet it is also true that much of the world's writing is done by people who do not consider themselves "writers" but who nonetheless need to communicate effectively through their written texts. As Janice Redish and colleagues have shown, these nonprofessional writers often need to use page design, graphics, and type style to make their messages clear and accessible. And, of course, we need to consider the relationship between writing and reading. As students learn to make wise use of visual elements in their own writing, they can also develop a critical awareness of ways other people are using those elements to advance their own ends.

In essence, then, we argue that teachers of rhetoric and composition find themselves and their students already immersed in a world in which visual elements are central to communication even though most of us have no training to help us function effectively in this world. Perhaps the integrative principles described in this chapter will constitute a bridge of shared features linking the visual and the verbal, a bridge that will help us cross into a new conception of our work as teachers, scholars, and "writers."

Works Cited

Andreasen, Nancy. "Linking Mind and Brain in the Study of Mental Illnesses: A Project for a Scientific Psychopathology." *Science* 275(1997): 1586–93.

Axelrod, Rise, and Charles R. Cooper. *The St. Martin's Guide to Writing.* 5th ed. New York: St. Martin's, 1997.

Barton, Ben F., and Marthalee S. Barton. "Toward a Rhetoric of Visuals for the Computer Era." *Technical Writing Teacher* 12 (1985): 126–45.

Becker, Alton L. "Literacy and Cultural Change: Some Experiences." *Literacy for Life: The Demand for Reading and Writing.* Ed. Richard W. Bailey and Robin Melanie Fosheim. New York: MLA, 1983. 201–15.

Burke, Kenneth. *Counter-Statement.* Berkeley: U of California P, 1968.

Doheny-Farina, Stephen. *The Wired Neighborhood.* New Haven: Yale UP, 1996.

Elbow, Peter. "Introduction: About Voice and Writing." *Landmark Essays on Voice and Writing.* Ed. Peter Elbow. Davis, CA: Hermagoras, 1994. xi–xlvii.

———. *Writing without Teachers.* New York: Oxford UP, 1973.

Festinger, Leon. *Toward a Theory of Cognitive Dissonance.* Stanford: Stanford UP, 1957.

Flower, Linda. *Problem-Solving Strategies for Writing.* New York: Harcourt, 1981.

Gibson, W. Walker. *Persona: A Style Study for Readers and Writers.* New York: Random, 1969.

Keyes, Elizabeth. "Typography, Color, and Information Structure." *Technical Communication* 40 (1993): 638–54.

Murayama, Veronica. "Schizophrenia: What It Looks Like, How It Feels." Axelrod and Cooper 173–76.

Odell, Lee, and Christina M. Prell. "Rethinking Research on Composing: Arguments for a New Research Agenda." *History, Reflection, and Narrative: The Professionalism of Composition, 1963–1983.* Ed. Mary I. Rosner, Beth A. Boehm, and Debra Journet. Stamford, CT: Albex, 1999.

Piaget, Jean. *Six Psychological Studies*. Ed. David Elkind. Trans. Anita Tenzer and David Elkind. New York: Vintage, 1968.

Redish, Janice C. "Understanding Readers." *Techniques for Technical Communicators*. Ed. Carol M. Barnum and Saul Carliner. New York: Macmillan, 1993. 14–41.

Redish, Janice C., Robin M. Battison, and Edward S. Gold. "Making Information Accessible to Readers." *Writing in Nonacademic Settings*. Ed. Lee Odell and Dixie Goswami. New York: Guilford, 1985. 129–53.

Saddler, Heather. *What, Me Depressed?* Brochure. Xerographic copy, 1996.

Schriver, Karen. *Dynamics in Document Design: Creating Text for Readers*. New York: Wiley, 1997.

Williams, Joseph. *Style: Ten Lessons in Clarity and Grace*. 6th ed. New York: Longman, 2000.

Young, Richard E., Alton L. Becker, and Kenneth L. Pike. *Rhetoric: Discovery and Change*. New York: Harcourt, 1970.

CHAPTER ELEVEN

Inventing the American Research University: Nineteenth-Century American Science and the New Middle Class

DANETTE PAUL
Brigham Young University

ANN M. BLAKESLEE
Eastern Michigan University

The American perspective of the history of science, as exemplified in Reingold's *Science in Nineteenth-Century America,* generally begins with British and European "great men of science" such as Copernicus, Newton, and Darwin, then moves almost immediately to Watson and Crick and onto twentieth-century Americans, primarily at large research institutions.[1] This pattern indicates four assumptions about American science: first, a seamless and natural transition from seventeenth-, eighteenth-, and nineteenth-century British and European scientists (primarily British) to twentieth-century American scientists; second, a parallel development of science in the nineteenth century in Great Britain and the United States (i.e., similar cultural and economic forces in operation); third, the inferiority of American science until the twentieth century; and fourth, the natural evolution of the American research institution from European models. Given these assumptions, we seem to have little reason to examine nineteenth-century American science or its relationship to the development of the modern American research university. However, closer examination of the actual players on either side of the Atlantic reveals distinct class differences between American and

British scientists, and, consequently, very different motivations and arguments for advancing science. Such an examination also reveals quite different outcomes in regard to how science developed and how it achieved its place in the modern American university.

For the most part, British scientists before the twentieth century were gentlemen with enough leisure and curiosity to wonder how the world worked and with enough money to pursue the answers. American scientists prior to the twentieth century, on the other hand, were middle-class men with enough curiosity to wonder how to make the world work better and with enough hope to believe the answers would result in both money and leisure. In other words, American scientists had a distinctly practical bent; they seemed more interested in scientific invention than in theories. In this chapter, we argue that the distinct characteristics of American science, which were closely tied to middle-class values, played an important role in transforming the traditional liberal arts college into the American research university.

Discovering how science was established in American universities entails considering the larger social and cultural contexts for this establishment and the rhetoric that surrounds and supports those contexts. In *The Cultural Meaning of the Scientific Revolution,* Margaret Jacob argues that genius or perseverance alone cannot account for the place achieved by or the meaning assigned to science in our culture; larger historical/contextual factors must be considered in any attempt to account for the integration and use of science in contemporary American society (4–5). Far from a haphazard occurrence, the integration of science into American universities was a purposeful strategy that resulted from the interrelationships among various social and cultural influences. These influences are apparent in the rhetoric that situates science in the university; they acted persuasively to effect change in late nineteenth-century American culture and education.

The shift in American scientific activity in the late nineteenth century is thus best understood as rhetorical. We argue that the proponents of science acted rhetorically in securing the position of science in the university. First, they appealed to the values of the developing middle class, and then they negotiated the contrasting rhetorics of pure and applied science, thus redefining the meaning and role of higher education in American society. We examine the goals and structure of the early American liberal arts college; scientific activity before the modern university, contrasting the American and the British developments of science; the growing number of young middle-class men; and, finally, the goals and structures of the modern research university, looking in particular at the development of Johns Hopkins University, which is considered the first modern American research university.

America's "Old Time" College: Ancient Authority and Mental Discipline

To understand how science gained dominance in the modern American university, we must first understand the goals, structures, and values of the earlier liberal arts college, what Bledstein calls the "Old Time College." A careful analysis of these factors reveals that the assumptions underlying the goals and structure of the old time colleges were antithetical to the development of a curriculum with science at its center.

A Religious Education

From the founding of Harvard in 1636 up through the beginning of the nineteenth century, most colleges in America were established and run by religious institutions. Naturally, this foundation affected the goals of the university in terms of curriculum. According to *New England's First Fruits,* the first generation of New Englanders wanted "to advance learning and perpetuate it to posterity; dreading to leave an illiterate ministry to the churches when our present ministers shall lie in the dust" (qtd. in Hofstadter and Hardy 1). William and Mary's charter was established so "that the church of Virginia may be furnished with a seminary of Ministries of the gospel and that the youth may be piously educated in good letters and manners" (qtd. in Hofstadter and Hardy 2). Yale's objectives are also to make their students "fitted for publick employment in both church and civil state" (qtd. in

Hofstadter and Hardy 2). As other scholars have noted (Bledstein; Veysey; Dewey), a broader survey of college charters would find similar goals for students: to prepare them as ministers and leaders in educated society. These goals led to a four-year regime of classical training for children of the American gentry to promote piety and strength of character. Even faculty were selected and rewarded not on the basis of their scholarship and expertise, but on the basis of their moral character—practices influenced by a theological orthodoxy that characterized seventeenth-century Puritan society (Veysey 25, 45). Scientific knowledge, in particular, was viewed as suspect and often as unnecessary; the human soul was the vital force that activated mind and body, and science could not measure the soul or discover its properties [2] (Veysey 22). In short, the role of education was not to teach science but to develop the mental and moral faculties of the soul.

However, in some ways the religious training itself did not undercut the study of science as much as the goals that old time colleges shared with established British universities. Although placing a heavier emphasis on moral goodness, the old time colleges' goals of preparing sons for the ministry or for society were much the same as the goals of the universities in England that trained the sons of aristocracy and gentry for their place in society. The similarities became more marked over time when the percentage of graduates who trained for the ministry dropped from approximately 70 percent in the beginning (approximately 1650 to 1700) to less than 10 percent at the beginning of the nineteenth century (Hofstadter and Hardy 6–7).

Furthermore, the educated leaders in early colonial America were often from the gentry or wealthy merchant class and therefore had been educated in established British universities, such as Cambridge (John Winthorpe and Roger Williams) or Oxford (Richard Mather). Naturally, they looked to their own education for a pattern on which to establish the new universities. Harvard's charter, for example, is very similar to Cambridge's. The founders' desire to recreate Cambridge prompted them to change the town's name from Newtowne to Cambridge in honor of some of the founders' alma mater. Not surprisingly, the founders borrowed the British universities' curriculum and their teaching methods. Therefore, the old time colleges offered a curriculum consisting of the medieval liberal arts. Students were expected to know Latin and Greek and, later, mathematics. They continued the study they had begun in their grammar schools and were taught primarily through lectures and drills.

An Upper-Class Education

This educational system, however, was more than the routine of the way things were done. It was built on aristocratic assumptions about education and truth that privileged the status quo. And in privileging the status quo, it ran contrary to the goals and purposes of modern science. As Hofstadter and Hardy have argued, important assumptions underlie this type of educational system: assumptions about whom education is for, what knowledge is, and how students learn (11–15). The question about whom education was for in the old time colleges is the easiest to answer: "Education was for gentlemen; it was designed to create among them a common core of central knowledge that would make them a community of the educated" (11). This assumption made education a form of initiation, not a quest for knowledge. As this education was an entrance to an already established lifestyle, knowledge had no practical application beyond the ability to speak, read, and write like a gentleman. What counted as knowledge was also clearly laid out. According to Hofstadter and Hardy, "a particular conception of knowledge was also tacitly or explicitly assumed. Knowledge was thought of as a certain more or less fixed quantum of truth" (14). Clearly, the notion of a fixed body of knowledge stands in direct opposition to the nineteenth-century scientific ideals of discovery and progress. Furthermore, in a system of fixed knowledge, experimentation and, to some extent, observation were unnecessary.

How students learned in this system is equally clear. Knowledge was presented by the professor and consumed by the students (as has been well documented by Berlin). This methodology was supported by "a particular theory of the nature of the mind . . . . The object of education was to exercise a form of mental discipline which would train the faculties of the mind [such as memory, reason, imagination, and judgment] for their uses, much as an athlete trains his muscles" (Hofstadter and Hardy 14–15).

Therefore, students in American colleges received a classical training guided by the "banner of mental discipline," which focused on drills for intellectual exercises (Veysey 9; Dewey; Berlin).

These conditions created a system which introduced students to a stable world of knowledge and instilled in them habits and manners that would allow them to take their "respectable place in society" (Veysey 4) rather than allow them to change that world with new knowledge and new career paths. Built on these elitist values, American education, despite the economic conditions of its students, was a thoroughly upper-class affair. As a result, empiricism did not replace ancient authority as a powerful intellectual tendency in American colleges until at least the 1870s (Veysey 126). Therefore, the cultural context of America before the beginning of the nineteenth century did not leave room for the inclusion of empirical science in its curriculum or for arguments for its inclusion.

Scientific Activity before the Modern University

Scientists as "Amateurs"

Given the incompatibility of the goals of science and those of the traditional "classical" education, it is clear why science before the nineteenth century was considered an avocation or hobby and generally not associated with colleges or universities. Scientific "amateurs," generally called natural philosophers, pursued investigations usually because of personal interest. In fact, the term *scientist* was not coined, nor was science considered a career, until the late nineteenth century (Kronick 104, 127). Science's dramatic change in status from an interesting hobby to a prestigious career over the course of the nineteenth century and the arguments and persuasive appeals that surrounded this change are key to understanding the role of science in contemporary society. The development of science in Britain has been the subject of a great deal of study (Atkinson; Bazerman; Kaufer and Carley). Because of the rise of industrialization and the middle class during this same period in both England and America, the rise in science in both countries is assumed to be similar.

However, careful examination of the actual events in each country indicates several significant differences in the ascendancy of science in the nineteenth century in the United States and in Britain. In particular, differences in the social class of the scientists and social structures of each country led to different motivations for the scientists; therefore, the scientists aligned themselves with different social forces and made different appeals to effect a change in science's status in each country. British scientists, as members of the upper class of a stable, highly structured society, constructed their scientific ethos based on the upper-class values of elitism and scholarship to effect a change in the role of science in Great Britain. On the other hand, American scientists, as members of the middle class in a highly fluid society, constructed their scientific ethos based on the middle-class values of utility, progress, and individuality to bring about a change in the role of science in the United States. In this section, we will briefly discuss the development of science in Britain, primarily as a means of comparison, and then focus on the development of science in America.

The Development of Science in Britain

As noted earlier, for the most part British scientists prior to the twentieth century were gentlemen with enough leisure and curiosity to wonder how the world worked (in other words, pure science) and with enough money to pursue their interests. More serious "scientists" who did not have wealth but had connections were funded by patrons. Whether hobbyists or serious scientists, most early British scientists belonged to scientific societies. The first and most prestigious scientific society in England was the Royal Society of London, which held its first meeting in 1645 and received a Royal charter in 1662. Scientific societies were an important part of the development of science in Britain for several reasons: first, these societies built on the upper-class ideal of a community of scholars; second, they operated within the established class structure because of the support they received from the aristocracy (most notably, the king); third, they regulated activities and maintained standards of performance, spreading news through their publications and meetings. In other words, these societies to a large extent controlled the ethos and rhetoric of nineteenth-century British science.

Although scientific societies, particularly the Royal Society, saw themselves as a radical departure from the university system (Kaufer and Carley 351), the societies adopted many of the upper-class ideals of that system. In line with the upper-class education of their members, these societies considered themselves an elite community of scholars and like-minded gentlemen. There were certain things a gentleman should know; enlightened gentlemen recognized science as one of those things. Russell's observations of late seventeenth-century scientists support these assertions. He argues that two features "embodied, more or less, in all scientific academies of the day were a preoccupation with open communication, and a sense of cultural superiority" (71). These values of open communication within an elite group of gentlemen helped to establish and secure a place for science within the stable social structure of British society.

To help create feelings of cultural superiority and social stability, these scientific societies actively recruited established members of the upper class. The Royal Society, for example, originally attempted to limit membership to serious scientists, but it soon opened its ranks to any member of the peerage of a baronet or higher to curry favor and patronage with wealthy members of the aristocracy. In addition, the leaders of the Royal Society rhetorically situated the society within the status quo, creating a safe and secure ethos for the organization. As Russell notes, Spratt's history of the Royal Society "deliberately played down the puritan sympathies of many of its founders" (70), while at the same time the society was "flooding" its membership with the peerage and the clergy. And naturally, the society's royal charter, though without financial support from the crown, added particular prestige to both the society and science.[3]

To provide open communications and to further scientific scholarship, scientific societies held meetings, presented demonstrations, and eventually created publications. Because members of the societies met for an open exchange of ideas, those ideas were subject to considerable scrutiny. The public discussions of ideas both in the meetings and through correspondence led to standardization (e.g., the Newton/Hooke debate; see Bazerman;

Gross). Furthermore, the correspondence eventually led to the founding of scientific journals (Bazerman; Kaufer and Carley). The societies offered "prize essays" to encourage research and publication in their journals (Veysey 125; Kronick 125). However, the journal system was not without its challenges. Instead of regularly publishing in society journals, scientists frequently submitted articles to popular magazines because of the public's interest in their work. Also, popular publications often proved more efficient publication vehicles since society journals could take years to accumulate sufficient materials to publish a volume. Because the specialized discourse that today prevents public access to much scientific work did not yet exist, the popular press also ensured wider exposure of a scientist's work (Kronick 104; Jacob).

This persuasive combination of appealing to upper-class values and broadly publishing results led to a top-down dissemination of scientific information that fueled the ascendancy of science in Britain at the end of the nineteenth century. British science largely bypassed the established educational system; however, because of Britain's highly structured social system, it was able to recreate the upper-class system within scientific societies, creating a community of scholars primarily interested in "pure" science.

The Development of Science in America

While science in Britain was successful in creating a place for itself in society by appealing to upper-class values, the same strategies were not as successful in nineteenth-century America because the ascent of science in America took place in a substantially different cultural context and was therefore supported by a different rhetorical context. First, because of the highly fluid structure of American society, a top-down approach, especially one outside of the colleges, would not have been effective. Second, because nineteenth-century American scientists were primarily middle-class men, they were motivated not only by their curiosity about the way the world worked but also by the ambition to make the world work better for them. Science, particularly applied science in the form of inventions, was a potential means for both social and economic progress and therefore for personal and professional advancement. Although some attempts were made both to build on upper-class values and to use scientific societies, nineteenth-century American science succeeded in becoming a powerful force in America primarily by building on the middle-class values of utility, progress, and individuality.

At first glance, the American attempt to promote science seems remarkably similar to the British attempt. Both largely bypassed an educational system that was antithetical to the goals of science, and both tried to establish societies to fill in the gaps in the educational system. In 1743–44, one hundred years after the founding of the Royal Society, Benjamin Franklin founded the first American learned society, the American Philosophical Society (APS). Franklin's leisure seemed to be one of his motivating factors. According to Franklin, "The first drudgery of settling new colonies is now pretty well over, and there are many provinces in circumstances that set them at ease and afford leisure to cultivate the finer arts, and improve the common stock of knowledge" (*APS Year Book* 298). A short time later, Franklin formed "a society of the 'most ingenious and curious men'"(*APS Year Book* 298).

However, there are several important differences between the British and American societies. First, the Royal Society was formed to explore "new philosophy or experimental philosophy" (Ornstein 93), whereas the APS was formed "to promote useful knowledge in the colonies" (*APS Year Book* 298). This broad concept of "useful knowledge" also resulted in a wider range of topics. While the Royal Society focused on "remarkable discoveries, inventions and experiments in the improvement of Mathematics, Mechanics, Astronomy, Navigation, Physics and Chemistry" (Ornstein 104), the American Philosophical Society, both in goals and practices, explored more diverse topics. Indeed, the areas of interest listed in the original charter focus first on practicalities, such as "Plants . . . and Methods of Propagating them . . . Improvements in vegetable Juices . . . Curing or Preventing Diseasing . . . [and] New mechanical Inventions for Saving Labour" (*APS Year Book* 273). Only in concluding does the document mention "And all philosophical Experiments that let Light into the Nature of Things, tend to increase the Power of Man over Matter and multiply the Conveniences of Pleasures of

Life" (*APS Year Book* 273). Americans were primarily interested in practical ways of improving the quality of life.

Most important, the members of the organization considered themselves primarily a "middling" sort of people. In eighteenth-century America, "middling" was not directly related to economic conditions, but rather to the ideology of rational moderation (Bledstein 9). Jackson Turner Main estimates that "70 percent of the white population" belonged to "a middling, property-owning class" (273). The members' perception of themselves as belonging to this middling class had several consequences. Although the ideology of the middling class valued individual achievement over class or rank, during this period it also balanced its individuality with communal needs. This ideology is reflected in the inclusive language of the APS charter. Unlike the exclusivity of the Royal Society rhetoric, the 1780 charter from Pennsylvania "guaranteed that the APS might correspond with learned individuals and institutions 'of any nation or country' on legitimate business at all times 'whether in peace or war'"(APS Homepage). In reality, the inclusive rhetoric was for white males (although women of rank and distinction could become members—the first being the Russian Princess Dashkova, the president of the Imperial Academy in St. Petersburg in 1789) (ASP Homepage). Nevertheless, the society saw itself as open to all learned individuals. The APS, then, reflected the values of the middle class: it was a private enterprise rather than government sponsored, it focused on practical knowledge, and it used an inclusive rhetoric in describing its membership.

The American Association for the Advancement of Science (AAAS) also used inclusive rhetoric in its founding documents in 1848. According to its charter, anyone was allowed to join, whether scientist or layman (AAAS Homepage). Even women seemed welcome. The first woman, astronomer Maria Mitchell, joined in 1850, and two more women followed before 1860. Furthermore, the minutes for these meetings were widely reported in the newspapers (AAAS Homepage). This inclusiveness was part of the association's mission, which was to "advance education in science, and increase the public's understanding and appreciation of the promise of scientific methods in human progress" (AAAS Homepage).

The American organization that most closely reflected the Royal Society in the nineteenth century—i.e., government sponsored, experimental philosophy, exclusive membership—was the National Academy of Sciences. But the National Academy, modeled on the Royal Society, was not a powerful force in American science until the twentieth century, after science had been successfully established in American culture. The bill to establish the National Academy was signed by President Lincoln and Congress without much fanfare in 1863 when the states were preoccupied with war rather than scientific advancement. The organization was exclusive to the point of excluding three well-known scientists from its ranks. Plagued by infighting, the National Academy probably would have died a slow death if it had not been for a large bequest from one of its members (Reingold 202). Reingold sums up the situation thus: "What was the significance of the founding of the National Academy of Sciences? Strangely enough, the most important aspect of the founding is that nothing happened. Most other great national academies became forces for research in their country. But in America, no powerful general scientific bodies came into being" (202). Clearly, the upper-class values at the core of this institution did not and could not find an audience in a largely middle-class society. Therefore, top-down approaches, such as the National Academy of Science, failed to integrate science into American society in a meaningful way, as they had in Britain. The change in science's place in American culture could only take place by aligning science with the values of the middle class.

The values of utility, progress, and individuality became tropes in science's argument for inclusion both in the culture and in the universities. Invention, which embodies these values, became the central metaphor for nineteenth-century science in the United States. While contemporary readers see a clear distinction both in substance and prestige between science and applied science or technology, this distinction was not so clear in the nineteenth century. In the early and mid-nineteenth century, "science" referred to a deductive, nonempirical enterprise characterized by well-organized bodies of principles concerning any area of knowledge or speculation (Veysey 133–34). The distinction was further blurred because the prototype of the American scientist, Benjamin Franklin, was both scientist and inventor.

In addition, the American success in invention led to higher prestige for applied sciences than for pure sciences, a marked difference between British and American science. Throughout the nineteenth century, Americans excelled in invention, as Edward Byrn exclaims in *The Progress of Invention in the Nineteenth Century* and Nathan Reingold laments in his *Science in Nineteenth-Century America*. The American reputation for invention went beyond a self-congratulatory praise of "good old-fashioned" American ingenuity. Europeans were also aware of this reputation. For example, in 1830 Frenchman Michael Chevalier noted that "in Massachusetts and Connecticut, there is not a laborer who has not invented a machine or a tool" (qtd. in Bledstein 18). And when American Joseph Henry visited England to present his work on electromagnetics to the British association, he was asked about the design and speed of steamboats (Reingold 86). While Henry's experience suggested to him the poor reputation American science had with the British because of the focus on applied science, many Americans saw this inventiveness as a triumph. In 1900, reviewing the achievement of invention in the nineteenth century, Russell waxes poetic: "[T]he speculative philosophy of the past is but a too empty consolation for short-lived, busy man, and seeing with the eye of science the possibilities of matter, he has touched it with the divine breath of thought and made a new world" (3). For Russell, invention had in effect created America. By the end of the nineteenth century, applied science had successfully integrated itself into the American character, body and, perhaps, soul. This close identification was possible because of the close alignment of science with middle-class values.

The force behind the ascendancy of science most consistent with the values of the emerging middle class was that of utility. In a highly fluid society, in a new country with seemingly unlimited resources, new rules, methods, and traditions were needed for facing new problems. Science was to serve the interests of society by providing knowledge for solving middle-class problems and for enabling individuals to define new career patterns, new occupations, and new identities (Bledstein 333), such as using the resources, moving west, and creating labor-saving devices. Both the APS and the AAAS used the language of utility in their charters and both specifically mentioned mechanical and labor-saving devices. One organization that eventually joined with the APS called itself The American Society for Promoting Useful Knowledge (*APS Year Book* 299). The goal of this organization was specifically "to strengthen the colonies economically as well as politically"(*APS Year Book* 299). Clearly, these societies used the rhetoric of utility to promote science.

Indeed, the American focus on utility is evident in the close ties between science and private enterprise, marking another difference between the Royal Society and the American scientific societies. While the Royal Society presented some reports on trade early on, this type of article became increasingly rare as time went on (Bazerman 66). In American societies, many of the early leaders had both academic and economic interests in science. For example, the first president of the AAAS was William Reified, "meteorologist, geologist and promoter of the railway and steamship developments" (AAAS Homepage). Railroads and mines required new inventions to improve methods and technologies, and those profiting from their development turned to science for the answers and were willing to fund the search for them. Both Yale's and Harvard's science schools, founded in the nineteenth century, were named after wealthy railroad magnates who provided large donations in an attempt to incorporate science into American universities. Promoters of science, whether for their own benefit or for the nation's, in both their language and their action aligned science with the middle class's focus on utility.

The middle-class value of progress was also closely tied to the ascent of science in the nineteenth century. For middle-class Americans, progress included improving their equipment, taming the land, and increasing their social status. According to Bledstein, in the nineteenth century the concept of "middling" was replaced by the new middle class; however, "'middle' no longer referred to an equilibrium between the extreme social orders of the aristocracy and the peasantry. It referred to the individual as 'escalator,' moving between the floors of the poor and the rich" (20). The new middle class became increasingly connected with economics, and the members of this group highly valued individuality. As Clark and Halloran argue, "the ideal of striving for individual advancement . . . [became] central to middle-class culture in the nineteenth century" (7).

Science seemed to many members of the middle class to be a way to move up the economic and social escalator. This perspective was supported by the life stories of several prominent scientists/inventors whose rags-to-riches progress argued that science was for individuals with upward mobility, men such as Benjamin Franklin, Thomas Edison, and Nathaniel Bowditch. Franklin started off as a printer's apprentice and became one of the nation's founding fathers. Edison sold newspapers to supplement his father's poor income and became perhaps the most inventive man in America's history. According to Reingold, "Bowditch was the poor boy who rose to a position of responsibility in the business world" (11). Reingold likens him to a Horatio Alger hero who happens to have a passion for mathematics and astronomy. Bowditch, however, earned his fortune through the practical application of navigation sciences and in business using his mathematical gift to solve actuarial problems. The lives of these men demonstrated that scientific training could lead to social and economic success for enterprising individuals.

As demonstrated, discussions of science were intertwined with the middle-class values of utility and progress. Toward the middle of the nineteenth century, Americans became more focused on their individual progress. For a growing number of middle-class youth (discussed further in the next section), the motivation to study science shifted from the good of society to individual progress. This large group created the most powerful force and argument for pushing science into the universities; thus science in America gained prominence from a middle-class groundswell rather than through the top-down elitist system that propelled science to prominence in England.

Middle-Class Youth in America: A New Culture Influenced by Science

In the late nineteenth century, two distinct classes existed in America: the traditional aristocracy and the new middle class—"crude but vital America" (Veysey 265). By the 1890s, one-third of the American population was middle class, and a significant proportion were young males in their twenties and thirties (Bledstein 35, 204). This group of middle-class Americans became a dominant cultural force in the late nineteenth century. Bledstein uses the phrase "Culture of Professionalism" to refer to the values of ambition and social mobility that characterized this new group and that between 1840 and 1915 dominated American social thought and institutional developments (ix, 53). These values influenced middle-class perceptions of education; rather than as a means of disciplining and building character, education was now viewed as a means of succeeding and getting ahead. An academic degree came to be seen as a mark of social mobility or an insurance policy against downward mobility (Veysey 265–66). However, the old time college, guided by its credo of mental discipline, failed to assimilate and accommodate these new values immediately (Dewey). The persistence of the new middle class, and the force of its values, made eventual change in the educational system inevitable.

Individual members of the middle class made some early attempts to change the university system. For example, the gifts of self-made men such as Yale's Joseph E. Sheffield helped to create schools for scientific training within some universities. Specialized schools were developed to provide the job training that the traditional universities did not. Clark and Halloran use the example of the Rensselaer school, one of the earliest technical institutes: "Its philosophy might be characterized as 'populist applied science' in that it understood that new scientific knowledge was common property to be spread widely for the general improvement of the populace" (8). But these attempts did not have nearly the drive of a critical mass of young men hungry for advancement. Their influence and beliefs formed the larger context against which the modern university evolved.

During its assimilation into the "new world environment" (Veysey 439), the American university, in response to middle-class values, acquired a foundation it had previously rejected: science. Scientific thought appealed to the new middle class as the nation industrialized and as the middle class developed its notions of professionalism and professional authority. Science offered these individuals a new sense of control and authority over their world.

Acquiring that control and authority now required training: "During a fairly difficult and time-consuming process, a person mastered the esoteric but useful body of systematic knowledge, completed theoretical training before entering a practice or apprenticeship, and received a degree of license from a recognized institution" (Bledstein 86–87). Hence, a solid scientific base became necessary for professional authority in the late nineteenth century. And once a "professional" acquired that base, his clients or customers were expected to trust him and respect his authority: the professional's "claim to power [lay] in the sphere of the sacred and the charismatic. . . . [He] controlled the *magic circle of scientific knowledge* which only a few, specialized by training and indoctrination, were privileged to enter, but which all in the name of nature's universality were obligated to appreciate" (emphasis added; Bledstein 90). Science began to replace teachings of antiquity as the new authority in American colleges and in doing so redefined the missions and roles of these colleges.

Through its promises of authority, control, and prestige, science appealed emotionally to the new middle class. It also possessed a rational or logical appeal. Americans looked more and more to the rational character of science to explain natural phenomena that were previously dismissed as beyond their understanding. They also looked to its "magic" and its charismatic powers, and they respected the authority of science. Middle-class professionals began justifying their actions by appealing to a special kind of knowledge, "scientific fact" (Bledstein 105). As expectations of science to answer questions about the world heightened, there was a perceived need for greater amounts of these "facts." The middle class set in motion a force that would occupy a central place in American culture and in the universities that trained individuals to function in society.

Scientific knowledge offered the means by which individuals could increase their understanding of the world and thus their ability to control and succeed in the world. The notions of professionalization and scientific knowledge, in turn, began to sustain and perpetuate each other: as the number of professions increased, so did the need for scientific knowledge and a scientific base for the new professions. Likewise, as scientific knowledge increased, so did possibilities for new professions and the increased specialization of existing ones. Conditions in late nineteenth-century America illustrate this mutual enhancement. Between the 1870s and 1880s, at least two hundred learned societies were founded (e.g., the American Chemical Society in 1876, the American Society of Naturalists in 1883, and the American Physical Society in 1889). These societies provided structure for and established and raised the standards of the various professions. For example, by 1850 the American Medical Association, which was founded in 1847, saw medical degrees from certified institutions replacing the questionable licensing practices of the older privileged medical societies (Bledstein 191–92). The diploma increasingly came to serve as a license of entry into the professions, and the institution of higher education emerged as seminal and necessary for success, its function being to legitimize the authority of professionals by appealing to "the universality and objectivity of science" (Bledstein 121, 123–24). Science, acting rhetorically through its emotional and rational appeals to new middle-class values, began to redefine the meaning and role of higher education in American society.

The Evolving University: Influences on Its Reform

By the 1830s and 1840s, a new culture was emerging in the United States that would demand a more scientific and practical training: a middle-class culture characterized by ambition and desire for mobility and influenced by the factual and practical character of scientific knowledge (Bledstein). Many of the institutions established to satisfy this ambition and desire were primarily technical institutions, like Rensselaer. But the youth of this culture began entering and influencing the old time American colleges by the middle of the nineteenth century.

The new American university evolved to support the new middle-class values: to serve and promote the professional authority in society and to enable individuals to advance and succeed (Bledstein x). This evolution was gradual; middle-class individuals did not simply transform the old time colleges. The middle-class student was an influential force in the colleges, but several other forces, including science, interacted to gradually effect change. Though many of the forces that influenced the changes were in place before the middle of the century, the changes themselves took place primarily between 1860 and 1900. Some of the changes, including debates about the aims of higher education, did not occur until the first few decades of the twentieth century (Veysey 2, 252).

Initially, applied sciences, particularly invention, fueled the middle-class interest in science. However, as the middle class became more committed to individual advancement and professionalism, its interest in research or pure science increased because science was seen as increasingly elite and specialized. This interest was further influenced by the importation of European ideas, primarily the German research model. All of these forces can be viewed and analyzed rhetorically because of the ways in which they appealed to and influenced various groups.

Pure Research and the German Ideal

The new empirical science had to win approval to attain its place in the new university. The approval of this new kind of science required that science and its proponents use different strategies to appeal to their audience. In particular, pure science made an appeal to elitism, focusing on the middle class's increasing interest in professionalism as a method of personal advancement and a way to improve social status. In the late nineteenth century, more and more Americans—especially those with wealth or with recognized academic ability—studied in Europe and were influenced by European ideals. Germany in particular held values that appealed to the American intellectual. To Americans, the German professors represented complete intellectuals whose system allowed them to examine natural and historical phenomena rigorously and precisely within the framework of the academic institution—to pursue knowledge for its own sake (Bledstein

315–16; Veysey 127). Thus the German system seemed to provide a method of "professional" intellectualism, accompanied by status-signifying titles, such as Doctor and Ph.D.

The ideal of pure research was imported by Americans who admired the German university system:

> Americans observed that among all the educational systems of Europe, only the German one came close to recruiting the best talent in the state and supporting original work of national significance. In England, for instance, leading thinkers like John Stuart Mill, Herbert Spencer, and Charles Darwin worked independently of the educational structure. (Bledstein 324)

Americans tended to idealize the German system, seeing it as a system that offered individual advancement. The English system, as well as the French, resembled the old time American college in favoring the aristocracy and providing "gentlemanly" rather than scientific or scholarly training.

In reality, the German system also favored the elite by restricting its clientele and reinforcing a classed society. Specialized research in Germany was viewed as a creative act and was not recognized as a professional career; support came not from university departments but from a competitive patronage system (Bledstein 314). Thus Americans were selective in the ideals they adopted from Germany, although in some cases they misinterpreted the way things actually were. Nevertheless, Germany provided a model for the new American research ideal, which influenced the aims and structure of the new university and brought with it the underlying value of elitism. Johns Hopkins University in Baltimore was the first American university built on this model. Established in 1876, Johns Hopkins valorized pure research and graduate training, and served as a national example of the new research ideal. However, the increasing prominence of elitist values in American science created an interesting rhetorical situation for science and its proponents who had aligned themselves so closely with middle-class values. The rhetorical appeals of science began subtly to shift, changing from a rhetoric of inclusion and practical value for society to a rhetoric of freedom and opportunity for individual progress.

Johns Hopkins: A Case Study

Johns Hopkins provides an interesting case study for examining how science helped transform old time colleges into modern research universities, and how one university negotiated the changing rhetoric of American science to win support from both the trustees and the local community. In addition, the discourses surrounding the establishment of Johns Hopkins and the emergence of its mission regarding graduate education provide insight into the role rhetoric played in situating science at the center of the modern American research university. This case is important for three reasons. First, although Hopkins was not the first university to experiment with the "new education," it was the first to completely incorporate the new education principles of an elective curriculum and graduate training, principles which complemented the training of scientists. Graduate training led to an elite class of scientists, furthering the professionalization, if not the mystification, of science. Second, graduate education led to the next generation of educators who went to other universities and re-created the Johns Hopkins system in those universities, making Hopkins the model for the new education system in America. And third, as Benjamin Peirce put it, Hopkins was "a great advance in the university system in this country and . . . the only American institution where the promotion of science is the supreme object" (qtd. in Hawkins 3). The rhetoric that accompanied this advance played a seminal role in situating science and establishing its place in the modern university.

Despite its clear focus on research, or pure science, in order to survive Johns Hopkins had to take into account the public's view of science as democratic and practical and as critical to upward mobility. This negotiation between the university's desire for pure science and the public's desire for applied science and the rhetorics that accompanied those desires sowed the seed for science's current status in contemporary American culture. To examine the founding of Johns Hopkins, we will take a brief look at where Johns Hopkins fits into the larger context of American universities; then we will examine the goals of the university and, finally, the rhetorical means by which the university sold these goals to the local community.

Founding Johns Hopkins

Johns Hopkins was not founded until 1876; therefore, as mentioned previously, it was neither the first university to introduce modern science into American colleges nor the first to experiment with what educators then called "the new education" (Hawkins 7). The first university to show serious interest in the emerging areas of empirical science was Yale. As early as 1801, Yale's president, Timothy Dwight, recognized the middle class's interest in empirical science. Therefore, he hired Benjamin Silliman, a young law student, to go to Europe to get the appropriate training (Clark and Halloran; Reingold). Silliman, though never a brilliant scientist, eventually created the *American Journal of Science and Arts,* one of the first scientific journals in the United States. In addition, he was instrumental in founding the Sheffield Scientific School at Yale (Warren 158–60). In the early years, however, the school received little support. Silliman's lectures were considered outside the standard curriculum and therefore were electives, carrying only a few credits. Given its tentative status, this program that focused on applied and agricultural chemistry was seen by most students as providing little return, and conservative board members did not believe "direct practicality should be any concern of the liberal arts curriculum" (Kelley 181). These feelings, and lack of support by Yale presidents, particularly Noah Porter (Hawkins 15), left Yale playing catch-up with other universities' science programs at the end of the century.

Although most of the advocates for science and practical education were outside the university during the first half of the nineteenth century, around midcentury some of the other universities were starting to seriously consider scientific and practical education, especially as they lost students to technical schools. Harvard founded the Lawrence Science School in the 1840s. The Morrill Act of 1862 created land-grant universities for teaching agriculture and scientific subjects. And the Massachusetts Institute of Technology was founded in 1865. However, these institutions still offered a standard curriculum based on classical education, with additional courses in technical and scientific subjects. With the introduction of these new courses, many schools started to experiment with the European elective system (Hawkins 7).

Cornell—a half private, half public institution—and Harvard led the way in offering electives; however, due to the constraints posed by trustees, the public, or both, these universities could not completely adopt an elective system.

The trustees of Johns Hopkins believed they were free of these constraints. Johns Hopkins's will left half of his seven-million-dollar estate to found a university. According to Peirce, it was a testament "happily free from all definite ideas" (qtd. in Hawkins 3). The only condition stipulated in the will was that the university provide "a 'judicious' number of scholarships for deserving candidates from Maryland, Virginia, and North Carolina" (Hawkins 3). The trustees voted in favor of new education and hired Daniel Coit Gilman, a science professor and administrator associated with educational reform (Hawkins 17), to be the president of the new university. Gilman's goals for educational reform were similar to the trustees'—to provide "new educational ideas and opportunities for 'young men bent on progress'" (Hawkins 18). These goals reflected the rhetoric of the new middle class while also incorporating Gilman's focus on pure science and research. Gilman and the trustees wanted to build a graduate university with a national reputation. Their plan was to admit only students of advanced standing, to create an elective system which would allow the students the freedom to pursue the course of research they chose, and to give scholarships based on academic merit that would provide gifted students freedom from financial concerns. These goals supported the creation of an intellectually elite group of scientists. In trying to re-create the educational atmosphere of the European educational centers, the leaders and trustees also adopted the upper-class values of those systems. The difference was that at Johns Hopkins, intellectual ability and academic degrees rather than birth were the entrance into the "magic circle."

Contrasting Rhetorics

The attempts by Johns Hopkins trustees to create an elite school focused on pure science highlighted the contrast between the various rhetorics used to advocate science. Gilman soon realized that the desire to re-create the educational atmosphere of the European education centers had to be considered within the cultural context of nineteenth-century America. On the one hand, applied science had been successfully integrated into American culture through arguments that science was practical, commercial, and available to all, i.e., on the strength of middle-class values. On the other hand, pure science argued that science was specialized knowledge for men of intelligence and taste. This argument was similar to the elitist argument made in Britain. However, while both pure and applied science also existed in Britain, this dilemma and the conflicting rhetorics that surrounded it did not. Because of Britain's highly structured social system, this distinction was a matter of class. For example, British surgeons who trained through apprenticeships were skilled laborers and held the title of Mister. General practitioners who attended the university were professionals and held the title of Doctor. The negotiation between research and applied science is a distinct characteristic of American science.

Gilman was familiar with the conflict between these two perspectives. Before coming to Johns Hopkins, Gilman had directed the University of California, recently established through the Morrill Act. In California a group of farmers called the Grangers had worked against Gilman, believing that his interest in research science "pervert[ed] . . . the vocational purposes of the Morrill Act" (Hawkins 23). The Grangers made sure that the Baltimore papers were aware of their concerns, and soon the *American* was publishing editorials blasting the idea of a university serving only graduate students. The *American* attacked the idea on two grounds: it was impractical and it was elitist. A graduate education, the *American* argued, would not provide Baltimore's youth with a solid education; instead it would give them "'the glittering stone' of 'elegant culture'" (Hawkins 24). Both the Grangers and the *American* used the rhetoric of inclusion and practical value for society to define how American science should be taught.

The Balancing Act

Clearly, Gilman and Johns Hopkins trustees needed a different rhetorical approach to achieve their goal of an elite graduate education and to win the middle-class community's support. This negotiation would eventually lead to a rhetoric of freedom and opportunity for individual progress. The first step in the compromise resulted in the university admitting a small number of undergraduates (twenty) and offering public lectures to specialized groups within the community. An examination of the *Johns Hopkins University Circulars: 1877* indicates how Gilman balanced community desires with the school's primary focus. The section called "The General Statement in Respect to the Plan of this University" opens with a clear statement of the university's goals: "The Johns Hopkins University provides advanced instruction, not professional, to properly qualified students, in various departments of literature and science" (*Johns Hopkins* 14). It then outlines the types of students who will be attending the university. In this description of the students, we see Gilman's deliberate attempt to use rhetoric that meets the expectations of the middle class, voiced so strongly by the local community, while at the same time defining his own goals for the university, which correspond with the more elitist perspective. The first description focuses on graduate students, Gilman's primary interest: "(a) those who have already been admitted to an academic degree, and who desire to prosecute their studies with or without reference to the attainment of a higher or different degree" (14). Then the undergraduates are described; however, they are carefully defined, both to show goodwill to the community and to distinguish college education from university education, as "(b) those (and especially students from Maryland and its immediate neighborhood), who desire to receive what is commonly known in this country as a college training" (14). The final category of students is also designed to show goodwill and preserve the elitism of the school: "(c) those who desire to avail themselves of the opportunities which are afforded by the laboratories of Chemistry, Physics and Biology, or attend some particular course of lectures in other branches of learning without reference to graduation" (14). In this way, Johns Hopkins provided opportunities for particular segments of the local population to have access to specialized knowledge without compromising the quality or exclusiveness of the Hopkins degree.

The *Circular* drives home the point of community service in the next section, at the same time balancing the university's obligation to the community with the individual responsibility of the students. "Members of the University" begins with a statement of the university's goodwill: "The authorities of the University, desiring to promote as far as possible the higher education of this community, have admitted to certain special courses of study those who are not able . . . to devote all their time to university work" (14). However, they again reinforce their goals for the university, stating:

> At the same time, the faculty are desirous of maintaining the principle that success as university students depends in most cases upon exclusive devotion to the subjects at hand, upon prolonged and regular efforts . . . and upon the freedom from external cares and occupations. (15)

Only those students who are willing to follow this rigorous course of study are afforded the title of Member of the University (15). This statement makes a clear argument for an elite system while simultaneously building on the middle-class work ethic (which values effort over rank) and on the American obsession with freedom for individual achievement.

The argument for freedom of choice continued with the offer of a completely elective system. According to the *Circular* of 1877, students could take courses in one of eight general areas: "1. Greek. 2. Latin. 3. Modern Languages. 4. Philosophy, History, etc. 5. Mathematics. 6. Physics. 7. Chemistry. 8. Biology" (21). Interestingly, the only freedom a student had to avoid proficiency in at least one science was to pursue "a literary training not rigidly Classical" (22). Focusing on the middle-class values of merit based on effort, freedom of choice, and individual achievement, Johns Hopkins's leaders and faculty sought to privilege an elitist pure science without violating the expectation of the local community.

The administration and faculty continued to use rhetoric focused on middle-class values (freedom and equal opportunity) to privilege pure science by distinguishing it from applied science and by dissociating it from commercial enterprises. The 1877 *Circular* states in the first line that the courses of study at Johns Hopkins were "not professional" (14). For the educators of Johns

Hopkins, the connection to the commercial world tainted pure science with invention. In "A Plea for Pure Science," an address to the American Association for the Advancement of Science in 1883, a physics professor from Johns Hopkins, H. A. Rowland, argued against a commercial connection with science, citing invention as the primary cause of this connection. He begins by looking at America's success and then states that he had "discovered a worm which threatened the ripe fruit" of success: invention for commercial advancement (31). He uses three important appeals to middle-class values. First, he argues that success from inventions is not the result of rewarding individual merit. He states: "[T]he proper course [of American science] is to consider what must be done to create the science of physics in this country, rather than to call telegraphs, electric lights and such conveniences, by the name of science" (31). According to Rowland, inventors lack originality and class: "some obscure American . . . steals the idea of some great mind and enriches himself" because he "had a mind that possessed the necessary element of vulgarity" (31). Furthermore, honoring these inventors is rewarding them for stealing others' original ideas. Next, he argues that inventions make us dependent clones:

> To-day [sic] the railroad and the telegraph, the books and newspapers have united each individual man with the rest of the world: instead of his mind being an individual, a thing apart by itself, and unique, it has become so influenced by the outer world and so dependent upon it, that it has lost its originality to a great extent. (Rowland 32)

Here, Rowland claims that Americans are losing freedom and originality, two of the defining characteristics of Americans at this time.

His final argument is that the commercialization of science is primarily responsible for these events. He then makes the connection between applied science and commerce explicit. "Commerce, the applications of science, the accumulation of wealth, are necessities which are a curse to those with high ideals, but a blessing to that portion of the world which has neither the ability nor the taste for higher pursuits" (Rowland 34). The worst result of this connection is that unqualified teachers are undermining the education of our youth. "Men receiving the highest salaries and occupying the professor's chair, are to-day [sic] doing absolutely nothing in pure science but are striving by the commercial applications of their science to increase their already large salary" (38). Ironically, Rowland's own arguments demonstrate the central role of invention and commerce as late as 1883 in integrating science into American life. Perhaps recognizing this, he attempts to show the proper relationship between applied and pure science: "Americans have shown no lack of invention in small things; and the same spirit, when united to knowledge and love of science, becomes the spirit of research" (40). This refiguring of science offered a new way of thinking about science as exploration.

Rowland's speech, which, as Hawkins notes, reflected the ideals of his colleagues, demonstrates the adoption of one of the upper-class values of European education: preservation of a community of elite scholars. Rowland's claims that those involved in applied science are "vulgar" and lacking in "taste" echo the British aristocrats' complaints about the rising middle class. Applied science is tasteless because it does not pursue truth for its own sake, a constant theme of addresses at Johns Hopkins. However, Hawkins points out that "the workers at Johns Hopkins rarely followed their own injunction that one should serve truth without looking behind it for any other good" (293) when selling pure science to various audiences. Even Rowland, after telling a commencement-day audience of the value of physics in and of itself, continued by explaining "the great value of the kind of minds [physics] made—minds careful and humbly aware of the possibility of error" (293), sounding very much like those making arguments for classical education.

While these types of arguments helped to change the perceptions of science in the United States by privileging research science over inventions, they did not eliminate Americans' interest in inventions, nor could they ever sever the ties between the academic and commercial worlds. For example, Johns Hopkins was one of the first of several universities founded by self-made men of business such as Carnegie, Stanford, and Rockefeller (University of Chicago) rather than by government or religious organizations. Furthermore, Johns Hopkins was maintained at first primarily by the dividends from B&O Railroad stock. Therefore, despite the educators' desire to divorce themselves from the commercial world, Johns Hopkins could not completely escape the commercial connection, tied as it was to the commercial enterprise of the B&O Railroad. Every time a serious drop in the stock threatened the survival of the young university, trustees and local leaders discussed the possible need for a vocational curriculum (Hawkins). In 1889 a tremendous drop in the value of the stock brought about serious changes in the student population. Although Gilman tried to cover the loss of revenue by soliciting large donations from wealthy friends of the university, the gifts alone were not sufficient. Recognizing the potential for funding from undergraduate tuition and alumni, Johns Hopkins dramatically increased the number of undergraduates admitted to the university.

As this review of the early history of Johns Hopkins University demonstrates, even the most successful attempts to promote science in the United States by re-creating the upper-class education of European universities were mediated by the values of the middle class. With its early promise of lightening the load of pioneers trying to build a new nation and its later promise of individual attainment, the rhetoric of applied science so successfully incorporated middle-class ideals that it continued through the nineteenth century to be the driving force for moving science into the university even as the European ideals of pure science became the dominant view of science. These forces created a new rhetorical approach to advocating science that emphasized freedom and opportunity for individual progress. Because of the changing attitudes about professionalization and upper mobility, an elitist system became acceptable if it offered opportunities for personal advancement based on individual merit.

Conclusion

This overview of science in nineteenth-century America offers a substantially different view of the development of science in the United States from the development of science in Britain. Unlike

Britain's top-down system, which focused on pure science, the ascendancy of American science in the nineteenth century was first fueled by American inventiveness and middle-class values. The force of the middle-class youth entering universities for technical and scientific training pushed science into the universities. Once there, the contrasting rhetorics of pure science and applied science became apparent and eventually became a matter of conflict. Because American science had already successfully aligned itself with central middle-class values and because American science had previously rejected or ignored elitist systems, a negotiated version of science developed which privileged research science but still valued the practical and commercial results of that science.

These strains of commercialism, elitism, and practicality and the rhetoric that surrounds them still affect the way we think about science and run science programs today. While the American culture has awarded research science an almost godlike status as the arbiter of truth, we demand from even the most esoteric research a nod toward practical application, usually in the research article's introduction or conclusion. The big business of big science is sustained by research and development in large corporations and government grants. In the last two years, both the National Institutes of Health (NIH) and the National Science Foundation (NSF) changed their rating requirements to include the primary criterion that research must have an "impact on society" (Mervis 26). When American taxpayers complain that our science is not focusing on basic research and then refuse to support any project that does not demonstrate practical applications, they are simply following a well-worn pattern in the development of American science and perpetuating a well-established rhetorical pattern. Science rhetorically positioned itself in American culture by playing up its connection to middle-class capitalist values of practicality, progress, and individuality while also appealing to a pure research ideal. Its success has created a highly technological and capitalistic society that reveres an elite but practical science.

Notes

1. This pattern is also reflected in much of the research on the rhetoric of science, as demonstrated in two book-length studies: Gross's *The Rhetoric of Science* and Prelli's *A Rhetoric of Science.*

2. However, science and religion were not seen as mutually exclusive. Increase Mather, for example, was very interested in science and founded the first scientific society in Boston.

3. Although some have argued how successful the society was in actually achieving status with the upper class (Kaufer and Carley; Russell), especially given its slow start, it was well established by the beginning of the nineteenth century, and was and continues to be one of the finest of such institutions, along with the Academie Des Sciences in France (Ornstein).

Works Cited

The American Association for the Advancement of Science (AAAS). Homepage. 18 Feb. 1998 <http://www.aaas.org/>.

The American Philosophical Society (APS). Homepage. 18 Feb. 1998 <http://www.amphilsoc.org/>.

The American Philosophical Society Year Book—1996. Philadelphia: American Philosophical Society, 1997.

Atkinson, Dwight. "The Philosophical Transactions of the Royal Society of London, 1675 to 1975." *Language in Society* 25 (1996): 333–71.

Bazerman, Charles. *Shaping Written Knowledge: The Genre and Activity of the Experimental Article in Science.* Madison: U of Wisconsin P, 1988.

Berlin, James A. *Writing Instruction in Nineteenth-Century American Colleges.* Carbondale: Southern Illinois UP, 1984.

Bledstein, Burton J. *The Culture of Professionalism: The Middle Class and the Development of Higher Education in America.* New York: Norton, 1976.

Byrn, Edward W. *The Progress of Invention in the Nineteenth Century.* New York: Munn, 1900.

Clark, Gregory, and S. Michael Halloran. "Introduction: Transformations of Public Discourse in Nineteenth-Century America." *Oratorical Culture in Nineteenth-Century America: Transformations in the Theory and Practice of Rhetoric.* Ed. Gregory Clark and S. Michael Halloran. Carbondale: Southern Illinois UP, 1993. 1–26.

Dewey, John. *Democracy and Education: An Introduction to the Philosophy of Education.* New York: Macmillan, 1916.

Gross, Alan G. *The Rhetoric of Science.* Cambridge: Harvard UP, 1990.

Hawkins, Hugh. *Pioneer: A History of the Johns Hopkins University, 1874–1889.* Ithaca: Cornell UP, 1960.

Hofstadter, Richard, and C. DeWitt Hardy. *The Development and Scope of Higher Education in the United States.* New York: Columbia UP, 1952.

Jacob, Margaret. *The Cultural Meaning of the Scientific Revolution.* New York: Knopf, 1988.

Johns Hopkins University Circulars: 1877. Baltimore: Johns Hopkins, 1877.

Kaufer, David S., and Kathleen M. Carley. *Communication at a Distance: The Influence of Print on Sociocultural Organization and Change.* Hillsdale, NJ: Erlbaum, 1993.

Kelley, Brooks Mather. *Yale: A History.* New Haven: Yale UP, 1974.

Kronick, David A. *A History of Scientific and Technical Periodicals: The Origins and Development of the Scientific and Technical Press, 1665–1790.* New York: Scarecrow, 1976.

Main, Jackson Turner. *The Social Structure of Revolutionary America.* Princeton: Princeton UP, 1965.

Mervis, Jeffrey. "NSF Adopts New Guidelines." *Science* 276 (4 Apr. 1997): 26.

Ornstein, Martha [Bufenbrenner]. *The Role of Scientific Societies in the Seventeenth Century.* 3rd ed. Chicago: U of Chicago P, 1938.

Prelli, Lawrence. *A Rhetoric of Science: Inventing Scientific Discourse.* Columbia: South Carolina UP, 1989.

Reingold, Nathan, ed. *Science in Nineteenth-Century America: A Documentary History.* New York: Hill, 1964.

Rowland, H. A. "A Plea for Pure Science." *Popular Science Monthly* 24 (1883): 30–44.

Russell, Colin A. *Science and Social Change in Britain and Europe, 1700–1900*. New York: St. Martin's, 1983.

Veysey, Laurence R. *The Emergence of the American University*. Chicago: U of Chicago P, 1965.

Warren, Charles H. "The Sheffield Scientific School for 1847 to 1947." *The Centennial of the Sheffield Scientific School*. Ed. George Alfred Baitsell. Freeport: Books for Libraries, 1950. 156–67.

Chapter Twelve

Scientific Writing and Scientific Thinking: Writing the Scientific Habit of Mind

Carol Berkenkotter
Michigan Technological University

What does it mean to write science? What is the relationship between scientific writing and scientific thinking? How do the grammar and genre conventions of scientific writing drive concept development? How does the learning of scientific language affect students' development of scientific concepts that are themselves the products of formal instruction? These are some of the questions that relate to the broader issue of the relationship between how children and older students learn the kinds of complex ideation that we associate with literacy and how they come to acquire the written language in which scientific concepts are couched. The knowledge of concepts such as "system" is abstract, and the language of the sciences and the social sciences is itself a system of abstractions.

L. S. Vygotsky theorized that scientific concepts—the products of formal school instruction—require children to instantiate meanings that are systematic, structured, and hierarchically organized. These meanings are couched in the "written speech" of the academic disciplines. In other words, the disciplinary knowledge that children encounter through formal instruction is represented in linguistic forms and conventions quite unlike those of their mother tongue. Vygotsky grasped that both second language learning and the reaming of scientific concepts had an important semantic component. He astutely observed that "to a limited extent reaming a foreign language also requires mastering the semantic aspect of foreign speech, just as the development of scientific concepts requires a mastery of scientific language (i.e., the mastery of scientific symbolism)" (223).[1]

In the past decade and a half, scholars working in the areas of systemic functional linguistics, applied linguistics, and North American genre analysis have investigated the evolution of scientific English (Bazerman, *Shaping*; Halliday; Halliday and Martin). Their studies can help us better understand the intimate relationship between students' use of scientific English, with its specialized register, and *professional vision* (Goodwin), i.e., a characteristic thought-style accompanying individuals' use of certain tools and artifacts that transform the world into categories and events relevant to the work of an institution or profession (609–10). Scientific language, like other forms of language, has both a sociocultural history and a logogenesis, studies of which bring to light the intricate interrelationship between cognitive, sociocultural, historical, semantic, and linguistic factors (see Atkinson; Gunnarsson; Valle). Gunnarsson, for example, from a sociohistorical perspective observes:

> Scientific language and discourse emerge in a cooperative and competitive struggle among scientists to create the knowledge base of their field, to establish themselves in relation to other scientists and to other professional groups, and to gain influence and control over political and socioeconomic means. . . . Historically language has played a central role in the creation [differentiation] of different professions and academic disciplines, and it continues to play an important role in the development and maintenance of professional and institutional cultures and identities. (98)

Gunnarsson is speaking here as an applied linguist who has specialized in historical studies of the evolution of discourse in the professions of economics and the law, two varieties of Language for Specific Purposes (LSP). From his Systemic-Functional Linguistics (SFL) perspective in studying the historical development of scientific English grammar, M. A. K. Halliday proposes, "The evolution of science was the evolution of scientific thought. But thought—not all thought, perhaps, but certainly systematic thought—is constructed in language, and the powerhouse of a language is its grammar" (12). This is the concept of *logogenesis* in a nutshell. What implications does Halliday's claim have for those of us who daily meet with and teach students the discursive conventions of written English, as we understand them? What implications does it have for those of us who teach students for whom spoken English is not the mother tongue? And, finally, what implications does it have for those of us who see racism, sexism, and classism fostered by training students in the tacit norms, values, and ideology instantiated in scientific English's grammatical and rhetorical constructions? These are issues I want to address in this essay; however, before I do, some explication of the Hallidayean approach to scientific English is necessary.

I can illustrate Halliday's notion of logogenesis by examining the following two sentences, which at first glance may look alike but which are actually quite different from one another (I have extrapolated sentence 1 from sentence 2):

1. Ground water *flows* in an easterly direction.
2. Ground water *flow* is in an easterly direction.

In sentence 1, "water" is the subject of the sentence and "flows" is the verb. This sentence communicates a process occurring in space and, by implication of the verb "flows," in time as well. In sentence 2, we see the verb transformed into a noun which becomes the subject of the sentence. This nominalization of the verb dramatically alters the syntax and meaning of sentence 2. The process instantiated in the syntax of sentence 1 has now become static and arrested in time. By changing the verb "flows" into the noun "flow," the writer has created an entity, "ground water flow."

Sentence 2 was taken from the paper of a college-level engineering student; thus we are seeing a common lexical construction (lexicalization) indicating a register he uses for writing about the objects of study in his academic discipline (environmental engineering). This sentence is a part of this student's repertoire; by this time in his academic career (his junior year), he has learned how to deploy such constructions in his speaking and writing. He uses the noun string "Ground water flow" as a lexical item, without conscious attention to its construction. What this student is not aware of as he writes is the history of discursive practices that have led to his deployment of this and other similar syntactical constructions in his prose. He does not know that the grammatical transformation of "Ground water *flows* in an easterly direction" to "Ground water *flow* is in an easterly direction" is a semantic artifact of the historical development of an elaborated code for expressing a set of meanings that has come to be perceived as being constitutive of scientific thinking and reasoning.[2]

The Process and Function of Grammatical Metaphor in Scientific English

Beginning with the publication of the first scientific journal, the *Philosophical Transactions of the Royal Society* in seventeenth-century England, a system of written communication—scientific English—has gradually emerged in professional journals read by scientists. The first contributors to the *Transactions* found themselves in the position of writing to reviewers and readers who were not present to witness (and therefore to confirm or disconfirm) the phenomena being described. Thus, to deal with the rhetorical problems of basing knowledge claims on that which could not be witnessed directly by peers, the scientist-writer required a set of linguistic tools and semantic resources to communicate what he had observed in conducting experiments. In particular, the cognitive demands facing the first publishing scientists in the seventeenth century required "the kind of grammar that is prepared to throw away experiential information, to take for granted the semantic relations by which elements are related to one another, so that it can maximize technical information" (Halliday and Martin 118).

Halliday's work on the evolution of the grammar of scientific English illustrates some of the techniques that scientist-writers developed in response to these rhetorical exigencies (see also Bazerman, *Shaping*; Zuckerman and Merton). He suggests that the major tool in the scientist-writer's tool kit was *grammatical metaphor*, i.e., the substitution of a noun or nominative construction for verbs and adjectives, as we saw in the two sentences described earlier (79–82). The original historical function of grammatical metaphor (or grammatical transformation, as it is sometimes called) was to create a set of causal relationships that would form the linguistic scaffolding for scientists' knowledge claims. Over time, however, grammatical metaphor, with its heavily nominalized syntax, has become a staple in the scientific genres, as well as many other professional genres. Grammatical metaphor serves an important rhetorical function: it enables the writer to package a lengthy series of antecedent arguments. Scientist-writers did this by transforming experiential statements into nominalized constructions that they placed in the subject slot at the beginning of a sentence. In this sentential position, the nominalization functioned as a springboard for the new information that appeared after the verb. For example, instead of writing "from those colours *we could argue that* the heterogeneous Rays diverge and separate from one another," Newton, in his *Opticks*, instantiated the claim in the nominalization, "a *diverging* and *separation* of the heterogeneous Rays . . . by means of their unequal Refractions" (emphasis added; Halliday and Martin 60–61). A similar instantiating technique can also be seen in a contemporary biologist's use of such nominalizations, as the following two sentences illustrate. (I have extrapolated and generated sentence 1 from sentence 2, the biologist's.) Sentence 1, which we might think of as the original experiential argument, depicts a sequence of activity and consequences occurring in the biologist's lab (clause subjects and verbs are italicized):

1. When *we injected* a single dose of *Candida albicans* into C3H/ HenN strain mice, *we observed* that the *plasma fibrinogen levels* in their blood *had* significantly *increased*.

In contrast, in sentence 2 the experiential and local information has been nominalized. The writer has transformed the verb "injected" into the noun "injection," which now appears in the subject position of the sentence. She has also added the verb "caused":

2. [One intraperitoneal dose] of *Candida albicans caused* [a chronic (longer than 2 months), significant elevation of plasma fibrinogen levels] in [mice of strain C3H/HeN.] (Riipi and Carlson 2750; bracketed material shows transformations of italicized subjects and verbs appearing in sentence 1.)

What results from this kind of nominalization of agents and processes are sentences that are much more toxically dense than sentences in other rhetorical contexts; that is to say, these contain far more content words signifying entities in the clauses. The rhetorical effect of the grammatical transformations that we see in sentence 2 is that a knowledge claim that was initially *experiential* becomes one that is *imputational*. This transformation occurs when "One . . . dose," rather than "we" appears in the subject slot, initiating the action of the verb "caused." Thus the imputational claim, "*One dose* of Candida albicans *caused* a significant elevation of" is constructed from the experiential antecedent claims, "we injected . . . we observed . . . ."

Note also that in contrast to its position at the end of the sentence in sentence 1, the clause "fibrinogen levels in their blood had significantly increased" is nominalized in sentence 2 as "significant elevation of fibrinogen levels" and foregrounded as thematic information. What I am suggesting with this example is that the nominalized syntax of sentence 2 functions to alter the relationship between the subject, verb, and object of sentence 1. The argument contained in initial chronological sequence of events in sentence 1, "*When we did* x, y occurred," has in sentence 2 become a *black box* (Pinch and Bijker 22), i.e., a form of semantically codified knowledge that obscures the experiential narrative of local observation that preceded it. The reader only sees that "*One . . . dose of Candida albicans* (x) *caused* y."

What were the long-term discursive consequences of this recontextualization of experientially derived information? Halliday suggests that in early scientific writing, Newton and his peers used grammatical transformation to package experiential statements with the effect of presenting a sequence of logically linked statements. Through such packaging, what was initially the argument "*When we did x, we observed y occurring*" becomes reformulated as "*x caused y to occur.*" From a systemic functional perspective, Halliday contends that

> [w]hat the scientists did was to take resources that already existed in English and bring them out of hiding for their own rhetorical purposes: to create a discourse that moves forward by logical and coherent steps, each building on what has gone

before. And the initial context for this was the kind of argumentation that was called for by the experimental method in physical science. (Halliday and Martin 64)

By using constructions such as these, scientist-writers from Newton on were able to "create a new variety of English for a new kind of knowledge" (Halliday and Martin 81), a kind associated with experimental methodology: general principles derived by the scientist reasoning from experiments, principles that were in turn capable of being tested through further experiments.

From this brief discussion of the history of grammatical metaphor it can be seen that the features we now associate with scientific prose developed from seventeenth-century scientist-writers' need to "stretch the grammar" into syntactical forms that would function as the vehicle for scientific propositions. Over the last two hundred years, the use of grammatical metaphor has spread through the knowledge-producing disciplines and through professions such as law, medicine, and psychiatry. Along with such features as technical taxonomies (such as botanical or medical or psychiatric classification systems), special expressions, and lexical density (see Halliday and Martin 69–85), grammatical metaphor has become a staple in the professional and academic writer's tool kit. Scholars and researchers within a number of disciplines, not only in the natural sciences but in the social sciences and humanities as well, deploy these features in their writing (see Secor).

What was once a much more experientially based discourse has become over time a *discursive technology* (Luke x) which aids the scientist-writer (or other professional) in achieving her communicative intentions. Little of this history is known, of course, to the children and adolescents who are socialized in various educational settings and activities into using the syntax of scientific argument. This fact takes on significance when we consider that it is difficult to separate scientific discourse (and the reasoning that is codified in the discourse) from its linguistic context, i.e., the syntactic structures and grammar in which scientific language has come to be cast over the last three centuries. From a Vygotskian perspective, the heavily nominalized syntax of scientific writing can be seen to be the tools for organizing and manipulating perceptions of the world, so that these objects [i.e., the abstractions that are the products of nominalization] and their appropriate manipulations become the very means of thinking that are difficult to escape once engaged with, but difficult to engage with when approached from any other form of intellectual life. (Bazerman, *Constructing* xx)

Enculturation into a Second Language and More: Writing the Scientific Habit of Mind

It is no accident that an enormous amount of attention in rhetoric and composition has been directed toward demystifying scientific and social scientific discursive practices—and concomitantly, with few exceptions (Geisler; MacDonald; Berkenkotter and Huckin), little attention directed to the discursive practices of humanists. MacDonald suggests two reasons for this asymmetry. First, the models for undermining "foundationalist" notions and, alternatively, showing the social construction of academic knowledge (for example, Gilbert and Mulkay; Knorr-Cetina; Kuhn; Latour and Woolgar; Latour) were studies of discursive practices in the physical sciences. She raises the specter of "physics envy" when she suggests, "Perhaps those of us in the 'soft sciences' and humanities envy our more prestigious colleagues in the 'hard' sciences and want to bring them down to our level" (8).

MacDonald suggests that the second reason humanists generally pay scant attention to demystifying the features of texts written by other humanists has to do with the "exotic" character of writing in the sciences and social sciences: "In the field of rhetoric and composition studies, scientific and business writing have for some time been recognized as not natural—not the sort of thing we teach in freshman composition, for instance, and therefore marked by being treated in separate courses" (8).

Despite the reforms in various disciplines resulting from writing-across-the-curriculum programs at many U.S. campuses, this implicit, institutionalized assumption still drives many if not most first-year writing curricula. And a multimillion- (if not billion) dollar textbook industry continues to support the status quo by turning out textbooks predicated on the view that there are "generic" forms of academic discourse to be mastered at the first-year level. The fact that many first-year composition instructors have turned to computer-mediated tools for teaching and learning has not altered the basic conservative structure of first-year writing instruction. In fact, this conservatism (and the assumptions on which it rests) appears to derive from the naturalization of norms reflecting humanistic epistemology and ideology.

From this (subject) position comes the view that learning to speak the language of the scientific disciplines and professions too often colonizes the writer's "voice" (a term instantiating a romanticist set of presuppositions), thus separating her from personal knowledge and meaning. To be sure, there is a strong connection between students' learning a disciplinary language or register and enculturation into the habits of mind of that community. However, this enculturation is as true for students trained in the humanities as it is for students studying to be climatologists, environmental engineers, or social psychologists. As students move from one discipline to others in their general education courses, they learn to code-switch. In fact, I would venture to suggest that the ability to code-switch is a predictor for undergraduate student success. At the graduate level and in professional schools such as law, business, medicine, and engineering, enculturation is at the heart of students' or apprentices' professionalization. Gunnarsson suggests:

> [E]very professional group, like other social groups, is also formed by the establishment of an internal role structure, group identity, group attitudes, and group norms. The need for a professional identity, for a professional we feeling, for separation from the out-group[s], has of course played an important role in the construction of the professional group language and constantly motivates people to adapt and be socialized into professional group behaviour. Socialization into a group also means establishing distance from people outside the group. (101)

In the study that my colleagues Tom Huckin, John Ackerman, and I conducted thirteen years ago, through participant-observation we tracked a graduate student's linguistic socialization into what was—at that time—a social science–oriented rhetorical-research community in the English department community at Carnegie Mellon University.[3] "Nate," the student of the study, expressed great anxiety at a senior professor's suggestion that his (and other graduate students') prose would come to reflect their thinking processes as research scientists:

> I always intended to be sensitized to the scientific canon, something I accept like father's lectures on handshakes, something I just need to do if for no other reason than you have to know something from the inside before you can ever fairly criticize it. I like to think analytically and I would hope that the bent toward research will satisfy an itch I've had for a long while. . . . But the line that chilled me was Young's conclusion that our training and experience will be reflected by our writing which will be the index of our assimilation of the scientific habit of mind. This is almost a Frankensteinian notion of what will happen to my mind. First I don't think that my writing will change. Of course I will learn patterns, but I have never been one to equate format with how someone composes. Form is etiquette. Handshakes. (Berkenkotter, Huckin, and Ackerman 18)

This excerpt, taken from one of Nate's self-reports, reveals him reflecting for the first time on the kinship between discipline-based thinking and writing. His initial response to this view is that formats and conventions are superficial—"etiquette," or "[h]andshakes," as he puts it. A few months later, he begins to evaluate how difficult the processes of learning to write social science expository prose will be:

> I feel like I'm butting heads finally with ACADEMIC WRIT-ING—and it is monstrous and unfathomable. Young, Waller, and Flower [professors in the students' program] write differently than me. I shouldn't lump them together because I know that they are quite different—and what I see is only a final product—and that they have much more experience doing all kinds of writing—and that I should not compare myself with people—but I feel that they have access to the code and I do not. (Berkenkotter, Huckin, and Ackerman 21)

These comments suggest Nate's awareness of a linguistic and semantic code that is an intellectual and social code as well—a code the understanding and use of which signifies membership in a community of practice (Lave and Wenger). It is true that he was an advanced learner entering a professional program. But it is even more the case that much younger students read, hear, and must be capable of deploying their knowledge of scientific English beginning in the middle school years and, in some cases if the student is precocious, much earlier.

Students in the United States are introduced gradually to the conventions of scientific English in the course of their reading (which now includes CD-ROMs and electronic databases), in the instructional language of the teacher, and through engaging in classroom activities. There is little if any explicit instruction, however, in the genres or the register of scientific English as a specialized register, much less in its grammar or syntax. Few public school language arts teachers or, at the university level, composition instructors use with their students an English for Special Purposes (ESP) approach, an approach used by applied linguists teaching English as a Second Language (ESL) to non-native speakers. Unlike English composition instruction, ESL teachers help students develop an awareness of the grammatical and syntactical forms of scientific and social science genres. Despite the growth of ESL and ESP programs in U.S. universities to serve the needs of a growing multicultural population, the institutionalization of written English language instruction in English departments (rather than in applied linguistics programs) has meant that the attention to linguistic form and semantics that Vygotsky saw as crucial to written language instruction has not materialized.

Although some researchers (Freedman; Freedman, Adam, and Smart) contend that the learning of disciplinary languages occurs mostly through a process of immersion, it may be a sin of omission *not* to bring to students' conscious awareness the conventions of scientific English. This is an argument that Tom Huckin and I advance in the last chapter of our book, *Genre Knowledge in Disciplinary Communication*. The forms of argument of science and the concepts those forms embody are instantiated in textual conventions and linguistic forms quite unlike those that students are encouraged to use in their language arts or English classrooms (cf. Reid; Cope and Kalantzis). Language arts/English and science classrooms are profoundly different semiotic contexts, contexts in which children and older students learn very different systems of meaning. In order to succeed in the university, these students must "learn how to mean" in registers and genres that are often alien, and therefore foreboding, to English instructors. However, as teachers of language we need to realize that every discipline (or aggregate of disciplines such as the natural or social sciences) constitutes its own practices through linguistic conventions that its members use to communicate with one another. Likewise, every discipline has its own *doxa*: as teachers of language, we must learn to see beyond ours. But this is not an easy task by any means: the fish are the last to see the water.

Notes

1. We can see with hindsight that Vygotsky was farsighted in his view that learning scientific concepts also involved the learning of an unfamiliar semantics.

2. A rival hypothesis by Tom Huckin (personal communication) is that "ground water flow" is simply a lexicalization which developed not as grammatical transformation but independently out of the increasing need for lexical items to characterize new conceptual entities. In any case, "ground water flow" is a reification of a process.

3. The cross-disciplinary character of the English department at Carnegie Mellon University in the early to mid-1980s made it possible for graduate students to become interdisciplinary hybrids, conversant in both social scientific and humanist registers and genres. The role of Richard Young in making possible this kind of unique cross-disciplinary training within an English department has not yet been fully recognized or appreciated. See Klein (*Crossing Boundaries*) on the rise of composition studies as a "contested territory along the borders of literature, literary criticism, and rhetoric" (67).

Works Cited

Atkinson, Dwight. *Scientific Discourse in Sociohistorical Context: The Philosophical Transactions of the Royal Society of London, 1675–1975*. Mahwah, NJ: Erlbaum, 1999.

Bazerman, Charles. *Constructing Experience*. Carbondale: Southern Illinois UP, 1994.

———. *Shaping Written Knowledge: The Genre and Activity of the Experimental Article in Science*. Madison: U of Wisconsin P, 1988.

Berkenkotter, Carol, and Thomas N. Huckin. *Genre Knowledge in Disciplinary Communication: Cognition/Culture/Power*. Hillsdale, NJ: Erlbaum, 1995.

Berkenkotter, Carol, Thomas N. Huckin, and John Ackerman. "Conventions, Conversations, and the Writer: Case Study of a Student in a Rhetoric Ph.D. Program." *Research in the Teaching of English* 22 (1988): 9–44.

Bijker, Wiebe E., Thomas P. Hughes, and Trevor Pinch, eds. *The Social Construction of Technological Systems: New Directions in the Sociology and History of Technology*. Cambridge: MIT P, 1987.

Cope, William, and Mary Kalantzis, eds. *The Powers of Literacy: A Genre Approach to Teaching Writing*. Pittsburgh: U of Pittsburgh P, 1993.

Freedman, Aviva. "Show and Tell? The Role of Explicit Teaching in the Learning of New Genres." *Research in the Teaching of English* 27 (1993): 222–51.

Freedman, Aviva, Christine Adam, and Graham Smart. "Wearing Suits to Class: Simulating Genres and Simulations as Genre." *Written Communication* 11 (1994): 193–226.

Geisler, Cheryl. *Academic Literacy and the Nature of Expertise: Reading, Writing, and Knowing in Academic Philosophy*. Hillsdale, NJ: Erlbaum, 1994.

Gilbert, G. Nigel, and Michael Mulkay. *Opening Pandora's Box: A Sociological Analysis of Scientists' Discourse*. Cambridge: Cambridge UP, 1984.

Goodwin, Charles. "Professional Vision." *American Anthropologist* 96 (1994): 606–33.

Gunnarsson, Britt-Louise. "On the Sociohistorical Construction of Scientific Discourse." Gunnarsson, Linell, and Nordberg 99–126.

Gunnarsson, Britt-Louise, Per Linell, and Bengt Nordberg, eds. *The Construction of Professional Discourse*. London: Longman, 1997.

Halliday, M. A. K. *An Introduction to Functional Grammar*. London: Arnold, 1985.

Halliday, M. A. K., and J. R. Martin. *Writing Science: Literacy and Discursive Power*. Pittsburgh: U of Pittsburgh P, 1993.

Klein, Julie Thompson. *Crossing Boundaries: Knowledge, Disciplinarities, and Interdisciplinarities*. Charlottesville: UP of Virginia, 1996.

Knorr-Cetina, K. *The Manufacture of Knowledge: An Essay on the Constructivist and Contextual Nature of Science*. Oxford, Eng.: Pergamon, 1981.

Kuhn, Thomas S. *The Structure of Scientific Revolutions*. 2nd ed. Chicago: U of Chicago P, 1970.

Latour, Bruno. *Science in Action*. Cambridge: Harvard UP, 1987.

Latour, Bruno, and Steve Woolgar. *Laboratory Life: The Social Construction of Scientific Facts: How to Follow Scientists and Engineers through Society*. Princeton: Princeton UP, 1986.

Lave, Jean, and Etienne Wenger. *Situated Learning: Legitimate Peripheral Participation*. Cambridge: Cambridge UP, 1991.

Luke, Alan. Introduction. Halliday and Martin x–xiii.

MacDonald, Susan Peck. *Professional Academic Writing in the Humanities and Social Sciences*. Carbondale: Southern Illinois UP, 1994.

Newton, Isaac. *Opticks, or A Treatise of the Reflections, Refractions, Inflections, and Colours of Light*. 1704. New York: Dover, 1952.

Pinch, Trevor J., and Wiebe E. Bijker. "The Social Constructions of Facts and Artifacts: Or, How the Sociology of Science and the Sociology of Technology Might Benefit Each Other." Bijker, Hughes, and Pinch 17–50.

Reid, Ian, ed. *The Place of Genre in Learning: Current Debates*. Geelong, Australia: Deakin UP, 1987.

Riipi, Linda, and Eunice Carlson. "Tumor Necrosis Factor (TNF) is Induced in Mice by *Candida Albicans*: Role of TNF in Fibrinogen Increase." *Infection and Immunity* 58 (1990): 2750–54.

Secor, Marie J. "Style as Argumentation in Literary Criticism." CCCC Annual Convention. Stouffer Hotel, Nashville. 18 Mar. 1994.

Valle, Ellen. "A Scientific Community and Its Texts." Gunnarsson, Linell, and Nordberg 76–98.

Vygotsky, L. S. "The Development of Scientific Concepts in Childhood." *Problems of General Psychology*. Vol. 1 of *The Collected Works of L. S. Vygotsky*. Ed. Robert W. Rieber and Aaron Carton. Trans. Norris Minick. New York: Plenum, 1987. 167–242.

Zuckerman, Harriet, and Robert K. Merton. "Institutionalized Patterns of Evaluation in Science." *The Sociology of Science: Theoretical and Empirical Investigations*. Ed. Robert King Merton. Chicago: U of Chicago P, 1973.

PARTICLE: PEDAGOGICAL APPLICATIONS OF RHETORIC

Viewed as a particle a unit has appropriate or typical distributions in temporal and spatial patterns, in classes or systems of classes each of which constitutes a higher level unit.

YOUNG, BECKER, AND PIKE, *Rhetoric: Discovery and Change*

The essays in this section focus primarily on situated explorations of literate practices and pedagogies as they are enacted in specific programs and courses. These may be understood as snapshots of selections "from the dynamic whole [the profession]" (Young, Becker, and Pike, 123). In other words, these are scholarly moments captured from our disciplinary family album. Elenore Long's essay grapples with the complex relationship between disciplinarity and literate practices. Through three case studies, she provides a compelling look at how college-aged undergraduate mentors negotiate competing disciplinary positions that emerge from the scholarly literature they are assigned; from their personal histories that imbued them with deep, strong, tacit theories concerning reading and writing; and from the encounters they have with urban teen writers at a community literacy center. At the same time, she provides a metarhetorical analysis of how our discipline's multiple, competing and contradictory theories of literacy inform not only our perspectives but also our actions as scholars and teachers. She thus offers an important methodology for both studying and teaching multiple literate practices.

Sam Watson's essay tackles the following questions: "Should the aim of WAC be to get students to write like experts? If so, what might that mean?" In exploring these two important questions, Watson problematizes the easy dichotomy of expertise/naiveté, thus raising important issues relevant not only for WAC and all writing classes but for learning in all subjects. His essay thus provides a rich lens with and against which the next three essays on writing in and across the disciplines may be read. Greene and Nowacek explore the question: Can writing be taught? Drawing on two empirical studies of students negotiating new disciplinary discursive terrain, Greene and Nowacek examine how pedagogical activities, especially writing assignments and responses to these assignments, do and do not help students participate in the discourses of particular fields and, thus, learn those fields. Their careful analysis of how the students in their studies interpreted assigned writing tasks offers insight into the tacit assumptions teachers and students hold about writing—assumptions often at odds. In so doing, they provide a strong argument that challenges the "drop 'em in the deep end of the pool and they'll figure out how to swim" approach and urges us to consider the complex intersections among disciplinary knowledge and discursive processes and products.

Michael Palmquist provides an important behind-the-scenes examination of efforts to construct a WAC program and a networked WAC program at a large university. His discussion is situated in a larger examination of online writing centers, WAC programs, and online support for WAC. Along the way, he explicates two different approaches—a faculty-centered versus an integrated approach to WAC—and provides a rich discussion of how institutional contexts shape participation and resistance in WAC programs. His essay thus raises important considerations for those engaged, or about to engage, in similar ventures. Likewise, Sipple, Sipple and Carson trace the evolution of the development of a WAC program, and in the process offer an important model—a rich, flexible process—for other WAC programs. Their comprehensive heuristic, "Institutional Audit," provides a valuable tool that holds powerful implications for curricular change beyond WAC programs.

This final section invokes what motivated Richard Young's initial journey into rhetoric. He was drawn to this rich terrain because, as he explained along with Becker and Pike in their introduction to *Rhetoric: Discovery and Change*, he was "convinced that rhetoric was potentially an important part, perhaps the most important part of a college student's education; yet [he] was dismayed by the intellectual emptiness and practical ineffectiveness of conventional courses" (xi–xii). In these snapshots, the contributors in this section demonstrate an intellectual depth that promises a practical effectiveness as well.

Work Cited

Young, Richard E., Alton L. Becker, and Kenneth L. Pike. *Rhetoric: Discovery and Change*. New York: Harcourt, 1970.

CHAPTER THIRTEEN

The Rhetoric of Social Action: College Mentors Inventing the Discipline

ELENORE LONG
Bay Path College

Acentral problem currently occupying the field of rhetoric and composition is literacy's relationship to social action. Do educators make the link, for instance, by helping students master a repertoire of rhetorical strategies? by engaging students in the practice of cultural critique? by cultivating mutuality and respect in the multicultural classroom? The heart of the disciplinary debate is the argument over theoretically informed practices aimed at literate social action. Yet, while the debate poses alternative arguments for and against a whole range of educational priorities, a more difficult problem emerges when we shift the ground to ask: How are these competing arguments transformed in local, situated action? Clearly, how we as theorists, researchers, and teachers work to forge the link between literacy and social action is problematic. But even more problematic is the question of how to teach students to understand the link. This chapter looks at college mentors working with inner-city teenagers at Pittsburgh's Community Literacy Center (CLC) as these students come to grips with competing notions of how literacy may sup-

Research on which this paper is based has been supported in part by the Office of Educational Research and Improvement/Development of Education (OERI/ED) for the Center for the Study of Writing and Literacy. The opinions expressed herein, however, do not necessarily reflect the position or policy of the OERI/ED, and no official endorsement by the OERI/ED should be inferred.

port social action. The inquiry asks: What is the nature of college students' learning when they are not only studying textual arguments for literacy in college but also practicing social action themselves at the center?

As students enrolled in an upper-division rhetoric course titled Rhetoric and the Writing Process: Community Literacy, college mentors are learners studying disciplinary arguments for literate social action. Yet they are also social agents supporting teen writers and structuring these teenagers' learning. This chapter traces what happens to mentors' theoretical commitments when these commitments are transformed into action. Analyzing the students' critical reflections, I argue that mentors actively invent the discipline for themselves by (1) making sense of disciplinary arguments within a specific problematic moment and by (2) qualifying these positions in terms of immediate constraints, emergent opportunities, and additional arguments in order to take action. In charting courses of action, college mentors struggle to be accountable to multiple interpretations, both of the situation at hand and of possible responses to it. Such intellectual struggle pushes mentors to experiment with rhetorical strategies in order to work out power relations and to cross cultural borders. Such struggle is at the heart of the disciplinary debate about literacy in the United States today.

Voices at the Table: An Overview of the Disciplinary Debate

The debate over literate social action is complex in part because both sides of the equation are contested. That is, the debate questions what counts as literacy, as well as what counts as social action. Moreover, the debate interrogates how exactly a given image of literacy supports a given image of social action. In the rhetoric course on community literacy, the problematic relationship between literacy and social action is often stipulated in terms of building "a more fair and equitable society." This representation of the problem is reflected in the following entry, which Wayne Peck—a team teacher for the rhetoric course—posted to the mentors on their electronic bulletin board:

> From: *Wayne Peck*
> There are problems all over the place. But let's try to major not in the minor [problems] but to major in the majors. These are the unresolved questions of how in the hell do you get a more fair and equitable society.

Peck's post invites mentors to "major in the major problems" that characterize literate social action. For mentors, Peck's invitation includes clarifying the work they see themselves doing at the center. In response to positions such as Peck's, mentors develop their own arguments for literate social action. Encoded in these positions are arguments from the larger disciplinary debate. The following section highlights four competing views of what one might consider the highest priority for someone wanting to support literate social action.

Contested Practice: Emphasize Grammatical Correctness

In "IQ and Standard English," Thomas Farrell argues, "For people today to develop abstract thinking, they need to know the grammar of a literate language. . . . In this country, that means learning the grammar of Standard English" (477–78). In her post, a mentor named Meg[1] takes a similar stance and questions the value that nonacademic literacy would have for urban teenagers at the CLC if they are to succeed in mainstream society:

> From: *Meg Anderson*
> What's the value of community literacy? Community literacy is nothing like academic literacy, which means there is no grammar. Obviously, academic literacy has higher value, because when teens talk in their own discourse, they come across as less than intelligent.

Contested Practice: Support Emancipation

Other mentors interpret the situation of mentoring through the Marxist lens of class struggle. Some turn to Paulo Freire's work with politically oppressed people—work that helps learners use literacy as a tool to critically analyze cultural myths, particularly those that position them in the passive role of consumers. Freire argues that literacy education emancipates learners when they learn to separate education from propaganda. Explicating a cigarette advertisement, for example, Freire explains that through emancipatory lessons, learners begin to perceive the deceit in a cigarette advertisement featuring a beautiful woman in a bikini: "The fact that she, her smile, her beauty, and her bikini have nothing at all to do with cigarettes" ("Adult" 409). Echoing Freire's commitment to critical consciousness, a mentor named Liz describes her goal for working with a teenager named Chaz:

> From: *Liz Trail*
> Freire talks about being aware of meaning and what you're thinking as you're doing it—getting at a meta-level about . . . culture, what it means, and what it means to mean and all that. Chaz has so much to say about what's going on in his world. That's what I want to be doing, helping him bring up that stuff he was never conscious of. Helping him to develop a consciousness that might not have been there. He wants to be a professional football player. I challenge that. He's a little guy, you know. I ask him to analyze this cultural thing—football, which I don't think is too much to ask from someone at this age level.

Contested Practice: Invite Free Expression

A third argument promotes literacy as free expression. Advocates of this position stress students' "own authority to make meaning as writers," not "what they have yet to attain in order to be able to write" (Willinsky 28). Mentors Elizabeth and Marta describe their notions of an ideal literacy project, one that gives top priority to self-expression over the goals of learning specific genres or writing conventions:

> From: *Elizabeth Kreski*
> It might be better simply to have the teen writers [write] about whatever they wanted, in whatever genre.
>
> From: *Marta Johnson*
> This leads me to question the writing standards of the English language. Apparently these standards don't work. So who's
>
> *continued on next page*

> trying to cling to them and why? I'm trying to say that it doesn't matter when you look at it [teens' writing] as communication. This person is trying to say something. Their goal may be just to get something off of their chest. Our goal as a collective is understanding and being a receptacle of that communication. If meaning reaches any number of us, that person was successful.

Contested Practice: Support Action-Oriented Problem Solving

John Dewey argues that effective instruction plunges students into "perplexing situations" which allow them to choose their own courses of action. Literacy, then, is a tool for asking tough-minded questions and responding to real problems. Shirley Heath and Milbrey McLaughlin argue that while schools typically fail inner-city teens, community programs often accomplish what schools do not because they can "provide opportunities for youngsters to build a sense of self-efficacy and a series of prevailing narratives of success in different . . . kinds of activities . . . and promote strong pride in . . . specific accomplishments" (24). Mentoring a teen who writes about problems she sees in her inner-city school, Keith crafts questions to invite the teen to translate her complaints about school into ideas for constructive change:

> From: *Keith Harter*
> I keep asking tough questions like, "What would you propose as a change?" and "How can you get adults to take you seriously?"

As the electronic bulletin board posts suggest, mentors' ideas reflect competing positions in the larger disciplinary debate. These disciplinary positions are voices that mentors confront as assumptions from their own experiences, as arguments that other people pose to them, as the agenda of the literacy center where they work as mentors, and as theoretical positions from academic texts. Yet mentors typically do much more than echo a favorite scholar or reinscribe an old habit of mind. But how much we see of the mentors' intellectual life depends, first, on the interpretive lens

we bring to the disciplinary debate over literacy's role in stimu-
lating social action.

Three Ways to Approach the Disciplinary
Debate over Literate Social Action

To this point, disciplinary scholarship has generally offered us
two basic frameworks for thinking about the scholarly ideas that
inform action. One framework looks for necessary and self-evident criteria. The second tells us to investigate the debate to locate the most reasonable argument for informing contingent
decisions. Yet, through tracing mentors' critical reflections, we
see a third alternative, one that a cognitive-rhetorical perspective
further illuminates. This perspective extends the distinction that
Chaïm Perelman and Lucie Olbrechts-Tyteca make between the
necessary and self-evident on the one hand, and the deliberative
and contingent on the other. The cognitive-rhetorical perspective
suggests that a person engages in the larger debate in order to
negotiate competing—even conflicting—disciplinary arguments.
As the following cases illustrate, mentors actively negotiate competing disciplinary arguments in order to take action and be accountable to those actions.

Read to Uncover Universal Principles
and General Truths

One way to read the disciplinary debate over literate social action is to look for criteria that are necessary to ensure that literacy supports social action. As Michael Bernard-Donals argues,
this approach provides theorists like himself with criteria for step-
ping outside the realm of the contingent to assess "which changes
of subject position constitute movements in the direction of the
good" (14). Similarly, in an essay titled "Reflections on Allan
Bloom's Critics: A Defense of Universal Norms," Mark Roche
advocates identifying what is necessary for educational reform
to work. Responding to Allan Bloom's argument in *The Closing
of the American Mind*, Roche writes:

> Not only do I think that some truths are not in flux . . . (they
> can be deduced *a priori*), . . . I also think that is a good thing,
> . . . and that the need for recognizing universal norms needs
> more supporters. . . . That we have moved too far away from
> what is universal and non-contingent is one of Bloom's claims,
> a claim that I am willing to take seriously. (135, 138)

The universal principles or general truths to which Roche refers
may be religious (as reflected in Freire's *Pedagogy of the Oppressed*; see also James Berlin's analysis of Freire) and are often
sociopolitical (as in Pierre Bourdieu and Jean Claude Passeron's
Reproduction in Education, Society, and Culture). Herbert Gintis,
for instance, argues along sociopolitical lines when he maintains
that radical structural changes in the larger society are necessary
before literacy education can effect any significant social change.

Reading the debate in this way one might also look for a
priori assumptions about language. A priori linguistic theories
assume, for instance, that specific features of language correspond
to universal patterns of thought (as Noam Chomsky suggests) or
have a fixed and autonomous status outside the immediate context in which they are used (as Thomas Cook, Judith Levinson-
Rose, and William Pollard maintain). As a result, discourse
conventions are considered "abstract, transcendent, and simultaneously present" rules rather than social compacts that emerge
from context (Hopper 21). Such a priori assumptions permeate
common notions of the relationship between literacy and social
action. Take, for instance, the current-traditional *The Practical
Stylist* by Sheridan Baker, still one of the most popular textbooks
today for teaching first-year composition. The textbook's premise
is that clear (i.e., "literate") ideas gain expression through a fixed,
prescriptive linguistic structure. David Olson has argued that from
such reasoning it follows that responsible literacy instruction is
text based, requiring students to produce texts that reflect this
"clear thinking."

Often sociopolitical arguments merge with arguments maintaining an a priori view of language. For instance, in their arguments regarding literacy as social action, David Bartholomae and
James Gee acknowledge the political and social factors affecting
linguistic norms, and they treat textual conventions as autono-

mous, prefigured entities. Thus they argue that literacy links to social action when instruction teaches students to imitate the discourses of prestige and power.

Reading in order to uncover universal principles or general truths provides a basis from which to dismiss other arguments in the debate. As a framework, it attempts to move the argument over literate social action out of the realm of contingent knowledge in order to argue what is necessary for literacy to support social action. Within this framework, the teacher or mentor serves to transmit literacy. This practitioner is a conduit—up front and personal, but a conduit nonetheless—for the transfer of literacy to be reproduced within a social structure.

Take a Text-Based Rhetorical View to Discern the Most Convincing Argument

A text-based rhetorical view reads the debate over literate social action to look for the most convincing text (Perelman and Olbrechts-Tyteca). From this perspective, the aim of arguments within the debate is to advocate a particular definition of literate social action. Each competing argument attempts to convince readers that its claims for literate social action are more reasonable and more justifiable than the others. The reader's task is to discern the worthiest argument.

This rhetorical view acknowledges that arguments for literate social action pertain to issues of human choice, not to universal principles or general truths. As such, these textual arguments must always deal with the contingent world, dismissing the claim that structural or a priori claims are somehow objective or "true" (Perelman; Perelman and Olbrechts-Tyteca). In the face of contingent knowledge about social issues, what constitutes moral public action? This is the question that governs the realm in which rhetoric thrives (Goggin and Long).

This text-based rhetorical approach underscores that the reasonableness of a claim is not self-evident but rather must be argued and agreed upon. An argument is judged reasonable when it resonates with its readers' values (Perelman; Perelman and Olbrechts-Tyteca). John Willinsky views an era of disciplinary history through this lens when he assesses the success of Peter Elbow's

Writing without Teachers. Willinsky maintains that in the 1970s and early 1980s, readers judged Elbow's argument to be reasonable because it resonated with the values they upheld as white liberal educators: values of free expression and individualism.

David Russell maintains that the current field of rhetoric and composition has largely lost sight of the classical understanding of how theory and practice inform one another. Instead, too often the field works from a simpler notion of "theoretical discovery lead[ing] to practical applications in problem solving" (176). Consequently, the emphasis in the current textual-rhetorical approach is on the interpretive task of selecting the best argument. Subsequent actions are considered to be merely informed by this theoretical deliberation, outside the parameters of the immediate rhetorical task. From a text-based rhetorical perspective, arguments over literate social action make up a contest of words that asks people to deliberate over the worth of competing texts. This interpretative approach views the debate as a textual performance of persuasion, governed by the slogan, "May the best text win."

Take a Cognitive Rhetorical View to Negotiate Competing Voices

Cognitive rhetoric draws on negotiation theory to suggest another framework for viewing this argument: negotiated action. Cognitive rhetoric is embedded within the rhetorical tradition already described. Among its aims is to account for how people deliberate in the discursive space between the necessary and the arbitrary (Flower, "Cognitive"). That is, unlike the first approach that looks for general truths, cognitive rhetoric emphasizes that the educator's task is more complicated than searching for universal truths to implement in practice. But cognitive rhetoric also differs from a text-based view of rhetoric by emphasizing discursive activity. Cognitive rhetoric maintains that the heartbeat of rhetoric is the constructive process of meaning making through which people transform conventional practices into inventive and purposeful literate action (Long and Flower).

Negotiation theory emerges from a cognitive-rhetorical orientation. This theory grows out of a whole host of process-tracing studies of writers composing texts (cf. Hull and Rose) and maintains that in moments of conflict, writers wrestle with competing voices for how to interpret and respond to their rhetorical situations: "voices of past experience and present opportunity—the voice of wisdom, . . . the voice of demand and doom, . . . the voice of possibility, . . . the voice of the discourse, . . . the voice of one's broad intentions and specific goals" (Flower, *Construction* 67). Negotiation theory attempts to account for writers' judgments as they interpret these multiple voices. The term *negotiation* describes this interpretive judgment in two senses of the term:

◆ writers do indeed *negotiate/arbitrate* power relations inherent in the social forces and inner voices that would shape writing, deciding whose demands to acknowledge, which goals to honor, where to compromise, and how to strike the balance; and

◆ writers *negotiate/navigate* their way through the space of the problem, charting the best possible path across a hillside strewn with obstacles and invitations, or envisioning the swift channel down the river that reaches many goals, satisfies as many constraints, and avoids as many difficulties as possible. (70)

As a lens for studying the problem of literate social action, negotiation theory suggests that when people find an argument convincing, they do much more than apply the argument to instructional methods. Consider, for instance, Lisa Delpit's argument in "The Silenced Dialogue" for providing minority students with direct instruction in standard written English. Delpit argues that the most urgently needed literate social action is that which teaches students to master mainstream discourse. She advocates that teachers provide students with explicit instruction in Standard English, as well as opportunities to practice using it within meaningful contexts for communication. If a teacher were to find this argument convincing, negotiation theory suggests that in moment-to-moment action that teacher would juggle Delpit's argument for direct instruction with familiar competing arguments, such as claims regarding issues of ethnic identity and her own personal commitments and habits of mind, as well as external pressures and the interpersonal dynamics of the classroom. Negotiation theory values the claims people build to account for their actions, but rather than performing discourse analyses of these accounts, it aims to understand the literate act in which people negotiate competing arguments for what to do (and how and why to do it). Transforming competing claims into a course of action, this act of negotiation is considered a highly rhetorical performance, in which individual cognition mediates public discourse (Flower, "Cognitive"; *Construction*).

To be sure, cognitive rhetoric, as well as the theory of negotiation that informs it, does not make the problem of literate social action any less controversial. But it does shift the focus from general principles and texts to situated, specific action. As an interpretive lens for reading the debate over literate social action, cognitive rhetoric stresses that judgment figures into the process of literate social action not only as a reader discerns the validity or worth of one argument over another; judgment continues to be part of the rhetorical process as individuals (such as college mentors at the Community Literacy Center) chart courses of action for themselves. For in charting these paths, individuals continue to engage in the act of meaning making. Without devaluing disciplinary arguments, cognitive rhetoric shifts the focus to situated individuals making difficult decisions in the face of competing, internalized public voices.

The Community Literacy Seminar

The college mentors featured in the following cases find themselves at an intersection between an academic seminar and a literacy project for inner-city teenagers at the Community Literacy Center. The formal aspect of this seminar asks students to learn to work as mentors, conduct observation-based inquiries, and read theories of literacy. The second aspect of the seminar is a literacy project for teenagers at the CLC, an intercultural community-university collaborative with an eighty-year history as a settlement house in an intercultural urban neighborhood (Peck, Flower, and Higgins). First and foremost, teens, mentors, and project leaders come together at the center as advocates for a common project: investigating problems that affect the lives of Pittsburgh's inner-city teens—situations involving street violence, drugs, teen pregnancy, and police-teen relations, for instance. Over the course of each project, teens produce a newsletter or video, and they hold a community conversation (a public assembly resembling a town meeting) to address the topic of the project.

College students work as mentors with teen writers in these projects. Unlike mentoring associated with a resident expert or coach, at the CLC the job of a mentor-as-supporter is not to offer good advice but to help the writer-as-planner consider strategically the rhetorical issues of purpose, key points, text conventions, and topic information (Flower, Wallace, Norris, and Burnett).

Supporting Literate Social Action: Three Case Studies

Given the kinds of conflicts that arise at the CLC, mentors' learning involves more than coming to some sudden realization or learning to adopt a politically correct set of attitudes. Rather, for mentors, learning depends on sustained and sometimes unsettling engagement with genuine open questions regarding their roles as mentors and the project of linking literacy to social action. The rhetorically rigorous aspect of their learning involves charting a course of action that strives to be accountable to competing—even conflicting—arguments concerning literate social action. It is in this activity, in the charting of a course of action, that I would argue mentors are not simply echoing arguments from the disciplinary debate but rather are actively inventing the discipline for themselves.

Gerald Graff has argued for the teaching of "the conflicts themselves" to revitalize American education. Mentoring at the CLC provides students with the chance to take this educational challenge one step further, drawing from the disciplinary debate to make judgments about how to create intercultural relationships. Not all mentors actively negotiate disciplinary issues all of the time. But as the case studies suggest, for the most part mentors do situate and qualify theoretical positions in light of other commitments that emerge from additional readings, discussions, and their connections with teen writers.

The following cases are grounded in an analytical method developed for my dissertation, "The Rhetoric of Literate Social

Action: Mentors Negotiating Intercultural Images of Literacy."
In a nutshell, mentors audiotaped self-interviews after holding
six of their mentoring sessions. Transcripts from these interviews
were coded for "conflict episodes." Blind to one another's codings,
co-raters identified conflict episodes with 83.5 percent reliability.

Direct quotes are taken either from these conflict episodes or
from mentors' final papers. For the argument I am making in
this chapter, what is important about this method of analysis is
this: The analysis indicates that mentors are not simply alluding
to disciplinary arguments as they mentor, but they are actively
negotiating the implications of these arguments for the central
problems they frame for themselves.

Case 1. Rachel: An Invented
Exchange with William Labov

While mentoring, Rachel frames her final project as an observation-based inquiry into the everyday cultural knowledge that teenagers bring to reading and critiquing advertisements she finds
genuinely perplexing—texts geared to seducing African American teenagers into buying malt liquor, fast cars, or $200 tennis
shoes. Based on her reading of William Labov and three other
discourse theorists (each with a different perspective on how to
conduct such an inquiry), she invents a discussion in which the
theorists advise her project.

RACHEL'S LITERATURE REVIEW

To begin the discussion, Rachel explains to the theorists the rationale for her inquiry:

> RACHEL: As a college student, I confront advertisements daily, but
> hardly give them a second thought. Any given day in Baker
> Hall, I might walk past an ad trying to persuade me to sign
> up for an American Express Card, for an LSAT prep course,
> or to send away for information about an academic seminar
> program. The message of any ad, I had assumed, was
> perfectly obvious to anyone who could read.
>   I realized this wasn't true when at the CLC I flipped
> open *Jet* and *Ebony* [two popular magazines targeting

African American readers]. There I saw advertisements that were not only unfamiliar to me, but downright perplexing as well. These ads were written for African American youth. So I've figured that the CLC teens might very well possess the cultural knowledge to clue me in on the advertisers' "intended" meanings. My question now is how to proceed.

In the invented debate that follows, the theorists challenge one another, as well as Rachel, as they lay out the assumptions undergirding their work in order to direct hers. Then, in the final conversational turn, Rachel challenges Labov—highlighting the intercultural focus of her project:

> LABOV: When I did my study, I compared the verbal behavior of an African American inner-city child when he was interviewed by a white interviewer with his response when interviewed by Clarence Robins, an African American. . . . The [second] time Mr. Robins met with Leon, he changed the social situation: he brought in potato chips, Leon's best friend. . . . As a result, the boys wouldn't stop talking. . . .
>
> RACHEL: But, Labov, I don't want to try and find an African American interviewer to conduct my inquiry. I'm a Jewish American 20-year-old, and I want to have the conversation. I want to see what I can learn firsthand. What this project is all about is finding a strategy for instigating intercultural conversation here at the CLC.

Rachel's project yokes the competing research perspectives of four discourse theorists with a problem that emerges for her from observations at the CLC, taking her on an exploration of the limits of her own cultural literacy and of the cultural resources of the CLC teens. Drawing again on the theorists to help her interpret the teens' comments as they unravel the specific logic of each advertisement, Rachel also identifies patterns emerging across interpretations, specifically "the distinction teens make between genuine and illegitimate authority, their strong sense of cultural unity, and their knowledge about the manipulative strategies of advertisers." Woven throughout her analysis are excerpts of dialogue between Rachel and each of the teens as they talk about— rather than shy away from acknowledging—how aspects of their world views differ.

As Rachel's project suggests, in order to establish a basis for understanding one another and improving collaboration, the community literacy seminar asks students to uncover the ways different people interpret or "read" a significant situation. A mentor named Kara, for instance, compared the ways in which she and two teen writers interpreted and approached the task of revision. And Dillon (a white mentor from Orange County, California) asked teen writers to help her better understand how teenagers express aspects of their cultural identities through discourse switching—reflecting, in the process, on her own cultural negotiations when teenagers asked her to perform publicly a role which they had scripted in Black English Vernacular.

The stipulation for these projects is that teenagers be included not solely as informants or as objects of inquiry, but rather as partners in interpreting a genuinely problematic situation or text. At its best, such inquiry fosters mutuality between mentor and teen—the kind of mutuality, for instance, that mentor Rachel and teen Terrel achieve when working through the contradictory codes in an automobile commercial published in magazines targeted at young African American readers. Part way through their audiotaped discussion of the ad, Terrel physically takes the recorder from Rachel and starts speaking directly into the microphone, explaining his critique of the advertisement. At this point, Terrel is not merely supplying answers to the mentor's questions, but articulating a point so that others might learn what he has to say.

Case 2. Keith: Agitating toward Productive Friction

Extending Freire's emancipatory pedagogy, Henry Giroux posits critical literacy as the exercise of power in acts of social resistance. From a historical perspective, Giroux contends that literacy is a double-edged sword: It represents "signifiers monopolized by the ruling class, [yet is] . . . also wielded for the purpose of self- and social- empowerment" ("Theories" 291). Critical literacy makes no promise to secure a state of emancipation. "To be literate is not to be free, it is to be present and active in the struggle for reclaiming one's voice, history, and future" (Giroux, *Teachers* 65). Critical literacy promises empowered struggle through opposition.

Critical literacy advocates educational practices that ask students to oppose existing injustices. Roger Simon explains: "Teaching and learning must be linked to the goal of educating students to take risks to struggle with ongoing relations of power" (375). Giroux theorizes that social structures are not determinant; thus social oppression is never complete ("Theories"). There is ready opportunity for resistance. He argues that human agency is positioned within the tension between social structure and resistance.

INVENTIVE PRACTICES FOR FOSTERING CRITICAL LITERACY

It is not uncommon for CLC mentors to have background in literary and cultural studies. However, Keith is particularly facile with this disciplinary set of ideas—"thinking tools" he calls them.[2] Keith explains having sought out additional courses in cultural theory beyond those required for his professional writing major: "I've gone outside and taken cultural theory classes just to inform what I'm writing about." As a mentor, he strives to translate what he has learned from his literary and cultural theory courses into a set of practices for fostering the critical literacy of Chanda, the teenage writer with whom he has been paired.

Guard against Homogeneity. To foster critical literacy, Keith decides he must first understand the power dynamics of the literacy center. He is interested in how teens, mentors, and literacy leaders relate among themselves. And with the school board as the audience for the document the teens are producing this semester, Keith is also interested in how power dynamics between the teens and this set of adults will affect the teens' efforts to enter into genuine dialogue with the school board.

Playfully, Keith positions himself at a slight distance from the CLC's project, always cooperating yet also keeping an eye out for stories that would otherwise have gone, if not unnoticed, at least untold. As Keith explains, he defines his stance according to Jean-François Lyotard's notion of "a theory of [language] games which accepts agonistics as a founding principle . . . [and invites] the inventiveness of the players in making their moves" (16–17). He is vigilant about broadening the stories participants tell about their experiences at the center, ensuring that "the main story not suppress the richness of the small narratives—and press them into a single mold." As reflected in his course journal and in his entries on the mentors' electronic bulletin board, Keith is particularly interested in incidents that bear witness to the fluidity of the power dynamics at the center. For instance, he documents an incident in which a teen writer assumes an unexpected power position by interrupting two literacy leaders' unsuccessful attempts to work a videocassette machine, thereby "tak[ing] control of the schedule and allow[ing] the daily program to proceed as planned." Keith elaborates:

> Tiana [a teen writer] stepped up to the plate. Just as Wayne [a literacy leader] was muttering something under his breath and apparently ready to shut down for the day, Tiana walked up to the VCR, pushed the right buttons, and got the show on the road. Without her, the entire day's plan would have flown out the window. With the slightest bit of maneuvering, the power dynamic between her and Wayne shifted. Wayne was at her mercy and grateful for her know-how.

For his course project, Keith analyzes the power dynamics at the center. He wants to understand the "circuits of power" linking writers, mentors, and literacy leaders. He explains:

> I try to notice—and to gauge—the different reactions when different people speak. . . . I've been trying to furiously take notes . . . about my perceptions about what's going on while the group sessions are happening. Part of that is that I want to know about concepts of power that are going on in that room.

For Keith, this inquiry has immediate application, for he wants to consider how he can legitimately support his teen writer's efforts to negotiate with members of the school board, who review the teens' ideas for restructuring the city schools.

Show Productive Frictions. Given his background in literary and cultural studies, Keith considers the teenagers' oppositional discourse of complaint and blame to be counterproductive—although some of his classmates would encourage such discourse as evidence of opposition to the dominant social structure. Keith argues that a more robust priority is to support generative dialogues between the teen writers and the school board members by locating what he calls "productive frictions":

> I want . . . Chanda to start thinking about possible alternatives to directly challenging the power position of the school board. You know, to think about other ways to get into the conversation. I am hoping to show her the possibility of other, more productive frictions.

Cope with a Foiled Attempt. Keith's goal as a mentor is to prompt Chanda to study "the system of power relationships" within their project for school reform. But one afternoon, his effort to carry out this goal backfired. "Damn! My strategy backfired," he reflected afterwards. "My questions . . . went over like a lead balloon." Keith explains that during a group discussion with the school board president, he was groping for a way to communicate with his teen writer without disrupting the discussion. So he decided to pass her a note. The note listed two questions which Keith had designed to prompt Chanda to analyze how the teens had positioned themselves in direct opposition to the school board president and how they could reposition themselves more strategically. Keith elaborates what went wrong:

> Chanda read the note, seemed to think about it for a minute, but didn't say anything. So I put the questions to the whole group. But then the questions were beaten into silence. I don't think anyone actually thought about either of them.

Had all gone according to plan, Keith's questions would have prompted Chanda to analyze power relations for herself and to help the group position itself more strategically in light of that analysis. However, strategies are not always effective and, as Keith recounts, they may even backfire.

In his final paper, Keith interprets the event further. After mentioning having felt "like I had been caught in grade school passing cartoons," he considers the event in terms of his effort to support literate social action. He writes:

> The result of asking these questions demonstrated power shifts but in an unexpected way. As a Mentor, having a question which I formulated left hanging in silence shifted my position in the roundtable. Mentors are constructed as authorities on writing and planning—a lack of response from the writers devalues that authority, at least to the Mentor. Here, I shifted my position in the power structure to that of less importance without improving the power position of my Writer.

Keith had wanted to support literate social action by having Chanda and the group consider power relations between themselves and the school board president. Instead, his intervention served only as another interesting event to account for in his study of the shifting locus of power at the CLC.

Ask Tough-Minded Questions. Even though Keith felt that during the note-passing incident he had temporarily constructed himself as a troublemaker, he stays committed to his goal of supporting productive friction between teens and school board members. His central tool for supporting this goal is to ask "tough-minded questions," a strategy in stark contrast to the "feel good" image of mentoring that he hears some other mentors advocating. While some mentors may be content merely being a pal to their teen writers, Keith is not:

> Some people—I don't know, like Rita—probably expect, you know, these kids to just bring up an idea and, "Oh, that's great. Now let's move on." I don't happen to share that sort of ideology. Chanda is a good writer, and she is very articulate. I'm there to push her thinking. I ask a lot of tough-minded questions. . . . I know this might sound arrogant. But I don't mean it to be. I just think that if she gets the experience or maybe is expected to push her thinking, then that might be one of the best things I could do, just give her something to base her subsequent thinking on.

Keith worries that all too often literacy instruction stifles students' growth. For an ethical and theoretically informed alternative, Keith turns to tough-minded questions to help Chanda prepare to meet with and write to members of the school board.

Keith's reflections underscore that he knows real cultural differences make it difficult to transfer theories of power from the university to the CLC. For one thing, Keith maintains that without adequately understanding issues of power from the writers' perspective, "we'd be denying our culpability in living in the master's house. . . ." For another, the very dynamics he is working to understand make teaching about power relationships difficult. That is, at least when seated at the table, the fluidity of his own status as mentor makes it difficult for Keith to find ground stable enough for building a scaffold. As a kind of scaffolding aimed at helping writers consider issues of power, passing a note proves ineffective. Nonetheless, as a committed mentor he is dedicated to Chanda's intellectual growth. So he translates the best he has to offer into tough-minded questions.

Case 3. Paula: Translating a Commitment to Freirian Pedagogy into Action

Paula comes to the CLC with an explicit commitment to Freirian pedagogy. Introduced to Freire in a previous rhetoric class, her commitment translates into an eagerness to work as a "co-learner" with the teen writers and literacy leaders. Following her visit to the CLC after three weeks of training on campus, Paula emphasizes the importance of equality: "I want us [her teen writer and herself] to be equals." And she argues that the CLC makes a difference in teens' lives precisely because of its commitment to equality:

> Unlike high school where unequal social status between students and teachers puts at-risk students even more at risk, the CLC grants everyone equal status, positioning all participants as co-learners [where, without the] . . . hierarchy of teacher-student relationships, . . . each person concentrates on their own learning.

While the effects of the CLC are interwoven into the fabric of teens' lives and thus are not always as profound as Paula suggests, her sense of the democratic underpinnings of the CLC's philosophy is not unfounded. Specifically, it resonates with an explicit respect for those who participate there, a respect articulated in several of the articles Paula had read as part of her training as a mentor. However, as we will see, her goal of achieving social equality proves problematic. Initially assuming an inherent—and positive—relationship between literacy and social equality, Paula struggles with how to instantiate her goal of equality.

LITERACY AND SOCIAL EQUALITY: THE ACADEMIC DEBATE

Paula's struggle resonates with vigorous, ongoing academic discussions of literacy: how to represent accurately the relationship of literacy to social equality. Theorists such as Mike Rose argue that literacy education has "the power to equalize things" (137). Others blast such an assumption. Strongest, perhaps, is Elzpeth Stuckey, who contends in *The Violence of Literacy* that "literacy is a system of oppression" (47). Drawing on Stuart Hall's theory of articulation, John Trimbur argues, however, that there is not "a fixed and necessary correspondence between literate practices and the social formation" (48)—that is, say, between literacy at the CLC and social equality there. Rather than being predetermined, the effect or role of literacy in lived experience must be articulated as "particular ideologies, political subjects, cultural practices, and social movements and institutions" that are uttered and combined within specific moments of history (Trimbur 42). Moreover, he contends that Rose's *Lives on the Boundary* is radical to the extent that it proposes "redefined standards and practices of literacy that are capable of promoting more equal social order" (48).

It is at this point in the disciplinary debate—the point at which theorists in the field of literacy work to articulate the dynamism with which discursive practices of social activity combine and recombine—that we hear a resonance with Paula's own negotiations in mentoring. The indeterminacy of literacy's relationship to social equality is a source of tension for Paula as a mentor. Granted, Paula's efforts to support social equality are not unique. As teachers we often work to maintain a sense of equality in the classroom. But the conflicts which Paula negotiates are especially interesting when considered in light of the course of action she constructs for herself as a conscientious and theoretically grounded mentor.

"I WANT US TO BE EQUALS."

During several of her first sessions as a mentor, Paula struggles with the desire to violate codes of equality within conversational discourse—where partners share turn taking, move freely among topics, and avoid stating "should commands" to one another—in order to provide her teen writer with explicit writing instruction. The conflict regarding social equality becomes all the more intense one afternoon when she leads a small group of teenagers in finalizing the script for the Community Conversation, the project's culminating event—a town meeting during which the teens will present their ideas on school reform.

The stakes are high this afternoon. The script is a big deal. All the teens know they will have parts to play, and they are waiting to find out their parts. The pressure is intense. The writing session this afternoon is necessarily the last before the prescheduled dress rehearsal and final Community Conversation, which school board members, teachers, and the center's funders will be attending. And not much of the script is actually written yet. In addition, the literacy leader who had previously worked with this group of teen writers is now absent, having stayed on campus for a faculty meeting. Discussing the situation later, Paula describes how the added responsibility brought with it a central concern: "I pretty much took charge, and now I'm struggling with that because this is the CLC where everyone is supposed to be equal." As Paula explains it, the challenge was to chart a course of action that would respect the writers' rights to be the "planners and thinkers" in developing the script, while at the same time ensuring that a specific, and rather large, writing task would get accomplished, and accomplished well, within a short time frame.

For Paula, learning at the CLC means actively appraising her course of action as a mentor in light of the competing pressures she feels obliged to honor, the multiple goals she is working to achieve, and the options she regards as viable. Consider first the pressure Paula describes. All of us working at the center that day knew Paula and the writers were under severe time constraints, and Paula had the responsibility of taking over for an absentee literacy leader. In her reflective self-interview, however, Paula addresses other pressures, including the emotional baggage carried over from the previous session. The session the previous Monday had not been a typical CLC writing day, though perhaps we can all relate to Paula's description of it: "Getting the ideas we needed and the little bits and pieces which we did Monday . . . was like pulling teeth. . . . We were all stuck, so getting going again today was really difficult." Moreover, there was simply a lot of writing to complete: "We had so many loose ends. We just needed to tie them up. I mean, we scrawled a few notes here and there on Monday, but we needed a format. We needed to get this thing in some kind of script form."

Intensifying Paula's sense of pressure were the specific goals she set for herself. In her reflection of the session, she describes trying to uphold three goals: (1) to support the purpose of the CLC, (2) "to have had a good day . . . after Monday," and (3) to complete the script for the skit. She articulates a felt difficulty stemming from the fact that she wants to encourage the teens to name their task for themselves, but she also realizes she needs to provide some leadership:

> I set the goal for us. . . . It was a big task, we had a lot of work ahead of us. And I said, "We're gonna write the script based on what we said the other day, and we're going to get it done." I set the goal for us, like right at the beginning of the day, and everyone knew this.

It might have been easy enough to have achieved any one of these goals: to have completed the skit, say, by railroading the writers or by writing it herself, or to have had a great day with little regard for productivity. What was difficult was simultaneously attending to all three goals.

In contending with this conflict, Paula names several options for mentoring but explains that she considered only one option to be genuinely viable. Her customary role was no longer available to her, for that role relied on having a literacy leader there to "lead the discussion," with "Allison [another mentor] and me jumping in from time to time." Another option, "going with the flow," did not fit the requirement of being as productive as the group needed to be that day. Considering that she could have

ELENORE LONG

"let Christine and the other writers do their own thing," Paula continues: "But I'm not sure I agree with that, 'cause sometimes it's not productive at all. Sometimes you have to give them something to go on, something to work towards. I mean everybody's like that. That's only human." In Paula's negotiation of the event, she is left with the option of working as the skit writers' facilitator. Part of what made that role difficult, she explains, is that "I was sort of playing the same role that Ms. Baskins [a literacy leader] plays in saying, 'This is what we're going to do today.'"

As Trimbur has claimed, "the rhetorical effect of ideas and practices" is not predetermined, but rather a product of the "practical joining together of discourse, institutions, and interests that social utterances and performances inevitably enact" (37). Trimbur argues that Rose's position in *Lives on the Boundary*, that "education has the power to equalize things," does not necessarily mean that education *does* equalize things. Rose's position is useful, argues Trimbur, to the extent it is detached from its usual political meaning of equal opportunity and rearticulated as political pressure. Paula, too, confronts the indeterminacy of her actions as a mentor. Interpreting this indeterminacy, as well as making judgments in the face of it, is a crucial aspect of a negotiated image of literate social action. As she considers the effects of having "set the goal for the day," we can hear Paula evaluate her mentoring discourse, consider her position within an institution, and consider its interests and the interests of writers. The episode captures part of her effort to ascribe—with the disciplinary resources available to her—"certain cultural meanings and political valences to [her] ideas and practices" (Trimbur 37).

It may strike some readers that applying such an interpretation to a rather minor event is to over-read it. However, I would argue that this interpretation works to illuminate some of the ways that rhetors work to forge possible links among discourse, institutions, and interests in everyday public life. In relation to Paula's interest in connecting literacy to social equality, it is indeed such pressure and activity that need to merge in dynamic concert if, as Trimbur has argued, efforts to reconstrue literacy are to participate in the "ongoing struggle for democracy and social justice" (49). Paula, then, is on to something here. After

— 312 —

suggesting several, some negative, interpretations of the rhetorical effect of her action, Paula comes to this provisional resolution:

> I think I made the community celebration more real to everyone because they got to read the script, and they realized that they were going to be doing this. Everybody had their parts and their lines. I think that started everyone realizing that "Wow, this thing is really going to happen."

Here, Paula's commitment to equality becomes a useful support for literacy. She moves away from her earlier notion that a CLC literacy project should be highly informal and conversational. Her position is rearticulated as a commitment to supporting literate activity in ways that invite teens to see themselves as participants with important arguments to make at a highly publicized and highly public community forum.

The negotiation indicates that Paula's commitment to social action (to being a supportive member in a place that gives "everyone equal status") had to be instantiated in the midst of numerous conditions. She represents the problem of equality as a generative source of conflict—a problem that calls her to negotiate situated judgments that will chart an interpretive course of action, one that is accountable to multiple strong arguments, real-world pressures, strong values, and group commitments. As Paula represents it, the "problem with equality" is that, as a goal, it cannot be simply assumed. Rather, it has to be constructed in the middle of existing—often countervailing—pressures and commitments to purposive rhetorical goals.

The Problem and Possibility of Literate Social Action

This chapter began as an exploration into the disciplinary problem of literate social action. It has shown specific ways in which the college mentors at the Community Literacy Center wrestle with critical issues within this disciplinary debate. More important, it extends Graff's contention that coming to understand a discipline as a site of contested knowledge constitutes valuable learning. That is, the mentors' reflections reveal that in mentoring, students not only are able to understand and deliberate over competing disciplinary arguments (as they do in Graff's model), but also to draw from the disciplinary debate to make judgments about what to do as literacy mentors. What is even more valuable and instructive for all of us involved in literacy education is that the mentors contend with disciplinary conflicts in generative ways, situating and qualifying theoretical arguments to build their own arguments that account for their judgments. Thus this chapter suggests that mentoring is a site of mutual learning. As the teenagers learn from working with the college mentors, so too the college mentors learn from working with the teenagers.

In these ways, this chapter underscores what the mentors' negotiations contribute to the disciplinary debate over literate social action. If we approach the debate over literate social action by holding out for universal truths, we will end up empty-handed. And if we are content merely to analyze the reasonableness of competing claims, literate social action will remain a theoretical construct that never moves outside the walls of the library. But mentors provide hope for moving beyond these two limited alternatives. Students such as Rachel, Keith, and Paula can teach us that there are alternatives to searching for ultimate truths or for authoritative claims. And their struggles also remind us that literate social action requires teachers and students alike to take risks. As Cornel West writes, "All facts are fallible, and all experience is experimental. . . . Unique selves acting in and through participatory communities give ethical significance to an open, risk-ridden future" (112–13). Forced to take action at the crossroads where theoretical debate and real-world literacy collide, mentors negotiate these risks as they build richer repertoires of new strategies for linking literacy to social action. Ultimately, they teach us that literate social action is born amid conflict and risk. They teach us that literate social action is made possible as we negotiate conflict and accept the risks required to build inclusive communities for effective problem solving in a complex world.

Acknowledgments

This piece grew out of a collaboration with many people: CLC teens; Carnegie Mellon University mentors; and community literacy leaders, including Joyce Baskins, Tim Flower, Gwen Gorzelsky, Lorraine Higgins, and Wayne Peck. I would especially like to thank Linda Flower, who has read previous drafts of this text. Linda Flower, Wayne Peck, and Jennifer Flach currently team-teach the mentors' seminar, now entitled Community Literacy and Intercultural Inquiry.

Notes

1. The names of mentors and teens have been replaced with pseudonyms.
2. When the study was conducted, courses in literacy and cultural theory served as the core curriculum for all students earning degrees in English at Carnegie Mellon University.

Works Cited

Baker, Sheridan. *The Practical Stylist.* 6th ed. New York: Harper, 1985.

Bartholomae, David. "Inventing the University." *When a Writer Can't Write: Studies in Writer's Block and Other Composing-Process Problems.* Ed. Mike Rose. New York: Guilford, 1985. 134–65.

Berlin, James. "Freirian Pedagogy in the U.S." *Journal of Advanced Composition* 12 (1992): 412–21.

Bernard-Donals, Michael. "Mikhail Bakhtin, Classical Rhetoric, and Praxis: Bakhtin and the Future of Rhetorical Criticism." *Rhetoric Society Quarterly* 22 (1992): 10–15.

Bloom, Allan. *The Closing of the American Mind: How Higher Education Has Failed Democracy and Impoverished the Souls of Today's Students.* New York: Simon, 1987.

Bourdieu, Pierre, and Jean-Claude Passeron. *Reproduction in Education, Society and Culture.* Trans. Richard Nice. Newbury Park: Sage, 1990.

Chomsky, Noam. *Language and Mind*. New York: Harcourt, 1972.

Cook, Thomas D., Judith Levinson-Rose, and William E. Pollard. "The Misutilization of Evaluation Research: Some Pitfalls of Definition." *Knowledge, Creation, Diffusion, Utilization* 1 (1980): 477–98.

Delpit, Lisa D. "The Silenced Dialogue: Power and Pedagogy in Educating Other People's Children." *Harvard Educational Review* 58 (1988): 280–99.

Dewey, John. *Democracy and Education: An Introduction to the Philosophy of Education*. New York: Free, 1944.

Elbow, Peter. *Writing without Teachers*. New York: Oxford UP, 1973.

Farrell, Thomas. "IQ and Standard English." *College Composition and Communication* 34 (1987): 470–84.

Flower, Linda. "Cognitive Rhetoric: Inquiry into the Art of Inquiry." *Defining the New Rhetorics*. Ed. Theresa Enos and Stuart C. Brown. Newbury Park: Sage. 171–90.

———.*The Construction of Negotiated Meaning: A Social Cognitive Theory of Writing*. Carbondale: Southern Illinois UP, 1994.

Flower, Linda, David L. Wallace, Linda Norris, and Rebecca E. Burnett. *Making Thinking Visible: Writing, Collaborative Planning, and Classroom Inquiry*. Urbana, IL: NCTE, 1994.

Freire, Paulo. "The Adult Literacy Process as Cultural Action for Freedom and Education and Conscientizacão." *Perspectives on Literacy*. Ed. Eugene R. Kintgen, Barry M. Kroll, and Mike Rose. Carbondale: Southern Illinois UP, 1988. 398–409.

———. *Pedagogy of the Oppressed*. Trans. Myra Bergman Ramos. New York: Continuum, 1970.

Gee, James P. "The Legacies of Literacy: From Plato to Freire through Harvey Graff." *Journal of Education* 171 (1989): 147–65.

Gintis, Herbert. "Education, Personal Development and Human Dignity." *Education and the American Dream: Conservatives, Liberals and Radicals Debate the Future of Education*. Ed. Harvey Holtz, Irwin Marcus, Jim Dougherty, Judy Michaels, and Rick Peduzz. Granby, MA: Bergin, 1989. 50–59.

Giroux, Henry. *Teachers as Intellectuals: Toward a Critical Pedagogy of Learning*. Granby, MA: Bergin, 1988.

———. "Theories of Reproduction and Resistance in the New Sociology of Education: A Critical Analysis." *Harvard Journal of Education* 53 (1983): 257–93.

Goggin, Maureen Daly, and Elenore Long. "A Tincture of Philosophy, A Tincture of Hope: The Portrayal of Isocrates in Plato's *Phaedrus*." *Rhetoric Review* 11 (1993): 304–24.

Graff, Gerald. *Beyond the Culture Wars: How Teaching the Conflicts Can Revitalize American Education.* New York: Norton, 1992.

Heath, Shirley Brice, and Milbrey W. McLaughlin, eds. *Identity and Inner-City Youth: Beyond Ethnicity and Gender.* New York: Teachers College P, 1993.

Hopper, Paul. "Discourse Analysis: Grammar and Critical Theory in the 1980s." *Profession* 88 (1993): 19–26.

Hull, Glynda, and Mike Rose. "Rethinking Remediation: Toward a Social-Cognitive Understanding of Problematic Reading and Writing." *Written Communication* 6 (1989): 139–54.

Labov, William. *Language in the Inner City: Studies in the Black English Vernacular.* Philadelphia: U of Pennsylvania P, 1972.

Long, Elenore. "The Rhetoric of Literate Social Action: Mentors Negotiating Intercultural Images of Literacy." Diss. Carnegie Mellon U, 1994.

Long, Elenore, and Linda Flower. "Cognitive Rhetoric." *Encyclopedia of Rhetoric and Composition: Communication from Ancient Times to the Information Age.* Ed. Theresa Enos. New York: Garland, 1996. 108–109.

Lyotard, Jean-François. *The Postmodern Condition: A Report on Knowledge.* Trans. Geoff Bennington and Brian Massumi. Minneapolis: U of Minnesota P, 1984.

Olson, David R. "From Utterance to Text: The Bias of Language in Speech and Writing." *Harvard Educational Review* 47 (1977): 257–81.

Peck, Wayne, Linda Flower, and Lorraine Higgins. "Community Literacy." *College Composition and Communication* 46 (1995): 199–222.

Perelman, Chaïm. *The Realm of Rhetoric.* Trans. William Kluback. Notre Dame: U of Notre Dame P, 1982.

Perelman, Chaïm, and Lucie Olbrechts-Tyteca. *The New Rhetoric: A Treatise on Argumentation*. Trans. John Wilkinson and Purcell Weaver. Notre Dame: Notre Dame UP, 1969.

Roche, Mark W. "Reflections on Allan Bloom's Critics: A Defense of Universal Norms." *Beyond Cheering and Bashing: New Perspectives on* The Closing of the American Mind. Ed. William K. Buckley and James Seaton. Bowling Green: Bowling Green State UP, 1992. 134–44.

Rose, Mike. *Lives on the Boundary: The Struggles and Achievements of America's Underprepared*. New York: Free, 1989.

Russell, David R. "Vygotsky, Dewey, and Externalism: Beyond the Student/Discipline Dichotomy." *Journal of Advanced Composition* 13 (1993): 173–97.

Simon, Roger I. "Empowerment as a Pedagogy of Possibility." *Language Arts* 64 (1987): 370–83.

Stuckey, J. Elspeth. *The Violence of Literacy*. Portsmouth, NH: Boynton/Cook, 1991.

Trimbur, John. "Articulation Theory and the Problem of Determination: A Reading of *Lives on the Boundary*." *Journal of Advanced Composition* 13 (1993): 33–50.

West, Cornel. *Keeping Faith: Philosophy and Race in America*. New York: Routledge, 1993.

Willinsky, John. *The New Literacy: Redefining Reading and Writing in the Schools*. New York: Routledge, 1990.

CHAPTER FOURTEEN

WAC, WHACK:
You're an Expert—NOT!

SAM WATSON
University of North Carolina at Charlotte

I hope you will hear this essay as a provocative question: Should the aim of writing across the curriculum (WAC) be to get students to write like experts? If so, what might that mean? I introduce this subject in the form of questions because I am not at all sure of the answers to either. One possible aim of WAC is indeed to train our students to write like experts, but such an aim always leaves me uneasy in a number of ways.

Students do not have the expertise, so why should they be expected to write as though they did? I might tell students, "The surest way for you to become an expert is to pretend that you already are one." There is surely something to that; it certainly seems sanctioned by ancient pedagogical practices of imitation. But I am paid by the taxpayers of North Carolina, and that state's motto is "To Be, Rather Than to Seem." I do not wish to turn our motto on its head. Both ethically and educationally, something would ring hollow if I did. And there may be more important matters we should be helping our students with. As a friend of mine, the parent of three college-aged girls, puts it, "I'm concerned about our children's colleges and how they do so little to help kids find themselves." Writing as if one were an expert when one knows oneself not to be—is that a promising route to self-understanding or to responsible citizenship?

Furthermore, few of our students will ever become experts in our field. None of them will become experts in all the fields they study and in which (we can hope) they find themselves writing. Then, too, there is the whole question of how experts actually do

write. We seem not to know a great deal about that; I certainly
do not. But the evidence suggests that, at least in the scholastic
world of academic expertise these days, the published texts of
expertise do everything possible to belie the contingent and im-
passioned processes of their own creation (Bazerman; Myers;
Gilbert and Mulkay). I fear that in ignorance my students (and
even I) would reduce the question of how experts write to something like: What do experts' resulting texts look like? That is a
very different question. Even if experts' texts provided us with
excellent writing (and they often do not), I am not sure I would
want to read our mimicries of them.

There also is the question of "expertise" in general. Our culture rewards it, perhaps even worships it, certainly depends on
it. But how well are we served by it? The calculations of the best
and the brightest got us into Vietnam but could not get us out;
this is a dated example, thank goodness, but its bitter lessons
linger. To bring matters closer to home, you and I are paid because somebody thinks we are experts in something. We are professors, after all, so our job presumably is to profess to our
students, to tell them what we know. Certainly that is the standard rationale for the academic research that deans and tenure
committees demand: we are to add to the storehouse of knowledge to which we are privileged so that within our guilds, if not
with our students, we might continue to have something to profess. A jaundiced reading, that? Perhaps, but I remind us that
academic kudos go to those who conduct the most specialized
research and publish in the journals with the most limited read-
ership; my inability to read your work, to make sense of it, marks
you as that much more the expert. Let us hope that the day Cheryl
Geisler fears does not come, "when it will be a faux pas to admit
the impact of our daily experience on our professional lives or
when it will be taken for granted that our research has no direct
bearing on our teaching, administration, or living" (247).

"I want to enrich my naiveté." This from my friend Henry.
Henry was a student of mine twenty-one years ago at UNC Charlotte. His life has been an interesting one—high school English
teacher, independent management consultant to businesses, fund-
raiser for a liberal arts college, manager of two almost-successful
congressional campaigns, divorced and remarried father of two,

lay reader in cosmology and quantum mechanics who finds thinkers on the cusp of science increasingly pointing him in the direction of poetry. Recently Henry told my first-year students that he values his failures, but the public hears little of those. Henry is also the president of our alumni association. "When I get introduced," he confides to me, "all they say is that I'm a successful banker." As indeed he is, a senior vice president in one of those tall money monuments that mark the Charlotte skyline. Henry the expert. Henry the failure. Henry the student still, seeking not to erase but to enrich his naiveté.

Expertise. Naiveté. I am a rhetorician, and if forced to choose between those two I opt for the latter, a choice that lands me amongst some interesting company. With Polus and Gorgias on the wrong side of Plato, for example, whose central complaint against us rhetoricians is that we have no rigorously principled art and we do not know what we are talking about. In Plato's world, we are forever naive, recklessly so.

Aristotle, as he arrays the realms of expertise, acknowledges a place for naiveté. It is the place of rhetoric. Aristotle says plainly, "The duty of rhetoric is to deal with such matters as we deliberate upon without arts or systems to guide us, in the hearing of persons who cannot take in at a glance a complicated argument, or follow a long chain of reasoning" (1357a). And he distinguishes between rhetoric and other disciplines:

> The better the selection one makes of propositions suitable for special lines of argument, the nearer one comes, unconsciously, to setting up a science that is distinct from . . . rhetoric. One may succeed in stating the required principles, but one's science will no longer be . . . rhetoric, but the science to which the principles thus discovered belong. (1358a)

And in my naiveté, I take some comfort from Isocrates, the father of humanism, who writes: "With this faculty [of language] we both contend with others on matters which are open to dispute and seek light for ourselves on things which are unknown" (256).

With the ancients as I have just invoked them, I have been implying that an expert is someone who knows something, something systematized, with a clarity and a rigor that the rest of us cannot claim. It is a definition which emphatically excludes me, and it excludes my students, too.

Surely what I am trading in here is not a definition but a stereotype, something that none of us really believes. But we seem to act as though we did; there's the rub. Else why would I be reading, in our professional books and journals, defensive apologies by authors who fear that their multiplicity of methodologies might make their work suspect in ways that can be hazardous to an academic career? Or others, finally somehow finding the courage to invoke the first-person pronoun? Then there is Ross Winterowd, in his Yule 1996 letter, characterizing the four decades of his CCC'ing. Says Ross, we began as Pentecostals, but then we began to discover systematic theology. So we became "High Church Episcopal, reading from *The Book of Common Prayer* and listening silently to the sermons. Now," says Ross, "we have gone beyond High Church; we are apotheosized, indistinguishable from the MLA." And he exhorts us:

> Brothers and Sisters, join with me to recapture our Spirit. Don't sit through the reading of respectable papers! Demand that the deacon talk to you. . . . When bearing your own testimony, make a joyful noise—and count yourself a failure if no one ever laughs with you or if not one member of your audience is outraged. . . . And join me in this resolution for 1997: we will bring joy and laughter back into composition-rhetoric. We will recapture our Pentecostal spirit.

What's going on here? Beyond a delightful display of Winterowdian outrage, perhaps Ross is helping us see that we are enchained by something we know better than to submit to, an image of expertise that we no longer believe in. Informing that image, it seems to me, are twin myths, which we might label the myth of autonomy and the myth of rigor. In our public posturings (including our publications, our professional conventions, and, alas, probably our classrooms as well), we act as though there is such a thing as an autonomous fact, an autonomous text which is a compilation of such facts (textbooks, of course, being the purest exemplar), an autonomous method, an autonomous expert. And we have the myth of rigor, too, which implies that impersonal and precise application of the correct methodology will underwrite if not guarantee any claims to truth we might care to make. Within those myths, we end up encased in a kind of rigorous mortis in which it becomes impossible to write or speak, impossible to think, and doubly impossible to do the two together. We have all been there, I submit; I certainly have, more times than I care to recall. Could it be that that is where our students end up also, the ones so conscientious that they find themselves blocked, laboring under expertise delusions of truly mythic proportions?

There is more to it than that, of course, thank goodness. If we acted under that myth of expertise—really, rigorously, and always—we would never have made it this far in our professional lives, or in our personal ones. We would never even have gotten out of bed this morning.

Well, what more might there be? I have been implying that "expertise" and "naiveté" are polar opposites, or dialectical ones, each defined by its contrast with the other. Perhaps that is not so? Perhaps there is naiveté which—quietly, usually unnoticed and unacknowledged—provides the heartbeat of expertise itself? William J. J. Gordon seems to think so. In *Synectics* he advises that if we need to solve a real-world problem, we had best not look only to the experts, whose very expertise often entails a sort of trained incapacity. We had best put together a team of people bringing various perspectives, and we should be sure to include some who are not expert in anything.

There is James Boyd White, scholar of the law, of civic culture, literature, and the classics, whose bearings could have come from the Isocrates and the Aristotle I have quoted:

When the resources of a certain kind of thinking run out, a common response is to give up in despair; the disconcerting discovery that the conceptual and logical apparatus of quasi-scientific rationality will not do for the understanding of life or literature or law leads to the announcement that we live in an incoherent and elemental flux in which no reasoning, no meaning, is possible. But to say that there is no meaning or knowledge of one kind is not to deny the possibility of other kinds, and in our actual lives we show that we know how to read and speak, to live with language, texts, and each other, and to do so with considerable confidence. But to do this we must accept the conditions on which we live. When we discover that we have in this world no earth or rock to stand or walk upon but only shifting sea and sky and wind, the mature response is not to lament the loss of fixity but to learn to sail. (77–78)

What might be the alignments between expertise and naiveté? For the remainder of this chapter, I would like to ask that question of three contemporary thinkers whose work seems to align in promising ways and for each of whom naiveté in some sense is central. Cheryl Geisler, with her understanding of rhetorical processes; Donald Schön, with his concern for reflective practices; Michael Polanyi, with his articulation of the dynamics of discovery: these three seem to have a good deal to say to each other and to us on the issues of expertise and naiveté.

In her meticulous and eloquent book *Academic Literacy and the Nature of Expertise*, Geisler argues that learners, whether lay or expert, inhabit two problem spaces: domain content, which is the available information and theories pertinent to the subject at hand, and rhetorical process, which includes the social culture within which one is living and, in texts, the metadiscourse markers which signal the contextualization of information, the adjudication of conflicts, the weighing of evidence, and the construction of lines of argument informing a claim of knowledge.

All learners live in both these spaces, content domain and rhetorical process. However, in the ways that schooling is currently constructed, the difficulty for the lay learner is that the two seem utterly at odds. Geisler says, "Schools ask students to leave their personal knowledge at the classroom door and move instead into a world of decontextualized facts. Academic knowing and contextualized understanding are taken to be at odds" (29). Students are led to construe texts "as autonomous repositories of knowledge, completely explicit in their content but utterly opaque in their rhetorical construction" (85). Students choosing not to leave their indigenous cultures behind reside on the ignorant side of what Geisler calls "the great divide," as passive consumers of the knowledge generated by experts.

Experts generate that knowledge not by working in the realm of content domain alone. Students who begin to enter the realm of a professional expertise find that "[a] process of rhetorical recovery is initiated. And what is recovered, strangely, are the temporal and human aspects of indigenous culture that students once thought they had to leave behind" (92). She continues, "Whenever expert practice is truly present—when knowledge is treated as something to be constructed rather than something to be found—both rhetorical process and domain content will necessarily be involved" (228). Experts indeed are persons in whose practice the two are tacitly integrated.

Expert practices are grounded in rhetorical processes which, on ancient authority, I have been calling naiveté. Geisler helps me think toward an understanding of expertise that is not at odds with naiveté but may be grounded in it. But she cautions that none of us can afford merely to look to experts for our understandings of expertise:

> [A]s long as research on expertise is written as the account of what other people do, the account will be a false account. Real reform can only be accomplished through an attempt to understand how our own practices of reading, writing, and knowing operate within the dual problem spaces of domain content and rhetorical process, thereby creating and re-creating the great divide. Only by engaging with this problem of reflection, seeking explanations which ring bells with our own experience, with what we ourselves do, will we be getting closer to the truth—and getting closer to change. The stakes for such change are high. As long as students think that they have to abandon the resources of their indigenous cultures in order to succeed in school and in the professions, a significant portion who refuse to take the move will be forced to drop out. A significant portion who do take the move will be crippled. And how many among us can say with confidence, "I am not crippled," or "I have not dropped out"? (94–95)

On the issues of expertise, Geisler invites us to reflection, which she characterizes as "the process by which each of the multiple worlds in our lives acknowledges and plays off against all of the others, generating a potential for change" (247).

Reflection may be the central word in Donald Schön's world. While Geisler's principle concern is for change of the academy and its literacy ways, Schön's is to help us understand and learn from ways that effective professionals go about working in the world beyond school walls. These persons have "know-how," which Schön contrasts with the "knowledge that" which school teaches. Our schooling does an efficient job, he acknowledges, of transmitting facts and theories to our students. If the world's demands were simply a matter of recalling facts or applying theories, such an education would be sufficient.

But the world does not work that way. The demands of any professional world in which we work, and of the civic world in which we live, are far more complex. Therein lies the rub—and a significant challenge for U.S. education. A person's mastery of "technical rationality," the information and procedures of any one narrowly defined academic discipline, is simply not enough, no matter how rigorous.

Whether as engineers or medical doctors, lawyers or teachers, our students need to become effective practitioners in their respective professions. Our civic health also depends on their becoming responsible citizens within the wider community. Effective practice, Schön finds, is not what "technical rationality" implies it to be, a matter merely of "applying" preexisting knowledge and theory instrumentally to solve problems which are already well defined. Donald Schön says there is also "an epistemology of practice implicit in the artistic, intuitive processes which some practitioners do bring to situations of uncertainty, instability, uniqueness, and value conflict" (49).

Through careful case studies of their actual work practices, Schön finds that effective practitioners do not just "solve" problems but define and redefine them: "Problem setting is a process in which, interactively, we name the things to which we will attend and frame the context in which we will attend to them" (40). Drawing on what Michael Polanyi has called their "tacit" or personal knowledge, effective practitioners experiment within the situation which engages them, shaping and reshaping what they are bringing to it in light of what they are finding within it. They engage in the sort of continuing "conversation with the situation" that Schön calls "reflective practice." Within the university, our students need to learn to become reflective practitioners: "All human beings . . . need to become competent in taking action and simultaneously reflecting on this action to learn from it" (Argyris and Schön 4).

Naming, framing, conversing, listening to others, learning from them and dealing effectively with them, all within a particular and problematic situation. Practicing reflection sounds messy, doesn't it? More like naiveté than expertise. And a lot like rhetoric, in the very oldest and best senses of that much-maligned word.

Ignorance. That is the word which Harry Prosch, co-author of Michael Polanyi's final philosophical book, uses to characterize Polanyi's expertise in philosophy (Prosch 192). A prolific research scientist, Polanyi found himself called to philosophy by horrific cultural (and rhetorical) exigency which was undermining the work of science itself, even though science is surely our culture's prime exemplar of expertise.

Polanyi's entry point into philosophy was to realize that prevailing understandings of science could say nothing significant about discovery, even though discovery is the heart of scientific work. Seeking to account for the dynamics of discovery, Polanyi articulates his philosophy of the tacit: "We can know more than we can tell," he insists, and what we can "tell"—our explicit knowledge—always and necessarily rests upon foundations of what we cannot say—the tacit understandings, beliefs, and commitments which define us and in terms of which we make what sense we can of the world beyond ourselves.

Visual perception offers an accessible if relatively trivial example of tacit knowing: I do not know and certainly could never tell how my eyes, brain, and mind work, but I accept these as generally reliable guides to a visual reality, I dwell within them indeed, attending from them to (or toward) something I am struggling to see; and in struggling toward a new focus, the lenses of my eye are quite likely to change shape in ways I am completely unaware of.

A scientific discovery is like that, too. "A good problem is half a discovery" (*Knowing and Being* 117), Polanyi says, but discovery is never achieved merely by routine, impersonal application of already-existing explicit theories, information, or methods. The scientist instead embodies these disciplinary frameworks and then goes beyond them, moving from all of these toward something which has remained problematic despite them. If the scientist achieves a discovery, seeing something which no one has seen before, the very discovery in some sense reshapes and renews the tacitly understood frameworks through which the scientist had pointed toward that discovery. In these ways, Polanyi says, "The process of examining any topic is both an exploration of the topic, and an exegesis of our fundamental beliefs in light of which we approach it; a dialectical combination of exploration and exegesis" (*Personal Knowledge* 267). Efforts at knowing inherently involve the informal, the personal, and all such efforts are hazardous; as optical illusions remind us, our discoveries can turn out to have been mistaken, and discoveries change their discoverers: "Having made a discovery, I shall never again see the world as before. My eyes have become different: I have made myself into a person seeing and thinking differently. I have crossed a gap, the heuristic gap which lies between problem and discovery" (*Personal Knowledge* 143).

Given the hazards, and given the largely tacit character of acculturation into an area of expertise (a science, say), communities of scientists serve utterly essential roles in the progress of scientific work. They acculturate and accredit new members, they point their members toward promising problems, and they adjudicate claims of discovery being advanced by community members. Some of the ways in which they do all of this are inherently informal, personal, tacit. In speaking of communities' actions, Polanyi often speaks a language that rhetoricians will find familiar, the language of jurisprudence, of opinion, belief, logical gap, persuasion, and yes, of conversion. It is a language of discursive practices:

> Like the heuristic passion from which it flows, the *persuasive passion* too finds itself facing a logical gap. . . . [The discoverer's] persuasive passion spurs him now to cross this gap by converting everybody to his way of seeing things, even as his heuristic passion has spurred him to cross the heuristic gap which separated him from discovery. . . . Proponents of a new system can convince their audience only by first winning their intellectual sympathy for a doctrine they have not yet grasped. Those who listen sympathetically will discover for themselves what they would otherwise never have understood. Such an act is a heuristic process, a self-modifying act, and to this extent a discovery. (*Personal Knowledge* 150–51)

What has happened to expertise in all of this? It seems to me that Polanyi is saying, as Donald Schön might put it, that experts engage in reflective practice *within* the domain(s) of their expertise, which Cheryl Geisler has called the content domain. And that what Geisler calls rhetorical processes are part and parcel of the affirmation of knowledge itself, within an accredited community, and are part and parcel of individuals' efforts to discover. It seems to me that a new and promising understanding of expertise is beginning to suggest itself: no longer a dialectical opposite to the naive person, perhaps an expert is someone who, to echo my old student Henry, seeks to enrich his or her naiveté. Perhaps an expert is someone who knows what he or she does not know and commits to finding out, within appropriate fields of discursive and reflective practice. Practices of language and reflection, the tacit and, yes, in some senses the naive—perhaps these are essential dimensions of expertise.

And what of our students' writing in all of this? The answer is not to pretend that expertise does not exist or to forget that a responsibility we share with our students is their enculturation into realms of expertise. In our students' writing, no one is well served if we sentence them to years of expressive self-indulgence. But we need to do much better than merely require that students mimic the published writing of experts. Such a stance forces students into roles as pretenders; it does not sanction their reflection and thereby discourages their reflection. It leaves aside the discursive practices that seem essential to the practice of expertise and certainly to its cultivation.

I wish that I were speaking the obvious, beating a horse now safely dead. But I am afraid that is simply not the case. Students often experience their writing as something which they (the naive) are forced to serve up to the expert (one of us) quite independent of their own concerns and their own thinking—writing is something to be delayed as long as possible, done with no more pain than necessary, escaped from as soon as possible. And I am afraid that our own best intentions often feed these negative attitudes.

Here is a recent student of mine, part of her response (reprinted with permission) to a letter I read to the class on our first meeting, in which I said something about who I was finding myself to be and what questions I was bringing to our time together, and in which I asked students to cultivate a "yes, but" attitude to whatever I might say about writing:

> Let me thank you for your letter. I really enjoyed having it as my introduction to the course. It is very rare that professors take a moment to introduce themselves, or want to know about us students. . . . I am very excited that within our expository writing course I will be able to explore my own ideas and improve my writing skills. I have always hated to write. As a student, I normally adjust my writing skills to the requirements of the teacher, but I feel that possibly this semester I will be able to include more of myself within my writing, without fear of a bad grade. I have always had a "yes, but" attitude in my life, but I have often suppressed it, so I would not offend others, or be impolite, and very rarely have I ever questioned teachers. In my experience many professors do not like their authority questioned, but I feel that questioning can only stimulate intellectual conversations where something new can be learned.

Among our students, is Trivia's experience isolated? I wish it were. But I am haunted by countless students who have heard our traditional injunctions against "I think" or "in my opinion" and similar textual markers of contingency, qualification, or uncertainty and have translated those injunctions into a belief that their own thinking belongs nowhere in their academic writing. And I am reminded of the assessment process that our English department recently began. A committee went through one hundred plus papers, all by graduating English majors at UNC Charlotte, and selected seven for the department as a whole to read. Though at least some committee members looked for a reflective paper to include in that group of seven, there was no such paper to be found.

Deeper understandings of expertise might help us work toward correcting this situation. An expert is someone who is in some senses naive, and our students are that. An expert is someone engaged in reflective practice within a problematic situation; as learners, goodness knows, our students are within such situations. An expert is aware of and engaged in practices that are inherently rhetorical; our students deserve that awareness and they need that engagement. Perhaps above all, we need to urge, encourage, and help them to experience their writing as a reflective medium that can deepen their understanding of a topic and our understanding of them. Such writing strengthens learning—and learners.

How might we lead students to write in such ways? Our deepened understandings of expertise can help, of course. We also can continue to push for greater acceptance of openly reflective writing in the publications of our own profession. (For superb examples, in composition studies see Hillocks and in philosophy see Kaplan.) Such writing is often far more readable, I submit, for both our students and for us as "experts": because the writing includes the writer making meaning, it invites us to locate claims with reference to the person making them, and that is actually a crucial dimension of our efforts to make what meanings we can—of the world, its texts, and, for that matter, ourselves.

Furthermore, such openly reflective publications provide better models for the writing our students need to be doing if their engagement is to be more than superficial. Laura Duhan Kaplan writes:

> [I]t is tempting, as a professional philosopher, to allow my work to remain superficial, to spin creative abstract theories about war and peace in response to the abstract theories of others. . . . When I do so, however, my work tells only the story of the latest fickle trends in my academic discipline. It does not confront my inner life, my aspirations, emotional ties, or attempts to find meaning. . . . At least I have chosen not to hide behind abstract but academically acceptable jargon which, if I use it correctly, masks all my personal confusions and imperfections. (137–38)

Particle physicist Andrew Pickering characterizes such confusions and imperfections—along with the constraints and potentials of the varied and intersecting material, social agencies, and intentionalities available to the researcher at any particular point in time—as "the mangle of practice," and he finds that original inquirers necessarily work within such a mangle. Certainly in our classrooms, even more than in our publications, we should let our students see us engaged in the mangle of practice as we work toward new understandings, some of which may eventuate in print. About this mangle Paul Connolly says: "In writing and science education, both, the strongest possible motivation to learn is . . . the social dynamic of doing the work itself, work in which there is genuine perplexity, which is addressed in the company of others, with curiosity not only about the outcome but about how to proceed." We can allow students to see that we have the courage of our own uncertainties.

If they hear our voices, our students will show us that they too can write reflectively; it seems to me that Ken Macrorie's far-too-easily-dismissed work on "I-searching" demonstrates precisely that. If we encourage students to write reflectively, whether within an "I-search" perspective or some other, their resulting texts will seldom read like the published works of experts, in which writers' struggles, their reflections, their rhetorical engagements often (and often appropriately) remain tacit, personal subtext to the page itself. But such reflective writing can be expected to strengthen the confidence, the understandings, and the commitments which undergird, inform, and sustain what we call "expertise" and which thus serve quite literally as the substance of such expertise.

Works Cited

Argyris, Chris, and Donald A. Schön. *Theory in Practice: Increasing Professional Effectiveness.* San Francisco: Jossey-Bass, 1974.

Aristotle. *Rhetorica.* Trans. W. Rhys Roberts. *The Basic Works of Aristotle.* Ed. Richard McKeon. New York: Random, 1941.

Bazerman, Charles. "What Written Knowledge Does: Three Examples of Academic Discourse." *Philosophy of the Social Sciences* 11 (1981): 361–87. Rpt. in *Landmark Essays on Writing Across the Curriculum.* Ed. Charles Bazerman and David R. Russell. Davis, CA: Hermagoras, 1994. 159–88.

Connolly, Paul. "The Mangle of Science Education." Unpublished essay, n.d.

Geisler, Cheryl. *Academic Literacy and the Nature of Expertise: Reading, Writing, and Knowing in Academic Philosophy*. Hillsdale, NJ: Erlbaum, 1994.

Gilbert, G. Nigel, and Michael J. Mulkay. *Opening Pandora's Box: A Sociological Analysis of Scientists' Discourse*. Cambridge: Cambridge UP, 1984.

Gordon, William J. J. *Synectics: The Development of Creative Capacity*. New York: Harper, 1961.

Hillocks, George, Jr. *Teaching Writing as Reflective Practice*. New York: Teachers College P, 1995.

Isocrates. *Antidosis*. Trans. George Norlan. Ed. T. E. Page. London: Heinemann, 1962.

Kaplan, Laura Duhan. *Family Pictures: A Philosopher Explores the Familiar*. Chicago: Open Court, 1998.

Macrorie, Ken. *The I-Search Paper*. Portsmouth, NH: Heinemann, 1988.

Myers, Greg. "The Social Construction of Two Biologists' Proposals." *Written Communication* 2 (1985): 219–45. Rpt. in *Landmark Essays on Writing Across the Curriculum*. Ed. Charles Bazerman and David R. Russell. Davis, CA: Hermagoras, 1994. 189–210.

Pickering, Andrew. *The Mangle of Practice: Time, Agency, and Science*. Chicago: U of Chicago P, 1995.

Polanyi, Michael. *Knowing and Being: Essays*. Ed. Marjorie Grene. Chicago: U of Chicago P, 1969.

———. *Personal Knowledge: Towards a Post-Critical Philosophy*. Chicago: U of Chicago P, 1958.

Prosch, Harry. "Polanyi and Rhetoric." *Pre/Text* 2 (1981): 189–95.

Schön, Donald A. *The Reflective Practitioner: How Professionals Think in Action*. New York: Basic, 1983.

White, James Boyd. *When Words Lose Their Meaning: Constitutions and Reconstitutions of Language, Character, and Community*. Chicago: U of Chicago P, 1984.

Winterowd, W. Ross. Letter to the author. Christmas 1996.

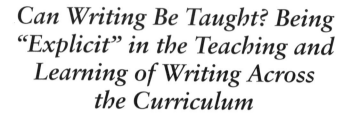

CHAPTER FIFTEEN

Can Writing Be Taught? Being "Explicit" in the Teaching and Learning of Writing Across the Curriculum

STUART GREENE
University of Notre Dame

REBECCA SCHOENIKE NOWACEK
University of Wisconsin–Madison

[W]e are learning that the ability of our students to master written English is hindered less by their deficiencies than by our failure, too often, to understand more precisely what is going on in them when they don't learn what we try to teach. Often, our very formulation of a problem keeps us from understanding it.

MINA SHAUGHNESSY (qtd. in Maher)

We practitioners, and our students, come to classes with theories about what it means to be literate and about how literacy is acquired—theories that are often unacknowledged or unexplored. Despite the hidden and sometimes incomplete nature of these theories, they influence how academic literacies are taught and learned. Therefore it is important for us to explore our literacy theories and their origins and, if appropriate, to revise and expand them in order to promote a repertoire of literate practices among our students.

ANN M. JOHNS, *Text, Role, and Context*

The authors would like to thank Barbara Walvoord and Terry Phelps for their helpful suggestions on an earlier version of this chapter.

In "Invention: A Topographical Survey," Richard Young proposes a distinction between the *art* of invention and mere *knack*. While knack is the product of "intuition and habit formed by long experience," the art of invention is a transmogrification of such a knack: "A knack becomes an art when what [the writer] does is made explicit in the form of reusable heuristic procedures." And, as Young concludes, "When this happens, the processes can be taught as well as learned" (1). In this essay, we would like to return to Young's distinction between knack and art, complicating two elements of their relationship. First, we explore what it means to make the processes of composition "explicit" when we are using writing as a means of teaching and evaluating disciplinary knowledge across the curriculum; we argue that what may seem "explicit" for members of a disciplinary community (such as the instructor) frequently remains tacit for individuals (like many of our students) struggling to achieve membership. Second, we return to and complicate Young's statement that "the processes [of invention] can be taught as well as learned" by exploring the difficulties of developing and implementing theories both of *teaching* writing and of *learning* to write. Although Young brought into focus for teachers of writing the kinds of strategies that can guide inquiry (e.g., defining what is at issue, formulating a rich question), we are seeing something different from what he envisioned: teaching often centers on text conventions, so that students are uncertain how to translate strategies for inquiry into specific things they can do as they formulate a problem. Moreover, notions about invention as an open-ended process of inquiry that can lead authors to contribute something new to a scholarly conversation get subsumed under an abiding concern for convention by both students and teachers.

Within this essay, we use the construct of authorship as a referent for understanding the process of invention Young describes. For Young, invention is a form of inquiry "concerned with discovering the subject matter of discourse"; it is invention that guides the discovery process "by heuristic procedures, that is, explicit plans for analyzing and searching which focus attention, guide reason, stimulate memory, and encourage intuition" (1). While invention, then, is a composition process equally applicable to all modes and purposes of writing—from grocery lists to doctoral theses to movie screenplays—we examine an aspect of invention demanded within academic writing. Authorship as we define it is a subset of invention, a subset coincident with an expectation writers are held to as they write across academic disciplines: to think critically in their efforts to contribute knowledge to a textual conversation, knowledge which is not necessarily found in source texts but is nonetheless carefully linked to the texts they read (Greene, "Making Sense"; Greene and Ackerman). Authorship is, in short, not only the state of having successfully written an essay appropriate for a given discipline, but perhaps even more important, it is the process through which writers determine what to do, why to do it, and how to do it.

Our notion of authorship is akin to Young's discussion of invention in that both constructs try to account for what is involved in the creative process, the features of which can be made explicit or "consciously directed" ("Concepts" 136). As Young has suggested, "We cannot teach direct control of the imaginative act or the unanticipated outcome, but we can teach" writers to read rhetorical situations and make informed choices about the appropriateness of their decisions about both text and context (136). We also build on Young's notion of rhetorical invention by calling attention to the extent to which the ways authors position themselves within a certain social space is contingent upon authority (e.g., a disciplinary community's conventions for inquiry, the academic institution, or a writer's expertise) and the topic of discourse or task at hand (cf. Dyson). Authorship, however, is a concept more bounded to academic writing than Young's more general concept.

In what follows, we complicate the picture of what happens when educators are explicit ("talk about what you think," "write an argument that . . ."), pointing to the kinds of well-learned strategies for writing that students bring to bear on what they believe they are asked to accomplish in their writing. If students are taught to focus their attention on the amenities of writing and text conventions, then it is difficult for them to shift their perspective to modes of inquiry that can foster authorship. Teaching invention is not simple. But if educators understand more about what is involved in learning to frame issues and develop arguments, we will be in a better position to teach modes of academic inquiry. After all, what educators attend to in studies of writing are often the strategies that we can teach.

We begin with some recent images of teaching that have appeared in two popular American films, images that advance a set of assumptions about both teaching and learning that not only persist in American popular culture but inform the practices of education observed in classrooms across the curriculum. The teachers depicted in both *A River Runs through It* and *Higher Learning* have a great deal of faith that the acquisition of writing ability can occur through repetition and practice, through immersion in a literate environment, or through sheer force. The assumptions underlying such practices appear to suggest that (1) writing can be learned, but it cannot be taught, and (2) writing is a generalizable skill that people can acquire in one setting and transfer to others.

After first examining images from these two films, we provide case examples from two studies that one of us conducted to show the extent to which explicitness is a relational term, suggesting that students make sense of what they are asked to do in the context of prior experiences of school and in their anticipation of how a teacher might respond to what they have written. Although we may design writing assignments that we believe will foster the learning we value, what we often find is that the learning strategies that once served our students so well at home or in their communities may seem less successful in the context of school (Heath). In fact, the strategies they have learned can be counterproductive (cf. Neuman and Roskos). Students may be quite capable of fulfilling the tasks we give them, but many of them are unaware of the ways in which the conventions they learned in one context may differ from those of academic discourse. For instance, in spoken language students are free to assert opinions without displaying evidence or to recount experiences without explaining what they mean. But in school, as Mina Shaughnessy has observed, we reward students' ability to sustain a play of mind upon ideas—teasing out contradictions and the ambiguities of statements. Therefore, when we admonish our students to "be specific," we need to be aware that the conditions for specificity may not be present for them. Similarly, the question, "What's your point?" may be difficult to answer because stu-

STUART GREENE AND REBECCA SCHOENIKE NOWACEK

dents have not developed certain habits of mind that would enable them to develop a sense of the direction they want to take.

Additionally, each discipline that students study embodies distinct ways of constructing knowledge that are merely implicit in the different genres of writing (e.g., a historical account or literary analysis) disseminated in these disciplines and in the very content that we impart to students. Underscoring students' confusion in negotiating different discourse practices, Ann Johns points out that students are often "unable to adjust to the implicit discourse rules of various disciplines." Students, she observes, "are seldom told about textual conventions, principally because the rules have become second nature to their instructors, who have already been initiated into disciplinary practices" (46). We would add that students are equally uncertain about the rules for inquiry in these practices. Thus it should not be surprising that the tasks that are so familiar to us may be formidable enough to discourage our students, just as travelers in a foreign land are discouraged when they do not speak the language of the country.

Some Prevailing Images of Teaching in American Popular Culture

We want to circle back now to think about the problem of explicitness that we are posing in the context of two films of the 1990s. In *A River Runs through It* (1992), based on Norman Maclean's autobiographical work of the same title published twenty years ago, we see a fundamental tension between two approaches to teaching and learning the art of fly-fishing; this tension is directly applicable to Maclean's experience of learning to write. At the outset of the film, we are given a portrait of Norman Maclean's relationship to his father, a Presbyterian minister and a fly fisherman. A moral teacher, he explains to Norman and his brother that "[m]an's chief end is to glorify God, and to enjoy Him forever," although he probably spent as many hours giving them instruction in fly-fishing as he did in all other spiritual matters. And fly-fishing for Maclean's father was definitely a spiritual matter. He also considered fly-fishing an art that could be learned and taught, an art "performed on a four-count rhythm

- 338 -

between ten and two o'clock." Maclean, the narrator in the film, goes on to tell us that he much preferred learning how to fish by simply "going out and catching a few, omitting entirely anything difficult or technical in the way of preparation that would take away from the fun." On the one hand, Maclean's father tries to make explicit the kind of technical expertise that is needed to catch a fish. For him, such knowledge is important, because to fish gracefully is to recapture the power, grace, and beauty of God. This is serious business, this idea of explicit teaching, although it may not be much fun. On the other hand, the young Maclean introduces the idea of immersion as a form of learning to fish. His approach is motivated by a different kind of faith: that one will simply acquire expertise through practice. Perhaps this will be the case for some who can learn through intuition, acquiring a knack—but what about others?

What interests us is that when writing becomes the focus of instruction, Maclean's father seems to reject explicit teaching in favor of the notion of immersion. In the film, we see the young author very tentatively bring something he has written to his father, who sits quietly composing a sermon in his office. The minister takes the paper from Norman, looks at it sternly, and then begins to circle some words and cross out others. When he is finished marking up his son's paper, he looks up and simply says, "Half as long." A similar scene is repeated two more times when, finally, his father tells Norman that it is "good" and that he can now "throw it away." What are we to make of this image of the beginning writer and his father? What constitutes good writing? What does this stern and seemingly inflexible man expect from his son and why? And once Maclean's father acknowledges the success of this piece of writing, will the son know better what to do the next time to produce an effective essay?

In this instance, writing is conceived as an art that can be learned and perhaps even taught, but not as the rhythms of fly-fishing might be learned and taught. If this conception has merit, it introduces a real conundrum for both students and the teacher of writing. The teacher is left with a sense that all he or she can do is create opportunities in which learning *might* occur. But what happens when students do not rise to the occasion? What do we do? Similarly, students may be left wondering how they can translate the advice teachers offer—whether it be the terse command "half as long" or detailed written comments—into actions they can take in different situations (cf. Ackerman). In other words, they are left with emerging intuition or knack but have not yet acquired the art of writing, in which such intuition is made explicit.

This notion that writing is an art that can be learned but not directly taught also runs through John Singleton's film *Higher Learning* (1995). The events that occur at what we come to know as Columbus University teach us all something about the assumptions that different ethnic and racial groups have about one another and the extent to which these assumptions are simply uninformed. In the film, the fact that people rarely try to understand one another leads to much violence and, ultimately, to the death of several students. The film is also about the role that one teacher plays in the lives of his students and his attempts to help them in their struggle to come to terms with their own ideas about the issues he raises in his political science class. At the beginning of the term, he tells his mostly first-year students that he expects them to take a stand on what they write, that he does not want them merely to summarize the positions other writers have taken. In this teacher-centered class, however, the students simply listen. They are not really invited to contribute to the well-prepared lecture their professor delivers. So perhaps we should not be surprised that his students are not quite sure what he means when he demands that they advance their own ideas in their essays. He sets up expectations but seems reluctant to talk explicitly about what he wants or how his students might manage the task he has given them. He behaves as though the force of his words will motivate these students to take a stand. This is his faith.

When a young woman, Kirsten, appears at his office door, we see a much more gentle, more nurturing professor who invites his student to sit down to talk about her paper. She is surprised that she did not do well because, she explains, she worked very hard on this paper. As much as her professor agrees that she has analyzed the reading effectively, he reiterates the point he made in class: "I want to see what *you* think," he tells her. And then he provides a brief example of what he has in mind. As he speaks, she interrupts, pulling out her notebook from a backpack to jot down what he says. That's a great idea, she remarks, unaware of her professor's impatience. That's my idea, he explains; you need to find your own topic. But nothing in this meeting between teacher and student indicates that the student understands what her professor means or suggests how she can fulfill his expectations. Nor is it altogether clear that he is aware of how difficult it can be for students to establish a position from which they might speak with authority, especially for those who have lived in silence in our classrooms.

A similar scene occurs later between the main character of the film, Malik, and this same professor. Again, the scene is the professor's office, which provides students with a relatively safe haven to talk about ideas they do not have the opportunity to discuss in class. Assuming the role of a mentor, the professor explains to Malik that, no, what you have written isn't what I want. You need to take a stand. Like Kirsten, Malik leaves—disappointed and uncertain about what he should do. During the course of the film, Malik begins to read about African American history and politics, and he talks with others about his ideas, although the source of Malik's motivation is not clear. At the end of *Higher Learning*, Malik returns to his professor with another draft of the essay. On this occasion, the professor reads and offers a smile, as if to say, yes, you've got it. This is a scene of hope in an otherwise violent and tragic story, one that calls attention to the importance of a teacher who is willing to reach out to his students with support and guidance in a kind of intellectual apprenticeship. In turn, we see some tentative recognition that an engagement with ideas can foster competence and lead students into the world. But this learning was, of course, new and quite fragile. What is more, we are never quite sure how Malik "got it." Nor do we know if in "getting it" he has stumbled on knack, or begun to grasp the art of authorship.

Together, these two films reflect models of instruction and student-teacher interaction that we see every day in U.S. colleges and universities. And what they should urge us to do is to reconsider our assumptions about the relationship between our instructional approaches and the kind of learning we believe our approaches foster. As instructors we need to adjust our angle of vision in order to focus on our students. Students can write force-fully, even elegantly, especially when they have something to say. However, our students do not always know what our expectations are, despite our efforts to design seemingly clear and cogent assignments. Unfortunately, our expectations are often merely tacit, even when we think we have made them explicit.

Strangers in Strange Lands[1]

To illustrate the dilemma that many real students face, we turn to our two studies. In the first, the student is asked to assume, among other roles, the complex roles of policymaker, play direc-tor, and literary critic in writing across the disciplines. In the sec-ond, we look in more detail at how students assume the role of historians of science. In discussing these two studies, we want to complicate educators' understanding of how students struggle to assume these roles and how students negotiate a fundamental tension between adhering to the conventions of academic writ-ing on the one hand and the conventions of academic inquiry on the other. As Victoria Purcell-Gates observes, reading and writ-ing are cultural practices that "are learned implicitly through participating within the culture. For those new to a culture," as the students we describe surely are, "the implicit must be made explicit," at least to the degree to which students become aware of the conventions for writing and conducting inquiry in an aca-demic context (98). We agree with Purcell-Gates, but we want to explore what it means to be explicit and what happens when educators are explicit.

A Four-Year Study of One Student Writing Across the Disciplines

For four years, one of us met with Laura, a student at a large midwestern public university who, at the age of twenty-five, had returned to college after working as an architectural drafter (Greene, "Can Writing Be Taught?").[2] All of her writing was col-lected during these four years, and she was interviewed at least once a semester during this period. Based on these interviews and a literacy autobiography she wrote as a first-year student in her beginning writing class, it was apparent that Laura received very little support from her parents, either psychological or financial, in deciding to return to college. Therefore, as she explained in her literacy autobiography, she "had to go it alone." Not unlike many first-year students, she was forced to negotiate the vast academic landscape without a guidebook, often unsure how to write a term paper or an essay exam (cf. Rose). Her initial experience in a sociology class was devastating. At the bottom of her first essay exam, her professor remarked that "this is not an essay" and that she should go to the University Writing Center. This experience seemed to reinforce Laura's sense that perhaps she did not belong. She felt out of place among traditional college students, aware that she had been labeled a nontraditional student by the university because of her age; she had also been tracked in high school into technically oriented classes. Someone had made the decision that Laura would not be college bound.

Drowning in a sea of conventions she did not understand, Laura was puzzled by the very language her professors used to describe the nature of academic work. In that first essay exam in an introductory sociology class, Laura was asked to present an argument for either affirmative action policies or policies that attempt to help the "truly disadvantaged," regardless of race. This exam represented the culmination of about five weeks of reading and lectures that focused on issues related to affirmative action and public policy, so presumably the students were prepared with the content knowledge to write such an argument. But imagine the effect the following exam question might have on a first-year student who has not been fully acculturated into the ways of thinking required for this sociological essay. The professor wrote:

> In your essay, you should first describe the relative standing of blacks and whites on important socioeconomic indicators, which is the basis for such policy proposals. Then present the evidence and interpretation of that evidence that best supports the policy you've chosen. Finally discuss what you think is the key weakness of your position. Can you modify the position to take into account the criticism? (Note: The aim here is to have

you think through the way policy arguments rely on social-scientific evidence and interpretation.)

Although teachers at the college level may have every reason to expect that students like Laura will know what an essay is—after all, we expect high schools to ensure that they have this knowledge—consider what she is asked to do: not only is she expected to (1) examine both the strengths and weaknesses of her own position, perhaps realigning her argument to account for others' criticisms, but she is also expected to (2) do so by thinking through the way policy arguments rely on social-scientific evidence and interpretation. In short, she is expected to think and write like a sociologist, one who is aware of what constitutes an appropriate sociological source of evidence to support an argument and who comprehends different socioeconomic indicators.

While the terms of the assignment might be familiar to some students, to ask writers to argue and to use evidence is to ask them to employ a set of conventions which vary from discipline to discipline; high schools cannot necessarily be expected to teach such discipline-specific conventions, and we cannot necessarily assume that students know them. After all, any discipline is comprised of different ways of thinking and using language. We should not be surprised that Laura was at a loss for words in writing her essay or that her professor was disappointed in the finished piece: Laura and her professor easily could have different conceptions of what it means to write this type of sociological essay, and there really was no opportunity to share these different ideas in class. Laura, like other students, had to accept some risk in committing herself to the approach she took in responding to this prompt to write about affirmative action. Although it is true that many students may have understood what this writing task required and did well, we also need to think about students such as Laura, Malik, and Kirsten who do not readily know what it means to read and write in and across the various disciplines of the university.

Laura did seek help at the University Writing Center and eventually learned what an appropriate response to this difficult question about public policy entailed. And she did well in this course. However, to think like a social scientist is different from thinking like a historian or literacy critic or, for that matter, writing like a scientist. Consequently, throughout her four years at the university Laura moved in and out of different classrooms, becoming immersed in cultures that often provided conflicting views of what it means to read and write in school. The tasks kept shifting and the assumptions underlying the assignments she was given kept changing. The exam question in sociology seems to represent one kind of thinking that university professors value—that is, the ability to interpret what others have said, formulate a well-thought-out position, and think critically about the strengths and weaknesses of that position. This kind of abstract, critical thinking also characterized what Laura was expected to do in a theater class. In this sophomore-level class, she was asked to imagine that she was the director of a play, *Trifles*. Given her role as director, "what kind of theater space would you want to put it in? Describe the space in detail." Additionally, she was asked to reflect upon and explain the choices she made, considering how these choices "might influence the reception of the play."

But instructors in other fields demanded a close reading of a single source of information. Her instructor in an introductory literature class asked in one assignment, "What does Georgia mean by saying that Aylmer has 'done nobly' in Hawthorne's 'The Birthmark?' Has he in fact done nobly?" To answer this question, Laura must support her answer with evidence from the story, a strategy that represents a marked departure from the invitation (given in sociology and theater) to include her own ideas and experiences in other classes. In her junior-level history course, she was asked to evaluate a statement by Polenberg: "[In the United States] there was no physical destruction, no redrawing of territorial lines, no change in the outward structure of government [after World War II]. Yet in more subtle ways the war exerted a profound impact upon the American people and their political, social, and economic institutions." Motivated by her prior experiences, Laura not only provided a close analysis of this statement in the context of the reading she was given in class, but she also brought in outside sources to support her opinion, a strategy valued by her teachers in sociology and theater. Interestingly, her history professor remarked in his written comments that he had wanted her to examine only the text he had given the class to read. Laura was, of course, puzzled by his comment. After all, she had begun to think and act independently, as many of her teachers wanted her to, but now she was actually criticized for taking real initiative.

We learn from this study of Laura's different assignments that Laura could not simply rely on her hard-earned knowledge about what it meant to write like a social scientist; instead, she had to read and interpret each new situation in order to figure out what was expected in drama, literary analysis, and history. Without the benefit of explicit instruction in how to conduct the kind of inquiry that Young envisioned, in order to determine what was at issue Laura had to rely on the prompts of an assignment, the ways in which a given professor engaged students in classroom talk, the comments she received on her papers, and the level of success she had achieved in the classes she took across the curriculum during previous semesters. The voices of past teachers' admonitions about how to write were as powerful as the voices of the teachers she heard in the present. Thus a certain logic motivated Laura's search for additional sources in writing her history paper; as it turned out, the choice she made was inappropriate in the context in which she wrote, one that emphasized text conventions apart from the spirit of open-ended inquiry that a theory of invention, and authorship, underscores.

Writing an Argument in the History of Science

To further complicate our understanding of how students approach the task of writing in a university, we turn to a study conducted in a first-year history of science course comprised of eleven honors students at a large public university in the Midwest. The seminar for honors students explored the events leading up to the discovery of the double helix and its assimilation into biology. However, the primary aim of the course was not to learn a specific set of scientific concepts; instead, as the instructor pointed out in her syllabus, she sought to teach her students "how to do research and writing in the history of science."

The purpose of the study was to understand the conditions that can foster students' sense of authorship as they integrate their interpretation of history through reading and then advance their own positions in what they write. Specifically, four questions motivated this project:

1. How does the instructor talk about writing and represent what it means to write in the history of science?

2. How do students interpret different writing tasks?

3. What patterns of discourse characterize the talk between students and the professor, and do these patterns influence what students write?

4. How do students organize their essays, and on what basis do they select information from reading, class discussion, and prior knowledge in developing their ideas?

For the purposes of our discussion, we will focus on the ways three of the nine participating students in the study interpreted and evaluated the task of writing an argument, first examining the introductions to the essays they wrote for class and then analyzing their retrospective accounts (Greene and Higgins), in which they described their interpretations of writing an argument. Although field notes were taken during the entire fifteen-week semester, these accounts were collected when students first received their assignment three weeks into the semester.

THE PARTICIPANTS

Kevin was majoring in computer science and hoped he might also major in music. Denise was majoring in molecular biology at the university and had taken bacteriology and genetics classes in high school. Anne had gone to a small private "laboratory high school" associated with a university and thought she might major in biology at the university she now attended; however, her fear of math had forced her to reconsider this choice, and she had declared "No major" in registering for courses. Table 15.1 provides additional details about these students' experiences with writing in school, based on interviews with the students before they wrote their essays.

Table 15.1. Students' Major at the University and Prior Experience Writing in High School

Student	Major	Writing in High School
Kevin	Computer Science/Music	Research Writing in English Creative Writing
Denise	Microbiology	Advanced Composition analysis of literature argument research writing
Anne	Undeclared	English persuasive writing debate History analysis argument

THE TASK

Writing an argument in this first-year history of science class entailed "assessing" the value of James Watson's *The Double Helix* for the historian of science. In the written assignment, the professor asked, "How useful is it [*The Double Helix*] as a document for giving us insight into the development of molecular biology (or insight into the scientific process in general in the early 1950s)?" She then offered some additional questions that she wanted her students to consider in formulating their answers:

♦ How accurate is the document—to what degree should we trust it, and in what areas?

♦ How broad or narrow is its scope? What information is included; what information (or what kind of information) is left out that you think would be helpful or necessary to formulate a fuller picture of the history involved?

♦ What does it tell us about the conduct of science that is useful to know and that might be lacking from other sorts of documents?

♦ What other sorts of documentation would you want to have access to, ideally, to gain a fuller picture of the early history of molecular biology?

Further, the professor wrote, "You do not need to address all of these questions; you might want to address others as well/instead. These are just suggestions. The essay should be about 1200–1500 words long (approx. 4–6 pages), and should make a coherent argument with a clear thesis statement that you support. (The argument itself may, of course, have multiple parts or subarguments.)" (For a full statement of the assignment, see Appendix 15.1.)

According to the professor, the purpose of assigning this kind of paper was to help students learn both the conventions of academic inquiry and of writing an argument. In an interview, she stated that she wanted to (1) give students practice in writing a "critical analytical essay, with a thesis, an argument, but without the added difficulties of doing research"; (2) help them formulate their own research problem, which is the next step in writing a research paper during the second part of the term: "This gives them something that's more manageable because it's based in readings that we read collectively"; and (3) give students practice in assessing documents, something that students will also do with the primary and secondary sources they find themselves while writing their research paper. Having students write in a course focusing on the discovery of DNA was critical because, the instructor observed,

> I think that helps them process the material and make it their own. Having made it their own, they will be less likely to forget it, to the extent that I want them to remember, as sort of an educated person, I want them to remember some things, general things about the history of biology, and that is what they are doing where this business of learning to formulate an argument is really crucial.

In short, the professor understood that writing could play a critical role in helping students learn the craft of writing an argument and learning to do the work of a historian.

THE PROFESSOR'S INTERPRETATION OF THE TASK

Focusing on her goal of teaching students to read, write, and think critically, the professor explained in an interview that she "wanted [her students] to weigh what they thought was useful and not useful," although she did not make explicit what she meant by the word "assess" in the written assignment. "It's kind of a deliberately vague word," she observed, "but then I have a lot of specific suggestions below [the subquestions]. It's a general word so that they have to figure it out. Because it could mean a lot of different things, but whatever they're doing, they're kind of, they're being asked to critically examine this book and consider how historians should have used it." In other words, she not only asked her students to assess what they were reading, but to do so in the role of historians of science ("Assess the value of James Watson's *The Double Helix* for the historian of science."). This meant, for the professor, that students would have to think about how a historian of science uses a document, "finding something out about the past, not simply giving their opinion of how *The Double Helix* read as a story." And, finally, by "argument," another key term in the assignment, she meant that "the pieces of writing provide evidence and logic that sustain the pieces, that is, by logically piecing together pieces of evidence, they will create a case for the thesis it asserted in the introduction, as I hope I've made clear."

TEACHING STUDENTS TO WRITE AN ARGUMENT

To prepare students to write an argument, the professor provided a sequence of assignments that encouraged students to think about the nature of scientific discovery and the nature of authorship, in particular how authors such as James Watson project their persona in their writing and the extent to which an author's presentation of an argument could be judged as reliable. As she pointed out in an interview, these assignments grew out of a central problem she posed at the beginning of the semester, one that centered on the relationship between memory and history.

> I find that a really interesting problem [focuses on] the relationship between memory and history and how the scientists are constructing their own history, and how that is related to ... the way historians might write history.... And so I want[ed] them to think about the differences between autobiography or

memoirs and history, and get a sense of what it is a historian can do in analyzing these kinds of writings that we've been looking at and synthesizing.

Of equal importance was the professor's concern for the relationship between the "development of the ideas in research and their dissemination through textbooks. How did anybody," she reflected in an interview, "how did the double helix get to be such a big actor in our culture, it's a very strange thing." Like other educators, she conveyed a sense that textbook representations of scientific discovery gloss over, even ignore, conflict within a scientific community and the process of scientific discovery, a cycle that is anything but the linear process many textbooks suggest (cf. Johns 46–48; Myers).

In addition to asking students to write weekly response papers based on the assigned readings, which included different and conflicting points of view on how the structure of DNA was discovered, she asked students to complete the following structured assignments:

> RESEARCH MINIPROJECT on what the textbooks say about the double helix story. LOCATE a biology textbook in the stacks in [. . .] Library that discusses the discovery (or at least mentions it) and bring it in. You should also submit a one-page analysis that focuses on how the discovery is treated: To what extent does the textbook discuss the historical events leading up to the discovery of DNA? How does the textbook present the scientific method?

> RESEARCH: Find out biographical information about ONE reviewer (at least the following: birthdate, education, disciplinary affiliation, and, if possible, then current institutional position). Write down your source(s), providing complete bibliographical information as specified in your style manual.

> ONE-PAGE RESPONSE: What effect does knowing biographical information about the reviewer have on your reading of the review?

As the professor pointed out in the interview, the goals of the miniproject and response papers aimed at encouraging students to read different sources of information critically and helping them understand the problems of "doing history." One such problem can be formulated as a question that she discussed in class: "Can you get at what really happened and, if not, what do you do?" In developing a method for answering this kind of question, historians, she told them, would have to explain "why you do what you do . . . with justification."

Guiding students through the process of formulating an argument, the professor also gave students a handout that defined the function of an argument, treating this kind of writing as a general skill that informs her suggestions about how students might organize their essays. (See Appendix 15.2 for the complete handout, "Essay Writing Guide.")

> The first thing to realize about [your] essay is that it must make an argument and not merely cram as many facts as possible onto the page. You are writing to persuade the reader (ANY reader) to believe what you are saying. . . . (2) tell the reader what your position on the question is; and (3) present an argument with evidence to demonstrate the correctness of your position. But before you write anything you must form your own opinion. (Or at least, before you write anything anyone will see.)

Students had two weeks to complete the task. They had the opportunity to submit a draft to the professor for comments and to work with other students in peer response groups, where they received additional written comments.

STUDENTS' WRITTEN RESPONSES TO THE ASSIGNMENT

Included below and unedited, the three students' introductions to the essays they wrote in response to the assignment represent three different ways of approaching the task they were given. Together, these students' approaches underscore a critical problem we have sought to address in this chapter: that explicitness in language, in this case academic discourse, is a function of the knowledge that specific readers/writers use to interpret meaning. Meaning is never given. Instead, the students in this study construed terms such as "assess," "thesis," and "argument" in ways that made sense to them—not just in the context of writing response papers in this class on DNA, completing a miniresearch project, or reading a handout on argument. As we will demonstrate, students' approaches to the assignment also reflected their prior knowledge about how to write an argument using evidence, knowledge based on their experiences of writing in other school contexts.

Perhaps students rely on these previously learned strategies because the "behaviors and ways of seeing" (Purcell-Gates 98) implicit in their professor's understanding of what it means to write an argument in the history of science were less clear to them. The professor's understanding is to some extent revealed in the way she structured the assignment ("to critically examine this book [*The Double Helix*] and consider how historians should have used it . . . , finding something out about the past, not simply giving their opinion of how *The Double Helix* read as a story") and in her interview with the researcher. Still, though the professor's careful sequence of assignments may represent her effort to make her expectations clear, her students had to take risks as they interpreted the terms of the assignment and translated their understanding of terms such as "argument" in fulfilling the task. These risks existed because these terms do not have clear definitions; students' approaches easily could have come into conflict with their professor's authority. Moreover, the task could be daunting because the kind of inquiry that the professor attempted to foster was fairly open-ended (cf. Emig 39). There was no right or wrong answer to the prompt asking students to assess the value of *The Double Helix*, although the inquiry the professor encouraged was very much in keeping with the spirit of Young's notion of invention. Students had the opportunity to integrate their interpretations of their reading, weighing different and conflicting points of view in advancing their own arguments.

In his paper, Kevin compares James Watson's account in *The Double Helix* of how Watson discovered the molecular structure of DNA to Watson and Crick's earlier published account in the journal *Nature*. In essence, he chose to address one of the subquestions in the assignment, "How accurate is the document [*The Double Helix*]—to what degree should we trust it, and in what areas," without addressing the larger concern in the assignment of how historians should have used Watson's book, as the professor might have expected. In the written assignment, the main question the professor asked was: "How useful is it [*The Double Helix*] as a document for giving us insight into the development of molecular biology (or insight into the scientific process in general in the early 1950s)?"

> James D. Watson's *The Double Helix* presents a scientifically important historical event—the discovery of the structure of DNA—as a personal account, and does not claim under false pretense to describe or outline *the* scientific method, rather it is a chronicle of the way in which James Watson and Francis Crick tackled the issue. Watson goes so far as to include a sort of disclaimer, saying that it presents "[his] vision of how the structure of DNA was discovered" (Watson 3). I hesitate to believe that there is any one way in which science should be conducted; instead I think that individuals—or teams—use whatever methods work in their unique instances.
>
> In my opinion, the general conception of the scientific method arises from the presentation, not in the implementation. In other words, the presentation, in the form of a scientific paper, may not accurately represent the techniques used but may instead distort the facts in order to fit a more commonly accepted notion of how science is performed. In the words of P. B. Medawar: "Is the scientific paper fraudulent? Yes: it misrepresents scientific thought" (Medawar 42). Watson and Crick's paper, as it appeared in *Nature*, deviated significantly from the account given in *The Double Helix*.
>
> The article submitted to *Nature* contrasts rather sharply with Watson's personal account of the events leading to the discovery of the structure of DNA (Watson 237–241). The paper implies an order of events different from that in Watson's memoir, in that it portrays a nearly linear thought pattern, moving logically from step to step. We find this to be grossly incorrect upon reading *The Double Helix*, in which we learn of the true, non-linear progression of ideas flowing through Watson and Crick's minds. At one point Watson is having trouble falling asleep, and consequently his lively mind comes up with the idea that proteins are synthesized from RNA, which is in turn fabricated directly from DNA (Watson 89).

Denise analyzed the scientific method in molecular biology, also centering her response on one of the subquestions, "What does [*The Double Helix*] tell us about the conduct of science that is useful to know and that might be lacking from other sorts of documents?" She explains to her reader in the opening statement of her paper that "[t]he documentation of scientific discovery has a profound effect on current developments, and can have an immeasurable influence on scientists." However, unlike Kevin, she also makes an argument as a direct response to the broader concern of the assignment, advancing the position that "[*The Double Helix* alone] is not sufficient to provide accurate insight into the development of molecular biology and the scientific process during the early 1950's." Still, the primary emphasis of Denise's essay is indicated at the end of the second paragraph and beginning of the third, where Denise explains the value of the double helix. Specifically, she tells us that Watson brings to light the process by which he went about his work. "The personal relationships among Watson, Crick, Maurice Wilkins, Rosalind Franklin, and the others involved in the discovery of the structure of the DNA," Denise observes, "are entertaining to read about and help to spice up the book. More importantly, however, they also help to explain why the discovery took the course that it did." Rather than "critically examine this book and consider how historians should have used it," as the professor construed the task, Denise tells a story about the scientific method.

> The documentation of scientific discovery has a profound effect on current developments, and can have an immeasurable influence on scientists (Sayre, 108). Therefore, it is crucial for scientists to be accurate, truthful, and objective when reporting their findings to the scientific community and the public. Unfortunately, scientific research and experimentation does not make for the most interesting reading, and increasing the accuracy of a report does little to increase its readability. *The Double Helix*, James D. Watson's personal account of the discovery of the structure of DNA, is an exception to the bland, impersonal recordings most are accustomed to. Watson makes his story interesting to the reader while reporting the famous discovery he and Francis Crick made. *The Double Helix* is, in comparison to other scientific reports of discoveries, a colorful and entertaining read. Alone, however, it is not sufficient to provide accurate insight into the development of molecular biology and the scientific process during the early 1950's.

James Watson greatly increased the readability of *The Double Helix* by adding personal stories, jokes, and opinions among the scientific information pertaining to DNA. Although the focus of the book is his monumental discovery, he devotes a large portion of it to recalling social outings, relationships between the main characters involved in the discovery, and his own feelings about his work and those he worked with. Watson's unique narration gives the reader a better understanding for the personal aspect of science. It exposes the reader to not only the actions of one of the most famous scientists of our time, but his thoughts as well. These thoughts help to explain the process by which Watson went about his work; they not only tell what he did, but why he did it.

The personal relationships among Watson, Crick, Maurice Wilkins, Rosalind Franklin, and the others involved in the discovery of the structure of the DNA, are entertaining to read about and help to spice up the book. More importantly, however, they also help to explain why the discovery took the course that it did. Had these relations been different—had Watson and Crick encountered personality conflict while Franklin and Wilkins got along beautifully, for example—the story of DNA which we are familiar with might have been considerably altered. Anne Sayre certainly believes this, and she states in *Rosalind Franklin and DNA* that "it is very possible that the history of molecular biology might be rather different from what it is today if Rosalind and Maurice Wilkins had not hated one another at sight," (95). The interpersonal aspect of scientific research cannot be ignored by those interested in the true history and nature of research. While most other scientific reports overlook this aspect, Watson's book emphasizes it.

In contrast to Kevin and Denise, Anne's argument focuses on the broad concern stated in the assignment: the value of Watson's double helix for the historian of science. Her position is clear from the outset as she asserts that *"The Double Helix* is not a valuable piece of historical evidence because it presents an inaccurate picture of events surrounding the discovery of the structure of DNA, and it presents a scientific process which could be detrimental to science." Focusing on both the broad concern and the subquestion about the scientific process is very much in keeping with her professor's understanding of how students would go about completing this writing task.

If you read the *Double Helix* by James Watson for amusement and to learn a personal view of the discovery of the structure of deoxyribonucleic acid (DNA), you will not be disappointed. If you are looking for a book that can serve as an accurate historical account of the discovery, you need to put this book back on the shelf. I must warn that while this book is entertaining due to its light hearted approach and personal nature, the mocking of characters and drunken stories included in this account do not present a true picture of the history of molecular biology. *The Double Helix* is not a valuable piece of historical evidence because it presents an inaccurate picture of events surrounding the discovery of the structure of DNA, and it presents a scientific process which could be detrimental to science.

When reading the *Double Helix*, you learn early in the story that Watson openly dislikes Rosalind Franklin. Scientists are humans and are allowed to dislike one another, but when writing a historical account, one needs to be impartial enough to accurately describe the contributions and the role of the other people involved. This is where Watson fails. He allows his personal feelings to interfere with the scientific aspect, and creates a picture of Rosalind Franklin that is completely unrepresentative of her actual role in the discovery of the double helical structure of DNA.

Rosalind Franklin was one of the top x-ray crystallographers of the time when she went to work with Crick. Nevertheless, Watson treats her as a second rate scientist simply because he and Rosalind did not get along. An example of the lack of respect Watson had for Rosalind Franklin is the name by which he refers to her in *The Double Helix*. Scientists are generally addressed by their last names (or at least first names) in this account, all except for Rosalind Franklin. Instead of treating her as he treats other scientists, Watson refuses to call her Franklin or Rosalind, but rather by the childish nickname of "Rosy". When reading this book, you must make a conscious effort to remember that this is an immature game Watson is playing. There is no legitimate reason to call her "Rosy" because even her friends did not refer to her by this name. This is Watson's effort to convince the reader of Franklin's inferiority, so that we might agree with his opinion of her.

Given prior studies of how students interpret writing assignments (e.g., Flower et al.; Nelson), it may not be surprising that these three students approached the assignment in such different ways. What interests us, then, is not simply that these students interpreted the task in different ways; we are more interested in the logic that influenced the decisions they made in writing their essays—what they chose to foreground as they considered such prompts as "assess" and such terms as "argument," "thesis," and "evidence." In probing these decisions, it is not sufficient to look at students' texts alone; we must hear students' voices, listening to retrospective accounts that can provide some insight into how these students approached the process of writing an argument.

In the analyses that follow, we answer the following questions: How did students interpret what it means to write for a historian of science? What does it mean for these students to develop "a coherent argument with a clear thesis statement that [they need to] support" and that may have "multiple parts or subarguments"? And what makes writing this kind of essay difficult? These are the questions students were asked by the researcher on the day they received their assignment in class. Their answers can help us to understand how students conceptualize writing assignments. Further, by understanding the logic that motivates what students do, we can better speak with directness and sensitivity to how students learn and how we can be explicit in a way that will enable students to become authors.

STUDENTS' INTERPRETATIONS OF WHAT IT MEANS TO WRITE AN ARGUMENT

In this section, we provide excerpts from students' retrospective accounts to illustrate how they interpreted the task of writing an argument. This section is organized around three concerns: (1) how students understood the task, (2) the way they defined how a historian of science thinks, and (3) what made writing this kind of essay difficult. The ellipses in each excerpt represent pauses.

Reading the assignment aloud in a retrospective account, Kevin related his understanding of what his professor expected him to write to the kind of writing with which he was already familiar, reflecting on the format of an argument. "According to the way I learned in high school," he commented, that is . . . [pause] well she talked a little bit about it. She said the introductory paragraph with your thesis and maybe a short little thing to draw the reader in before that and then I do think it was a series of paragraphs with a controlling idea in each one . . . like she had us pick out some controlling ideas in Sayre. They should link together to form a good basis for your argument and then in order to prove each of the paragraphs you need to support.

Denise considered the nature of argument in much the same way as Kevin, conveying, at least implicitly, the kind of explanation many teachers of writing might find in a composition handbook. Of course, their accounts also demonstrate that they had begun to internalize the general criteria their professor provided in her handout on essay writing, such as supporting one's thesis (see Appendix 15.2): "A coherent argument," Denise mused,

> means just be able to have an idea and have your ideas support . . . and have the rest of the argument . . . support your thesis or your original idea. Not have like a wishy-washy, wish-washy thing, you know like, well it could be this and this but you're still arguing all in one point. Coherent argument. Just make it make sense.

Finally, Anne, whose essay, according to the professor, most directly addressed the value of Watson's book for a historian of science, takes the explanation of what constitutes an argument further. In this excerpt, she considers the point of view she might take and her audience's needs:

> Um. An argument where one can understand where you stand, what your point is, what you're arguing for um and um they can understand the points you're making um that they're clear to someone and it's not . . . it's something that someone that doesn't necessarily have a kind of background in here would be able to understand, I think. You know, something that's clear, it's just there. I don't know, there's more I suppose.

Like Kevin, she refers to her prior knowledge about writing when she tries to understand the difference between a thesis statement and an argument in the wording of the assignment:

> Your thesis statement . . . thesis statement I'd say in my opinion or from what I've been taught is kind of like what you're claiming, it's what you're, it's what like you're the point is like you're supposed to be getting out of the argument. The argument is going to support the thesis, the argument is going to be convincing the reader of your thesis statement. It's gonna be an idea however specific and then your argument's gonna go into detail and give the evidence and gonna be the part that's trying to convince you.

Together, these three students' accounts reveal the powerful influence of students' legacy of schooling and of the prompts their current teacher provides. Equally helpful in guiding Kevin's approach were the comments his professor offered in response to something Kevin wrote earlier in the term:

> If she reads it [his argument focusing on Watson] even if she doesn't agree with our thesis, if she had a different idea about how important it is, she'll read through our argument and if it's clear and makes sense and it's well supported and it's logical then I think that she'll say we did a good job. And in support for that I cite my last informal response I turned in about Sinsheimer; he's the reviewer that I wrote on and I wrote that I disagreed with him and I thought he was too mean in his review and stuff. But I mean I had a fairly clear argument, and she said, this is a good argument but I don't agree with you, but she still gave me a check plus.

If students' conceptions of writing an argument were for the most part general, they had an even less well-defined sense of how they could direct their arguments to the historian of science. Denise hesitated when she read and reread the language of the assignment: "Assess the value of James Watson's *The Double Helix* for the historian of science." She then went on to say,

> [T]he way that science is carried out and how. . . um . . . basically how people came to make their discoveries, how, um, what effect they have. It's hard to explain. Just the history of it, um, um I don't know, I don't know how to explain it. I mean I think I understand it, but ha ha . . . I don't know, I guess the role of certain people in certain discoveries in certain information and knowledge that is had throughout the years and to leading into new and different things.

Kevin offered, "[T]he historian of science is interested in people's opinions as well as the facts, I suppose." Anne provided a slightly more detailed explanation in commenting on the assignment:

> Assess what the value . . . how much of it is actually just like him being James Watson as a person and how much is it him being a scientist and like how much is actually relevant to explaining . . . assessing the value, kind of determining how much you feel is relevant as a historian of science he's gonna be, he or she, would be able to accurately . . . would take that information accurately and look back upon the scene and say "It's not . . . the thing's not very valuable" (let's see if I can finish a sentence) then it's not . . . it wouldn't reflect much in what actually happened, it wouldn't tell you much about it, but if it's valuable then it, despite how he wrote it, it'd tell you a lot about what actually was going on. I think it asks you how much you can believe and how much you can count on.

Still, no matter how sophisticated or how underdeveloped students' understanding was of what it means to argue in the context of writing for a historian of science, much of their success depended on a number of different factors.

In addition to those factors already discussed, we would also include how students dealt with the difficulty of translating what they knew into writing an argument they believed would fulfill their professor's expectations as a reader. For example, when asked in an interview what made the assignment difficult, Kevin simply pointed to not having sufficient time. And Denise suggested that she needed to learn how to assume a role she was not accustomed to playing in reading.

> [I]t's hard to really decide whether or not um, um, like the parts of the book are valuable or not, such as you know his [Watson's] own opinions. I mean, it's hard to um, I just have to look at it from a point of view, from the historian of science whereas, you know, I look at it from the point of view of someone just reading the book. I just have to take a different point of view than what I had originally taken while reading this, I guess.

To the difficulty of knowing how to read in a new way, Anne added the challenge of what students face when they are reading different and conflicting points of view and struggling to come to terms with what they think and believe. Specifically, she observed that

> I kept getting frustrated because in one way I could see both sides of this and if I had been like more, like if I had really hated the book or if I really felt that it helped a lot or whatever, it would have been a lot easier. But I, I read Sayre's book, maybe if I had read Crick's book it would have made it a lot easier, too. But I read Sayre's book and this book fully through, so it gave me total opposing sides but I saw both, but in terms of writing an argument, I couldn't, I couldn't figure out a way that I could think of it both ways and still like present an argument and not just a "well it's this, it's that" without, and still not come up with an argument. I couldn't find a way to do that, so I had to pick a way and then every, and I tried to pick both ways and I sat and made what I like, you know, what I, how I, trying to pick both sides of the coin and I chose by saying that I didn't think it was very valuable, you know, but then I kept second guessing myself along the way through. I mean I got like halfway through the paper and was almost ready to start over and try the other side, and I was like . . . That was my big problem.

Based on our analyses of three students' retrospective accounts, it is apparent that these students struggled with defining what it means to think like a historian of science, despite the instructor's efforts to develop a sequence of assignments that would make explicit the modes of inquiry characteristic of historians of science. Consequently, it was difficult for students to shape their arguments in ways that responded directly to the assignment: that students "assess the value of James Watson's *The Double Helix* for the historian of science." It was equally apparent that these three students' understanding of what it means to argue was very general, relating more to the format of a paper than to the elements spelled out in the handout the professor gave them (see Appendix 15.2). This handout emphasized using specific evidence to support one's claims and keeping the question "So what?" in mind as students wrote about the details of what they read concerning the structure of DNA and the extent to which they believed Watson's book was a reliable source. Implicit here is a fundamental tension between general advice about writing and the kind of discipline-specific inquiry that the assignment required. It may have been one thing for students to develop a coherent argument using criteria they had learned in school, but quite another to engage in an open-ended inquiry within a discipline with which they were not altogether familiar. Students' retrospective accounts help us to see the ways they tried to negotiate this tension and shed light on the complexities of writing.

More than this, however, these accounts complicate our notion of what happens when a teacher is "explicit." The ways students constructed the task (as opposed to the written assignment) seemed to be shaped mainly by five primary influences: (1) previous writing instruction in school; (2) comments their professor made on their response papers; (3) the professor's authority, exhibited through her expertise; (4) the students' ability to locate a position from which to write amid different and conflicting points of view in reading; and (5) the evaluative climate of the classroom.

Implications for Research and Teaching

One implication of the research presented here is that when we examine students' processes of composing—the thinking that often remains hidden behind the texts they produce—we find that a better predictor of what students will do than the assignment we give is the task they set themselves (Flower; Greene, "Making Sense"). Although we may assume that a writer's interpretation is a stable, integrated image of a task, writers can change goals and strategies throughout the process of composing because of their conflicting sense of whom they are writing for: the teacher, an interested reader, themselves, their peers, and so on. By examining students' assumptions about writing, we can begin to develop practices that build upon their knowledge and extend their emerging abilities to use language in different contexts.

Not unlike many instructors, the students in the studies described here appear to embrace the notion that there are general strategies for writing arguments, for reading a given text, and for thinking critically. And one could maintain that, indeed, many of us teach general strategies of invention, including the following: (1) identifying the issue, (2) formulating a rich question to guide inquiry, (3) generating evidence, and (4) identifying counterarguments. Similarly, Flower has underscored the value of teaching students to be metacognitively aware. This means that writers need to understand the kinds of discourse strategies that are appropriate in writing, the ways to use a repertoire of strategies for composing (e.g., employing different types of evidence, using a particular genre) and evaluating the appropriateness of their choices. But it is equally important to recognize the discourse practices in different communities that influence the inventional strategies that writers use. As Johns asserts, different "communities use written discourses that enable members to keep in touch with each other, carry on discussions, explore controversies, and advance their aims." Different genres represent "the values, needs, and practices of the community that produces them" (56; cf. Berkenkotter and Huckin).

Although we have not addressed how students' cultural backgrounds affect their choices in writing—for example, whether to include their own ideas—it is important for us to explore how rules of interaction in a particular culture and how traditions governing appropriate expression of feelings or beliefs have an impact on how students write (Heath; Valdes) and conduct inquiry. For instance, how does a student's perception of his or her intended reader (e.g., teacher, other students, self) and the cultural traditions governing interactions with such individuals influence the manner in which the student develops an argument? If the primary reader is assumed to be the teacher, then how will students from different cultural backgrounds write for such a reader? Do they limit how they argue or what they explain because the teacher is the sole audience? Do they consider different sorts of writing (e.g., persuasion) to be inappropriate for addressing an instructor?

Of particular interest to those teaching writing across the curriculum are the kinds of explanations about writing that instructors offer as a way to teach students how to use the knowledge they acquire within the conventions of writing and inquiry in a particular field. This kind of research can be especially relevant to students such as Laura, who often felt frustrated by the lack of connections between what she learned in one class and what was asked of her in another. Unfortunately, she felt that the rules distinguishing classes were all too arbitrary (cf. Chiseri-Strater; McCarthy). In turn, we can begin to understand more clearly the role that writing can play in learning to think and act within such diverse communities as history (cf. Greene, "Students"; Seixas; Voss, Carretero, Kennet, and Silfries) or the history of science by examining how different historical explanations actually influence what students write. Although studies have begun to sketch out the difficult navigations students are expected to perform through the varied disciplinary terrains of the university, further research needs to offer detailed analyses of *how* students make connections or distinctions between various disciplines—or what we as teachers can do to facilitate this process (cf. Nowacek).

In concluding this chapter, we want to return to the images in *A River Runs through It* and *Higher Learning*. These images portray teachers as gifted and knowledgeable and students as bright and energetic in their attempts to fulfill what their teachers expect of them. But we have also tried to challenge these images as incomplete, urging us to reexamine our assumptions about learning, to give voice to those assumptions that remain tacit, and to become students of different disciplines and of our students themselves. Creating opportunities for learning through immersion or repetition and practice will not suffice if we are to ensure that all of our students understand what it means to complete the tasks we give them. We will need to do more. We can teach them to assume the role of author. And by this we mean that we can teach writers to read rhetorical situations and make informed choices about the appropriateness of their decisions about both text and context. But teaching students to author texts, which is akin to the notion of rhetorical invention, will entail continuing our efforts as a research community to "make reasonable judgments about the adequacy of our theories . . ." (Young, "Paradigms" 39). The questions Richard Young asked twenty years ago persist as we strive to make explicit what remains merely tacit in cross-disciplinary writing: "To what fea-

STUART GREENE AND REBECCA SCHOENIKE NOWACEK

tures of the [writing] process must a theory of invention respond? Is the process the same for all kinds of discourse and rhetorical purposes? . . . Or are there different kinds of processes for which different theories of invention are appropriate and inappropriate?" (44).

Appendix 15.1

History of Science: The Double Helix

FIRST PAPER ASSIGNMENT:
Polished draft due Tuesday, October 8 (bring 3 copies TO CLASS)
Final version due Tuesday, October 15

Assess the value of James Watson's *The Double Helix* for the historian of science. How useful is it as a document for giving us insight into the development of molecular biology (or insight into scientific process in general in the early 1950s)? Some things you might want to consider in formulating your answer:

◆ How accurate is the document—to what degree should we trust it, and in what areas?

◆ How broad or narrow is its scope? What information is included; what information (or what kind of information) is left out that you think would be helpful or necessary to formulate a fuller picture of the history involved?

◆ What does it tell us about the conduct of science that is useful to know and that might be lacking from other sorts of documents?

◆ What other sorts of documentation would you want to have access to, ideally, to gain a fuller picture of the early history of molecular biology?

You do not need to address all of these questions; you might want to address others as well/instead. These are just suggestions. The essay should be about 1200–1500 words long (approx. 4–6 pages), and should make a coherent argument with a clear thesis statement that you support. (The argument itself may, of course, have multiple parts or subarguments.) However, we do not need to be rigid about the exact form of the argument. If you feel most comfortable writing a standard academic essay, you may do that. If you would rather imagine yourself offering advice to a friend, or a student, or someone else burning to know the early history of molecular biology who has been told that *The Double Helix* is a good place to start, you may do that. You may even imagine yourself writing a didactic letter to the journal Biology Teacher or presenting a paper at the International History, Philosophy, and Science Teaching Conference (a real conference held every other year) advising non-historians of science of the pleasures and pitfalls of using this book to teach students about the history of molecular biology. In any of these cases, you would want to develop a clear thesis and argument, but you might couch them slightly differently in your introduction, and the overall tone might differ somewhat, depending on which approach you take. (BE SURE to be clear which approach you're doing!)

Please attach to your draft a cover letter for your readers that highlights where you especially want advice. Are you uncertain whether you have articulated your thesis clearly? Do you want them to pay special attention to the ways you support your argument? the relationship of your conclusion to the evidence? your balance of different kinds of argumentation? Are you concerned that you are trying to cover too little? too much? Are there other issues you want them to focus on? The more responsibility you take for guiding your reader-editors, the more likely you are to get truly useful feedback.

Appendix 15.2

Essay Writing Guide

1. *Making an Argument*

The first thing to realize about an essay is that it must make an argument and not merely cram as many facts as possible onto the page. You are writing to persuade the reader (ANY reader) to believe what you are saying. Therefore, the first thing you need to do is ask yourself, "What do I think about this question?" Whatever the question, you need to (1) introduce the reader to the basic elements of the question as you will treat them in your answer; (2) tell the reader what your position on the question is; and (3) present an argument with evidence to demonstrate the correctness of your position. But before you write anything you must form your own opinion. (Or at least, before you write anything anyone will see.)

2. *Introduction*

A good introduction is indispensable to a good essay. Without it, the reader gets lost from the very beginning, and is likely to remain lost. The introduction must do two things:

a. It introduces the reader to the topic of the essay. This can be done in any number of ways, such as with a short anecdote (for a 5-page essay, any anecdote you use must be very short!), or by launching into the topic.

b. It tells the reader, in a few sentences, what you intend to say about the topic. That is, it lays out your thesis.

3. *Exposition and Argument in the Main Body of the Paper*

Once you have moved from the introduction to the main body of the essay, you face the task of giving your reader sufficient details about the topic so s/he can get some idea of what you are talking about. At the same time, you must present your argument and persuade the reader that your interpretation is a reasonable one. Combining these tasks is no easy matter, and even experienced writers often devote considerable effort to giving their essays a readable structure.

One thing that may help you to organize your essay is to keep in mind three questions that a reader will be asking when reading your essay:

1. What does the writer mean?
2. How do I know it's true?
3. So what?

These three questions should be in your head at all times. The first reminds you to take care in explaining yourself. Don't just assume the reader knows what you are talking about; make sure you have said enough for the reader to understand your point. Above all, DO NOT assume the reader is your Professor! You will do much better if you assume that your reader is a reasonably well-educated person who knows nothing specific about the subject and who has to be told certain things in order to understand what your essay is about.

The second question reminds you that you must provide specific evidence for your claims. In the case of this essay, all the evidence will be likely to come from primary sources; if you use direct quotations, you MUST use footnotes or endnotes to cite where your evidence comes from. It does not matter exactly what citation format you use, but it should be consistent.

The third question reminds you that you must work hard to see that everything in the essay has some recognizable function. Don't just throw in "interesting" facts to take up space: "It is interesting that Paracelsus lived in Southern Germany and Vesalius in Italy." No, it isn't, unless you explain why that little tidbit is important (for example, by going on to say that medical education was different in the two countries and this gave them different conceptions of the profession). Everything you do and say must advance the essay toward your goal: persuading the reader of the reasonableness of your judgment.

Finally, one more word of advice about the main body of the paper, and that is to take the reader by the hand and lead him step-by-step along the way. Historians are very lazy creatures, and given half a chance they will completely lose track of your argument. Good writers provide plenty of signposts of where things are and where they are going. Remember that the reader cannot peer into your mind; therefore, you must do everything possible to make the essay completely transparent. For example, don't leave the answer to the "So what?" question for her. Tell her what the connection is. You can do this along the way, but a good place to reinforce it is in your conclusion.

4. *Using Footnotes and Endnotes*
   Historical essays of the kind described above need evidence. A footnote or endnote basically tells the reader, "Here is my evidence for this particular point." Footnotes and endnotes are mostly used to display a writer's evidence. But they have two other functions as well. First, they sometimes are used to explain or expand something said in the main body of the text. Writers do this to avoid getting too far away from their point. Second, notes are also used to give credit to another writer when you are using that person's ideas. You must give credit for someone else's ideas, even when you have put them into your own words (and, of course, when you are using someone else's words you must use quotations). Failure to do so is plagiarism, which is a serious academic offense.

Notes

1. This heading is taken from McCarthy.

2. All student names in this study are pseudonyms. Excerpts from student papers and interviews are reprinted with permission.

Works Cited

Ackerman, John M. "Translating Context into Action." *Reading-to-Write: Exploring a Cognitive and Social Process*. Ed. Linda Flower et al. New York: Oxford UP, 1990. 173–93.

Berkenkotter, Carol, and Thomas Huckin. *Genre Knowledge in Disciplinary Communication: Cognition/Culture/Power*. Hillsdale, NJ: Erlbaum, 1995.

Chiseri-Strater, Elizabeth. *Academic Literacies: The Public and Private Discourse of University Students.* Portsmouth, NH: Boynton/Cook, 1991.

Dyson, Anne. *Social Worlds of Children Learning to Write in an Urban Primary School.* New York: Teachers College P, 1993.

Emig, Janet. *The Composing Processes of Twelfth Graders.* NCTE Research Report No. 13. Urbana, IL: NCTE, 1971.

Flower, Linda. *The Construction of Negotiated Meaning: A Social Cognitive Theory of Writing.* Carbondale: Southern Illinois UP, 1994.

Flower, Linda, Victoria Stein, John Ackerman, Margaret J. Kantz, Kathleen McCormick, and Wayne C. Peck, eds. *Reading-to-Write: Exploring a Cognitive and Social Process.* New York: Oxford UP, 1990.

Greene, Stuart. "Can Writing Be Taught?" Danish Network for Second Language Pedagogy. Odense University, Denmark. 19 May 1995.

———. "'Making Sense of My Own Ideas': Problems of Authorship in a Beginning Writing Classroom." *Written Communication* 12 (1995): 186–218.

———. "Students as Authors in the Study of History." *Teaching and Learning in History.* Ed. Gaea Leinhardt, Isabel Beck, and Catherine Stainton. Hillsdale, NJ: Erlbaum, 1994. 133–68.

Greene, Stuart, and John Ackerman. "Expanding the Constructivist Metaphor: A Rhetorical Perspective on Literacy Research and Practice." *Review of Educational Research* 65 (1995): 383–420.

Greene, Stuart, and Lorraine Higgins. "Once Upon a Time: The Role of Retrospective Accounts in Building Theory in Composition." *Speaking about Writing: Reflections on Research Methodology.* Ed. Peter Smagorinsky. Thousand Oaks: Sage, 1994. 115–40.

Heath, Shirley Brice. "Sociocultural Contexts of Language Development." *Beyond Language: Social and Cultural Factors in Schooling Language Minority Students.* Los Angeles: Office of Bilingual Bicultural Education, California State Department of Education/ Evaluation, Dissemination and Assessment Center, California State U, 1986. 143–86.

Higher Learning. Dir. John Singleton. Perf. Jennifer Connelly, Ice Cube, Omar Epps, Michael Rapaport, Kristy Swanson, and Laurence Fishburne. Columbia/Tristar, 1994.

Johns, Ann M. *Text, Role, and Context: Developing Academic Literacies.* New York: Cambridge UP, 1997.

Maclean, Norman. *A River Runs through It.* Chicago: U of Chicago Press, 1976.

Maher, Jane. *Mina P. Shaughnessy: Her Life and Work.* Urbana, IL: NCTE, 1997.

McCarthy, Lucille P. "A Stranger in Strange Lands: A College Student Writing Across the Curriculum." *Research in the Teaching of English* 21 (1987): 233–65.

Myers, Greg. *Writing Biology: Texts in the Social Construction of Scientific Knowledge.* Madison: U of Wisconsin P, 1990.

Nelson, Jennie. "This Was an Easy Assignment: Examining How Students Interpret Academic Writing Tasks." *Research in the Teaching of English* 24 (1990): 362-96.

Neuman, Susan B., and Kathleen A. Roskos. "Bridging Home and School with a Culturally Responsive Approach." *Childhood Education* 70 (1994): 210–14.

Nowacek, Rebecca S. "Disciplinary Learning in the Interdisciplinary Classroom: A Study of the Relationship between Talking and Writing." Diss. U of Wisconsin–Madison, in prep.

Purcell-Gates, Victoria. *Other People's Words: The Cycle of Low Literacy.* Cambridge: Harvard UP, 1997.

River Runs through It, A. Screenplay by Richard Friedenberg. Dir. Robert Redford. Perf. Craig Sheffer, Brad Pitt, Tom Skerritt, Brenda Blethyn, Emily Lloyd, Edie McClurg, Stephen Shellen. Columbia Pictures, 1992.

Rose, Mike. *Lives on the Boundary: A Moving Account of the Struggles and Achievements of America's Educational Underclass.* New York: Penguin, 1989.

Seixas, Peter. "The Community of Inquiry as a Basis for Knowledge and Learning: The Case of History." *American Educational Research Journal* 30 (1993): 305-26.

Valdes, Guadalupe. "Bilingual Minorities and Language Issues in Writing." *Written Communication* 9 (1992): 85–136.

Voss, James F., Maria Carretero, Joel Kennet, and Laurie N. Silfries. "The Collapse of the Soviet Union: A Case Study in Causal Reasoning." *Cognitive and Instructional Processes in History and the Social Sciences*. Ed. Maria Carretero and James F. Voss. Hillsdale, NJ: Erlbaum, 1994. 403–29.

Watson, James. *The Double Helix: A Personal Account of the Discovery of the Structure of DNA*. 1968. Ed. Gunther S. Stent. New York: Norton, 1980.

Young, Richard. "Concepts of Art and the Teaching of Writing." *The Rhetorical Tradition and Modern Writing*. Ed. James J. Murphy. New York: MLA, 1982. 130–41.

———. "Invention: A Topographical Survey." *Teaching Composition: Twelve Bibliographic Essays*. Ed. Gary Tate. Fort Worth: Texas Christian UP, 1986. 1–43.

———. "Paradigms and Problems: Needed Research in Rhetorical Invention." *Research on Composing: Points of Departure*. Ed. Charles Cooper and Lee Odell. Urbana, IL: NCTE, 1978. 29–47.

CHAPTER SIXTEEN

Notes on the Evolution of Network Support for Writing Across the Curriculum

MIKE PALMQUIST
Colorado State University

If we focus on behavior—behavior we want to change or behavior we want to nurture, such as a traditional practice in the teaching of writing or particular ways of increasing student writing throughout the university community—we begin to look at things in a different way.

RICHARD YOUNG, Interview

What would it mean to look at writing across the curriculum (WAC) in a different way? Over the past five years, my colleagues and I have wrestled with our discovery that WAC as it is typically conceptualized—what we have come to think of as "WAC Orthodoxy"—does not work on our campus.[1] Yet we have remained committed to the goals that inform most WAC programs: increased use of writing in disciplinary courses, increased exposure to the conventions and writing strategies employed in various disciplinary communities, and support for faculty who express interest in using writing in their courses. In addition, we have pursued two goals that inform many, although by no means all, WAC programs: direct support for student writers, including those who are not enrolled in WAC courses, and the creation of a campuswide community of writers.

Efforts to meet these goals began at my institution when members of the English faculty started an aggressive program of WAC outreach in the late 1970s. Their efforts ultimately targeted not only faculty at the university, but also public school teachers across Colorado.[2] When I joined the faculty in 1990, WAC seminars were a regular occurrence, and I participated in them enthusiastically. Unfortunately, it was clear by then that our cumulative efforts had resulted in relatively low faculty participation across the university.

In 1992, reasoning that a new approach was in order, we obtained external funding to explore technological support for WAC (Palmquist, Zimmerman, and Kiefer). Our initial discussions helped us clarify our goals about what our new WAC program should entail, but before we began to implement the program we spent a year evaluating student, faculty, alumni, and workplace perceptions about writing. The results of our exploratory studies challenged our expectations about what our WAC program should ultimately look like (for reports of these studies, see Thomas; Vest, Long, and Anderson; Vest et al.; Zimmerman and Palmquist; Zimmerman et al.).

As we struggled to balance our goals for WAC with what we had learned during our first year of study, we found that the idea of "designing a WAC program" had itself become an obstacle to success. The WAC movement, although fostering diversity in the implementation of individual programs, is informed by a set of expectations—an orthodoxy, if you will—about what a WAC program is, what it does, and who it serves. Perhaps predictably, we found ourselves wrestling with such commonplace issues as whether to focus on writing to learn or on writing in the disciplines, whether to house the program inside or outside the English department, and whether to offer new writing-intensive courses or additional courses in composition, journalism, speech, and technical communication. Unfortunately, we also found that we were at times losing sight of the instructional and institutional goals that had led us to consider designing a WAC program in the first place. Designing the program seemed to have become our primary goal.

Faced with institutional and faculty resistance of various flavors (Couch; Kaufer and Young; McLeod; Soven; Swanson-

Owens), we decided to step back from the goal of designing a WAC program per se and focus instead on exploring strategies for reaching the goals that had led us to propose a WAC program. Not surprisingly (in retrospect), we began to enjoy modest success. As Richard Young suggests, we found that focusing on specific goals brought about greater success than focusing on broader issues of program design.

In this essay, I explore how our focus on reaching specific goals—or more accurately, our focus on issues of implementation—has allowed us to create a writing-across-the-curriculum program on a campus that exhibited extraordinary indifference to two decades of previous WAC efforts. Our approach to WAC, as the title of this essay suggests, makes extensive use of network and multimedia technologies. It is also influenced by scholars who have argued that campus writing centers and a direct focus on student writers can play a pivotal role in WAC. In the following sections, I discuss scholarship in each of these areas. I then turn to a discussion of the Online Writing Center at Colorado State University. I conclude with a discussion of future directions in network support for WAC, with attention to the WAC Clearinghouse, a consortium project involving faculty from several colleges and universities.

Unorthodox WAC: Arguments
for Direct Student Support

> Because of the uncertainty of our knowledge and the rapidity of change in the field, we believe that constructive change is necessary if any writing program, certainly any WAC program, is to be sustainable. What is stable and persistent as the program evolves is a set of principles that give the program its identity.
>
> RICHARD YOUNG AND CHRISTINE NEUWIRTH,
> "Writing in the Disciplines"

If WAC can be said to have an orthodoxy, it lies in its almost unrelenting focus on faculty as a primary audience (Russell). To borrow a phrase from the 1980s, most WAC programs seem to have adopted a trickle-down approach to writing instruction (see

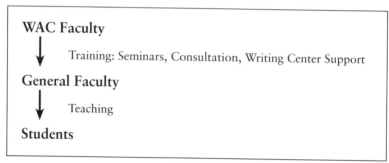

FIGURE **16.1.** *A traditional top-down WAC model.*

Figure 16.1). Seminars and outreach efforts, as a result, are typically targeted at faculty rather than at students. Once faculty have gained a sufficiently robust understanding of how writing can or should be used in their classrooms, they can in turn provide writing instruction—or, at the least, opportunities to write —to their students. As a result, most WAC programs invest heavily in seminars that train faculty to use writing in their classes (Walvoord, "Getting Started"; Young and Fulwiler; Young, "Designing for Change").

This approach has a great deal of merit: if teachers do not assign formal writing or ask students to capture their thinking on paper, then students are much less likely to practice disciplinary conventions or to write to learn. As a result, our WAC efforts include a strong focus on faculty seminars and outreach.

We are concerned, however, about focusing our efforts solely on faculty. Two of the primary goals that have shaped our WAC program are providing direct support for student writers regardless of which courses they are taking and fostering the creation of a campuswide writing community. To meet these goals using a faculty-centered approach would require that most, if not all, faculty on our campus actively participate in our WAC program.

Our experiences, as well as those of other WAC scholars, suggest that such massive participation on the part of faculty at our institution is unlikely. Indeed, despite the tendency of most WAC programs to invest heavily in faculty training and outreach, faculty are the most likely—and typically the most vocal—sources of resistance to WAC initiatives (Couch; Kaufer and Young;

McLeod; Soven; Swanson-Owens). The importance of faculty resistance should not be underestimated; as Susan McLeod points out, it can "gradually wear away even the most firmly established institutional program" (343). Our interviews with faculty and our review of WAC scholarship indicated that faculty resistance typically took one or more of three forms: (1) lack of expertise and/or inclination to teach and respond to writing (Holladay; Strenski), (2) concern that incorporating writing into courses would reduce the amount of instruction provided in the content area (Russell), and (3) programmatic concern about replacing existing courses with writing-intensive courses (an issue of particular importance at public institutions operating under state-mandated ceilings on the number of credits that can be required for graduation).

As we struggled to meet our goals, we found ourselves reflecting on differences between our campus and those on which a faculty-centered approach to WAC has proven successful. In contrast to many smaller, liberal arts colleges, for instance, we found that our faculty as a whole did not seem to focus the majority of their efforts on teaching. The moral force behind the argument that WAC helps students become better writers and thinkers was not compelling to faculty faced with large classes and demanding research agendas. Nor did they welcome our efforts to institute courses that could be team taught by communication and disciplinary faculty or to institute specific courses that focused on communication skills. There simply were not enough "extra" course credits available, they told us, to support our proposals. Finally, we found ourselves faced with a small but rather vocal minority of faculty who expressed disbelief that undergraduates needed additional work on communication. To these faculty, our efforts were at best misguided and at worst a capricious waste of their time.

It seemed clear that a strictly faculty-centered WAC program would not work on our campus: reaching our goals of providing direct support for student writers and creating a campuswide writing community would require a different approach. Over time, our cumulative efforts coalesced into what I have termed an "integrated approach" to WAC (Palmquist et al., "Audience"; see Figure 16.2). Our approach is characterized by the following:

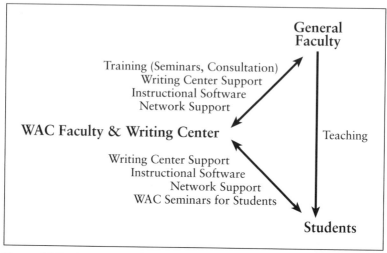

FIGURE 16.2. *An integrated approach to WAC program design.*

◆ continued focus on faculty training and outreach

◆ additional focus on direct support for students

◆ use of network technology to support access to tutors, teachers, and classmates

◆ use of the World Wide Web to provide resource materials for writers and instructors

◆ use of the campus writing center as the visible focus for writing on our campus

As we worked to implement our integrated approach, we found ourselves consulting a range of work, not all of which might initially be seen as compatible. We found ourselves exploring scholarship that views faculty, to use Richard Young's phrasing, as "agents of change" within the institution. At the same time, we discussed Tori Haring-Smith's "bottom-up" approach to WAC, which views students as the primary audience for WAC efforts.

We also found ourselves persuaded by arguments that the campus writing center—even though it evolved to help students less prepared for college writing—can play an important role in WAC instruction (Griffin; Harris, "Writing"; Holladay; Russell).

We found David Russell's observation that the campus writing center could play a central role in a WAC program particularly compelling. Noting that this approach is a "less common model," he observes that it provides "another means of getting around the problem of recruiting faculty whose time and interests may not allow them to restructure their courses to include more writing" (289). Finally, we found ourselves turning to the campus computer network in general—and the World Wide Web in particular—as a vehicle for reaching out to both students and faculty.

Technological Support for Writing Across the Curriculum

> We may be more successful if we shift emphasis away from formal programs to specific things faculty are more likely to accept, like student dialogues via electronic bulletin boards that supplement class work.
>
> RICHARD YOUNG, Interview

WAC Scholars Consider Technology

The development of computer support for writing across the curriculum has in some ways paralleled and in other ways lagged behind the adoption of computer support for composition instruction. WAC scholars, like their colleagues in computers and writing, were initially drawn to the potential of using computers to reduce the tedious work of instructing students in grammar and mechanics. In 1984, Muriel Harris and Madelon Cheek, extending the earlier work of Kate Kiefer and Charles Smith on the collegiate version of Writer's Workbench, carried out a project in which they analyzed and subsequently returned papers sent to their writing lab by engineering students. Harris and Cheek observed that the program, which analyzed several aspects of style and mechanics, "allowed us to add into an already overloaded teaching schedule some writing assistance that we could not have offered otherwise" (5). Commenting on the use of the program to support writing across the curriculum, they noted:

[O]ur use of WRITER'S WORKBENCH generated interest among engineering faculty and encouraged them to consider its potential as a writing tool. This can lead to a stronger interest in writing instruction within their classrooms, drawing them into the writing-across-the-curriculum movement via the computer. (5)

Other WAC scholars also recognized the potential usefulness of computers as a way to draw faculty into a WAC program. In 1988, writing about computers as a way to extend the WAC movement, Gordon and Mansfield recalled, "At a workshop at Drew University in the summer of 1985, Elaine Maimon expressed the hope that the computer would give the writing-across-the-curriculum movement a 'shot in the arm'" (9). Arguing that using computers to carry out disciplinary activities is a form of disciplinary thinking comparable to writing in the discipline, Nicholas Gordon and Susan Mansfield concluded that "it makes sense to expand a writing-across-the-curriculum project into a computers-across-the-curriculum project" (11).

Writing across the curriculum as computer across the curriculum did not, however, gain a foothold in the imagination of most WAC scholars. WAC scholars did not begin exploring in earnest the uses of technology to support WAC until the early 1990s. Even then, as Barbara Walvoord notes in 1996, it would still remain far from the mainstream of the WAC movement. In a call for serious consideration of technology in WAC, she wrote:

But WAC can no longer just introduce the idea of handwritten journals; it must deal with network bulletin boards, distance learning, and multimedia presentations by both students and teachers, as lines blur between writing and other forms of communication and between classrooms and other learning spaces. ("Future" 72)

Writing Centers and Computers

While WAC scholars have been relatively cautious in their adoption of technological support, their colleagues working in writing centers took note of the potential of computers and computer networks to support their work early in the 1980s. These interests would eventually lead to the development of online writing labs and online writing centers, which have the potential to significantly change the way WAC is implemented and supported on a number of campuses.

Mason expressed a sentiment common to many who saw computers as a means of reducing the tedium of writing instruction. In the *Writing Lab Newsletter* in 1982, he argued, "If one has the financial and human resources, one should install a battery of microcomputer stations for CAI [computer-assisted instruction] in the writing lab" (3). Within the year, additional articles appeared in the newsletter discussing CAI and in some cases advocating its use as a replacement for face-to-face tutoring (Southwell).

As computers became more common in writing centers, additional uses were found for them. In 1984, Joan Garcia Kotker discussed the benefits of using computers during tutoring sessions with developmental students, while L. H. Holmes argued one year later that bringing computers into the writing center would help reduce its association with remediation.

Between 1986 and 1989, mirroring a comparable shift in the computers and writing community (Hawisher; Stracke; Sullivan; Weiss), articles began appearing that explored the uses of word processing in the writing center (Crisp; Marshall; Scharton). Also at this time, while the uses of network computing were beginning to be explored in the composition classroom, WAC and writing center scholars began the process that would lead to online writing centers and online writing labs (Kinkead, "Computer Conversations," "Electronic Writing Tutor").

Writing Centers and WAC Programs Move Online

In 1996, Jane Lasarenko noted that she had found "93 self-styled OWLs," or Online Writing Labs. These OWLs fulfill a variety of purposes, ranging from those that serve as little more than online advertisements for campus writing centers, to those that offer online aids such as handouts and links to other online resources, to "Full-Fledged" OWLs, which "offer a complete set of online services, including online manuscript submission and feedback."

The development of OWLs is relatively recent, occurring primarily since 1995, with additional OWLs coming online on a regular basis. The movement toward online writing labs and online writing centers, however, has a comparatively long history. Early work on the concept dates at least to 1987, when Richard Young and Christine Neuwirth proposed to the Buhl Foundation a project that would establish an online writing center to support writing in the disciplines at Carnegie Mellon University. Their proposal, which was expanded significantly and resubmitted in 1988, called for:

- creation of a new first-year writing-in-the-disciplines course that would provide training in "argument for either general and specialized audiences," exposure to "rhetorical forms and methods necessary for effective participation in the upper-level disciplinary courses," and "use of the computer network support system" (10)

- faculty training workshops in writing instruction and use of the computer support system

- creation of a network program that would connect students seeking help with any other student or faculty member who was currently working on the computer network

- access to online consultants (either trained faculty or graduate students) who could provide delayed feedback in situations in which immediate feedback was unavailable or did not sufficiently answer the initial request for help

- access to software that would support writing instruction

Young and Neuwirth's vision of a network-supported writing-across-the-curriculum program, although not funded by the Buhl Foundation, laid out the principles that would later inform the development of many online writing labs and online writing centers. In their proposal, they called attention to functional similarities between their network support system and traditional writing centers, as well as to the potential of the system to help create intellectual communities:

These are, of course, the traditional and important functions of conventional Writing Centers found at almost every college and university in the country, though in conventional Centers they are carried out between students and consultant face to face. However, because of the computer network, the Support System can perform other functions that cannot be performed by conventional Writing Centers. The most unconventional of these and perhaps in the long run the most important for both the university and the student is the creation of an environment in which collaborative learning can take place spontaneously and freely. The network makes possible the creation of University-wide intellectual communities of students and faculty, admission to which requires only a willingness to participate seriously in any of the on-going, campus-wide dialogues conducted over the network. (11)

When Young and Neuwirth submitted their proposals to the Buhl Foundation, they were at one of the few institutions to possess a computing infrastructure capable of supporting such an endeavor. The experimental Andrew computing system provided access for faculty and students from public labs, offices, homes, and dorm rooms to sophisticated network communication tools and to a now widely adopted file system. In addition, between the mid-1980s and early 1990s, Neuwirth and her colleagues created several software tools that could be used to support writing processes and interaction about writing:

- ◆ CECE-Talk, a chat utility that allowed students to collaborate in real time and record a transcript of the discussion (Neuwirth, Palmquist, and Gillespie; Neuwirth, Gillespie, and Palmquist)

- ◆ Comments, which allowed students to exchange drafts of papers with classmates and teachers via the network (Neuwirth et al., *Comments*)

- ◆ Notes, a hypertext program that supported working from sources (Neuwirth et al., "Notes")

- ◆ PREP Editor, which supported commenting in a variety of forms and is the core technology employed in Houghton-Mifflin's CommonSpace software (Neuwirth et al., "Issues")

The Buhl Foundation's decision against funding the project may have delayed the broader movement toward online writing labs and online writing centers, but elsewhere other scholars were also exploring the potential uses of computer networks to support writing instruction. Another early project was Dawn Rodrigues and Kate Kiefer's Electronic Writing Service at Colorado State University (Rodrigues, Kiefer, and McPherson; Rodrigues and Kiefer). Begun in 1989, the project was envisioned as a virtual lab that could be used "as the hub for Writing-Across-the-Curriculum activities" (Rodrigues, Kiefer, and McPherson 3).

The Electronic Writing Service (EWS) provided students, faculty, and staff at the university access to "a variety of computer-assisted writing aids that have been developed or customized by English Department faculty and graduate students, including style analysis programs, prewriting templates, and revision guides" (Rodrigues, Kiefer, and McPherson 3). Writers accessed EWS via electronic mail. Requests for specific documents were listed in the subject line of the message, while requests for style analysis of various kinds were accomplished by inserting the text of the document into the body of the message. The long-term goal of the project was to "expand the EWS by collaborating with other faculty to develop writing aids for courses in all content areas across the curriculum" (3). This goal reflected Kiefer's 1991 vision of the writing classroom of the future, in which the network played a central role in a writing-across-the-curriculum program.

Despite its potential, EWS would enjoy only limited success. Providing network access to Writer's Workbench (which conducted the style analyses for EWS) raised issues about sound use of style analysis programs, noted Kate Kiefer in a 1997 interview:

> Some faculty outside the department wanted to use Writer's Workbench in ways that were inconsistent with our goals as a composition program. And Writer's Workbench is easy to misuse. Unless you have a sensitivity to language or an understanding of what the program can and can't do, you can easily find yourself focusing exclusively on surface issues.

In addition to concerns about how EWS was being used, technical difficulties plagued the project, and it was discontinued in 1991.

In 1991, Purdue University's OWL went online in the form of a similar e-mail request system (Harris, "Hatching"). Unlike the Electronic Writing Service at Colorado State University, however, Purdue's OWL was linked directly to the campus writing center. "E-mail was another way to reach students when we were physically closed," said Muriel Harris, who initiated the project with Dave Taylor (personal interview). Students accessing the Purdue OWL could obtain handouts on various writing issues and interact directly with writing center tutors. Purdue's OWL would shift from a strictly e-mail-based service to a gopher-based system in 1993. In 1994, Purdue's OWL moved to the World Wide Web (http://owl.english.purdue.edu).

Unlike the earlier efforts at Carnegie Mellon and Colorado State University that were designed to provide support for WAC, Purdue's OWL focused primarily on extending the writing center. This focus on the writing center would subsequently mark the majority of efforts to establish online writing labs and online writing centers.

By 1995 a number of writing centers had established an online presence. In addition, Dakota State University's OWL, one of the first in the country, was established because the campus lacked a writing center (Ericsson). A special issue of *Computers and Composition* on "Writing Centers Online," edited by Christine Hult and Joyce Kinkead, came out in 1995. In it several scholars addressed issues related to providing network support for campus writing centers (Harris and Pemberton; Healy; Nelson and Wambeam), online tutoring (Coogan; Jordan-Henley and Maid), and online support for training tutors (Chappell; Johanek and Rickly; Strenski et al.). In the following issue of *Computers and Composition*, a set of related articles, written by scholars affiliated with Michigan Technological University's writing center, critiqued the connection between writing centers and computers, calling attention to the need to foreground the human within an increasingly technological space (George; Grimm; C. Selfe; D. Selfe).

By 1996 the number and variety of OWLs had grown immensely. Writing as part of the Coverweb in the Spring 1996 issue of *Kairos*, J. Paul Johnson observed, "The long list of 'online writing labs,' or OWLs, compiled by the University of Maine's Writing Center Online offers testament to the range of writing services establishing an identity in cyberspace. Clever and memorable as it is, the acronym OWL can hardly begin to describe the work accomplished in this variety of sites." That work includes:

- a gopher or Web site that promotes a "real" writing center (e.g., with photos, hours, location, maps, philosophy statements)

- access to electronic handouts, handbooks, or other local reference material

- access to electronic texts from global net sites

- access to Internet or other network searches

- links to homepages of the local writing community

- a local publishing environment for student writers of electronic texts

- connectivity to local forums or global listservs on writing or writing topics

- links to MOOs and MUSHes for writers

- one-to-one tutorials by means of computer-mediated communication (e.g., private chat rooms, form-based e-mail paper submissions)

- a pointed philosophical mission of redefining traditional notions of academic literacy

Although the movement to put writing centers online had strong roots in the WAC movement, it was clear by the mid 1990s that comparatively little work was being done to provide network support for writing across the curriculum. The visions of network-supported WAC programs put forth by Young and Neuwirth at Carnegie Mellon and Rodrigues and Kiefer at Colorado State University had not yet become reality. After they pulled the plug on the Electronic Writing Service, however, Rodrigues and Kiefer joined with other colleagues and tried a new approach.

WAC Online: The Online Writing Center at Colorado State University

So much of what's written in WAC seems to be on program design. We need narratives of what's happening.

RICHARD YOUNG, Interview

As a graduate student at Carnegie Mellon University in the late 1980s, I worked closely on several research projects with Richard Young, Christine Neuwirth, and David Kaufer. The majority of these projects focused on the impact of technology on writing and writing instruction. As a result, I was familiar with their thinking about the role computers could play in WAC. When I joined the faculty at Colorado State University in 1990, I shared those ideas with my new colleagues, who had been working toward the same goals.

The Online Writing Center at Colorado State University is in many ways a product of the work conducted in the late 1980s at the two universities. Although we could not have predicted the particular form it has taken (the World Wide Web, among other things, was still years away), it is informed by many of the same goals.

In 1991, following the demise of the Electronic Writing Service, Don Zimmerman and I began collaborating with Kate Kiefer and Dawn Rodrigues on a successor to the program. We envisioned a project that would provide closer links to the writing center, direct support for students as well as faculty, and resource materials that writers could consult as needed. In 1992, after several attempts to obtain funding, we received support from the Colorado Commission on Higher Education (Palmquist, Zimmerman, and Kiefer).

Our funding supported the study of computer support for writing instruction and the development and assessment of a network-supported, writing-across-the-curriculum program.[3] We spent the first year conducting baseline assessments of writing needs and attitudes on our campus and in the engineering professions (the target audience for our initial WAC efforts; for reports of these studies, see Thomas; Vest et al.; Zimmerman and Palmquist; Zimmerman et al.). In the second year, we began developing and assessing alternative designs for the Online Writing Center, using Asymetrix Multimedia ToolBook as a development platform. In the third year, we concentrated our efforts on developing content for the Online Writing Center. In the fourth year, we shifted our development efforts to the World Wide Web and began direct support of writing in courses in electrical, civil, and mechanical engineering. In the final year of external funding, we expanded our support for courses to other departments across the university.

The Online Writing Center (http://www.colostate.edu/Depts/ WritingCenter) emerged by 1997 on our campus as a highly visible means of supporting writing across the curriculum (see Figure 16.3). We are enjoying success in attracting participation not only from faculty who have responded to our previous WAC efforts (seminars, outreach), but also from some who had resisted those efforts. The central strategy we have used in enlisting support for the Online Writing Center is to position it as an extension of the classroom and a service to teachers and students. Perhaps the most important technique contributing to this strategy is the online assignment, a variation of the syllaweb concept (the practice of putting course syllabi and other materials on the World Wide Web).

The online assignment, as we have implemented it, attempts to replicate (in an abbreviated form) the product and process of giving a writing assignment. In a classroom, an instructor typically hands out the assignment, discusses its key points, and answers student questions about the assignment. Occasionally, the instructor will also provide example texts and point students to additional resources that might be of use in completing the assignment. On the Online Writing Center, we provide the equivalent of the assignment sheet, add commentary from the instructor on key points of the assignment, in some cases provide annotated example texts, and provide links to resources that students can use to complete the assignment (see Figures 16.4 and 16.5).

In addition to online assignments and annotated example texts, we also provide a wide range of materials that support composition instruction, technical communication instruction, and writing in the disciplines. These reference materials, implemented as hierarchically structured hypertexts with cross-links, function as online textbooks (see Figure 16.6). In some cases, such as our reference unit on argumentation,written by Donna LeCourt, they exceed five hundred screens in size. Most of the reference materials provide direct support for students, but several, including an extensive unit on writing across the curriculum written by Kate Kiefer, provide support for faculty. As this essay

FIGURE **16.3.** *Colorado State University's Online Writing Center homepage.*

is being written, fifty-two reference units are available on the Online Writing Center, with several in preparation. Reference materials address a range of issues, including writing processes, working with sources, speeches and presentations, types of documents, and critical reading.

In addition to reference materials, the Online Writing Center also offers access to interactive tutorials. The tutorials are designed to help students generate text that can be used at various points in their composing processes. Invention tutorials, for instance, ask students to answer questions or explore issues related to their assignments. Revision tutorials ask them to analyze critically such issues as how they have addressed their audience or supported their claims. Tutorials are designed to be relatively brief, but writers can return to a tutorial and start working on it at the point they left it. When they have completed the tutorial, writers can save or print their text, or paste it into a word processor.

MIKE PALMQUIST

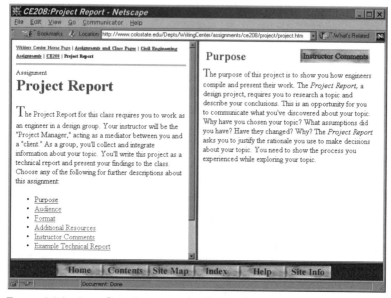

FIGURE 16.4. *An online writing-in-the-disciplines assignment.*

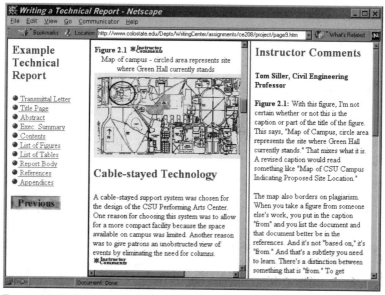

FIGURE 16.5. *An annotated example text.*

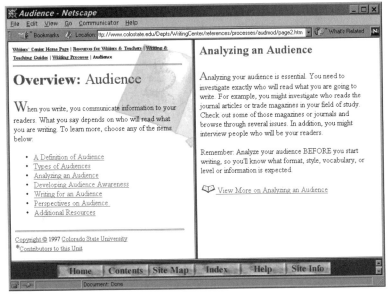

FIGURE **16.6.** *A reference unit on audience.*

Two communication services offered through the Online Writing Center have proven popular with students and faculty. The "Send a Paper" program, a forms-based electronic mail program, allows students to send text-based copies of their papers to a teacher or writing center tutor. Class "Web Forums," located on the class pages we have set up on the Online Writing Center, allow students to engage in threaded discussions of issues related (or sometimes unrelated) to class. We are currently investigating additional communication services, including chat rooms and the potential of VRML-based MOOs (more simply, interactive chat rooms presented using virtual reality).

A final set of materials available through the Online Writing Center is external links. We have provided links to our university library, to library databases, and to various library services on and off campus. We have also provided an extensive set of links to Web-based materials for writers and teachers. These include links to other online writing centers and to WAC sites.

As we have worked on the Online Writing Center, we have found our greatest success working with individual faculty and students (Palmquist, Kiefer, and Zimmerman). A faculty member who experiences success with the Online Writing Center has proven to be our best way of enlisting additional faculty in that department. We have also found success through making presentations to faculty groups and administrators. After a recent presentation to our university's leadership forum, for instance, I was approached by several faculty who expressed interest in putting their writing assignments online.

More important in terms of the long-term success of the program, presentations to faculty and administrators have helped us secure long-term funding for the program. Following a series of presentations in the winter and spring of 1996, our university administration approved a new tenure-track faculty line to direct our writing center and head up WAC efforts on campus. In the following year, we sought approval (and received strong indications that we would be successful) for base funding for our writer/programmer and a graduate teaching assistant to support further development of the Online Writing Center. One of the keys to our success in attracting institutional funding for our program has been the strong support of our department chair, our dean, and our associate deans. Keeping them informed of our efforts has been a high priority throughout the project, and we are now seeing the benefits associated with that decision.

Similarly, our interactions with individual students have proven to be the foundation for positioning the Online Writing Center as the focus of a campuswide community of writers. Students who have had good experiences after submitting a paper by means of electronic mail or who have found our reference units or tutorials helpful have begun to spread the word about the Online Writing Center. A sizable number of first- and second-year students have learned about the Online Writing Center through its use in our composition program. And a growing number are being exposed to it through disciplinary courses. Our interactions with students in our courses, in the campus writing center, and online suggest that a growing number of students are becoming aware of—and are starting to use on a regular basis—the resources available through the Online Writing Center.

The Future of Network Support for Writing Across the Curriculum

> What is going to keep this movement from going the way of other movements that Russell has chronicled over the past century?
>
> RICHARD YOUNG, Interview

As we have worked to develop the Online Writing Center—and, more to the point, to develop a working writing-across-the-curriculum program on our campus—we have constantly found ourselves faced with questions about where to go next. The decision to focus on students has been extremely important in the long-term development of our program, for instance, as has the decision to shift the project to the World Wide Web. Focusing on students has meant that we have had to confront directly the issue of large numbers of papers coming across the network to tutors in our writing center. Our tutors initially resisted the idea of commenting by means of e-mail. They argued that they could do a better job face to face. We agreed with them, but pointed out that many of the students sending the papers would not come to the writing center in the first place; reaching out to them electronically would both help them with their writing and potentially provide them with the incentive to come in for face-to-face discussions.

We also found ourselves facing the question of what to do when a faculty member teaching a class of eighty students wanted to require all of his students to send their biweekly writing assignments to our tutors. We have resolved that issue for now, largely by pointing out that we did not have the tutoring resources to support mass submissions of papers for review, but we know we will face it again, and we are working to secure funding for additional tutors, either from central administration sources or from the departments who make heavy use of the tutoring services offered by the writing center.

One of the logical extensions of our goal to directly support students is to provide WAC seminars for students. In 1997 we began those seminars, offering them through the campus writing center. Graduate student interns, taking a tutoring course for credit under the direction of our writing center director, Laura Thomas, have been involved in developing the workshops, as have our regular tutors. The materials they have developed for the seminars are being used as the basis for expanding existing or writing new reference materials for the Online Writing Center.

Additional projects we are exploring involve the use of database programs to make it easier for faculty to update assignments on the Online Writing Center—something that must now be done manually by our writer/programmer, Luann Barnes. Our university is in the midst of evaluating products that might be used to accomplish this task. Our hope is that the product selected by the university committee conducting the evaluation will be compatible with our current design. We are also interested in evaluating the use of work-group software that will allow us to more easily exchange and comment on student writing, and scheduling software that will allow students to more easily set up face-to-face meetings with tutors.

One of the most intriguing projects we are currently pursuing is the WAC Clearinghouse (http://aw.Colostate.edu/resource-list.htm), a Web site that is being developed with the involvement of several scholars from around the country, among them Christine Hult, Bill Condon, Gail Hawisher, Martin Rosenberg, Kate Kiefer, Linn Bekins, Paul Prior, and Sharon Quiroz. Like other WAC sites on the Web, such as WAC Page, maintained by Larry Beason at Eastern Washington University (http://ewu66649.ewu.edu/WAC.html), and the Computer-Supported Communication Across the Curriculum site maintained by Donna Reiss (http://www.tc.cc.va.us/tcresourc/faculty/tcreisd/dreiss/ecacsite.htm), the WAC Clearinghouse provides information about WAC issues and concerns. It also provides a discussion forum for a range of WAC issues, a place to share scholarship on WAC, and resources on teaching and program design.

As increasing numbers of WAC scholars begin to explore network support for WAC, we are seeing additional innovations in program design and implementation. Some of these are discussed in publications that focus on electronic support for writing across the curriculum, such as the edited collection *Electronic Communication Across the Curriculum* (Reiss, Selfe, and Young), while others appear as essays in journals (Walvoord, "Future") and new collections addressing mainstream WAC issues (e.g., an essay by Reiss and Young in a collection by McLeod and Miraglia on the future of WAC, under consideration for publication). Other reports of innovations in network support for WAC have been or will be discussed in workshops and presentations at recent and upcoming national WAC conferences.

The Online Writing Center represents an approach to WAC that seems to have strong potential for long-term success. Exploring ways to make it easier for faculty to use writing in their courses appears as though it would work in situations in which faculty are at least willing to consider using writing. As we have found, however, each campus faces its own set of challenges. On our campus, many of the more common approaches to WAC did not enjoy the success they did elsewhere. As a result, I have no illusions that our approach will necessarily translate well to other institutions. But I am confident that the principle of identifying specific behaviors we want to change is more likely to bring about long-term success than focusing on creating a general program. I am also confident that the benefits of network communication will play an increasingly important role in the design of existing and new WAC programs. If so, we will have made clear progress toward looking at WAC in new ways.

Notes

1. I would like to thank my colleagues for their support, goodwill, and insights as we have worked together on this project: Kate Kiefer, Don Zimmerman, Dawn Rodrigues, David Vest, Luann Barnes, Michel Muraski, Steve Reid, Donna LeCourt, Tom Siller, Laura Thomas, Lauren Myracle, Laurel Nesbitt, Stephanie Wardrop, Brenda Edmands, and Kathy Zellers. I am grateful for comments on drafts of this essay from Kate Kiefer, Donna LeCourt, and Donna Reiss. And I am particularly indebted to Richard Young for his thoughtful responses to this essay, for his insights into the process of creating and maintaining successful WAC activities, and for his friendship.

2. The Writing-to-Learn Project began at Colorado State University in 1984 when Kate Kiefer, Steve Reid, Jean Wyrick, and Bill McBride began meeting with high school language arts teachers. Later that year,

they expanded their efforts to teachers from other disciplines. The project continued through the 1980s and ultimately involved elementary through high school teachers from seven school districts across Colorado.

3. The Transitions study followed four teachers and 187 students in eight classrooms. Each teacher taught the same course in a traditional and a computer-supported writing classroom. We interviewed students and teachers, collected student drafts, collected teaching materials and logs, observed the classrooms, collected network communications, and surveyed students. A complete report of the study is found in Palmquist, Kiefer, Hartvigsen, and Godlew's *Transitions: Teaching Writing in Computer-Supported and Traditional Classrooms.*

Works Cited

Beason, Larry. "WAC Page." Eastern Washington University. <http://ewu66649.ewu.edu/WAC.html>.

Chappell, Virginia A. "Theorizing in Practice: Tutor Training 'Live from the VAX Lab.'" *Computers and Composition* 12 (1995): 227–36.

Coogan, David. "E-Mail Tutoring, a New Way to Do New Work." *Computers and Composition* 12 (1995): 171–81.

Couch, Ruth. "Dealing with Objections to Writing Across the Curriculum." *Teaching English in the Two-Year College* 16 (1989): 193–96.

Crisp, Sally. "You Can Teach an Old Dog New Tricks: Observations on Entering the Computer Age." *Writing Lab Newsletter* 11.3 (1986): 12–14.

Ericsson, Patricia. "WAC Learns to Fly: The Birth of an OWL." Computers and Writing Conference. Columbia, MO. 22 May 1994.

George, Diana. "Wonder of It All: Computers, Writing Centers, and the World." *Computers and Composition* 12 (1995): 331–34.

Gordon, Nicholas, and Susan Mansfield. "Computers Across the Curriculum: A Confluence of Ideas." *Computers and Composition* 6 (1988): 9–13.

Griffin, C. W. "Programs for Writing Across the Curriculum: A Report." *College Composition and Communication* 36 (1985): 398–403.

Grimm, Nancy Maloney. "Computer Centers and Writing Centers: An Argument for Ballast." *Computers and Composition* 12 (1995): 323–29.

Haring-Smith, Tori. *A Guide to Writing Programs: Writing Centers, Peer Tutoring Programs, and Writing-Across-the-Curriculum.* Glenview, IL: Scott, 1987.

Harris, Muriel. "Hatching an OWL (Online Writing Lab)." *ACE Newsletter* 9.4 (1996): 12–14.

———. Telephone interview. 1997.

———. "The Writing Center and Tutoring in WAC Programs." McLeod and Soven 154–74.

Harris, Muriel, and Madelon Cheek. "Computers Across the Curriculum: Using WRITER'S WORKBENCH for Supplementary Instruction." *Computers and Composition* 1 (1984): 3–5.

Harris, Muriel, and Michael Pemberton. "Online Writing Labs (OWLs): A Taxonomy of Options and Issues." *Computers and Composition* 12 (1995): 145–59.

Hawisher, Gail E. "Studies in Word Processing." *Computers and Composition* 4 (1986): 6–31.

Healy, Dave. "From Place to Space: Perceptual and Administrative Issues in the Online Writing Center." *Computers and Composition* 12 (1995): 183–93.

Holladay, John. "Institutional Project Grant: A Report on Research into Writing-Across-the-Curriculum Projects." Report no. JC880422. Monroe County Community College, MI. ERIC 1987. ED 298 995.

Holmes, Leigh Howard. "Expanding Turf: Rationales for Computers in Writing Labs." *Writing Lab Newsletter* 9.10 (1985): 13–14.

Johanek, Cindy, and Rebecca Rickly. "Online Tutor Training: Synchronous Conferencing in a Professional Community." *Computers and Composition* 12 (1995): 237–46.

Johnson, J. Paul. "Writing Spaces: Technoprovocateurs and OWLs in the Late Age of Print." *Kairos* 1.1 (1996). <http://english.ttu.edu/kairos/1.1/index.html>.

Jordan-Henley, Jennifer, and Barry M. Maid. "Tutoring in Cyberspace: Student Impact and College/University Collaboration." *Computers and Composition* 12 (1995): 211–18.

Kaufer, David, and Richard Young. "Writing in the Content Areas: Some Theoretical Complexities." *Theory and Practice in the Teaching of Writing: Rethinking the Discipline.* Ed. Lee Odell. Carbondale: Southern Illinois UP, 1993. 71–104.

Kiefer, Kate. "Computers and Teacher Education in the 1990s and Beyond." *Evolving Perspectives on Computers and Composition Studies: Questions for the 1990s.* Ed. Gail E. Hawisher and Cynthia L. Selfe. Urbana, IL: NCTE, 1991. 113–31.

———. Personal interview. 1997.

Kiefer, Kate, and Michael Palmquist. "WAC Clearinghouse." Colorado State University. <http://aw.Colostate.edu/resource_list.htm>.

Kiefer, Kate, and Charles Smith. "Textual Analysis with Computers: Tests of Bell Laboratories' Computer Software." *Research in the Teaching of English* 17 (1983): 201–14.

Kinkead, Joyce. "Computer Conversations: E-mail and Writing Instruction." *College Composition and Communication* 38 (1987): 337–41.

———. "The Electronic Writing Tutor." *Writing Lab Newsletter* 13.4 (1988): 4–5.

Kotker, Joan Garcia. "Computers and Tutors." *Computers and Composition* 1 (1984): 6–7.

Lasarenko, Jane. "PR(OWL)ING AROUND: An OWL by Any Other Name." *Kairos* 1.1 (1996). <http://english.ttu.edu/kairos/1.1/index.html>.

Marshall, Rick. "Word Processing and More: The Joys and Chores of a Writing Lab Computer." *Writing Lab Newsletter* 11.10 (1987): 1–4.

Mason, Richard G. "Computer Assistance in the Writing Lab." *Writing Lab Newsletter* 6.9 (1982): 1–5.

McLeod, Susan H. "Writing Across the Curriculum: The Second Stage, and Beyond." *College Composition and Communication* 40.3 (1989): 337–43.

McLeod, Susan H., and Margot Soven, eds. *Writing Across the Curriculum: A Guide to Developing Programs.* Newbury Park: Sage, 1992.

Nelson, Jane, and Cynthia A. Wambeam. "Moving Computers into the Writing Center: The Path to Least Resistance." *Computers and Composition* 12 (1995): 135–43.

Neuwirth, Christine M., Terilyn Gillespie, and Michael E. Palmquist. *A Student's Guide to Collaborative Writing with CECE-Talk: A Computer Network Tool.* Pittsburgh: Carnegie Mellon U, Center for Educational Computing in English / Annenberg-CPB, 1988.

Neuwirth, Christine M., David S. Kaufer, Ravinder Chandook, and James H. Morris. "Issues in the Design of Computer Support for Co-Authoring and Commenting." *Proceedings of the Conference on Computer-Supported Cooperative Work.* Los Angeles: ACM, 1988. 183–95.

Neuwirth, Christine M., David S. Kaufer, Rick Chimera, and Terilyn Gillespie. "The Notes Program: A Hypertext Application for Writing from Sources Texts." *Hypertext '87 Proceedings.* Chapel Hill: ACM, 1987. 345–65.

Neuwirth, Christine M., David S. Kaufer, Gary Keim, and Terilyn Gillespie. *The Comments Program: Computer Support for Response to Writing.* Pittsburgh: Carnegie Mellon U, CECE-TR-3, Center for Educational Computing in English, 1988.

Neuwirth, Christine M., Michael E. Palmquist, and Terilyn Gillespie. *An Instructor's Guide to Collaborative Writing with CECE Talk: A Computer Network Tool.* Pittsburgh: Carnegie Mellon U, Center for Educational Computing in English, 1988.

Palmquist, Mike, Kate Kiefer, James Hartvigsen, and Barbara Godlew. *Transitions: Teaching Writing in Computer-Supported and Traditional Classrooms.* Greenwich, CT: Ablex, 1998.

Palmquist, Mike, Kate Kiefer, and Donald E. Zimmerman. "Creating Community through Communication Across the Curriculum." *Electronic Communication Across the Curriculum.* Ed. Donna Reiss, Dickie Selfe, and Art Young. Urbana, IL: NCTE, 1998. 57–72.

Palmquist, Mike, Dawn Rodrigues, Kate Kiefer, and Donald E. Zimmerman. "Enhancing the Audience for Writing Across the Curriculum: Housing WAC in a Network-Supported Writing Center." *Computers and Composition* 12 (1995): 335–53.

Palmquist, Mike, Donald E. Zimmerman, and Kate Kiefer. *Colorado State Center for Research on Writing and Communication Technologies.* Proposal to Colorado Commission on Higher Education Programs of Excellence. July 1992.

Reiss, Donna. "Computer-Supported Communication Across the Curriculum." Tidewater Community C. <http://www.tc.cc.va.us/tcresourc/faculty/tcreisd/dreiss/ecacsite.htm>.

Reiss, Donna, Dickie Selfe, and Art Young, eds. *Electronic Communication Across the Curriculum.* Urbana, IL: NCTE, 1998.

Rodrigues, Dawn, and Kate Kiefer. "Moving toward an Electronic Writing Center at Colorado State University." *Writing Centers in Context: Twelve Case Studies.* Ed. Joyce A. Kinkead and Jeanette G. Harris. Urbana, IL: NCTE, 1993. 216–26.

Rodrigues, Dawn, Kate Kiefer, and S. McPherson. "English Department Offers Electronic Writing Service." *Vector* 7.5 (1990): 3–4, 16.

Russell, David R. *Writing in the Academic Disciplines, 1870–1990: A Curricular History.* Carbondale: Southern Illinois UP, 1991.

Scharton, Maurice. "The Third Person: The Role of the Computer in Writing Centers." *Computers and Composition* 7 (1989): 37–48.

Selfe, Cynthia L. "Three Voices on Literacy, Technology, and Humanistic Perspective." *Computers and Composition* 12 (1995): 309–10.

Selfe, Dickie. "Surfing the Tsunami: Electronic Environments in the Writing Center." *Computers and Composition* 12 (1995): 311–23.

Southwell, M. G. "Computer-Assisted Instruction in the Comp-Lab at York College/CUNY." *Writing Lab Newsletter* 7.8 (1983): 1–2.

Soven, Margot. "Conclusion: Sustaining Writing Across the Curriculum Programs." McLeod and Soven 189–97.

Stracke, Richard. "The Effects of a Full-Service Computer Room on Student Writing." *Computers and Composition* 5 (1988): 51–56.

Strenski, Ellen. "Writing Across the Curriculum at Research Universities." *Strengthening Programs for Writing Across the Curriculum.* Ed. Susan H. McLeod. *New Directions for Teaching and Learning* 36. San Francisco: Jossey-Bass, 1988. 31–41.

Strenski, Ellen, and TA-TALKers. "Virtual Staff Meetings: Electronic Tutor Training with a Local E-Mail Listserv Discussion Group." *Computers and Composition* 12 (1995): 247–55.

Sullivan, Patricia. "Human-Computer Interaction Perspectives on Word-Processing Issues." *Computers and Composition* 6 (1989): 11–33.

Swanson-Owens, Deborah. "Identifying Natural Sources of Resistance: A Case Study of Implementing Writing Across the Curriculum." *Research in the Teaching of English* 20 (1986): 69–97.

Thomas, Laura H. "Educating Electrical Engineers for Workplace Communication: A Qualitative Study." MA thesis. Colorado State U, 1994.

Vest, David, Marilee Long, and Thad Anderson. "Electrical Engineers' Perceptions of Communication Training and Their Recommendations for Curricular Change: Results of a National Survey." *IEEE Transactions on Professional Communication* 39 (1996): 38–42.

Vest, David, Marilee Long, Laura H. Thomas, and Michael E. Palmquist. "Relating Communication Training to Workplace Requirements: The Perspective of New Engineers." *IEEE Transactions on Professional Communication* 38 (1995): 11–17.

Walvoord, Barbara E. "The Future of WAC." *College English* 58 (1996): 58–79.

———. "Getting Started." McLeod and Soven 12–31.

Weiss, Timothy. "A Process of Composing with Computers." *Computers and Composition* 6 (1989): 45–59.

Young, Art, and Toby Fulwiler. *Writing Across the Disciplines: Research into Practice*. Upper Montclair, NJ: Boynton/Cook, 1986.

Young, Richard E. "Designing for Change in a Writing-Across-the-Curriculum Program." *Balancing Acts: Essays on the Teaching of Writing in Honor of William F. Irmscher*. Ed. Virginia A. Chappell, Mary Louise Buley-Meissner, and Chris Anderson. Carbondale: Southern Illinois UP, 1991. 141–60.

———. Telephone interview. 1997.

Young, Richard E., and Christine M. Neuwirth. "Writing in the Disciplines: Computer Support for Collaborative Learning." Proposal to the Buhl Foundation. May 1988.

Zimmerman, Donald E., and Michael E. Palmquist. "Enhancing Electrical Engineering Students' Communication Skills." *Proceedings of the IEEE International Professional Communication Conference*. Philadelphia: IEEE, 1993. 428–31.

Zimmerman, Donald E., Michael E. Palmquist, Kathleen E. Kiefer, Marilee Long, David Vest, Martha Tipton, and Laura H. Thomas. "Enhancing Electrical Engineering Students Communication Skills—The Baseline Findings." *Proceedings of the IEEE International Professional Communication Conference.* Banff, Canada: IEEE, 1994. 412–17.

CHAPTER SEVENTEEN

Pedagogical Invention and Rhetorical Action in Writing Across the Curriculum

Jo-Ann M. Sipple
Merrimack College

William L. Sipple
Bay Path College

J. Stanton Carson
Robert Morris College

Great scholars are often appreciated more for individual and sometimes seemingly unrelated contributions than for the totality of their work and the comprehensive changes their gifts make possible. This essay argues that no area offers a clearer lens for viewing the comprehensive nature of and change made possible by Richard E. Young's work[1] than writing across the curriculum (WAC), and that no specific case brings that lens more into focus than writing across the business disciplines (WABD) at Robert Morris College. In this one instantiation of his praxis, Young was able to bring together for an entire academic community a system he created out of the following of his lifelong professional and scholarly concerns: classical rhetoric and its adaptation for modern uses, especially as related to his seminal work in tagmemic/problem-solving rhetoric (Gorrell, "Teaching of Rhetoric," in the *Encyclopedia of Education* and particularly Young, Becker, and Pike, *Rhetoric: Discovery and Change*); the use of nineteenth- and twentieth-century psychological and educational research in modern contexts, especially the function of epistemic rhetoric; and the importance of systematic and structural approaches, including effective invention and other heuristics, and the connection of sound pedagogical practices—notably collaborative classroom strategies and evaluation designs—to earlier theoretical and practical concerns.

Over the last twenty-five years, writing across the curriculum has grown into one of the largest educational reform movements in the United States. A number of surveys, including Carol Hartzog's, Susan McLeod's, and data from five RMC/PBS videoconferences (W. Sipple, "Robert Morris"), have indicated the movement's growing strength. As Elaine Maimon, Barbara Walvoord, and others have pointed out, WAC's impact has gone beyond literacy, learning, and writing in the disciplines to long-term positive change in faculty lives and practice (Walvoord 63). Yet the future of WAC remains clouded. In a recent article on the subject, Barbara Walvoord notes that a number of "assessments, predictions, and proposals for the future of WAC are characterized by a pervasive sense of uncertainty" (Walvoord 58). In the face of this uncertainty, ensuring the future of the movement has become a formidable task. It remains as true today as when James Kinneavy said it in 1983: WAC is both one of our best hopes for improved literacy and learning and a movement on which the jury is still out.

Few areas have offered more opportunity to explore the various theories and applications of Richard Young's work than writing across the curriculum. No institution has been more of a laboratory for those theories and practices than Robert Morris College. Young himself has pointed out that the WAC movement in the United States became a comfortable home for ideas he had had for a number of years. In a 1991 interview, Carson traces Young's attraction to WAC "as a natural outgrowth of [Young's] continuing interest in rhetorical theory, invention, and the pedagogy of writing, professional concerns that appeared in his personal journals as far back as graduate school" ("Writing" 69). The matching of these interests is perhaps nowhere more evident than in WAC's and Young's parallel concern over the functions of writing. In his famous bibliographic essay "Recent Developments in Rhetorical Invention," Young argues that rhetoric has been, in some sense, epistemic from its beginnings, in that it has always been concerned with "issues of coming to know and how others can be brought to know" (7). He maintains, however, that from the eighteenth century until recently, the focus on rhetoric shifted to its communicative function at the expense of its epistemic function. In the 1960s, the disciplinary paradigm returned to the ancient recognition of the connection between language and learning, articulated more recently in the popular press by William Zinsser: "Good writing and clear thinking go hand in hand" (58). Modern rhetorical studies continue to repudiate what Young has labeled "current-traditional" rhetoric in favor of a view that recognizes the dominance of the ancient art of invention (Young, "Recent Developments" 2). Young also believes that this rhetorical process must be adapted in the form of rhetorical action to various disciplines and situations; hence the need for pedagogical invention. Writers can develop and apply defined sets of heuristics (strategies) to arrive at more precise thinking about the subject matter of their disciplines. So strongly situational is writing, Young suggests, "[t]hat it makes sense to speak of the ethnolects of various disciplinary communities" ("Recent Developments" 11).

These assumptions, Young's paradigm for a new rhetoric articulated in 1970, foreshadow those of WAC seminal researchers James Britton et al. and Janet Emig, and the connection has been noted by Young himself: "[WAC] depends heavily on work in modern invention" ("Recent Developments" 10–11). This emphasis on invention in WAC programs is praxis for Young. Good invention theory is carried out in Young's vision of effective planning for WAC programs.

Just as a well-crafted paragraph or longer piece of prose begins with rhetorical invention—i.e., articulated planning—so writing-across-the-curriculum programs that have been built to last rely on a well-articulated planning process that integrates fully both pedagogical and rhetorical invention as well as pedagogical and rhetorical action. This praxis is the basis of Young's ability to have placed so many important invention strategies at the heart of the numerous writing-across-the-curriculum programs he fostered, evaluated, directed, or advised across the country.

One of the major premises of the WAC program at Robert Morris College (RMC), where Young advised extensively, is derived precisely from his concept of "writing in the disciplines," a cornerstone of successful WAC programs. That premise is that writers can develop and apply defined sets of heuristics or writing strategies to help them think more effectively about the subject matter of their disciplines. In the college's writing-across-the-curriculum program, Young was able to facilitate faculty expertise across the disciplines by leading them to discover or invent appropriate pedagogies that would host the rhetorical practices necessary to think more comprehensively and precisely in their disciplines. The end result was that particular faculty reenvisioned their courses to integrate write-to-learn tasks or the "small genres," in Young's words, of writing across the curriculum. In these reconfigured classes, instances of pedagogical invention design by the faculty immerse students in the repeated and varied writing tasks of rhetorical action to help them better achieve course objectives and become active learners.

The strategic plan to accomplish these parallel ends of pedagogical invention and rhetorical action, sometimes juxtaposed as rhetorical invention and pedagogical action, involved the faculty first in the following planning process strategies:

- Articulating the theoretical assumptions behind the program: developing a paradigm

- Establishing the goals or ends of the program

- Designing the program and evaluation activities (means) to arrive at the desired program goals

- Developing a community of collaborators through a forum for generating conversation about WAC on campus

- Designing a research component to go hand in hand with both the program and the evaluation activities

- Determining the organizational position of the program

- Documenting the planning process (J. Sipple)

Each of these strategies, when applied to planning WAC at RMC, reflects an aspect of Young's own lifelong concern with issues of the epistemic nature of rhetoric ("Recent Developments" 7). Thus the sum of strategies for planning to build WAC programs that last equals more than the litany of axioms derived from Young's work; it indeed epitomizes Young's weltanschauung —a coming together of pedagogical invention and rhetorical action in the best sense.

Establishing Program Goals

With Richard E. Young as main consultant and collaborator, the primary goal at RMC in 1985 was to establish a program in which faculty from all disciplines engaged their students in numerous and various opportunities to use writing as a means of helping them better achieve course objectives. Robert Morris College's curriculum, while becoming increasingly diversified, still maintains business and related professional education as its core. Our corollary purposes, related to the primary, were to help faculty from all subject areas redesign courses around the full integration of write-to-learn activities and to provide an environment for faculty collaboration in both the evaluation and research efforts to improve the program continuously. Young pointed out that course planning by the faculty was crucial to integrating write-to-learn activities because students could then practice their discipline-specific language, or ethnolects. In other words, the write-to-learn activities enabled students to think more precisely about the disciplines they were studying (see Appendix 17.1 for a sample of course-specific write-to-learn activities). Both faculty and students, therefore, were engaged in pedagogical invention as well as rhetorical action.

The Paradigm for WAC at RMC

The tenets of this paradigm stem directly from Young's lifelong, professional concerns, such as sustained rhetorical invention and action, as well as from his work enabling the institution's faculty to succeed in the art of sustained pedagogical invention and action. Impressive as it is, his application of these principles is not as important as his ability to integrate them seamlessly into a discovered pedagogy that changed the academic life of one college.

Thus the pedagogical inventions by the faculty at Robert Morris College are founded on the following premises derived mainly from Janet Emig, Elaine Maimon, and Richard Young, respectively: (1) writing is a mode of learning (Emig); (2) each academic discipline that shapes the writing of its practitioners is driven by its own specialized procedures, conventions, and terminology in an interactive process between writing and learning (Maimon et al.); and (3) writers can develop and apply defined sets of heuristics or writing strategies to help them think more effectively about the subject matter of their disciplines (Young, Becker, and Pike). At Robert Morris, these assumptions have been translated into pedagogical inventions and practices across ten academic departments (predominantly in the business disciplines); faculty reenvision their courses to integrate write-to-learn tasks, immersing students in repeated and varied writing tasks in every academic department that will help them better achieve course objectives.[2]

Designing the Program and Evaluation Activities

While it is not too difficult to identify classroom practices that innovatively challenge students in write-to-learn pedagogy in most WAC programs, it is more difficult to implement a more often neglected aspect of pedagogical invention, namely evaluation. Thus, as faculty redesigned courses using innovative classroom activities, they also measured their own students' performances by designing experimental evaluations for each of their classes. We also knew that if we wanted to change attitudes toward writing and student-writing behaviors, we had to begin with the faculty. Therefore, our program and evaluation activities extended beyond the students to the faculty and administration. They included the following four major activities for faculty and students:

1. Faculty reenvisioned their courses, planning the full integration of writing as means to helping students better achieve course objectives.

2. Students used writing-to-learn tasks more frequently and variously in targeted courses across the disciplines to achieve more sophisticated thinking and learning in a discipline.

3. Both faculty and student attitudes toward writing changed significantly when faculty and students engaged in courses containing fully integrated writing-to-learn principles. Students and faculty saw writing as more than a means for testing student knowledge at the end of the learning experience and were inclined to use it more and variously during the learning experience and on the way to more finished products. Writing became the means to the end rather than the end itself.

4. Through a multiple-measure approach to program evaluation, we identified expert teacher-planning processes and corresponding student-learning processes, discipline by discipline and course by course.

Based on the assumption that we can make cross-disciplinary research and practices happen, we asked faculty to target one of their courses in which they integrated writing-to-learn tasks as a means of helping students gain entry into the discourse community (defined by Clifford Geertz, "Growth," *Local Knowledge*) of the discipline they were studying. To provide ample context for such an ambitious task, we established the following environment: representative faculty from each of the academic departments were chosen each year to participate in forty-five hours of intensive seminar work for the purpose of considering the uses of writing to learn in a particular targeted course, culminating in an exemplary course design. Not until the subsequent semester did these faculty implement their course designs, which integrated writing to learn with disciplinary content. Both during and after the implementation semester, these faculty, as well as the program director and outside evaluators, measured the results of the faculty's planning processes and the students' corresponding learning processes, discipline by discipline and course by course.

Just as individual teachers must determine the means by which students can best arrive at course goals, so writing program directors must determine means by which students, faculty, and administrators can collaboratively arrive at the institution's program goals (or ends). The effectiveness of the means-ends relationship is best verified through a rigorous plan for evaluation. At both the course and program levels at Robert Morris College, we have designed a multiple-measure approach to evaluation as a necessary means of providing reliable evidence about the program's effectiveness. For a number of reasons, we needed to show conclusively that we succeeded or failed in arriving at program goals. The future of the program in terms of continued funding, continued faculty and student involvement, continued administrative encouragement and support, and possibilities for dissemination of program goals outside the institution all were contingent on the kinds of evaluation results that bore enough weight to convince many audiences of the program's worthiness. At the later stage of accountability, we found that we were successful in persuading our respective audiences—ourselves, administrators, other faculty, students, and various funding agencies—of the depth and extent of evaluation evidence. Hard data are, as Witte and Faigley argue, privileged in the minds of most administrators, evaluators, and funding agencies. Wherever possible, our multiple-measure approach provides for both the collection and analysis of hard data as well as for the inclusion of other, "expert-opinion" kinds of evaluation (5).

Table 17.1 demonstrates the depth of evaluation activities we established as sufficient means to justify the continuation of the program. Across the top of the horizontal axis, adapted from Algo Henderson's cross-sectional chart, are the kinds of evaluation used in our multiple-measure approach. Down the left side of the vertical axis are the issues, or what is to be evaluated. Listed at the points of intersection between the vertical and horizontal axes are the evaluation instruments used. This cross-sectional chart illustrates the importance of planning both program and evaluation activities as necessary means to arrive at program goals. Evaluation activities should be determined early in the planning process rather than separately and retrospectively in building writing-across-the-curriculum programs. Young insisted throughout his nearly twenty years of collaboration with us that each pedagogical invention and rhetorical action in the program find its way into the evaluation plan.

TABLE 17.1. Evaluation Design

What Is to Be Evaluated / Kinds of Evaluation	Internal		External	Metaevaluation
	Formative	Summative		
Effectiveness of Planning Seminars	writing responses by faculty participants faculty-participant surveys	faculty participant survey	XXXXXXXXXXXXX	XXXXXXXXXXXXX
Effectiveness of Targeted Courses	contribution to taxonomy of writing evaluation by ind. faculty participant writing activities throughout pre- & post-course design	pre- & post-course designs evaluations by individual faculty course plans	on-site WPA evaluation visit	evaluation designs by individual faculty participants evaluation design of whole program
Integration of Writing-to-Learn Activities in Targeted Courses	taxonomy of small genres faculty-participant surveys student-participant surveys	final copy of taxonomy faculty-participant surveys student-participant surveys	on-site WPA evaluation-team visit protocol interviews protocol analysis	protocol analysis—experimental design
Effectiveness of Winter Research Seminars	participants' written responses to weekly agendas and writing materials	faculty-participant surveys course plans	on-site WPA evaluation-team visit (analysis of data by external team)	analysis & conclusions drawn from pre- & post-faculty surveys designs by faculty
Impact of Writing-to-Learn Activities in Targeted Courses	preimplementation information faculty surveys administrative surveys student surveys	post-course design info: faculty surveys student surveys administrative surveys	design of sets of writing activities performed by students pre- & post-implementation of targeted courses	coding schemes & analysis of pre- & post-implementation protocols
Implementation of Targeted Courses	class visits protocols interviews	analysis of class visits, protocols & interviews Writing Program progress report	on-site WPA team protocol analysis	design of protocol analysis protocol analysis of faculty/students
Probability of Long-term Establishment of WABD	XXXXXXXXXXXXX	analysis of: administrative surveys faculty surveys student surveys	on-site WPA team recommendations	longitudinal case studies research design

Although we suspected, as is the case in most programs, that evaluation and program activities would change in later cycles (as some of ours certainly have), the plans of the present activities serve as blueprints that can be altered or dismissed at later stages of implementation. For example, in the first year faculty met regularly in seminars with Richard Young. In subsequent years, however, in an effort to make the program more cost effective, faculty met with WABD-trained mentors and colleagues from their respective academic departments. We anticipated having to adjust or alter the program and evaluation activities even further in later cycles of the program, but we had plans on which to base those decisions.

Designing a Research Component

Perhaps some skeptics will question the practicality of planning a research component in every writing-across-the-curriculum program. Art Young and Toby Fulwiler in their 1986 book *Writing Across the Disciplines: Research into Practice* argue for such research, based on three issues: (1) through research, individual faculty members have evidence to support their professional accountability in their respective disciplines; (2) the diagnostic function of applied research enables program administrators to verify what works and what does not, thereby discovering wherein lie the weaknesses and strengths of particular programs; (3) the persuasive function of research is without equal in convincing a variety of faculty, administrative, and student audiences of the importance of writing across the disciplines. As Art Young would have it, the writing-across-the-curriculum program at Michigan Technological University has initiated a number of research efforts by faculty in all disciplines. Some results of this research are reported in Young and Fulwiler's *Writing Across the Disciplines*, earlier research efforts appear in their 1982 *Language Connections*, and still other results appear in articles by Michigan Tech faculty in various disciplinary journals (e.g., Watson in *Mathematics Teacher*; Stinson in *WLA Newsletter*).

At Robert Morris College, we too designed a research component derived from our evaluation plans. In addition to analyzing a number of attitude surveys distributed among faculty, students, and administrators in an experimental design for our multiple-measure evaluation, we have invented a form of talk-aloud protocols (J. Sipple) to discover planning processes that teachers use when they design writing assignments in their courses.

The protocol/interview method proved to be a useful tool for evaluating the faculty workshops offered as part of the Writing Across the Business Disciplines program at Robert Morris College. Combining protocols with postprotocol interviews for evaluation purposes allowed program directors to determine in some detail how the workshops affected the teaching and attitudes of the participants. The method revealed that faculty who had participated in the WABD-training workshops differed significantly from nonparticipants on measures of attitude and teaching behavior. Participants typically viewed writing assignments as a powerful means for encouraging student learning rather than as only a means for testing content knowledge or improving writing skills. And they were more likely than nonparticipants to develop assignments that furthered the learning objectives of their courses and that were integrated into the course structure.

The protocols and interviews conducted in this evaluation provided the program directors with valuable information about the views of faculty on student writing, attitudes, and needs and about their approaches to the design of writing assignments. Such information would not have been so readily available through other, more conventional assessment methods used in isolation, such as surveys, classroom observations, student evaluations, or close analyses of assignments and student papers—methods which were used to evaluate other components of the WABD program. The protocol/interview method complemented and clarified data obtained from these other sources. As a general principle of design, those who planned the WABD evaluation project devised multiple, complementary methods of evaluation keyed to the distinctive features and educational objectives of the various components of the program (Blakeslee, Hayes, Sipple, and Young).

The data we accumulated through transcriptions of audiotaped teacher and student protocols showed that teachers who participated in intensive WABD writing seminars had more clearly defined strategies for planning the nature, function, use, and variety of the student writing they assign than those who did not participate (Sipple and Stenberg). For example, in an experimental design conducted during the first year of implementation, we discovered that faculty who had participated in the first-year seminars (experimental group) could call upon a larger repertoire of planning strategies for designing writing tasks (rhetorical invention) than faculty who had not participated (control group). Note that the faculty from the experimental and control groups teaching identical courses were paired (see Appendix 17.2). The results are compiled in Table 17.2.

At first glance, it may be surprising to find that 75 percent of the nonparticipants were trying to improve student writing while none of the participants were trying to teach writing or improve writing skills. On closer analysis, we find that the participants were trying to use writing in many ways to aid students during the learning process. The well-intended nonparticipants thought that their formal writing assignments, used to test student knowledge, would teach students how to write as well. The WAC participants had established clearer and more focused goals for their uses of writing.

We have been able to draw some conclusions about our program based on these data and others like them. First, in a formative way, the data we have been accumulating through protocols continue to help us monitor faculty seminars, classroom practices, and other writing-across-the-curriculum activities. Through analyses of these data, we have not only been able to discover what works and what does not in our program, but we have also been able to make necessary adjustments along the way.

Second, teacher protocol analysis permits us to make a number of summative evaluation statements:

1. We can judge the success of our forty-five-hour intensive faculty seminars. Our protocol analyst, Nancy Penrose, offered these summative statements about these data:

   Overall, seminar participants differed from nonparticipants on measures of attitude and teaching behavior. Participants typically view writing as a means for learning rather than as a testing device or an opportunity for practicing writing skills. Their use of writing in the classroom reflects these

Table 17.2. Teacher Attitudes toward Planning Writing Assignments

Teacher Attitude toward Planned Writing Task	Participants in WABD	Nonparticipants
	(percent agreeing with stated attitude)	
The teacher realizes that creating an an assignment is a rhetorical task.	30	13
The teacher is concerned that students see the purpose of the writing.	30	0
The teacher has thought about the task in concrete, operational terms—has considered the subtasks involved.	100	88
The teacher is sensitive to students' abilities and acts on that information by modifying the writing task, providing extra guidance, etc.	90	25
The teacher hopes that the writing assignment will help improve the students' writing skills.	0	75

attitudes. Participants are more likely than nonparticipants to develop assignments that further the learning objectives of their courses and that are integrated into the course structure. . . . The results of the present analyses indicate that the faculty seminars provide an effective means for communicating the fundamental principles of the writing-across-the-curriculum program and for changing the way writing is used in courses at Robert Morris. (54–55)

2. The protocol analysis corroborates the findings from our analyses of teacher-attitude surveys: participants have changed their conception of writing assignments and the place of such assignments in course designs and, more important, have acted on that information in their own courses and in attempts to influence their departmental colleagues in discussions about the various uses of writing.

3. The protocol analysis reveals that participating faculty know how to plan for and design writing tasks that aid learning and, further, that they know how to plan courses that integrate writing-to-learn tasks.

4. The protocol analysis reveals that faculty participants view writing much differently from nonparticipants. (This was especially true in the first two years of the program; in later years, the halo effect brought nonparticipants closer to this view.)

5. The faculty's experience with protocols has shown them the significance of their contributions to the institution's evaluation effort and has also provided them with a database from which to pursue collaborative and individual research (e.g., Lesnak; Morrison).

These evaluation data, which Ericsson and Simon argue are "the raw data in as hard a form as could be wished" (4), provided us with the beginnings of a database, which we continue to build in order to answer more precisely two different sets of research questions: (1) What are the planning processes teachers use to construct write-to-learn tasks? Can we derive models of teachers' planning processes? and (2) What are the writing processes students use to perform these write-to-learn tasks? Can we derive models of students' learning processes?

The issue tree in Figure 17.1 illustrates the two sets of research questions tied to using protocol interviews as the research methodology, questions that helped us accumulate the necessary data to begin answering these questions. In identifying faculty planning processes, our protocol analysis allowed us to examine whether faculty who participated in the writing-across-the-curriculum program designed writing assignments (rhetorical invention) drawn from principles learned in the faculty seminars in order to help students better achieve course goals. Likewise, in identifying student learning processes, our protocol analysis allowed us to examine whether the students participating in targeted writing-across-the-curriculum courses developed more expert learning processes in performing the writing assignments (rhetorical action) that had been designed to help them better achieve course goals. The instruments we used to measure these performances are the major evaluation tools of pedagogical invention.

A WAC Model to Disseminate Across the Nation

Perhaps the greatest tribute to the Robert Morris experiment in pedagogical invention and rhetorical action, and therefore to Richard Young's thinking behind it, has come in the form of a FIPSE (Fund for the Improvement of Postsecondary Education)

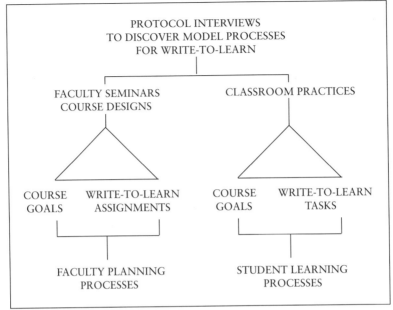

FIGURE **17.1.** *An issue tree.*

grant to Robert Morris College (1996) to disseminate the proven WAC model to six other institutions across the country: Babson College, Wellesley, Massachusetts; Bryant College, Smithfield, Rhode Island; Golden Gate University, San Francisco, California; Kent State University, Salem, Ohio; Mercyhurst College, Erie, Pennsylvania; and Southeastern University, Washington, DC.

Reiterating Young's concerns over WAC program longevity, the grant proposal argues that programs often fail because they are insufficiently woven into their institutional contexts. Through this three-year project (1996–1998), we disseminated our proven model of writing across the curriculum to achieve the following program goals:

1. Provide a structural approach to integrating WAC principles and practices into existing courses.

2. Train the collaborating institutions' (CIs) representatives who, in turn, will train their respective faculty in a long-term full implementation of this approach, through both faculty seminars and departmental mentor relationships.

3. Offer strategies to implement an evaluation system for these projects derived from the published Robert Morris design.

4. Provide the CIs with twenty RMC-PBS WAC Video Project videotapes, accompanying print materials, and our guidance for their effective use in sustaining their programs long after the grant period has ended.

5. Monitor through quantitative and qualitative measures our success in disseminating our program to the CIs in hopes of creating a flexible, efficient, and effective national model for implementation of WAC programs (Carson, "To Disseminate").

In addition to disseminating this proven model of WAC to six other institutions, we have developed yet another tool in our repertoire of pedagogical inventions for the six institutions and others to use. This latest tool of pedagogical invention is the Institutional Audit (W. Sipple, "Institutional").

The Institutional Audit

One lesson of the WAC program at Robert Morris College is its demonstration that curriculum is a solution to a perceived problem; curriculum is both a means and an end. Curricular change occurs in response to perceived problems. Curricular efforts often fail not because they lack intrinsic value but rather because they are inappropriate or unrealistic for their contexts. Solutions that are right for one institution may not work for other institutions because of such factors as institutional mission constraints, institutional image, budget priorities, internal or board politics, or symbolic ramifications. Hence, as Young advised the administration and faculty of Robert Morris, writing across the curriculum must be appropriate for the context and constraints of individual institutions, and these constraints are best identified early in the planning process.

Thus, before focusing on the roles of writing across the curriculum and on write to learn as means to redesign courses and create instructional materials and/or programs (pedagogical inventions), program designers should carefully define the particular problem they wish to solve in their institutions. Analyzing the environment in which the WAC program must survive is a useful way to identify that problem. An institutional audit is one way that curriculum leaders may focus on their particular institutional goals, missions, constraints, and resources so as to design plans and to implement changes that are appropriate and reasonable for their individual contexts. In the Institutional Audit exercise—an activity appropriate for administrator/faculty retreats or development seminars—curriculum leaders will begin to describe in detail the particular problem(s) they hope to solve through writing across the curriculum and related course redesigns, programs, and other curriculum materials and faculty activities. Continuing this activity with others at the institution is a good way to begin meaningful discussion and to create permanent change.

The Institutional Audit is intended to be a heuristic that increases the chances for successful planning of institution-specific WAC programs and activities. It should be flexible and adapted to individual needs. The audit systematically focuses attention on at least seven areas of concern for administrators and faculty planning WAC efforts: (1) the nature of the institution, (2) the instructional context, (3) the participants in the WAC initiative, (4) the necessary project resources, (5) political perspectives, (6) symbolic elements, and (7) personal perspectives. Within each section of the audit, the participants should generate their own answers and perspectives, and then compare, combine, and refine results.

Institutional Audit

(1) Nature of the Institution

(1a) Mission Statement: The mission statement provides the overall context within which you must create curriculum or invent pedagogy. Read your institution's mission statement: What are the key elements of your mission? Here you should consider your institution's mission in an operational sense—how do you implement the mission?

(1b) Vision Statement: Often the president or other administrators will articulate a vision that is used as a guide for long-range planning. Summarize your institution's vision statement or, if you do not have one, summarize what your administrators (deans, department heads, vice presidents) articulate as the vision for your institution. For example, your president may summarize the institution's vision in such a statement as "our graduates will be known for their superior communications skills." Many faculty are unaware of their president's vision—knowing the institution's vision is useful in planning specific curriculum.

(1c) Describe the parameters of your institution—in other words, review your internal organizational structure: organization of schools, departments, reporting structures; your curriculum review processes; your budgeting processes, etc. The insights here reveal how the curriculum leaders may have to proceed to effect change: how does information flow within the institution? What does one typically encounter in proposing change? In other words, identify the constraints within which you will be working.

(1d) With this contextual information in mind, make a list of those who will have direct influence on your WAC project (you may include administrators, faculty, students, etc.). Who are the chief stakeholders? Who will provide approvals for the project?

(1e) List who may be involved indirectly as a result of your WAC efforts (this list may include alumni, funding sources, trustees, employers, etc.). Within all institutions there are secondary stakeholders who may have an impact on the project. These include such groups as enrollment managers who must sell your curriculum to potential students and funding sources who may be asked to provide the resources needed for the project.

(2) Instructional Context

(2a) What major instructional or curricular problem(s) are you addressing currently at your institution? It is important here to focus on the real curricular issues you confront, rather than only on those narrowly defined within the WAC project itself. The intention in this section of the audit is to discover where in the institutional curricular priorities the WAC effort may reside and if there are ways to link it to the central curricular efforts of the institution. In other words, try to discover the problem to which WAC is a solution.

(2b) For whom is this a problem—faculty, students, administration, other constituents (employers, etc.)? Note why it is a problem for these constituents. In WAC a solution to a real problem is for someone. To succeed, the curricular change must be perceived as useful to all stakeholders.

(2c) List objectives that your various constituents may want to achieve through your WAC initiative as related to the resolution of this problem. Include pedagogical as well as rhetorical goals. At this stage of the discussion, it is useful to write objectives for the program. For example, "at the end of the implementation faculty will be able to demonstrate write-to-learn activities (rhetorical actions) appropriate for the pedagogical environment; these are designed for their specific fields"; or "administrators will be able to explain for an external audience the WAC program at this institution."

(2d) Summarize this discussion and write a problem statement that may help you focus your WAC training and development component of this project. Think about what you hope to achieve through this project and its relevance to the solution of real curricular problems.

(3) Participants in WAC Initiative

(3a) Whom do you hope to involve in the WAC initiative? List departments, individuals, etc. In other words, who is your audience for effecting this curricular change?

(3b) What are the prevailing attitudes of those whom you hope to involve in the WAC initiative? Are they supportive, open to change, positive, hostile? Will you have to "sell" the program within the institution? Who will help you?

(3c) What is your role in the organization of the WAC project? What is your role in effecting curricular change in your institution? What authority do you have "to make things happen"? It is important here for individuals to see their place in the overall hierarchy of decision making and authority. This frequently has an influence on the viability of curricular efforts by helping curriculum leaders identify strategies and develop arguments for effecting change.

(4) Project Resources

(4a) Based on your analysis of the institutional context in which your curricular solution must be achieved, describe your existing resources and support system: i.e., are there supportive administrators; are there adequate financial, technological, and human resources; can you rely upon positive attitudes among faculty and administration; is there institutional agreement on the direction of curricular change; will there be funds for faculty development? Describe a realistic framework within which the project must exist.

(4b) How supportive is your administration of new curricular efforts? What funding or resources have been allocated for this WAC project? What do you hope for as support for the project? How will the program be supported after initial funding is depleted? Administrative support is essential for systemic curricular change. Ultimately, those with authority must endorse the project and provide for long-term support.

(4c) What role do you play in the budgeting process? How do budget priorities get set in your institution? Where does the WAC effort fall in these priorities? Can the institution afford the project as envisioned? What might be a more realistic approach to achieving the same ends? In other words, you may have to develop more cost-effective approaches to the problem.

(5) Political Perspective

(5a) Describe the political ramifications of the WAC curricular initiative—what supportive and/or subversive elements may exist, what misperceptions may evolve, who may oppose the WAC efforts, why would faculty resist change, etc.? This is the context in which you work—think about the system for allocating scarce resources in your institution: what gets cut in the budget crunches?

(5b) From a faculty point of view, what departments and individuals stand to "win" or "lose" because of the WAC initiative? What may faculty perceive as "rewards" and "punishments" associated with participating/not participating in this project? By identifying these forces you will begin to see the subtext of the proposed change.

(5c) What kinds of arguments may you have to construct to win approval for implementing a WAC initiative, to enlist faculty support and participation, and to bring curricular change related to WAC efforts to implementation? This is a key element: the intrinsic value of the curricular effort often is not your most viable argument for effecting the change.

(5d) How is your problem similar to or different from political problems in other institutions? For insights, listen to the problems, constraints, and resolutions of your colleagues in other institutions.

(6) Symbolic Elements

(6a) How might your president describe the WAC effort in a report to the Board of Trustees? Here you should shift your perspective and try to envision how the top administration would perceive the WAC effort and the language the administration might use to describe it. How would you want the president to describe the effort?

(6b) What symbolic ramifications might you attach to your WAC initiative that may help to motivate faculty and enhance your institution's reputation and/or image? Frequently, names given to projects and attaching projects to worthwhile institutional goals empower a project with a symbolic force that will help to drive it forward. By identifying these yourself, you will help to shape the project and attach meanings to it that often, in effect, make the project larger than itself and win long-term institutional and foundation support.

(7) Personal Perspectives

(7a) What/Who do you see as the chief obstacle(s) to the success of this project? It is useful to be specific here and to name names (we do recommend that you keep this confidential, however). Knowing where the obstacles to a project reside is useful in effecting change and assessing the energy that it will take personally to make the change. What are you willing to invest in this effort?

(7b) What/Who do you see as your chief support(s) for this project? (Note: the same goes here for confidentiality and for being candid.) Knowing who will help you personally is a valuable part of planning change.

Conclusion

Richard E. Young's continued influence epitomizes his view of writing across the curriculum—a coming together of pedagogical invention and rhetorical action in the best sense. The fifteen successful years of the Robert Morris College Writing Across the Business Disciplines (WABD) program stand as testament to that influence.

Appendix 17.1

Sample Write-to-Learn Activities

Following a method described by Algo Henderson in "The Design of Superior Courses," faculty participants now construct a matrix that lists course goals across one axis and material to be covered across the other. At the intersection of goals and materials to be covered, the faculty member, following guidelines from Robert Mager's *Preparing Instructional Objectives,* designs instructional objectives—active learning tasks that are often opportunities for writing to learn. It is here that faculty develop "small-genre" write-to-learn tasks in redesigning their courses.

For example, one goal in Jay Carson's American Writers course is for students to be able to isolate problems in the text and use them as points of departure for writing about literature. Where that goal intersects with *Huckleberry Finn,* the following instructional objective appears: "Huck thinks of Jim as a friend but calls him a *nigger.* In about one page of your journal, explain."

This matrix approach is transferable to any field. For example, in the discipline of accounting we see that the course goal 1, "Identify terminology, conventions, and procedure," intersects with the first section of the professor's topics of instruction (or material to be covered), "Job-Ordered Cost Accounting System." At this intersection, Chris Stenberg designs two detailed write-to-learn tasks:

> **Writing Task 1:** I'm having trouble understanding the design of job-order cost-accounting systems. Maybe my problem is that I don't understand the job-cost environment. Can you help me by listing some operating characteristics of a job coster and then explain why this accounting system makes sense under these circumstances?

Writing Task 2: Let's pretend that you manage a print shop. I stop at your shop and ask if you can print 100 copies of an audit report. The report is 15 pages long and should be printed on a high-quality, white bond paper measuring 8.5 x 11 inches using black ink. You agree to print this job. I then ask you how much you will charge me. You set your selling price by multiplying your production cost by a factor of 2. If the cost of a job was $100, then you would set the selling price at $200. Before responding formally to my price inquiry, you must estimate the total production cost of this job. Write some notes describing how you will make this estimate. Be precise in describing your methodology.

A similar example, this one for remedial mathematics, can be found in another published piece of WABD literature, "Writing-to-Learn: An Experiment in Remedial Algebra" by Richard Lesnak. At the intersection of one of his course objectives and the topic, he writes the following write-to-learn task for his students: "Students write in natural language (as opposed to mathematical) a detailed, step-by-step procedure for factoring an expression completely." This task appears at the intersection of his goal "Ability to identify problems and select the proper computational technique" and his topic "Factoring."

Later in the course, at the intersection of his goal "Ability to analyze an incorrect solution for the purpose of determining the error in the solution" and his topic "Solving Equations," Lesnak includes the following write-to-learn task: Students must take completed "incorrect" solutions which the professor presents to them, upon which students respond with "a written description (again in natural language) of the procedural error before they solve the equation again correctly in mathematical terms."

Appendix 17.2

The Research Component

The general question asked in evaluating whether the seminars/workshops both persuaded and helped participants to integrate writing-to-learn activities into their courses was this: Did the workshops influence the participants' approaches to constructing writing assignments in ways that reflect the principles advanced in the workshops? We selected faculty writing assignments as the focus for this part of the evaluation project since they are suggestive of instructors' concerns and approaches to teaching writing. Further, the assignments created by workshop participants could be compared with those created by nonparticipants, with both sets of assignments being analyzed for evidence, or lack thereof, of the principles espoused in the workshops. The specific questions we asked about the assignments included: Did the participants in the workshops try to create writing assignments that promoted student learning, that helped students solve problems related to the course, that were integrated into the course structure, and that were manageable by the students?

To answer these questions, we developed what we call the "protocol/interview" assessment method. With this method, several workshop participants were asked to provide think-aloud protocols while they created a writing assignment for one of their classes. Immediately after completing this task, they were asked a series of questions about their goals in creating the assignment. Other faculty who taught comparable courses and who did not participate in the workshops were given the same tasks. Raters then examined the protocols and the answers to the interview questions to identify evidence bearing on each subject's approach to creating writing assignments. Because the subjects in the evaluation were observed while they were creating writing assignments and were interviewed soon after, we believe that the protocol/interview method provided sensitive indices of the subjects' approaches to this educationally important task. In contrast, we believe that interviews alone, because they are not so closely tied to performance of the task, are less likely to provide useful information than protocols and interviews together.

Subjects

The subjects were nine faculty members, five who attended Young's seminars and four who did not. The seminar participants were chosen to provide as broad a sampling as possible of the disciplinary areas at Robert Morris College. Each of the nonparticipants was chosen because he or she was in the same discipline and taught the same course as a participant.

Procedure

The subjects were asked to think aloud and to describe as fully as possible their main teaching/learning concerns while planning and composing a writing assignment for their classes. The instructions for the protocol read:

> Devise one writing assignment for your course. While you are devising the assignment, describe as fully as you can your main teaching/learning concerns. Talk aloud about what is going on in your mind while you are doing the task. Write the words for the assignment which you would have typed to hand to the student.

Following the think-aloud sessions, each subject was asked six questions designed to supplement the information obtained through the protocol. These questions concerned the objectives of the assignment, its use in the course, its relation to course goals, specific learning problems addressed by the assignment, and the intellectual demands it placed on students. The protocols and the postprotocol interviews were tape-recorded and transcribed for later analysis. These transcripts, together with the assignments and any written text or notes produced during the protocol session, constituted the data set for each subject.

Analysis

For analysis of the protocol and interview data, the raters were given the list of nineteen features shown below. These features were developed and used to evaluate each complete data set, including protocol and interview transcripts, written texts and notes, and the assignments created. Some of the features focus on the nature of the assignment created and the concerns suggested by it, while others address more explicitly the thinking and attitudes of faculty members while creating the assignments. Raters were asked to examine the data set for each subject to determine whether each of the nineteen features was present. Each data set was analyzed as a single unit; that is, all three sources of data (protocols, interviews, and writing assignments) were examined for evidence of each of the features under investigation. The raters did not know which data sets belonged to participants and which to non-participants.

Features of the Protocols, Interviews, and Assignments Addressed by the Raters

1. The writing assignment is designed to do more than test student knowledge. The writing assignment is designed to promote student learning/discovery.

2. The writing assignment leads the student to solving a particular problem in achieving course objectives.

3. The writing assignment is responsive to a learning problem that the teacher has identified.

4. The teacher is aware that the writing assignment is cultivating a level of cognitive ability.

5. The writing assignment is integrated into the ongoing learning process in the course.

6. The teacher has an awareness of different, varied ways of responding to student writing with a mind toward giving feedback to the student.

7. The teacher's response to student writing is integrated into the ongoing process of the course.

8. The writing assignment is manageable for the student given the allotted time, constraints, and the description of the writing assignment.

9. The teacher realizes that creating an assignment is a rhetorical task.

10. The teacher is concerned that students see the purpose of the writing assignment.

11. The teacher realizes that the assignment will provide him/her with valuable information about student learning/progress in the course.

12. The teacher has thought about the task in concrete operational terms; recognizes subtasks involved.

13. The teacher is sensitive to his/her students' abilities, e.g., thinks about how students might respond to the task.

14. The teacher is sensitive to students' abilities and plans to act on that information, e.g., by modifying assignments, providing extra guidance, etc.

15. The teacher is sensitive to student needs, e.g., the types of writing and other skills students will need in later courses or in their careers.

16. The teacher is sensitive to student needs and plans to act on that information, e.g., by modifying assignments, providing extra guidance, etc.

17. The teacher is sensitive to students' attitudes toward writing.

18. The teacher gives students a specific audience to write for.

19. The teacher hopes that the writing assignment will help improve students' writing skills (intentionally or as a side effect).

In addition to these nineteen features, raters assessed two additional features of the writing assignments, as well as the length of the protocols. These additional measures are shown in the following list.

Additional Measures Assessed by the Raters

20. Quality of the writing assignment rated on a scale of 1 (low) to 4 (high):

    1 = Low quality: confusing, purposeless, not integrated into course goals, etc.

    4 = High quality: well thought out and articulated, fits into course, helpful, etc.

21. Breadth of teacher's view of writing rated on a scale of 1 to 4:

    1 = Restricted view: writing equals grammar, correctness; writing takes place after thinking; writing is thought of in terms of number of pages; etc.

    2 = Larger view: writing is a medium for thinking and learning; writing is an occasion for exploration; etc.

22. Protocol length (number of transcript lines).

For more information, see Blakeslee, Hayes, Sipple, and Young.

Notes

1. See, for example, Young "Designing," "Impediments," "Some Presuppositions"; and Kaufer and Young.

2. When writing across the business disciplines (WABD) was implemented in 1985 at Robert Morris College, the original undergraduate departments numbered ten: Accounting; Business Education; Business Information Systems; Communications; Economics and Finance; Transportation; Management and Marketing; Quantitative and Natural Sciences; Social Sciences; Sport Management. Originally, twenty courses were redesigned, two per department. That number grew every year, and today there are well over fifty courses in twelve departments: Accounting, Communications, Computer and Information Systems, Education, Finance, Health Administration and Allied Services, Hospitality

Management, Management, Marketing, Quantitative and Natural Sciences, Social Sciences, Sport Administration.

Works Cited

Blakeslee, Ann, John R. Hayes, Jo-Ann M. Sipple, and Richard E. Young. "Evaluating Training Workshops in a Writing Across the Curriculum Program: Method and Analysis." *Language and Learning Across the Disciplines* 1.2 (1994): 1–31.

Britton, James, Tony Burgess, Nancy Martin, Alex McLeod, and Harold Rosen. *The Development of Writing Abilities (11–18)*. London: Macmillan, 1975.

Carson, J. Stanton. "To Disseminate the Proven WAC Model to Six Other Institutions Across the Country." FIPSE Grant Proposal, 1996.

———. "Writing Across the Business Disciplines at Robert Morris College: A Case Study." Diss. Carnegie Mellon U, 1991.

Emig, Janet. "Writing as a Mode of Learning." *College Composition and Communication* 28 (1977): 122–28.

Ericsson, K. Anders, and Herbert A. Simon. *Protocol Analysis: Verbal Reports as Data*. Cambridge: MIT P, 1984.

Fulwiler, Toby, and Art Young. *Language Connections: Writing and Reading Across the Curriculum*. Urbana, IL: NCTE, 1982.

Geertz, Clifford. "The Growth of Culture and the Evolution of the Mind." *The Interpretation of Cultures: Selected Essays*. New York: Basic, 1973.

———. *Local Knowledge: Further Essays in Interpretive Anthropology*. New York: Basic, 1983.

Gorrell, Robert M. "Rhetoric, Teaching of." *The Encyclopedia of Education*. Vol. 7. Ed. Lee C. Deighton. New York: Macmillan/Free, 1971. 549–54.

Hartzog, Carol. *Composition and the Academy: A Study of Writing Program Administration*. New York: MLA, 1986.

Henderson, Algo D. "The Design of Superior Courses." *Improving College and University Teaching* 13.2 (1965): 106-09.

Kaufer, David, and Richard Young. "Writing in the Content Areas: Some Theoretical Complexities." *Theory and Practice in the Teaching of Writing: Rethinking the Discipline.* Ed. Lee Odell. Carbondale: Southern Illinois UP, 1993. 71–104.

Kinneavy, James. "Writing Across the Curriculum." *ADE Bulletin* 76 (1983): 14–21.

Lesnak, Richard. "Writing to Learn: An Experiment in Remedial Algebra." *Writing to Learn Mathematics and Science.* Ed. Paul Connolly and Teresa Vilardi. New York: Teachers College P, 1989. 147–56.

Mager, Robert F. *Preparing Instructional Objectives.* Rev. 2nd ed. Belmont, CA: Pitman, 1984.

Maimon, Elaine, Gerald L. Belcher, Gail W. Hearn, Barbara F. Nodine, and Finbarr W. O'Connor. *Writing in the Arts and Sciences.* Cambridge, MA: Winthrop, 1981.

McLeod, Susan H. "Writing Across the Curriculum: The Second Stage and Beyond." *College Composition and Communication* 40 (1989): 337–43.

Morrison, Phyllis. "Preparing Business Teachers to Teach Keyboarding to Elementary School Students." *Business Education Forum* 40 (Mar. 1986): 25–29.

Penrose, Nancy. "Analyses of Faculty Protocols and Post-Protocol Interviews." *Close-Out Report to the Buhl Foundation.* Ed. Jo-Ann M. Sipple. Pittsburgh: Robert Morris College. Unpublished ms, 1986.

Sipple, Jo-Ann M. "A Planning Process for Building Writing Across the Curriculum Programs to Last." *Journal of Higher Education* 60 (1989): 441–57.

Sipple, Jo-Ann M., and Chris D. Stenberg. "Robert Morris College." *Programs That Work: Models and Methods for Writing Across the Curriculum.* Ed. Toby Fulwiler and Art Young. Portsmouth, NH: Boynton/Cook, 1990. 181–98.

Sipple, William L. "Institutional Audit." Unpublished ms. FIPSE Funded Dissemination Program, 1996.

——, exec. producer. *Robert Morris College Writing Across the Curriculum: PBS WAC Videoconferences and Resource Programs.* PBS Adult Learning Satellite Service, 1991–95.

Stinson, Robert. "Journals in the Geography Class." *WLA Newsletter* 15 (Spring 1980): 5.

Walvoord, Barbara E. "The Future of WAC." *College English* 58 (1996): 58–79.

Watson, Margaret. "Writing Has a Place in a Mathematics Class." *Mathematics Teacher* (1980): 518–20.

Witte, Stephen, and Lester Faigley. *Evaluating College Writing Programs.* Carbondale: Southern Illinois UP, 1983.

Young, Art, and Toby Fulwiler. *Writing Across the Disciplines: Research into Practice.* Upper Montclair, NJ: Boynton/Cook, 1986.

Young, Richard. "Designing for Change in a Writing-Across-the-Curriculum Program." *Balancing Acts: Essays on the Teaching of Writing in Honor of William F. Irmscher.* Ed. Virginia A. Chappell, Mary Louise Buley-Meissner, and Chris Anderson. Carbondale: Southern Illinois UP, 1991. 141–60.

———. "Impediments to Change in Writing Across the Curriculum Programs." *Composition in Context: Essays in Honor of Donald C. Stewart.* Ed. Ross Winterowd and Vincent Gillespie. Carbondale: Southern Illinois UP, 1994. 26–38.

———. "Recent Developments in Rhetorical Invention." *Teaching Composition: Twelve Bibliographical Essays.* Ed. Gary Tate. Fort Worth: Texas Christian UP, 1987. 1–38.

———. "Some Presuppositions in Decision-Making for Writing Programs." *An Olio of Notions Concerning the Politics of Writing Instruction.* Ed. Robert D. Narveson. Lincoln: U of Nebraska–Lincoln, 1987. 44–63.

Young, Richard, Alton Becker, and Kenneth Pike. *Rhetoric: Discovery and Change.* New York: Harcourt, 1970.

Zinsser, William. "A Bolder Way to Teach Writing." *The New York Times,* 13 Apr. 1985, natl. ed., sec. Education Life: 58.

INDEX

AAAS. *See* American Association for the Advancement of Science

Abstract, 229

Academic Literacy and the Nature of Expertise (Geisler), 324

Academic writing, case study of learning, 347–63

Accessibility, 208, 210, 212, 218–19, 221, 225, 230–31

Activity theory, 23, 85

Adams, Charles Francis, 45–46

Adaptive expectations, 34, 49, 53–54, 54

Addison, Joseph, 20

Ad Herennium, 179

Advertising, 137

Aleatory procedures, 185–86, 187, 189, 190

American Association for the Advancement of Science, 247, 250

American Chemical Society, 254

American Journal of Science and Arts, 258

American Medical Association, 254

American Philosophical Society, 246–47, 250

American Physical Society, 254

American research universities, 237–38

American science, assumptions about, 237 development of, 245–51

American scientists, 238

American Society for Promoting Useful Knowledge, The, 250

American Society of Naturalists, 254

American university research, model for, 255

Anagrams, 191

Analysis, protocol, 414–16

Ancient Rhetorics for Contemporary Students (Crowley), 158

Andreasen, Nancy, 227

Antifoundationalism, 90, 94

Antimethod, 193–94

Antimethodology, 193

Antiscientism, 90, 96–99

Appeals, types of, 159

Applebee, Arthur N., on textbooks, 166

Applied Grammatology (Ulmer), 191

Applied science, 245, 249, 252, 255, 260, 262, 264

APS. *See* American Philosophical Society

Arguing and Thinking (Billig), 83

Argument, 136, 140, 153, 154, 156
  as dominant form of discourse, 155
  as means of conveying truth, 154
  as mode of discourse, 152
  rhetoric confined to, 124–25
  structure of, 116–17
  in student papers, 352
  writing of, 349–50, 367, 368

Protocol data, analysis of, 427–29
Protocol interviews, 413, 417, 426
Protocols, talk-aloud, 413
Purcell-Gates, Victoria, on
    reading and writing, 342
Pure research, 255
Pure science, 245, 249, 255, 259,
    262, 264, 266
Purpose, 161–62, 162

Quadrivium, 38
Qualification, 118
Quarterly Journal of Speech,
    146–47
Questioning, 175
Quincy, Josiah, 45–46
Quintilian, 16, 19, 159, 181
QWERTY, history of, 30–35

Ramism, 18
Reading, 209, 364
  processes of, 209–13
Realism, 94–95
Reasoning, economic, 57 n. 2
"Recent Developments in
    Rhetorical Invention"
    (Young), 404
*Reconceiving Writing,
    Rethinking Writing
    Instruction* (Bazerman),
    61 n. 21
Redish, Janice, 209, 234
Reflection, 233
"Reflections on Allan Bloom's
    Critics" (Roche), 294
Reflective practice, 326–27
Reid, Thomas, 20
Reified, William, 250
Reingold, Nathan, 237, 248,
    249, 251
Relativism, 94, 96, 111
Religions, 11
Republic of Letters, 6
Research, x, 13, 425–26

cross-disciplinary, 67–74
development of scientific,
    238–50
pure, 255
scientific, 260
Reservation, 118
*Rethinking the History of
    Rhetoric* (Poulakos), 74
"Revival of Rhetoric, The"
    (Booth), 167 n. 1
Reynolds, Frederick, 183 n. 4
Rhetoric (Aristotle), 123–24, 133
Rhetoric (Hughes and Duhamel),
    152, 155
Rhetoric (Young, Becker, and
    Pike), xi, xxv n. 2, 1, 173
Rhetoric, 2, 37, 38–39, 116, 118,
    124–26, 261, 262
  Aristotelian, 148, 149, 154,
    155, 158, 164, 165, 166
  Big vs. Little, 92–93
  classical, 15–17, 23, 146, 147,
    158–61, 174
  current-traditional, 163
  curriculum for new, 100
  definition of, 83
  deliberative, 160
  as epistemic, 86–87, 93–96, 405
  faculties of, 174
  graduate programs in, xviii
  graduate study of, 38, 39,
    58 n. 5, 59 n. 9
  history of, 15–23, 173–74
  ignorance of classical, 148
  marginalization of, 37
  new, 23, 85, 173, 191, 196
  philosophical, 91
  purpose of, 133
  scientific, 238–39, 254, 259–60,
    265, 266
  sophistic, 128
  vs. sophistry, 129
  tagmemic, xi, xxi, xxii, xxv n.
    2, 69, 403
  as teachable art, 159
  technical, 91

EDITOR

Maureen Daly Goggin, assistant professor of rhetoric and composition and director of writing programs at Arizona State University, has published on the history of rhetoric, historiography, and the history of the discipline of rhetoric and composition in journals such as *Rhetoric Review* and *Rhetoric Society Quarter* and in a number of edited collections. Her book *Authoring a Discipline: Scholarly Journals and the Post–World War II Emergence of Rhetoric and Composition* explores the interdependent roles of journals, editors, contributors, and disciplinarity and the disciplinary history of rhetoric and composition.

CONTRIBUTORS

Charles Bazerman, professor of English and education at the University of California, Santa Barbara, is interested in the social dynamics of writing, rhetorical theory, and the rhetoric of knowledge production and use. His most recent book is *The Languages of Edison's Light.* Current projects include a rhetorical theory of literate action and an investigation of environmental information.

Steve Beatty is an instructor at Arizona State University. He holds an M.B.A., an M.F.A. in creative writing, and an M.A. in rhetoric and composition, and is currently completing his dissertation on the professionalization of creative writing for his Ph.D. in rhetoric and linguistics at Arizona State University.

Carol Berkenkotter is professor of rhetoric and communication at Michigan Technological University. She published with Thomas N. Huckin the book *Genre Knowledge in Disciplinary Communication: Cognition/Culture/Power* and has authored numerous articles on academic and professional genres. She is currently working on a book titled *Psychiatry's Rhetorics: The Curious Case of the Case Report.*

Ann M. Blakeslee is associate professor of English and co-director of writing across the curriculum at Eastern Michigan University. She teaches upper-level and graduate courses in technical communication. Blakeslee has studied the composing practices of physicists and has published articles addressing their journals, collaborative practices, and mentoring activities in *Technical Communication Quarterly; Science, Technology, and Human Values;* and *Journal of Business and Technical Communication.* Her book, *Interacting with Audiences: Social Influences on the Production of Scientific Writing,* is forthcoming.

J. Stanton Carson is professor of communications and director of language-across-the-curriculum programs at Robert Morris College. His dissertation, "Writing Across the Business Disciplines at Robert Morris College: A Case Study," was directed by Richard Young. Carson has published and consults regularly on WAC issues. Most recently, he has directed a U.S. Department of Education FIPSE grant for the dissemination of the Robert Morris College Writing Across the Business Disciplines (WABD) structural approach to integrating WAC into the curriculums of six other colleges and universities across the country.

Richard Leo Enos is professor and holder of the Lillian Radford Chair of Rhetoric and Composition at Texas Christian University. His research emphasis is on the history of rhetoric with a specialization in classical rhetoric. Much of his work deals with understanding the relationship between thought and expression in antiquity. He is the current editor of *Advances in the History of Rhetoric*, an annual publication of the American Society for the History of Rhetoric.

Eugene Garver is Regents Professor of philosophy at Saint John's University. Author of *Machiavelli and the History of Prudence* and *Aristotle's Rhetoric: An Art of Character*, he is currently writing about Aristotle's *Ethics* and about character in rhetoric and ethical argument. He studied in an NEH summer seminar with Richard Young in 1977.

Stuart Greene is Francis J. O'Malley Director of the University Writing Program at Notre Dame. He has published his research on composition theory, writing in the disciplines, and rhetorical theory in a number of journals and edited collections. He is co-editor of two books, *Educated in the USA: Readings on the Problems and Promise of Education* and *Teaching Academic Literacy: The Uses of Teacher-Research in Developing a Writing Program*. With Robert Kachur and Anne Clark, he is completing a textbook on argument titled *Inquiry and Argument: Entering the Conversation of Ideas*.

Winifred Bryan Horner is professor emerita of English, University of Missouri, and Radford Chair emerita of Rhetoric and Composition, Texas Christian University. She is the author or editor of numerous articles and eleven books dealing with rhetoric and composition. Her latest book is *Rhetoric and Pedagogy: Its History, Philosophy and Practice*. In 1988 she published *Rhetoric in the Classical Tradition*, which combined her two main interests: the history of rhetoric and the teaching of composition. She has lectured both nationally and internationally, including at Oxford University and the Universities of Turin, Amsterdam, Göttingen, and Edinburgh. She was a visiting research fellow at the University of California, Berkeley and a fellow of the University of Edinburgh. A Festschrift in her honor was edited by Theresa Enos and published in 1991.

Contributors

Robert Inkster is currently on leave from the English department serving as associate vice president for academic affairs at St. Cloud State University. His research interests include the intersections of rhetorical theory with epistemology and pedagogy and the role of rhetoric in contemporary professional life. His most recent publication is *The Writing of Business*, with Judith M. Kilborn. Inkster was a fellow in Richard Young's 1978–79 NEH seminar.

Janice M. Lauer is Reese McGee Distinguished Professor of English at Purdue University, where she founded a doctoral program in rhetoric and composition. She has received the CCCC Exemplar Award, has served on the executive committees of CCCC and NCTE, and currently coordinates the consortium of doctoral programs in rhetoric and composition. For thirteen summers she directed a two-week international rhetoric seminar. She has written on rhetorical invention, disciplinarity, writing-as-inquiry pedagogy, and empirical research; her publications include *Four Worlds of Writing* and *Composition Research: Empirical Designs*.

Elenore Long is associate professor of English and communications at Bay Path College in Longmeadow, Massachusetts. After completing a postdoctoral fellowship through the Community Literacy Center in Pittsburgh, Long directed for several years a Community House initiative called STRUGGLE. Her decade-long "internship" with colleagues at the Community House—including Wayne Peck, Linda Flower, Joyce Baskins, and Jennifer Flach—continues to inform her daily practices as a teacher and a writer.

Karen McGrane is director of information design and usability for the North American offices of Razorfish, Inc. Razorfish is a strategic digital communications company with eleven offices throughout North America and Europe and provides digital change management strategy, design, and technology services to leading companies and organizations across the world. Karen is pursuing a Ph.D. in rhetoric and communication from Rensselaer Polytechnic Institute and also holds B.A. degrees in American studies and philosophy from the University of Minnesota.

Rebecca Schoenike Nowacek is a graduate student in the composition and rhetoric program at the University of Wisconsin–Madison. Her scholarly interests include writing across the curriculum, disciplinary and interdisciplinary learning, and the negotiation of role taking in various academic and nonacademic contexts (including classrooms, writing centers, and song-writing groups). She is currently completing her dissertation, tentatively titled "Writing, Talking, Role-Taking: Disciplinary Learning in the Interdisciplinary Classroom."

Lee Odell is professor of composition theory and research at Rensselaer Polytechnic Institute. His current publications discuss the interaction between visual and textual information in both print and digital media. His most recent book, with Charles Cooper, is *Evaluating Writing: The Role of Teachers' Knowledge in Text, Learning, and Culture*. He has served as chair of the Conference on College Composition and Communication (CCCC) and of the National Council of Teachers of English (NCTE) Assembly for Research. His articles have received the CCCC Richard Braddock Award and the NCTE Award for Excellence in Technical and Scientific Communication.

Mike Palmquist is professor of English at Colorado State University, where he is a member of the composition faculty. His scholarly interests include writing across the curriculum, the effects of computer and network technologies on writing instruction, and the use of hypertext/hypermedia in instructional settings.

Danette Paul is assistant professor of English at Brigham Young University, where she teaches courses in composition pedagogy, rhetoric, and technical and professional writing. Her main area of research is the rhetoric of science. Her most recent work includes a study in *Written Communication* of rhetorical strategies in article introductions.

Joseph Petraglia is associate professor of rhetoric and writing in the English department at Texas Christian University. He is the editor of *Reconceiving Writing, Rethinking Writing Instruction* and the author of the recently published *Reality by Design: The Rhetoric and Technology of Authenticity in Education*. He is currently editing a collection on the subject of rhetoric education and is working on a manuscript examining disciplinary variations on the "rhetorical turn."

Karen Rossi Schnakenberg studied with Richard Young at Carnegie Mellon University and completed her Ph.D. in rhetoric there in 1996 with Richard Leo Enos and Richard Young as co-chairs of her committee. Her dissertation is a historical study of the revival of classical rhetoric in the 1950s and early 1960s. She is currently a senior lecturer in rhetoric and professional writing at Carnegie Mellon and director of the undergraduate programs in professional and technical writing. Her major areas of inquiry include the history of writing instruction, the pedagogy of writing, and the general question of how specialized knowledge crosses disciplinary boundaries and is communicated to nonexperts.

Jo-Ann M. Sipple has been professor of communications since 1981 and vice president for academic affairs since 1990 at Robert Morris College in Pittsburgh. During the early 1980s, she founded and established the college's writing-across-the-curriculum program, serving as its first director and advisor. Sipple's publications relevant to WAC include articles in *The Journal of Higher Education* and *Language and Learning Across the Disciplines*. She has taken a leave of absence from Robert Morris College to accept the position of interim vice president for academic affairs (1999–2000) at her alma mater, Merrimack College, North Andover, Massachusetts.

William L. Sipple, Ph.D., is provost and vice president for academic affairs and professor of communications and English at Bay Path College in Longmeadow, Massachusetts, and former professor and dean of the School of Communications and Information Systems at Robert Morris College in Pittsburgh. He has more than thirty years of experience in college teaching, higher education administration, media production, and technology/information management. He led the development of the Robert Morris College communications skills program. His publications focus on rhetoric, communications, technology issues, media management, higher education, and Renaissance literature. He has produced award-winning television projects for PBS, corporations, nonprofit organizations, and education, being recognized with Telly Awards, New York Festival Awards, International CINDY Competition Awards, and others.

Victor J. Vitanza is professor of English at the University of Texas at Arlington, where he teaches a variety of courses in literacy and electracy. He is editor of the journal *PRE/TEXT*, co-editor of *PRE/TEXT: Electra(Lite)*, and moderator of the *PRE/TEXT* list (www.pre-text.com). His most recent book is *Negation, Subjectivity, and the History of Rhetoric*; he is completing a book tentatively titled *Canonicity, Rape Narratives, and the History of Rhetoric*; and he has begun a book on James Berlin and cultural studies.

Sam Watson completed his doctorate at the University of Iowa with a dissertation that became the book *Michael Polanyi and the Recovery of Rhetoric*. A member of Richard Young's NEH seminar titled "Invention of Rhetoric" (1978–79), Watson has spent his career at the University of North Carolina at Charlotte teaching and fostering environments conducive to writing. As founder of a writing project there and as director of University Writing Programs (1993–1998), he has become increasingly convinced that cultures which foster writing also foster learning, that many academic cultures nurture neither activity, and that reflection is central to both.

This book was typeset in Adobe Sabon by Electronic Imaging.
The typeface used on the cover is Granjon.
The book was printed on 50-lb. Husky Offset by IPC Communications.